The New York Air Brake System; a Complete and Strictly Up-to-date Treatise, Containing, Detailed Descriptions and Explanations of All the Various Parts of the New York Air Brake

INTRODUCTION

It may be truthfully said that no other appliance connected with the running of railway trains requires the amount of study, and skill on the part of the operator, as does the modern air brake, with all the varied and improved devices which have from time to time been added to it, and those also, which no doubt will be added in the future as occasion demands.

The air brake undoubtedly stands at the head of the long list of appliances which today are considered absolutely necessary in the operation of railway trains; and when viewed from the standpoint of safety and convenience it is bound to retain its position at the top

As many of the great trunk lines of railways have adopted, and are now using the New York Air Brake, the study of this particular system as presented in the following pages cannot fail to be of the greatest benefit to all enginemen and trainmen.

Detailed explanations are given of the principles governing the construction and operation of the system, all the parts, and their various functions being described in language at once plain and practical.

The information given is strictly up to date, and includes descriptions and illustrations of all the latest improved appliances that have been added to the New York Air Brake equipment Although a certain amount of purely descriptive matter is indispensable in dealing with mechanical appliances, the fact still remains that the conditions connected with air brake practice demand in addition, a large amount of catechetical instruction to enable the student to prepare himself to successfully pass the rigid examinations to which he will be subject while in the line of promotion.

The answers to the questions are condensed as much as is consistent with reliability and truthfulness Train handling, both freight and passenger, is dealt with at length, and a full course of instruction given regarding the same. Brake leverage and braking power are also clearly explained, and simple rules given for their calculation

The greatest care and diligence have been exercised in the compilation of the book, and the highest authorities on air brake practice have been consulted in an earnest effort to make it complete in every detail. The reason that no references, or names of authors consulted are given in the text or on the Title page of the volume, was for the purpose of presenting these names and authorities in a single group, as witness the following list:

Calvin F Swingle, M. E., President National Institute of Practical Mechanics, Chicago, Ill.

Frederick J. Prior, M A. A., Author of "Operation of Trains," "What Stops a Moving Train"

Robert H. Blackall, Air Brake Expert D & H C Company.

W. W Wood, Air Brake Expert (Monon Route) C. I & L. Ry

Frank H. Dukesmith, Director Dukesmith School of Air Brakes

INTRODUCTION

W. G. Wallace, M E, Former President Traveling Engineers' Association.

C. B Conger, Air Brake Expert, and Author.

The Locomotive Firemen and Enginemen's Magazine.

* The Editors and Compilers gratefully acknowledge their indebtedness to the Air Brake Association for a portion of the text contained in the following pages; particularly that pertaining to the examination Questions and Answers.

NEW YORK AIR BRAKE SYSTEM

The
New York Air Brake Equipment

DUPLEX AIR PUMP.

The air cylinders of the New York pumps are located above the steam cylinders, whereas with the Westinghouse pumps the air cylinders are located on the bottom end. The low pressure cylinder of the New York pump has a volume capacity of about double that of the high pressure cylinder. The diameter of the steam cylinders is always the same as the diameter of the high pressure air cylinder.

Another feature in regard to the action of the New York pump is that there is only one steam piston in motion at any one time, for the reason that when a piston has made its stroke it waits for the other piston to make a stroke before it moves again. This is brought about by reason of the fact that the reversing-valve on one piston controls the action of the opposite piston.

The Duplex Air Pumps manufactured by the The New York Air Brake Company for locomotive service are of four different sizes, and are known as the Nos. 1, 2, 5 and 6. The dimensions of these pumps are as follows:

Pump No.	Diameter of Steam Cyl.	Diameter of L. P. Air Cyl.	Diameter of H. P. Air Cyl.	Stroke
1	5 in.	7 in.	5 in.	9 in.
2	7 in.	10 in.	7 in.	9 in.
5	8 in.	12 in.	8 in.	12 in.
6	7 in.	11 in.	7 in.	10 in.

The No. 1 and No. 2 differ somewhat from the No. 5 and No. 6 in design as well as in size, although the principle of operation is practically the same.

To meet the demand for a pump that would furnish air for a freight train of 100 cars, and still be sufficiently within its capacity to reduce the liability of failure to a minimum, the No. 5 pump was designed and perfected, and such structural changes made as to materially improve the design, and increase the efficiency and economy of the duplex air pump.

The valve gear of the duplex air pump is exceedingly simple, consisting of two ordinary D slide valves, similar to the same type of valve used in locomotives, actuated by valve stems which extend into the hollow piston rods and are moved by contact with the tappet plates bolted on the steam piston heads. The valve on one side controls the admission of steam to, and exhaust from the opposite cylinder, as shown, so that while one of the pistons is moving the other is at rest. This feature also allows the air valves to seat by gravity.

The air cylinders are known as the low pressure and high pressure cylinders, and in each type of the pumps that is herein described, the difference in the areas of the air cylinders is in the same proportion, the low pressure piston having twice the area of the high, and the

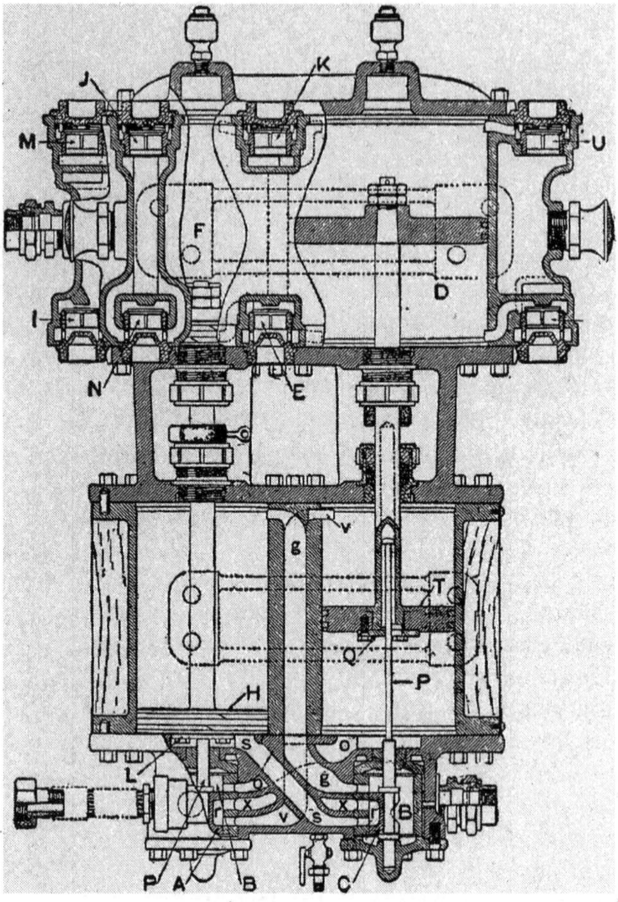

Fig. 1—Low Pressure Piston Moving Upward. High Pressure Piston at Rest.

high pressure the same area as the steam cylinders. Thus three measures of air are compressed with two measures of steam.

The operation of all the duplex air pumps is practically the same, the difference being in the arrangement of the air valves. The No. 1 and No. 2 have six air valves, viz., upper and lower receiving, upper and lower intermediate and upper and lower discharge valves, and the same air inlets for both cylinders. The No. 5 and No. 6 have separate air inlets for each cylinder, and eight air valves, viz., upper and lower receiving for low pressure cylinder, upper and lower intermediate, upper and lower receiving for high pressure cylinder and upper and lower discharge All air valves of the No. 5 pump are the same size and are interchangeable. This is also the case with those of the No. 6.

The No. 5 and No. 6 pumps are identical except in size, and as this type of pump is the later one, we will describe the operation of the No. 5.

By referring to Figures 1, 2, 3, and 4, it will be seen that each part has a reference letter and the pump pistons are shown in different positions. These letters will be used in the description of the operation, so that the movements can be easily followed, by referring to the cuts when reading the explanation

OPERATION

Before the pump has been started, both pistons will naturally be at the bottom of the cylinders, due to their own weight, or, if not completely down, will at least have dropped enough to permit the slide valves to fall to the bottom of the steam chests.

Assuming for convenience of explanation that the pistons are both down, when the pump throttle is opened live steam flows into both steam chests B, and is always present in them when the pump is taking steam. In this

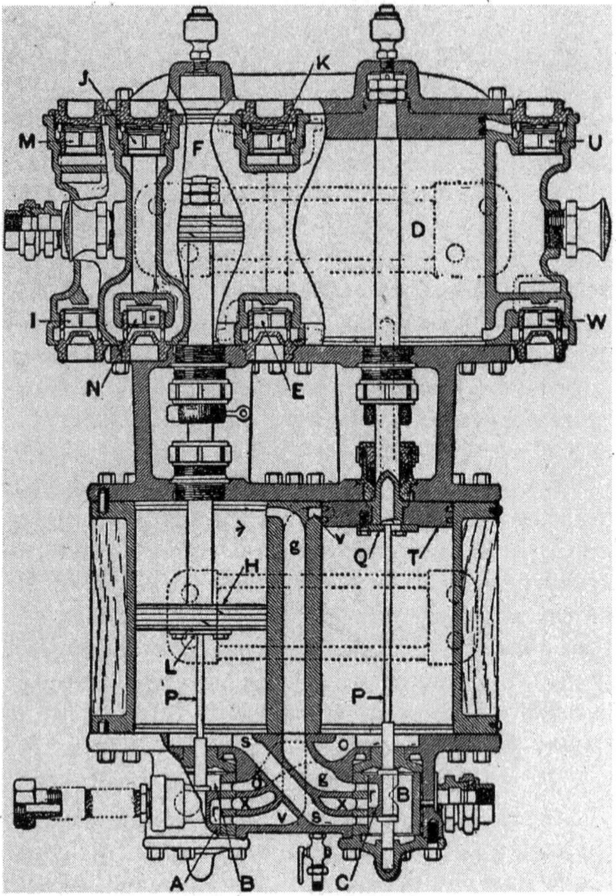

Fig. 2—High Pressure Piston Moving Upward. Low Pressure Piston at Rest.

instance only, steam is admitted to both cylinders at once, through port g to the upper side of piston H, which being at the bottom is merely held in that position, and through port o, to the under side of piston T, (Fig. 1). Piston T now moves upward and in doing so forces the air that is above the piston in low pressure cylinder D, through intermediate valve K, into the high pressure cylinder F. At the same time, the low pressure piston tends to create under it a vacuum, which is filled with air at atmospheric pressure through the air inlet at the right, and receiving valve W. Just before piston T reaches the end of its upward stroke, the tappet plate Q engages the button on the end of the valve stem P, which moves the slide valve C, to its highest position, allowing the steam above piston H, to pass through ports g, cavity r, in slide valve C, and the exhaust X, to the atmosphere, and live steam through port s, to the under side of piston H. As piston H moves upward (Fig. 2), the high pressure piston in cylinder F forces the air above it, which may be said to be under the first stage of compression, through discharge valve M, to the main reservoir, while its upward movement tends to create a vacuum under it in the high pressure cylinder F, which is filled with air at atmospheric pressure through high pressure receiving valve N.

Just before piston H completes its upward stroke (Fig 3), tappet plate L engages with the button on the valve stem, raising it with the slide valve A, exhausting the steam under piston T, through port o, cavity r, in slide valve A and the exhaust X to the atmosphere, and admitting steam through ports v to the upper side of piston T, moving it downward. During the downward movement of piston T, the low pressure piston in cylinder D forces the air under it which was taken in on its upward stroke, through the intermediate valve E to the under side of the piston in high pressure cylinder F, and

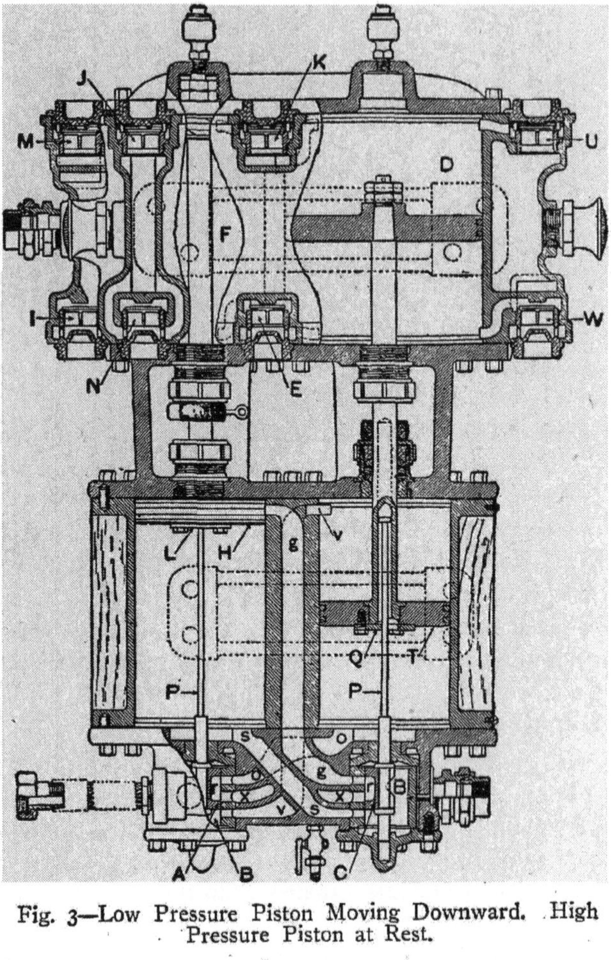

Fig. 3—Low Pressure Piston Moving Downward. High Pressure Piston at Rest.

at the same time cylinder D is filled with air at atmospheric pressure through the air inlet and upper receiving valve U. Just before the piston T completes its downward stroke (Fig. 4), the tappet plate Q, coming in contact with the lower tappet or shoulder on the valve stem P, moves the slide valve C to its lowest position, allowing the steam under the piston H to exhaust to the atmosphere through port s, cavity r, in slide valve C and the exhaust X, and admitting live steam to the upper side of piston H, through ports g, moving it downward. As piston H moves downward, the high pressure piston forces the air under it through the lower discharge valve I into the main reservoir, while the cylinder is filled above with air at atmospheric pressure through the air inlet at the left, and receiving valve J.

The completion of this stroke completes one cycle of the pump. The movements described are repeated through each succeeding cycle.

The air valves through which air is being received or discharged during the movements of the pistons are shown in the illustrations as being raised from their seats.

Before starting a pump, open the drain cocks in the steam and exhaust passages. Open the steam valve slightly at first, and run the pump very slowly until all the condensation has been worked out of the steam cylinders. Then the steam valve may be opened a little more, but the pump should be run slowly until a pressure of 50 or 60 pounds has been accumulated in the main reservoir. It should be run just fast enough to promptly restore the pressure in brake system, but never raced.

The steam cylinders should receive a constant supply of oil from the lubricator (about one drop a minute), and it is necessary to keep all joints between the lubricator and pump perfectly tight, so that no oil will be wasted.

NEW YORK DUPLEX AIR PUMP

NO. 5 DUPLEX AIR PUMP

Low Pressure Piston Completing Upward Stroke, High Pressure Piston at Rest.

No. 1.

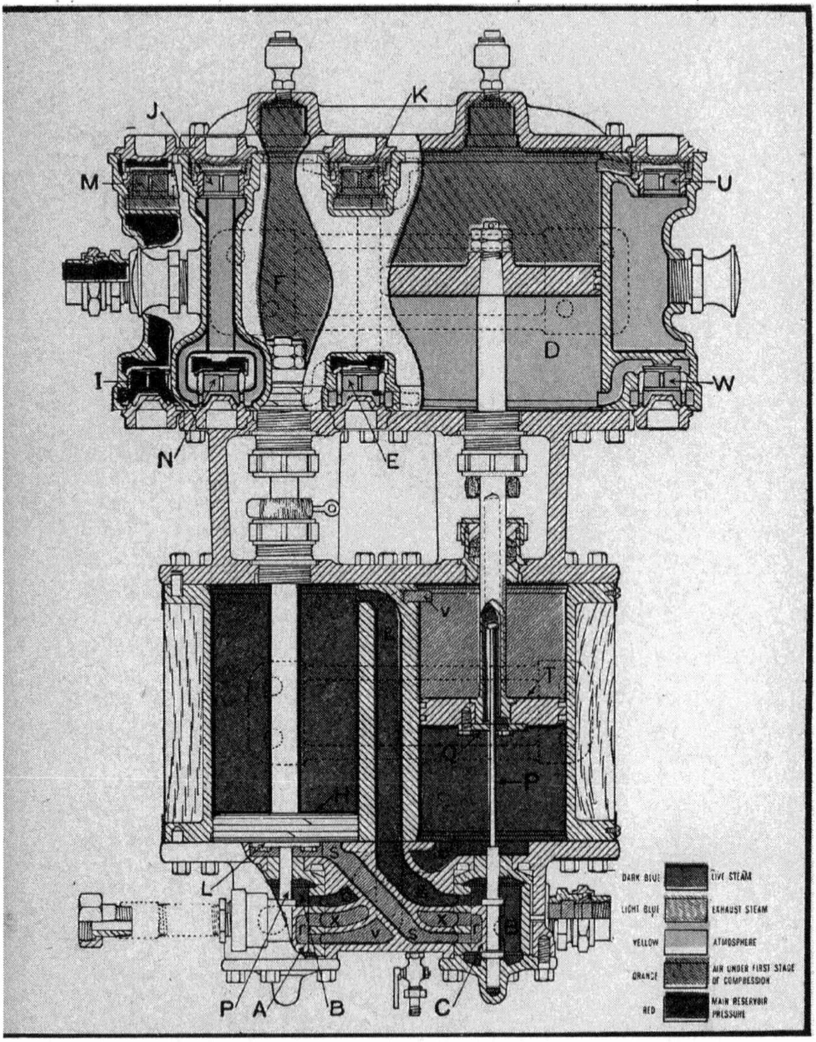

NO. 5 DUPLEX AIR PUMP

High Pressure Piston Completing Upward Stroke, Low Pressure Piston at Rest

No. 2.

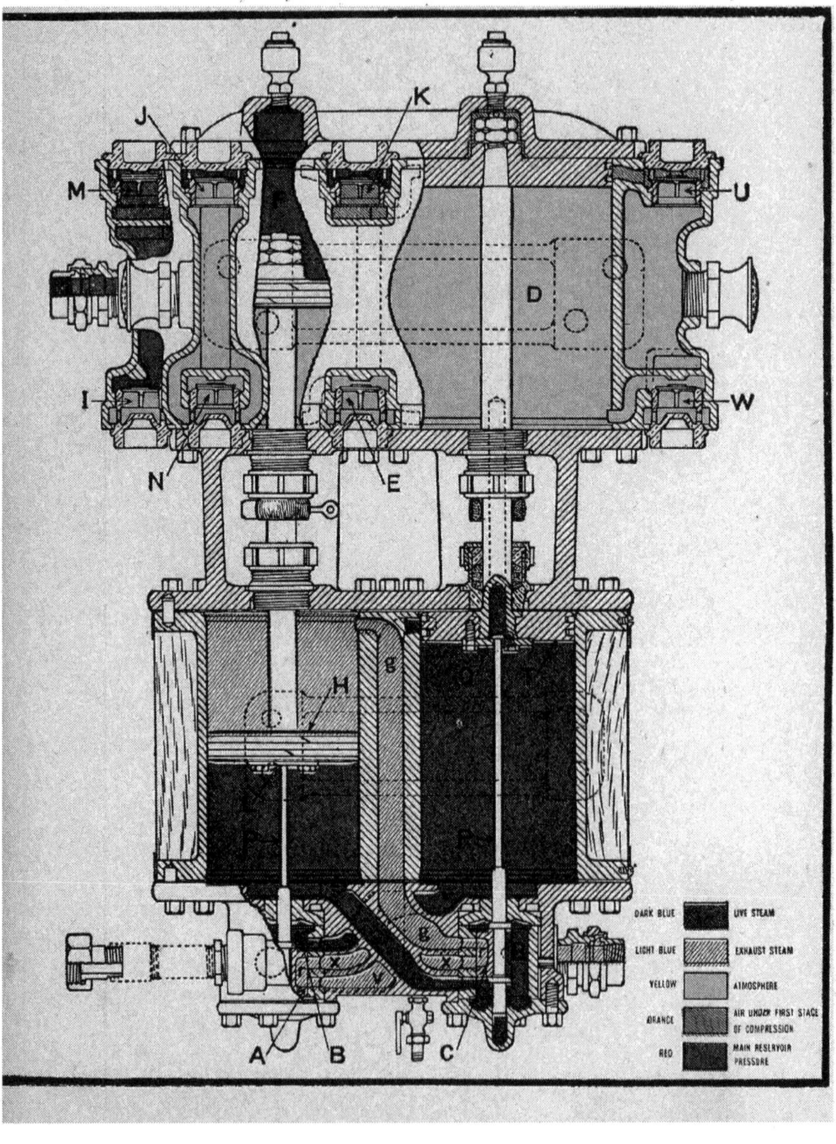

THE NEW YORK AIR BRAKE COMPANY

NO. 5 DUPLEX AIR PUMP

Low Pressure Piston Completing Downward Stroke, High Pressure Piston at Rest

No. 3.

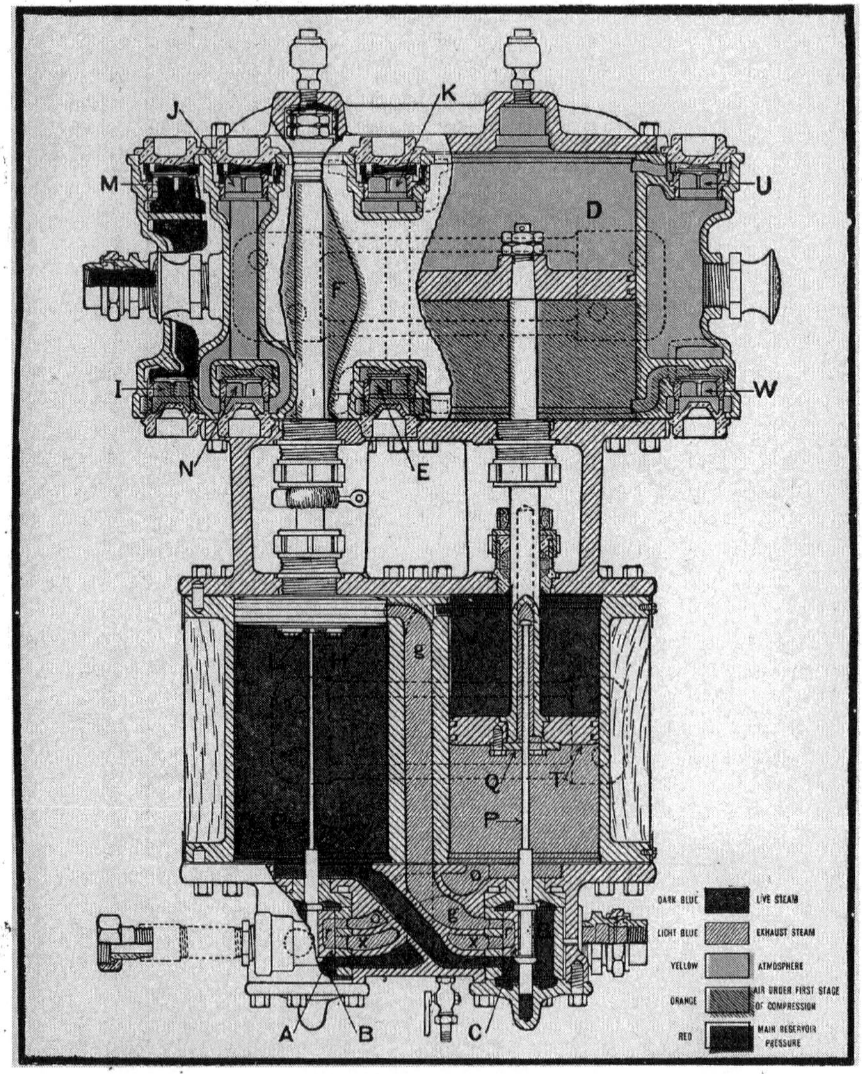

NO. 5 DUPLEX AIR PUMP

High Pressure Piston Completing Downward Stroke, Low Pressure Piston at Rest

No. 4.

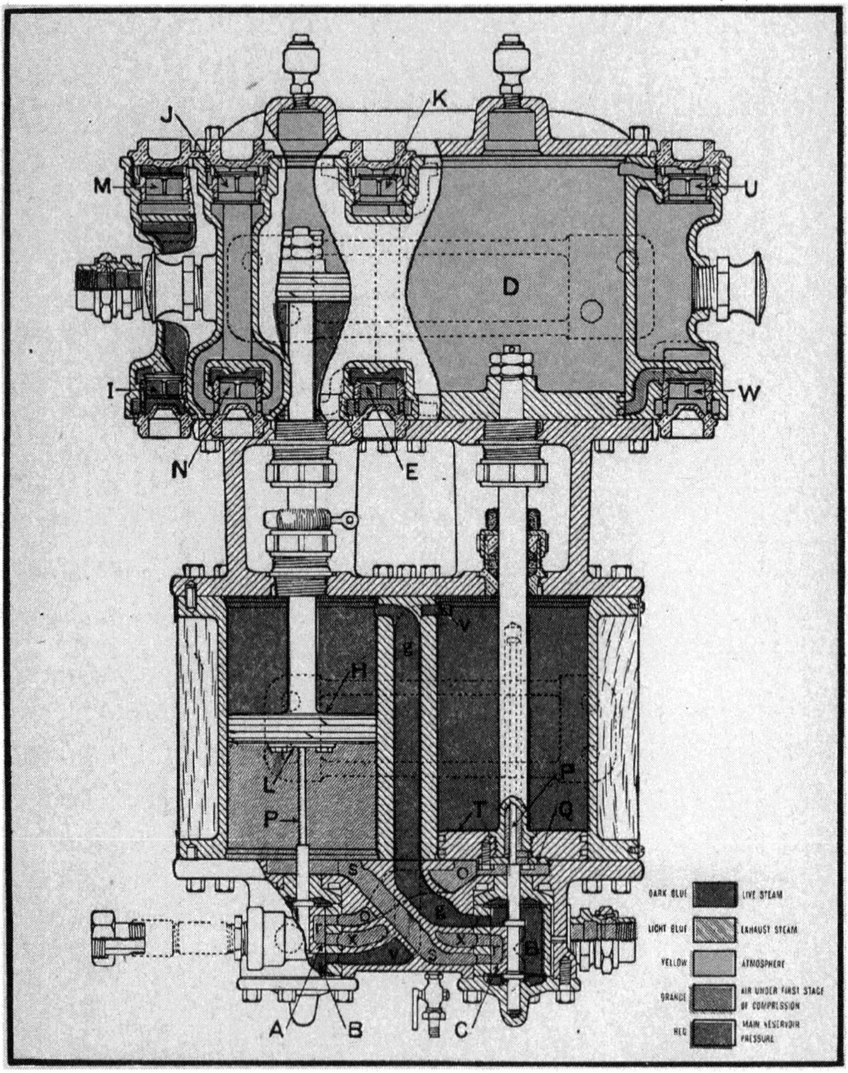

NEW YORK ENGINEER'S BRAKE VALVE

RELEASE POSITION

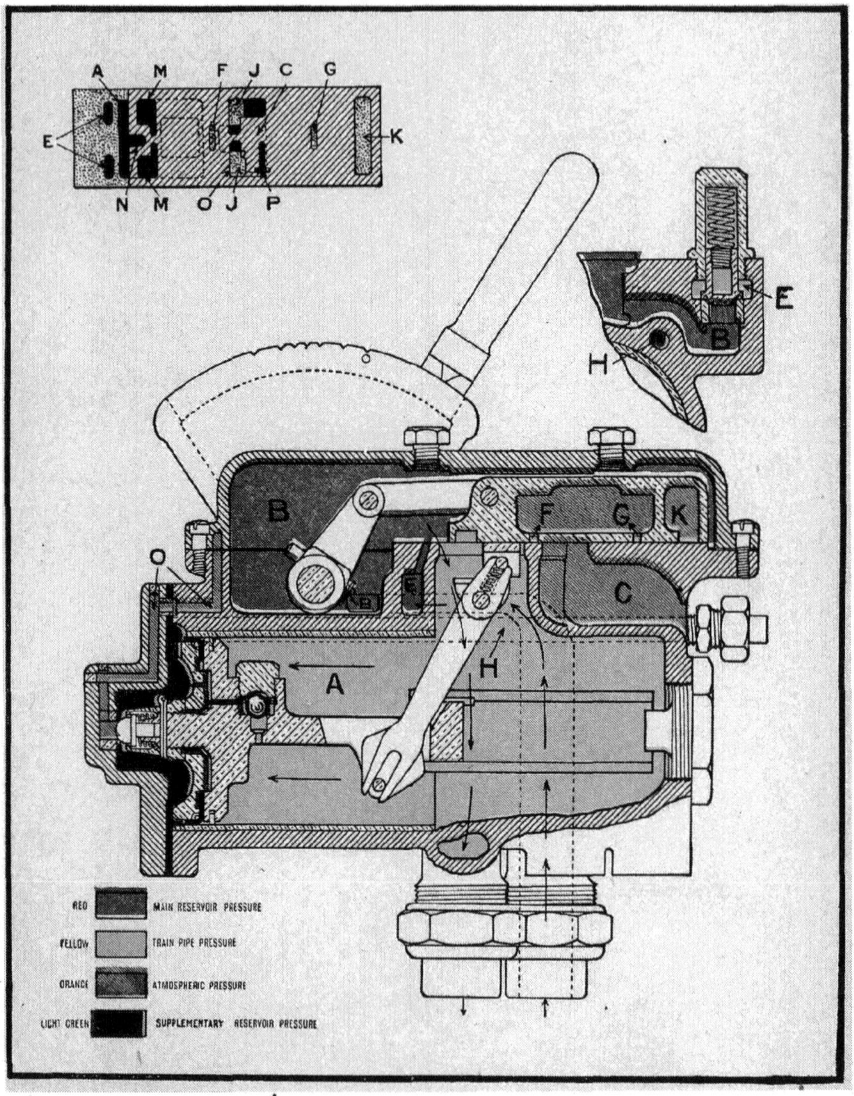

RUNNING POSITION

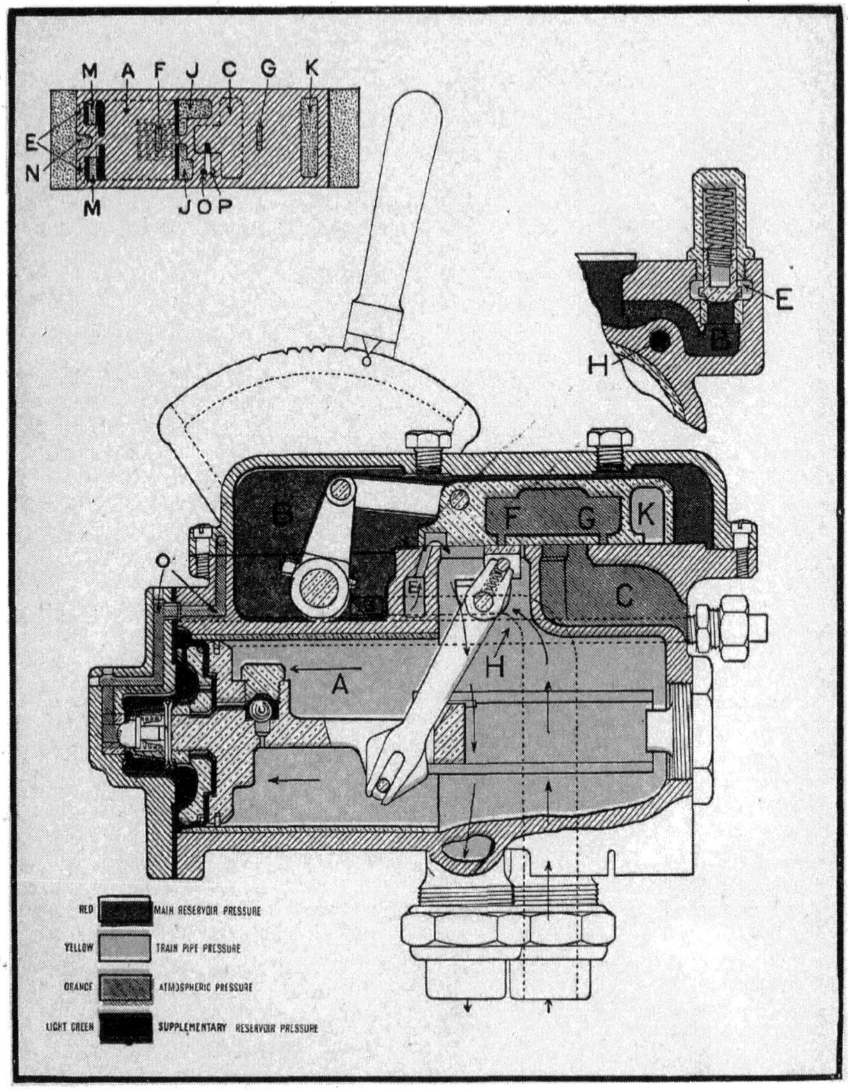

THE NEW YORK ENGINEER'S BRAKE VALVE

LAP POSITION

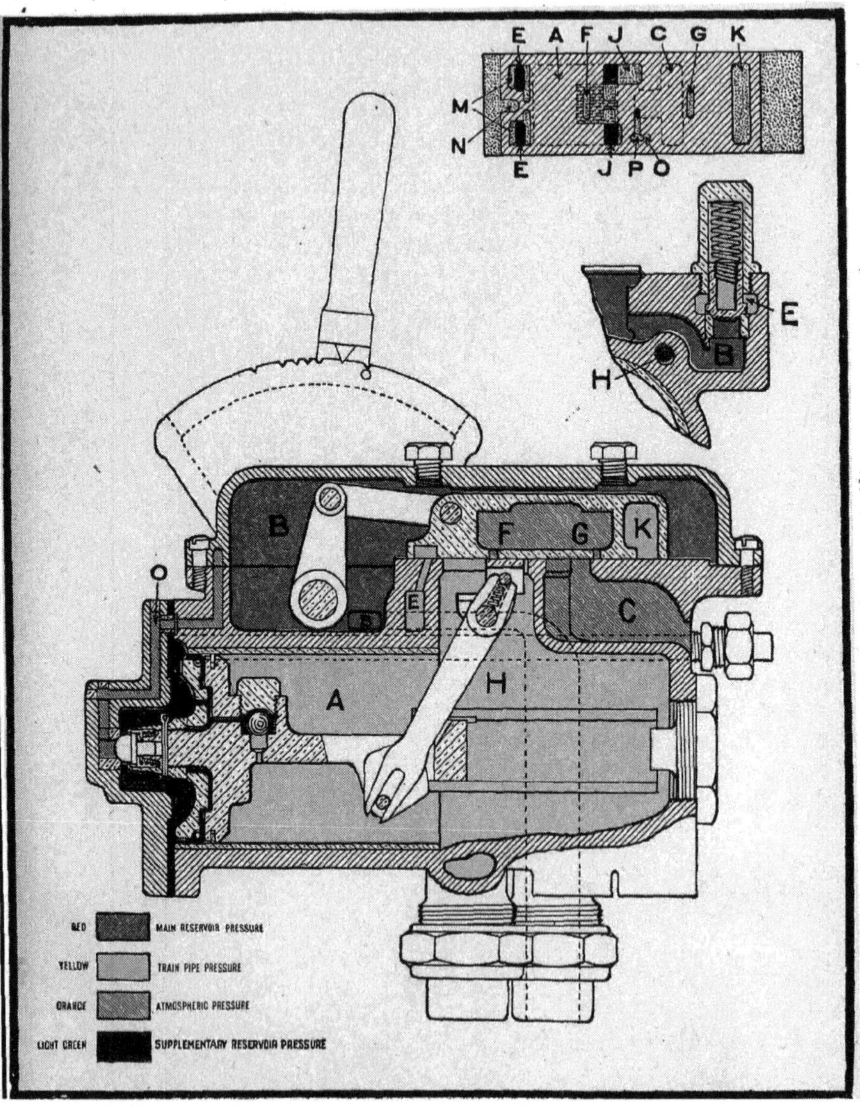

[Style B]

SERVICE POSITION

Automatic Lap

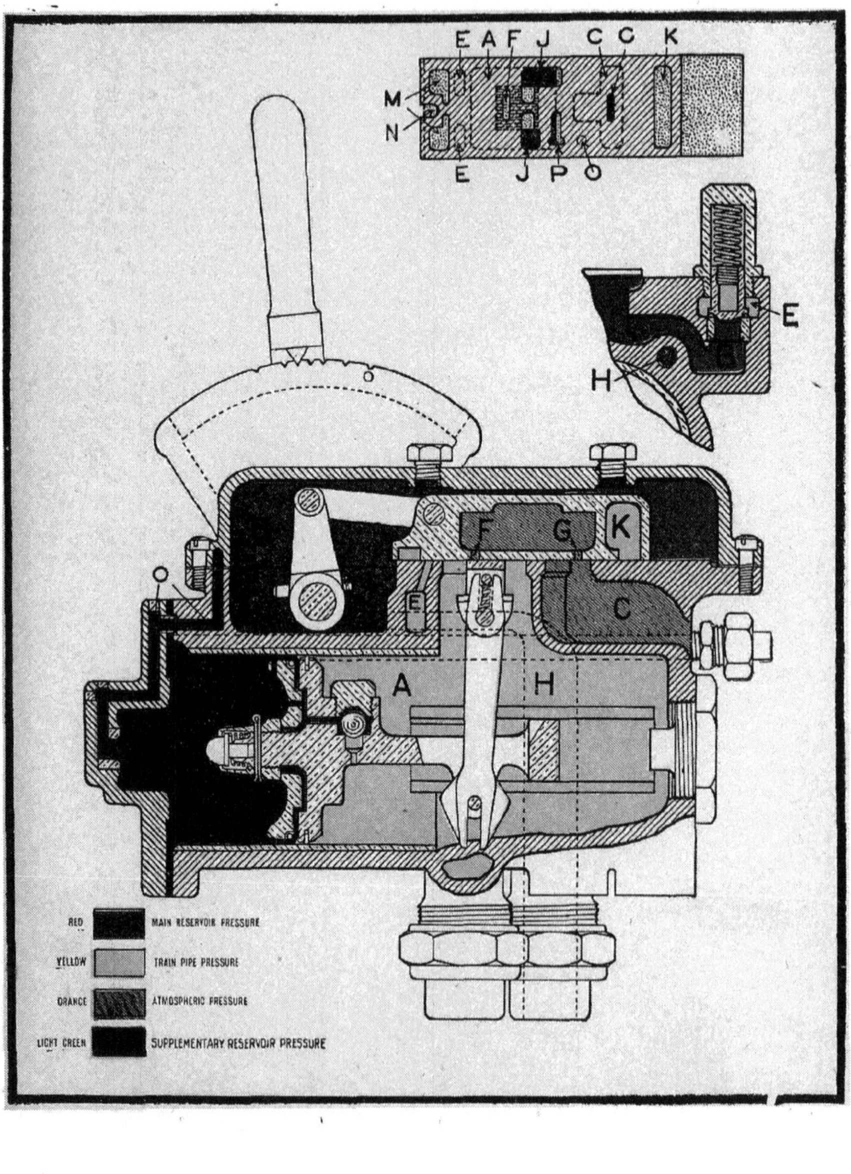

THE NEW YORK ENGINEER'S BRAKE VALVE

SERVICE POSITION

Exhausting

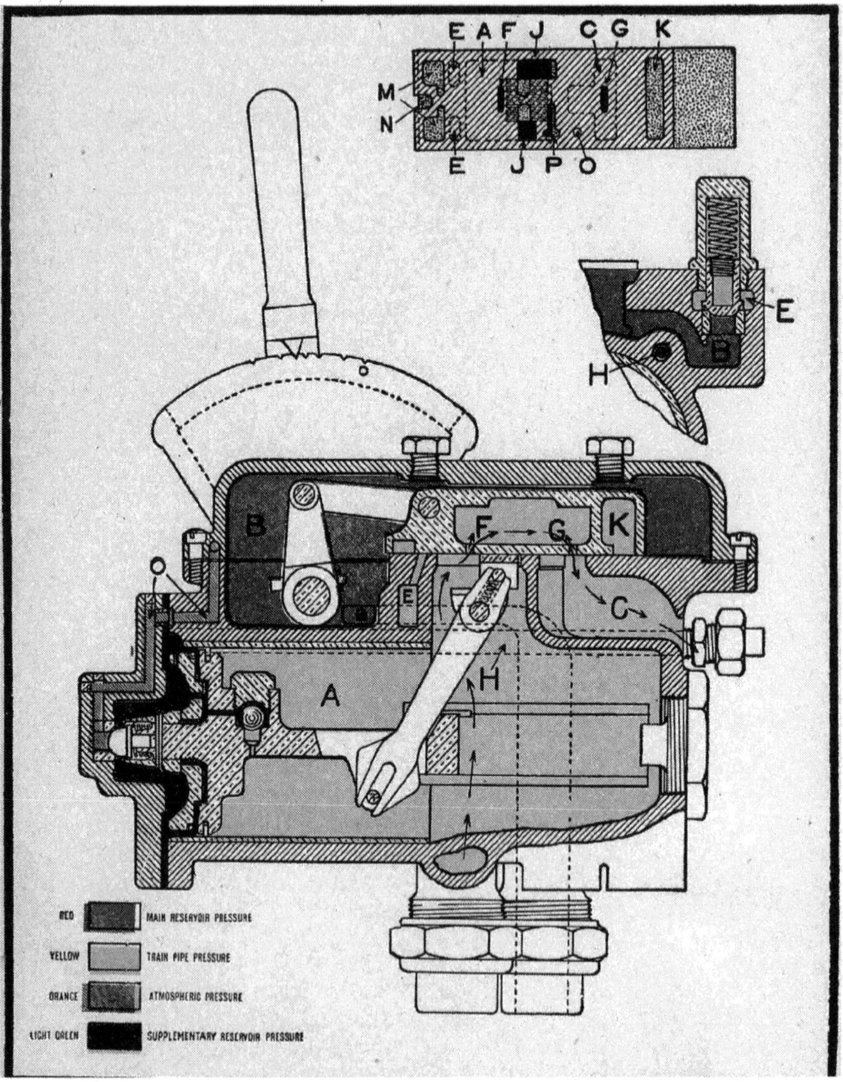

EMERGENCY POSITION

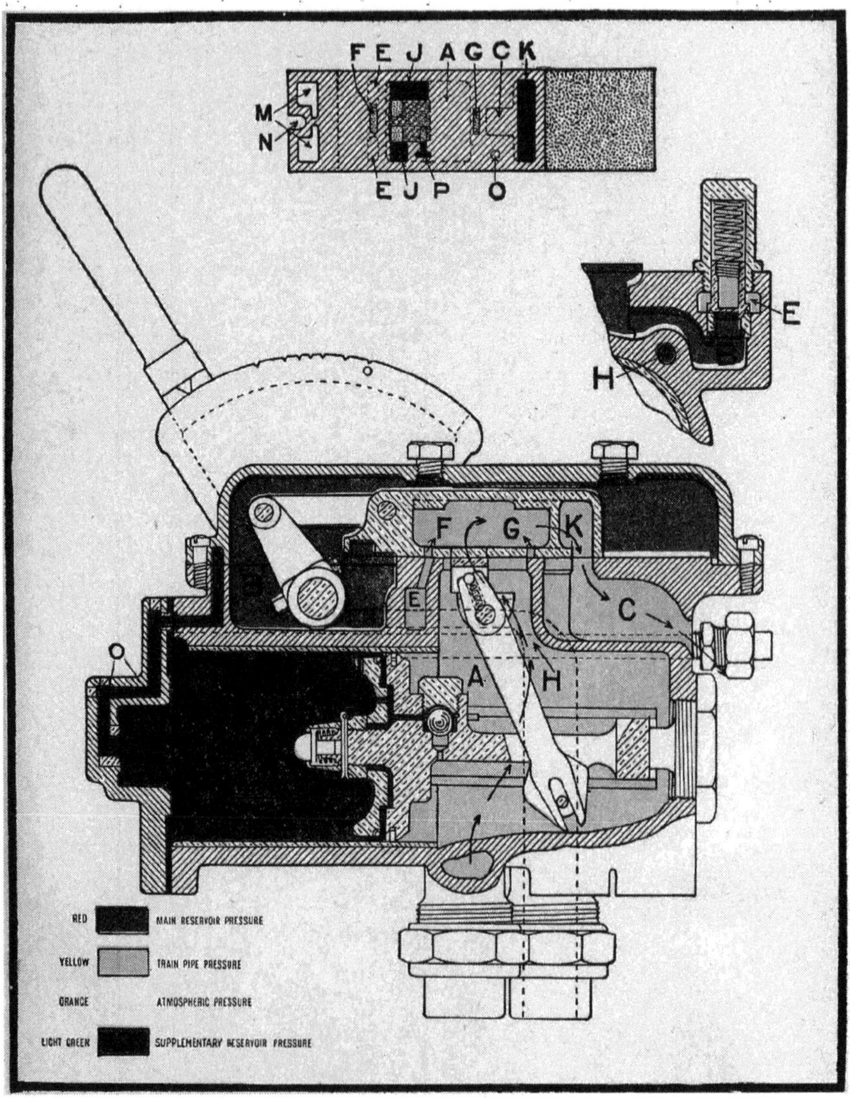

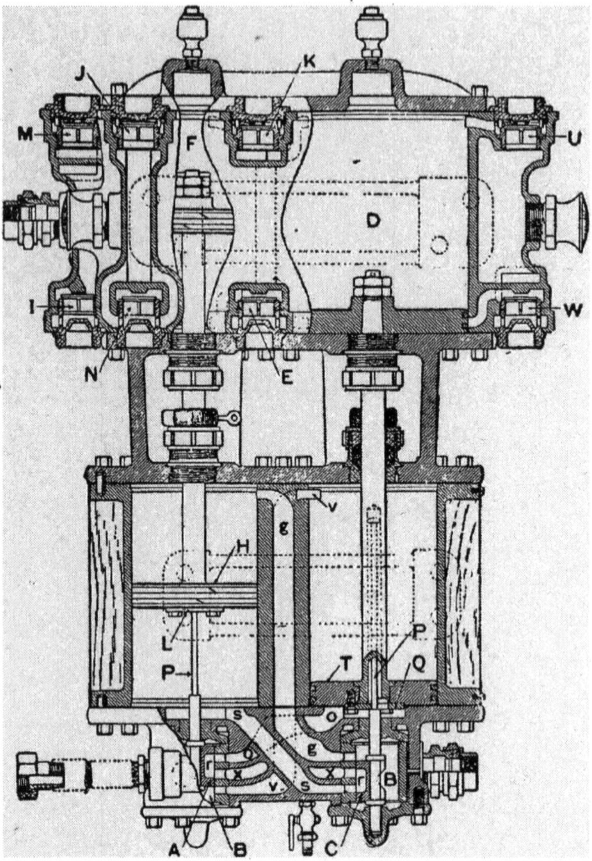

Fig. 4—High Pressure Piston Moving Downward. Low Pressure Piston at Rest.

Oil can leak away at the steam joints, where there is little or no indication of steam leakage.

The piston rods should be kept well packed, and good, clean swabs well oiled should be maintained on them.

AIR PUMP DISORDERS.

Broken or stuck air valves or seats will materially reduce the efficiency of the pump. They almost invariably cause the pump to work unevenly, and can usually be located by watching the action of the pistons. Leaky piston packing rings will also reduce the efficiency of the pump, and cause an uneven stroke. To detect them, pump up about 90 pounds in the main reservoir and stop the pump. Remove the oil cup. If there is a

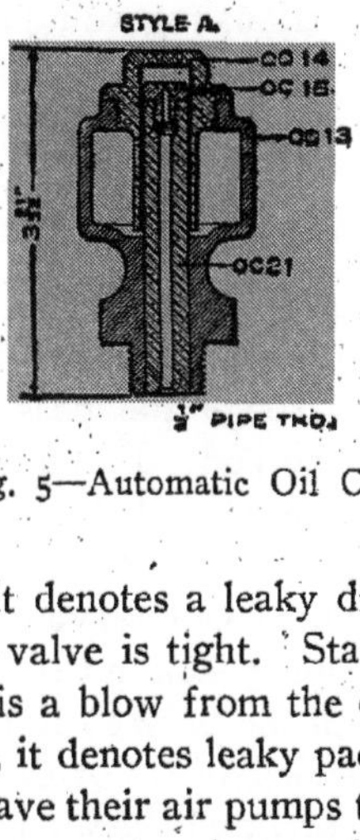

Fig. 5—Automatic Oil Cup.

continuous blow, it denotes a leaky discharge valve. If not, the discharge valve is tight. Start the pump again, and note if there is a blow from the oil cup hole on the down stroke, if so, it denotes leaky packing rings. However, most roads have their air pumps tested in the roundhouse, and they are supposed to maintain the standard pressure against a certain size orifice, the failure to perform which results in their removal for repairs.

Should the pump stop and refuse to go to work again,

first see that the governor is working properly, and that the pump is getting a full supply of steam, by opening the drain cock in the steam passage (see governor disorders). Sometimes a pump will stop on account of insufficient lubrication, and may be started by shutting off the steam for a few moments, opening the drain cock in the steam passage and again turning on the steam, letting the lubricator feed a few extra drops of oil. If it will not then go to work, it will undoubtedly be due to a break-down, which would have to be repaired in the shop or round-house, as engines are not usually equipped with tools and parts necessary to make such repairs on the road.

The general instructions regarding oiling, speed, drainage, etc., apply to the New York pumps the same as they do to the Westinghouse pumps.

AUTOMATIC OIL CUP STYLE A.

The action of this cup is as follows:

As the air piston makes its up-stroke, compressed air is driven upward through the passage drilled through the center post in the body of the oil cup, next passes downward inside the extended sleeve of the cap nut, and then through the regulating ports drilled in this sleeve, to the surface of the oil in the reservoir, on which it creates pressure. As the air piston makes its down-stroke, a vacuum is formed in the passage in the center port, and also inside the extended sleeve of the cap nut which envelops the center port, and the air pressure on the surface of the oil, created when the air piston made its upstroke, forces the oil on the down-stroke to the inside of the sleeve, and a small portion of it is drawn into the air cylinder through the hole in the feed cap, O C 15, which

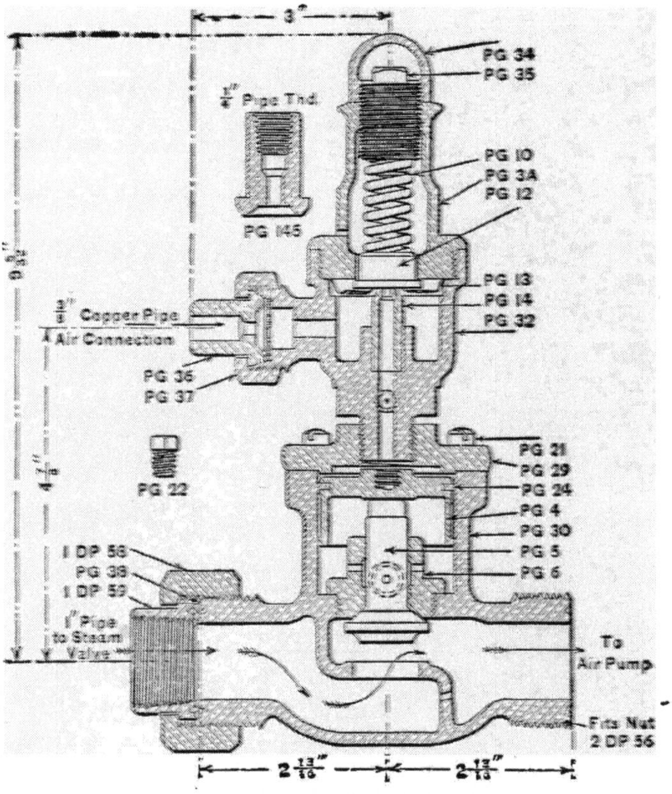

Fig. 6—Style C, New York Pump Governor, Steam Valve Open.

screws into the center port (Fig. 5). With this cup the quantity of oil fed to the air cylinder is governed by the diameter of the hole drilled in the feed cap, O C 15. The style A cup supplies oil to the air cylinders only when the pump is working, thus performing the service required of it with a maximum economy in the use of oil. It should always be filled before starting on a trip. Use only good cylinder oil, as other oils do not lubricate air cylinders on account of their low flash point. This cup

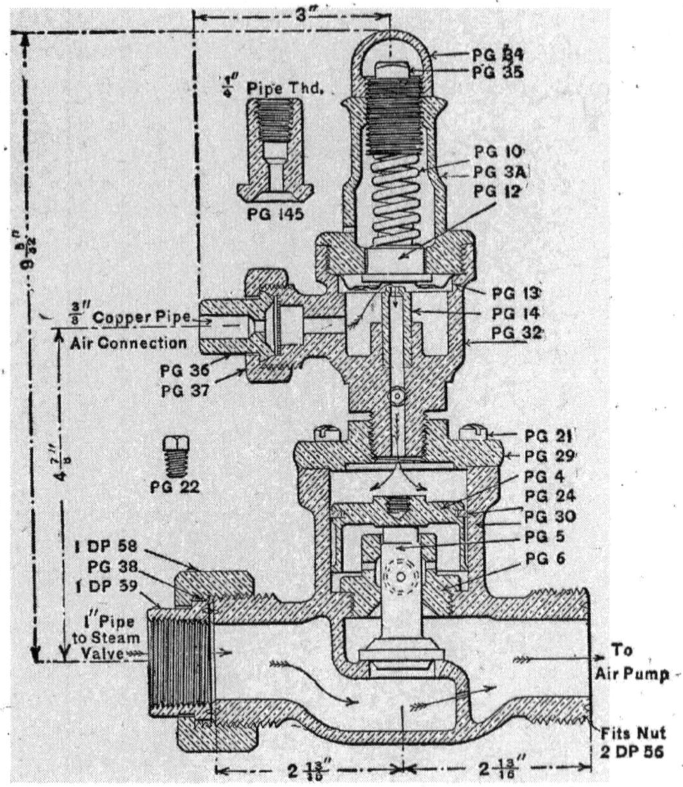

Fig. 7—Style C, New York Pump Governor Steam Valve Closed.

can be filled whether the pump is running or not, and it is a good plan to start the pump first so as to be sure that the small port in the feed cap O C 15 is open. Be careful not to enlarge it when cleaning it out.

NEW YORK AIR PUMP GOVERNOR.

The principles controlling the action of the New York pump governor are practically the same as with the

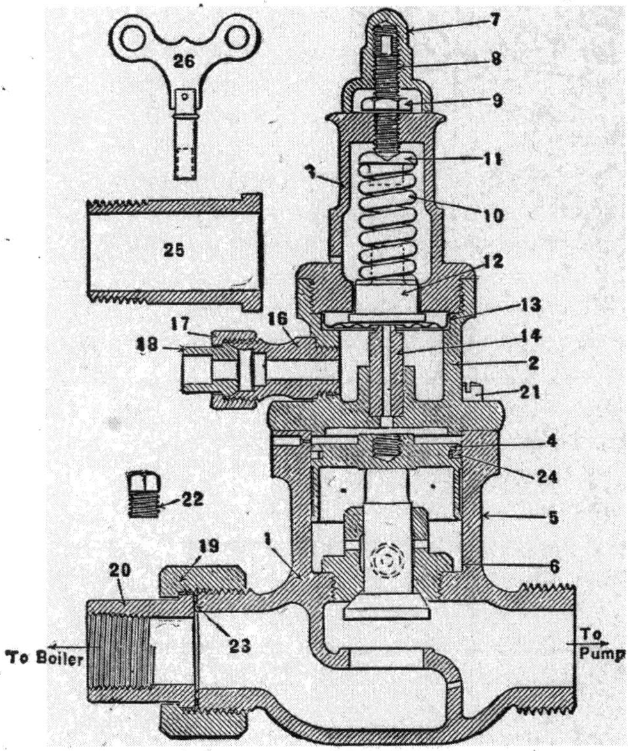

Fig. 8—Style A, New York Pump Governor.

Westinghouse. There is a slight difference in the construction, but not enough to make it necessary to redescribe the entire governor here. It has a diaphragm, regulating spring and a regulating nut, the same as the Westinghouse, but instead of having a diaphragm pin-valve like the Westinghouse, the diaphragm-valve in the New York governor closes the port leading from the diaphragm chamber to the steam piston. Another difference is that there is no spring under the steam piston as in the Westinghouse, so that the steam valve and the steam-valve piston are forced up by steam pressure alone, whereas with the Westinghouse both steam and spring are used to force the steam-valve piston up. There is an outlet port from the steam piston chamber to allow any back pressure to escape to the atmosphere, which is the same as in the Westinghouse. This vent port prevents the pressure from accumulating under the steam piston, for if not allowed to escape the air pressure on top would not be able to force the steam valve to its seat and shut off the pump, whereas, when steam is operating against the steam-valve alone it only requires about one-third as much air pressure on the large area of the top of the piston to overcome the steam pressure and force the steam valve down.

Figure 6 shows style C of the New York pump governor with the steam-valve open, and Fig 7 shows this same style C governor with the steam-valve closed.

The old style A New York governor requires a key with which to set the regulating spring, and is shown in Fig. 8

The New York duplex governor will be described and illustrated in the section on the Automatic Control equipment.

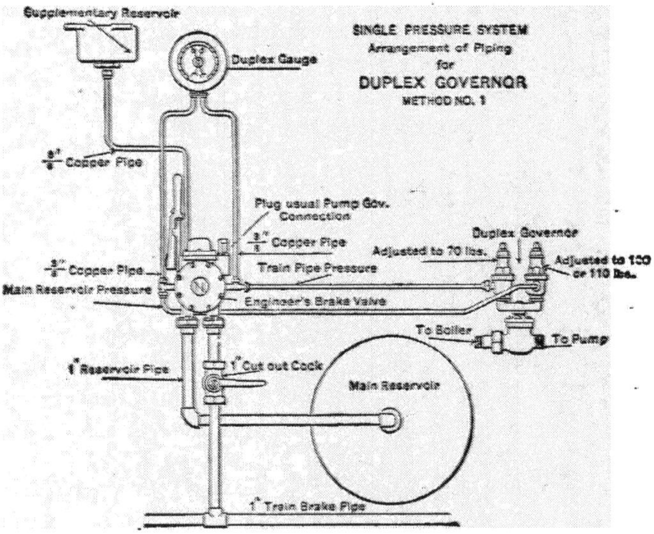

Fig. 9—New York Air Brake.

The method of piping the governor differs according to whether or not a single or double pressure is to be controlled.

The method of piping used in the single pressure system, that is, the ordinary automatic air-brake, is shown in Fig. 9. In this diagram it will be noted that the train-pipe pressure is connected to only one side of the governor, and is adjusted to seventy pounds, while the other side is connected to the main reservoir, and may be adjusted at ninety or a hundred pounds, or whatever number of pounds is considered standard on the particular road operating the device. Fig. 9 shows no cut-out cocks on the pipe leading to the Duplex governor, for the reason that with this method of piping the movement of the brake valve handle determines which side of the governor is operative. This will be explained more fully in the description of the engineer's brake valve.

Figure 10 shows the method of piping a single governor for a single pressure system. With the old style

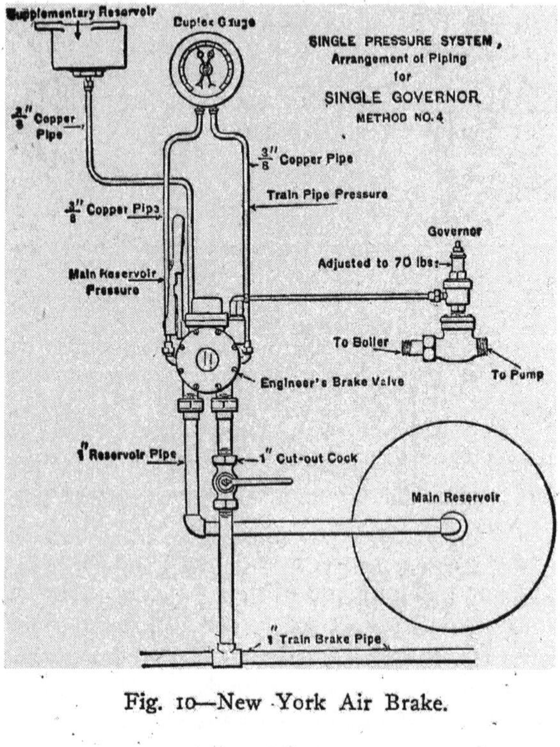

Fig. 10—New York Air Brake.

New York brake valve the single governor would be connected to the trainpipe, whereas with the Westinghouse system the single pump governor is always connected to the main reservoir.

Figure 11 shows a cut-out cock in the pipe leading from the low pressure side of the governor to a T connection with the train pipe, so that by cutting out the low pressure governor, the train pipe pressure will be raised

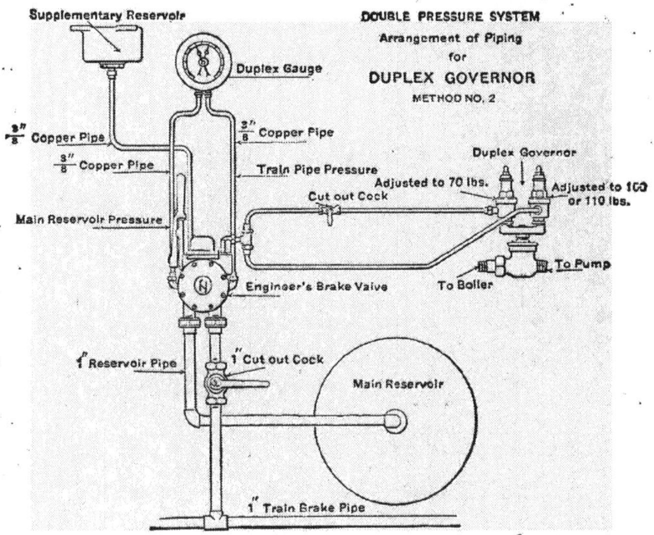

Fig. 11—New York Air Brake.

to one hundred or a hundred and ten pounds, as the case may be, according to what the high pressuer governor is set at. But it must be remembered that with this method of piping there is no separate governor control for the main reservoir pressure. (See New York Brake Valve.)

Figure 12 shows the triplex governor by which the main reservoir pressure is controlled in addition to giving two other degrees of control to the train pipe pressure as may be desired. With the triplex pump governor the main reservoir pressure can be adjusted at any point that may be considered safe. If it were the high pressure control system or the high speed brake it would be proper

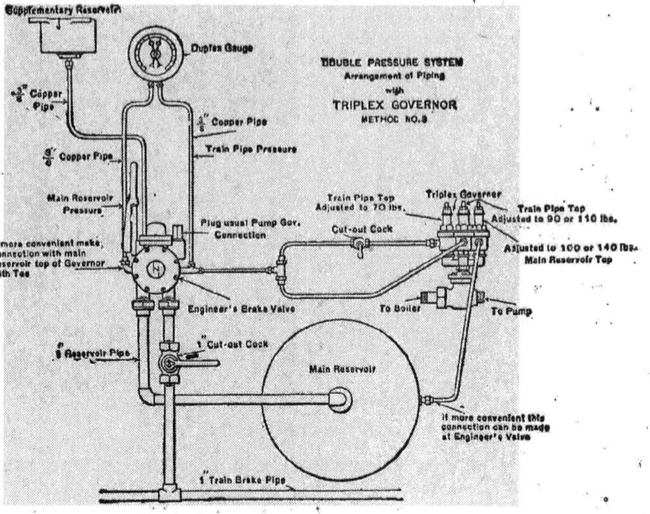

Fig. 12—New York Air Brake.

to set the main reservoir governor at one hundred and ten or one hundred and twenty pounds, and the middle pressure-top would be set at ninety or one hundred and ten pounds, and the remaining top at seventy pounds.

With the New York air brake valve on lap, service or emergency position, there is no connection between the brake valve and the train pipe pump governor, so that if the brake valve had only one governor, as shown in Fig. 10, and the handle of the brake valve should be left on lap, service or emergency position, there would be nothing to stop the pump, and consequently it would continue to operate as long as the steam in the boiler could move it, but when the Duplex governor is used and one governor pipe is connected to the train pipe and one to

General Arrangement of Brake Valve, Supplementary Reservoir, [illegible]

Fig. 13—New York Air Brake.

the main reservoir, as shown in Fig. 9, then if the brake valve handle should be on lap, service or emergency position the pump would have to shut off when the main reservoir pressure reached the point at which the main reservoir governor was set.

ENGINEER'S AUTOMATIC BRAKE VALVE, STYLE B.

CONSTRUCTION.

The construction of the Engineer's Automatic Brake Valve, Style B, is shown in the Figs. 14 to 20, inclusive.

Figures 14 and 15 are external views respectively of rear end and side. Fig. 16 is a cross section through the feed valve (rear view). Fig. 17 is a section through the side, showing travel of main slide valve, EV 114A*, and how graduating slide valve EV 110 is controlled by piston EV 104A. Fig. 18 is a cross section through the slide valve EV 114A (front view). Fig. 19 is a plan of the valve seat. Fig. 20 shows the face of the slide valve.

THE PRINCIPAL PARTS AND THEIR DUTIES.

Referring to Fig. 17 the main reservoir return pipe is connected to chamber B. The brake pipe is connected to chamber A. Discharge of brake pipe air to the atmosphere, for service application, occurs through ports F and G, in the main slide valve, and exhaust port C, in the slide valve seat, when the handle is placed in the service graduating notch; and for emergency applications, through ports J and K, in the main slide valve, and exhaust port C in the seat. The main slide valve also controls the flow of air from the main reservoir into the brake pipe.

---

* Note—On the figures 14 to 20, inclusive, the symbol EV is omitted from the reference numbers.

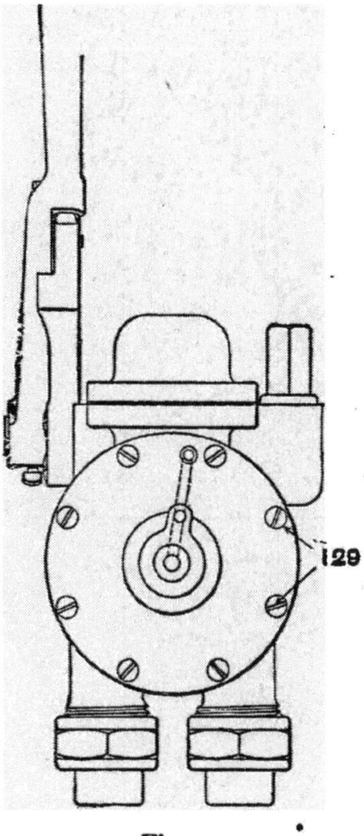

Fig. 14.

Small slide valve EV 110 is a cut-off or graduating valve, operated by piston EV 104A and lever EV 112. In service applications it automatically laps port F and stops the discharge of brake pipe air, when the brake pipe reduction, corresponding to the service graduating notch in which the handle is placed, has been made.

Piston EV 104A, which is exposed on one side to

brake pipe pressure, chamber A, and on the other to chamber D and supplementary reservoir pressure, through the agency of lever EV 112 causes valve EV 110 to move automatically whatever distance is neces-

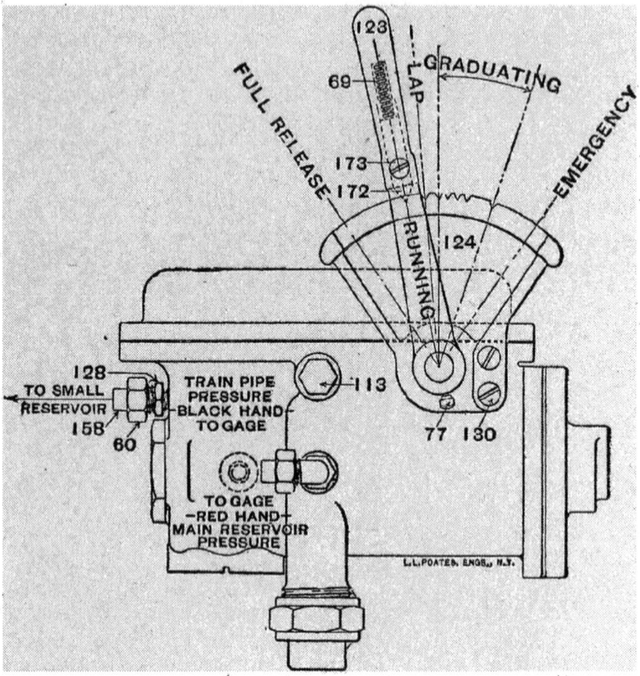

Fig. 15.

sary to close port F. Reducing brake pipe pressure (chamber A) by placing the handle in the service application position causes ball check EV 184 to seat and prevent the backward flow of air from chamber D to chamber A through piston EV 104A.

The supplementary reservoir pressure, therefore, will push piston EV 104A forward and move the small slide valve EV 110 as far to the right as the main slide valve was carried to the right, or until it closes port F.

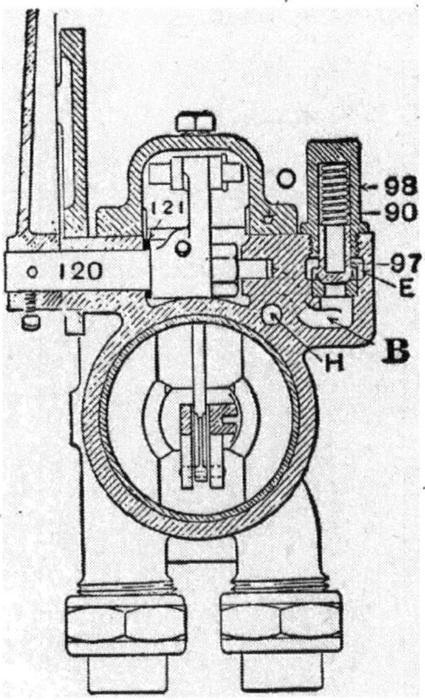

Fig. 16—Cross Section of New York Brake Valve, Showing Passage "H" in Body and Passage "O" in the Valve Cover.

Passage H (Fig. 17), runs lengthwise of the valve, one end leading to the supplementary reservoir, as indicated in the figure, while the other end leads to the space D, back of piston EV 104A.

In the release and the running position, air from chamber A passes through piston EV 104A to chamber D, thence through passage H to the supplementary reservoir until there is equal pressure on both sides of this piston, and the supplementary reservoir pressure is equal to the brake pipe pressure.

OPERATION.

The operation of the valve will be easily understood from Figs. 21, 22, 23, 24, 25 and 26, which show the various internal arrangements of valves and ports for each position of the brake valve handle.

RELEASE.

In this position (see Fig. 21), air is flowing direct from chamber B (main reservoir) into chamber A (brake pipe) past the end of valve EV 114A, through the large open-

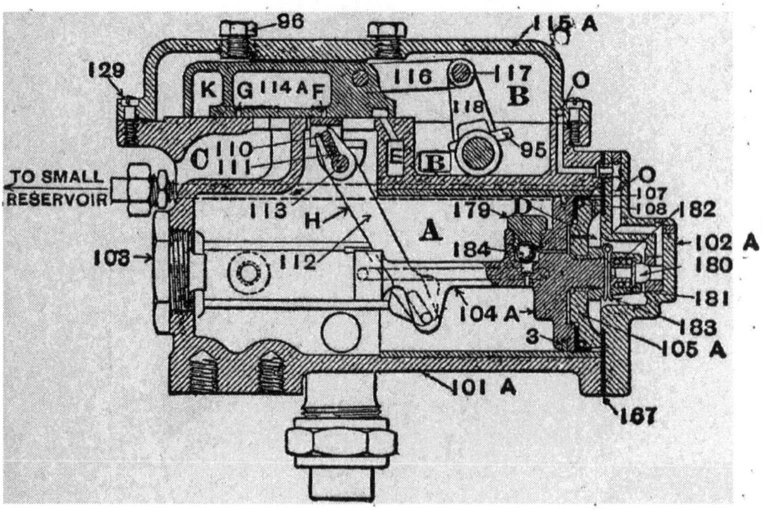

Fig. 17.

ing in the valve seat. This causes the brake pipe pressure to increase rapidly, and force the triple valve to release position.

Equalizing pistion EV 104A and small cut-off valve EV 110 are also returned to their normal positions, as shown, ready for another application.

When the handle is placed in release, a light puff of air will be heard at exhaust port C. This is air escaping from chamber D, through port O, which will reduce chamber D pressure sufficiently to allow piston EV 104A to return to its normal position and seat check valve EV

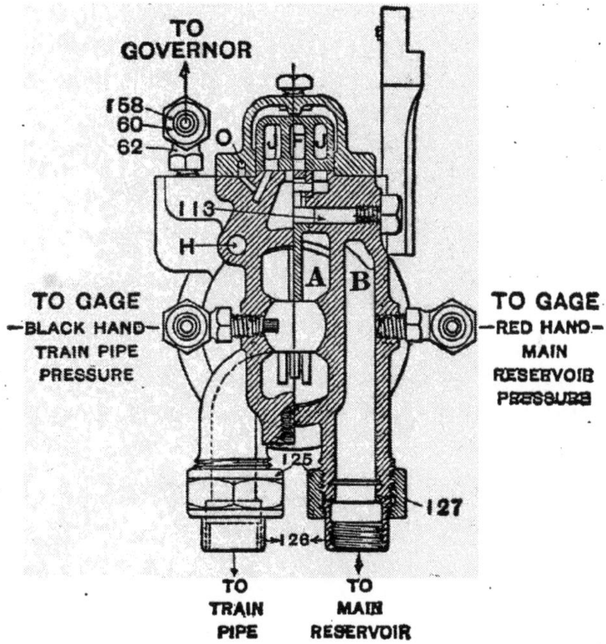

Fig. 18.

180, this check valve closing port O, and preventing further escape of chamber D air. Chamber D and the supplementary reservoir are charged as soon as check valve EV 180 seats, through ball check EV 184.

This is also true when the handle is returned from the application position to lap or to running position.

USE OF RELEASE POSITION.

When releasing brakes it is highly important, unless the train be unusually short, that the handle be placed in

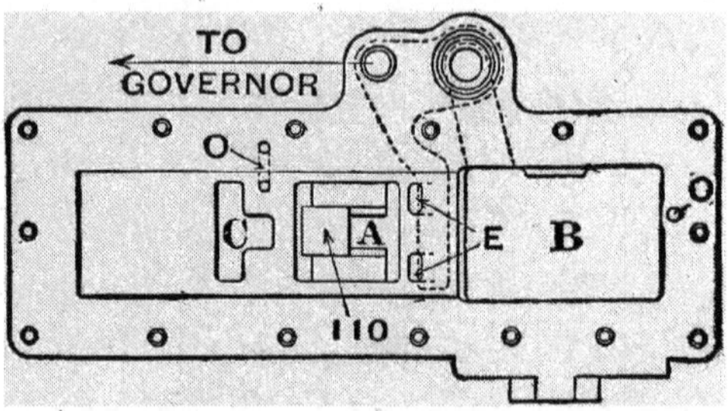

Fig. 19—Showing Port "O" in Main Slide Valve Seat.

"release" as shown in Fig. 21, and allowed to remain there until the red and the black hand, moving up to-

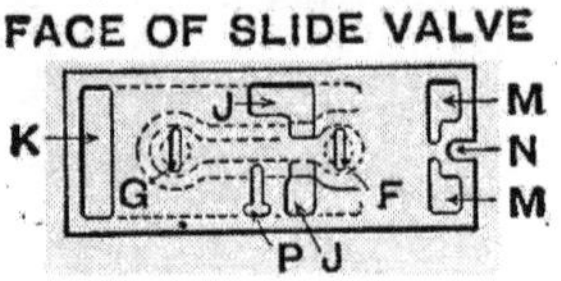

Fig. 20—Face of Slide Valve.

gether, reach the pressure for which the brake pipe pressure top of pump governor is adjusted, and the governor slows down the pump, then move the handle to running position, when the pump will accumulate the excess pressure.

The slowing down of the pump, when both gauge hands

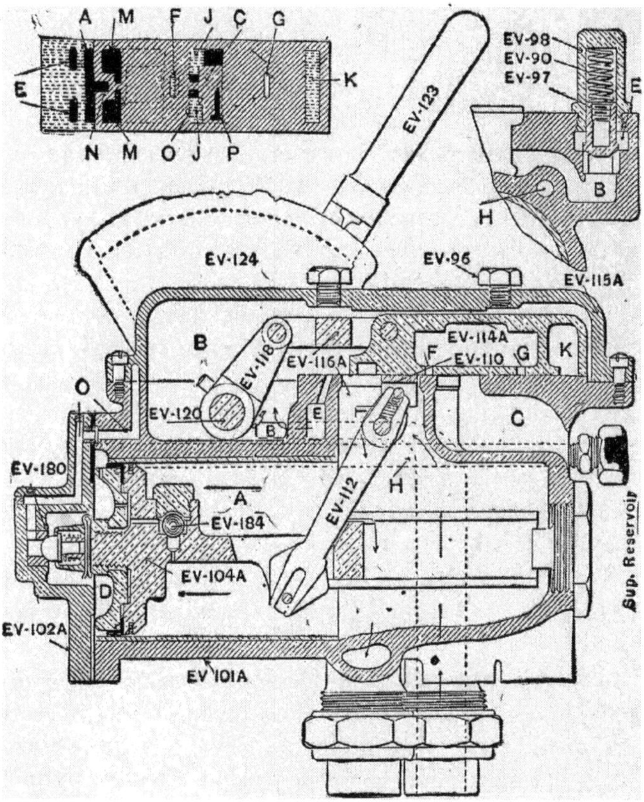

Fig. 21—Full Release Position of B-1 Brake Valve.

are at the brake pipe pressure figure indicates that the auxiliaries are recharged.

When handled in this way there is no danger of brakes "creeping on" on the front portion of the train during the time that the pump is accumulating sufficient excess pressure to lift the feed valve EV 97, and feed the brake pipe, while they are apt to do so if the handle is returned before the auxiliaries and brake pipe are fully recharged It might be remarked, however, that where large air pumps are employed, such as the No. 5 Duplex Pump, the time required to charge the main reservoir with 20 pounds excess is so short—about 20 seconds for a 60 thousand cubic inch reservoir—that there is very little chance of brakes creeping on even though the handle be moved to running position before the brake pipe and auxiliaries are fully equalized.

When charging trains in yards and terminals, and when recharging auxiliaries while descending grades, carry the handle in release position.

Under the above conditions of charging and recharging, time is of much more consequence than excess.

RUNNING POSITION.

In this position air from chamber B cannot flow directly into chamber A, but must pass the excess pressure, or the feed, valve, EV 97, before entering the brake pipe. The spring EV 90 has a tension sufficient to hold valve EV 97 on its seat against a pressure of 15 or 20 pounds, whichever amount of excess is carried, acting upwardly on it from chamber B.

Running position (see Fig. 22), is used, while the brakes are released and train is running, to accumulate the excess pressure in the main reservoir. Should brakes commence to "creep" on the drivers and front cars shortly after moving the handle to running from release position, move the handle quickly to release and back to running again once or twice. While running along with

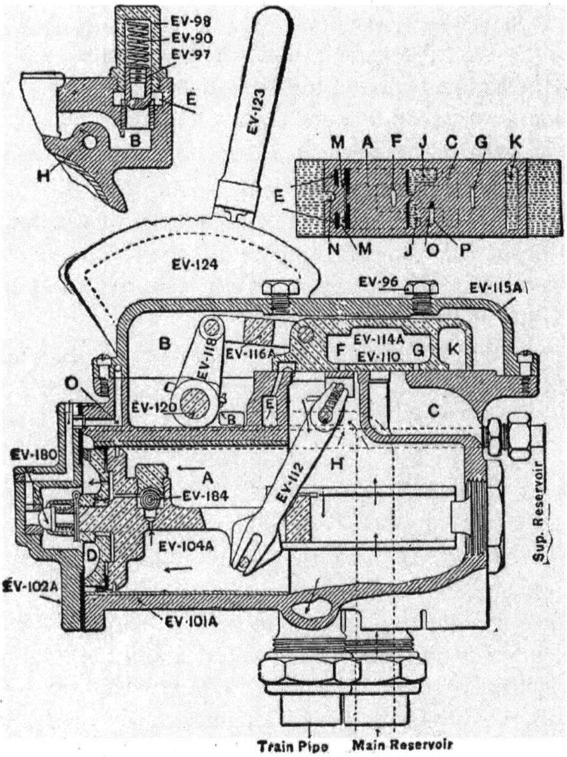

Fig. 22—Running Position B-1 New York Brake Valve.

all brakes properly released, do not practice moving the handle to release and then back to running as this will overcharge brake pipe, and surely cause the brakes to creep on.

POSITIVE LAP POSITION.

In this position (see Fig. 23), all communication between the main reservoir and the brake pipe, and between the brake pipe and the atmosphere, is closed. This position is used in making the two-application stop, to prevent over-charging of the brake pipe.

It is also used to test the main slide valve EV 114A, (see instructions on testing), and, should the equalizing feature become inoperative, to cut off the escape of brake pipe air when the required service reduction has been made, and hold the brakes applied.

Whenever the train parts or a hose bursts, the handle should be placed in positive lap position, to save main reservoir air.

An Important Use for Lap Position. The best method of stopping ordinary passenger trains at stations is by using the two application method.

This method requires that the service reduction on the first application be made heavy, while the speed of the train is high, applying the brakes with sufficient force to bring the train down to a speed of about ten miles per hour, within a few car lengths of the stopping point then releasing all brakes as nearly simultaneously as possible, by placing the handle in release position for a moment; then moving it to positive lap preparatory to the second and final application. A light reduction usually suffices for the second application and the brakes may be held on until the train stops, without producing severe recoil and jar at the stop.

The reason the handle is returned from release to positive lap position is to prevent overcharge of the brake

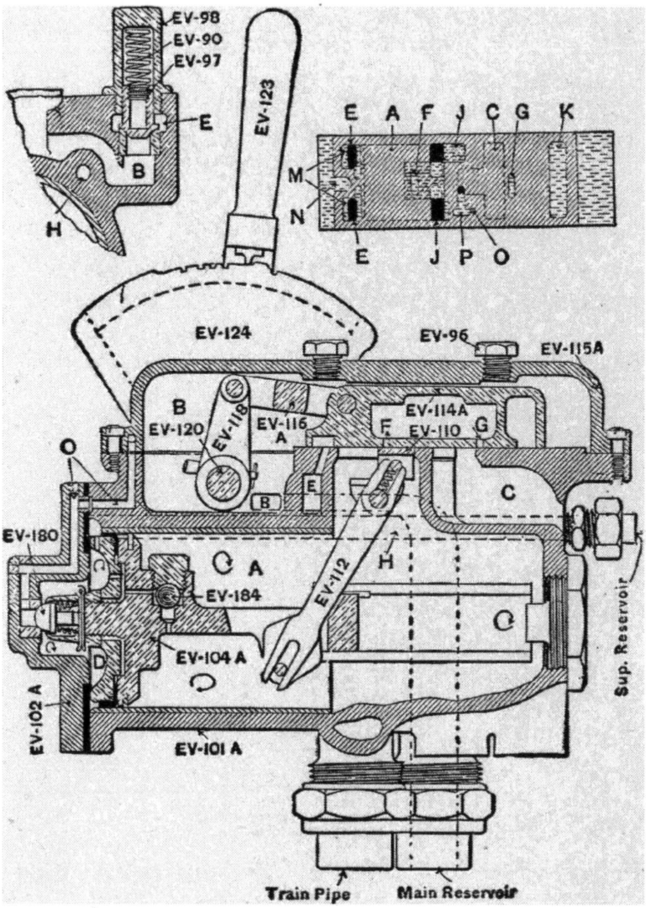

Fig. 23—Positive Lap Position, New York B-1 Brake Valve.

pipe, which, if it occurs, will cause tardy response of the brakes when the second and final application is made.

When the handle is placed in release position, the brake

pipe being short, the main reservoir air flows freely into it, and momentarily overcharges it. By quickly returning the handle to positive lap position, after first release,

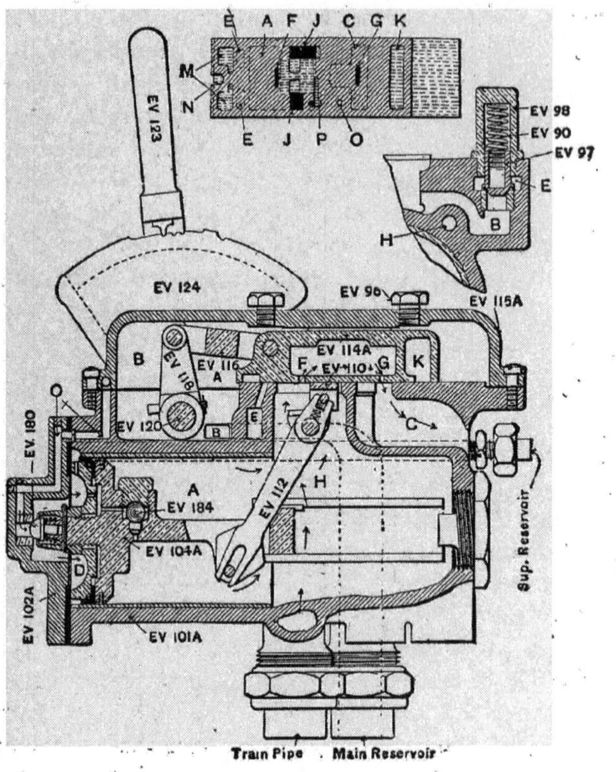

Fig. 24—Service Graduating Position, B-1 New York Brake Valve.

whatever over pressure there may be in the brake pipe is quickly taken up by the feed grooves in the triple valves, and a quick equalization of pressure between the auxiliary reservoir and the brake pipe is had. Thus, when the second application is desired, the triples respond promptly to the brake pipe reduction and the brakes apply promptly.

On modern long passenger trains, when releasing the brakes at moderate speed, the slack of the train should be held together by the use of the straight air brake, driver brake pressure retaining valves, or by restrictions placed in the driver brake triple valve exhaust ports. This precaution of holding driver brakes applied while train brakes are released is necessary on modern trains because of their greater length and weight and, consequently, the greater danger of breaking them in two On ordinary passenger trains, if but one application is used, the brakes should be released just before coming to a stop, to avoid shock caused by recoil of truck.

SERVICE GRADUATING POSITION.

In this position (see Fig. 24), ports F and G connect chamber A with exhaust port C and the atmosphere so that brake pipe air can escape gradually, and cause the brakes to apply gently with the necessary degree of force

Also port O in the slide valve seat is closed so that pressure in supplementary reservoir and chamber D can force piston EV 104A forward, and by means of lever EV 112 move cut-off valve EV 110 back to cover port F, when the brake pipe reduction is made that corresponds to the service graduating notch in which the handle is placed.

When it is desired to make a service application, the handle should be placed in the service graduating notch that will give the desired intitial brake pipe pressure reduction.

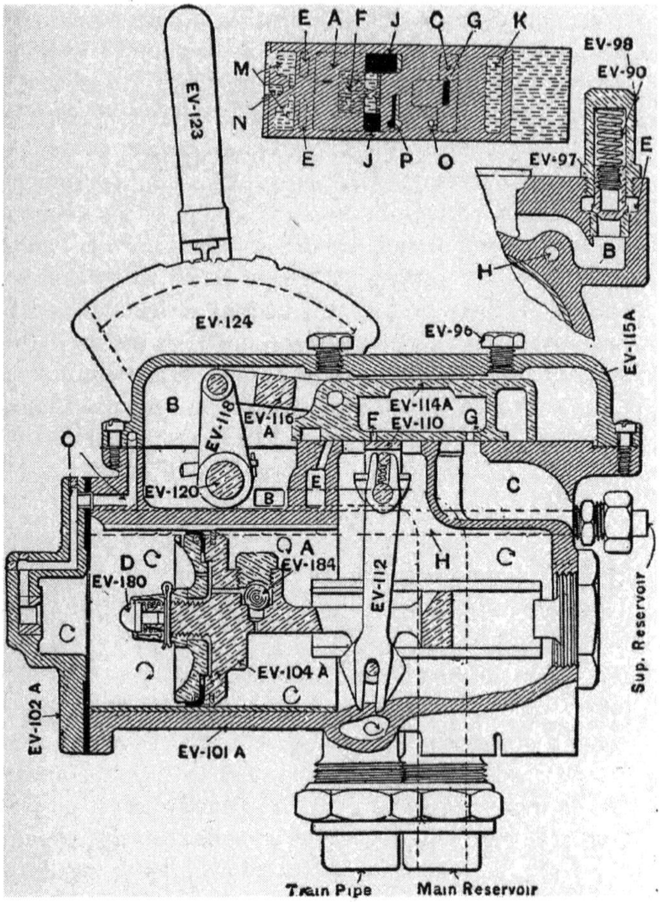

Fig. 25—Automatic Lap Position B-1 Brake Valve

Figure 24 shows the handle in the third service graduating notch.

Regardless of length of train the service graduating notches reduce brake pipe pressure as follows:

Brake Pipe Pressure	1st Ser Grad. Notch	2d Ser. Grad. Notch	3d Ser Grad. Notch	4th Ser Grad. Notch	5th Ser. Grad. Notch
70 lbs	5 - 5 lbs	8 - 3 lbs	11 - 3 lbs	16 - 5 lbs	23 - 7
90 lbs	5 - 5 lbs	9 - 4 lbs	13 - 4 lbs	19 - 6 lbs	27 - 8
110 lbs	6 - 6 lbs	10 - 4 lbs	14 - 4 lbs	21 - 7 lbs	30 - 9

The first figure in the column of notch reductions denotes the total reduction had when handle is placed in that notch; the second figures denote the reduction for that notch if handle is moved along successively from the first to the last notch, and the valve is allowed to lap automatically in each notch. The brakes are fully applied in service when the last graduating notch is used.

When the train consists of five or more cars the first graduating notch should not be used to make the initial service reduction; if less than five cars, the first service graduating notch should be used for the initial reduction.

When the train is very short, if the second graduating notch is used to make the initial reduction, there is danger of the triples applying in quick action, because of the small brake pipe volume to draw from.

AUTOMATIC LAP POSITION.

In this position (see Fig. 25), cut-off valve EV 110 has covered port F and stopped the escape of brake pipe air, and Fig. 25 shows the equalizing piston EV 104A moving forward, and cut-off valve EV 110 closing port F, the service exhaust port.

To make a further service reduction in brake pipe pressure the handle must be moved into the next service graduating notch.

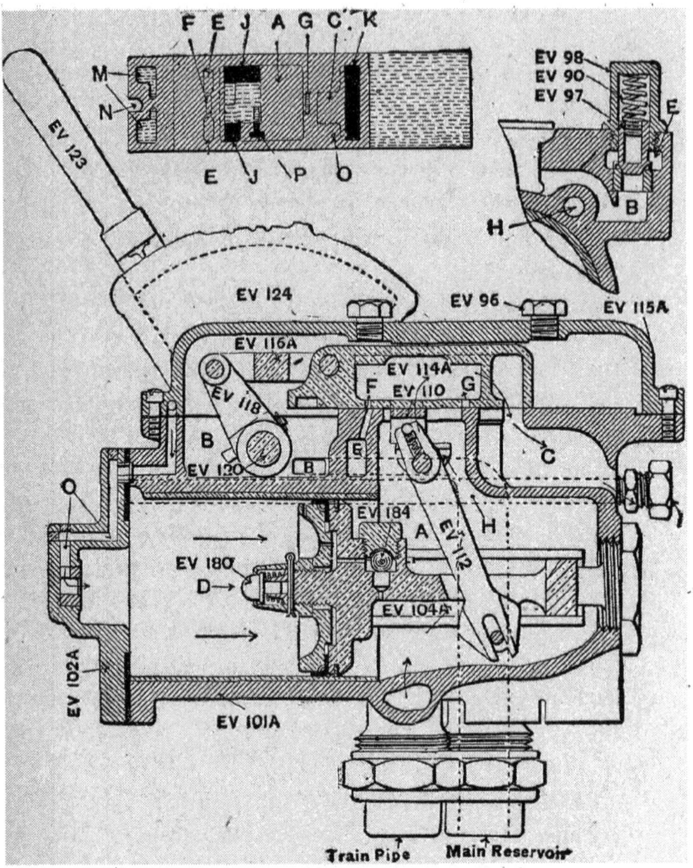

Fig. 26—Emergency Position, New York Brake Valve.

Should it happen that the automatic lapping feature did not operate perfectly, when making a service reduction, but instead allows the brake pipe exhaust to drag, move the handle back slowly a short distance, or until the exhaust ceases.

If, through accident, the pipe connecting the supplementary reservoir to the brake valve should become broken or disconnected, plug the connection at the brake valve; then in service applications, lap the brake valve by hand, returning the handle slowly to positive lap position after the required reduction in brake pipe pressure has been made.

EMERGENCY POSITION.

In this position (see Fig. 26), the brake pipe has a large, direct passage to the atmosphere, and the air can escape quickly through the large ports J and K in the slide valve EV 114A to the exhaust port C in the seat, thence to the atmosphere.

The emergency position is for the purpose of producing a quick, heavy reduction in brake pipe pressure so that all triple valves on the train will operate in quick action and apply the brakes in the shortest possible time.

Whenever there is danger of wreck or accident, which requires a quick stop to avoid, move the handle quickly to the emergency position and leave it there until the train stops or the danger is removed. This opens the brake pipe wide to the atmosphere, and all brakes apply with full force.

GENERAL INSTRUCTIONS.

Before starting out on a trip see that all pipe connections about the brake valve and engine equipment are absolutely air tight and that the piston travel of the driver brake is not over 5 inches; of the tender and engine truck brakes not over 7 inches.

See that the main slide valve EV 114A is properly lubricated and that the excess pressure valve EV 97 is clean. To lubricate the main slide valve, remove the oil plugs EV 96, place the handle in release and pour two or three drops of machine oil through the rear oil hole; move handle to emergency and pour the same through the front oil hole; replace oil plugs and work the handle back and forth a few times to spread the oil well over the seat.

To clean the excess pressure valve EV 97 remove cap EV 97, take out valve and clean with a little kerosene—do not scrape it—and replace perfectly dry Never put oil on the excess, or feed, valve when replacing it.

Do not attempt to lubricate the main slide valve or to clean the excess pressure valve while there is pressure in the main reservoir This should be attended to before air pump is started.

In setting the regulating spring of the excess pressure valve, place the brake valve handle in running position, and let the pressure pump up until the red hand of the gauge shows twenty pounds before the black hand begins to move. Should the black hand begin to move before the red hand reaches twenty pounds it indicates that the regulating spring needs to be tightened down, while, on the other hand, if the black hand of the gauge did not begin to move until the red hand had passed the twenty pound mark, then the regulating spring should be loosened up.

With the New York brake valve handle in running position the excess pressure is accumulated before the train-pipe pressure begins to show, but with the Westinghouse brake valve the excess pressure is not produced until after the train pipe is fully charged.

The new style brake valves B-2 and B-3 are virtually the same as B-1, excepting that they contain an additional function whereby the engine brakes are applied with straight air when the handle is in full release position These valves do not change the arrangement of triple valves and double check valves on the engine and tender, as these remain the same as before. Should it be desired to release an automatic application of the engine brakes while the train brakes are applied, it can be done by using the independent release valve. Another feature of the B-2 and B-3 equipment is the accelerator valve, which is operated by the exhaust pressure from the train pipe forcing a piston down, thereby creating a second opening from the train pipe to the atmosphere.

REPAIRS TO STYLE B AND B-1 NEW YORK ENGINEER'S BRAKE VALVES.

Dismantling.—The top cap EV 115 should first be removed and then the back cap EV 102A. The main slide valve EV 114A should be taken off, and the graduating or cut-off slide valve EV 110 lifted out; also the graduating valve spring EV 111. Next remove the graduating slide valve lever fulcrum bolt EV 113, after which remove graduating piston EV 104A.

Do not attempt to remove the nuts from piston EV 104A before taking it out of the brake valve body, as to do so would probably result either in springing the groove in the piston stem, or in breaking off the dowel pin in the valve body.

After the brake valve is dismantled the various parts should be placed in a bath of hot lye, and allowed to remain in it long enough to remove all the gum from the ports. It is not advisable to put the back cap lead gasket EV 167 in this bath as the lead would partly dissolve, and portions of the dissolved lead would adhere to other parts in the lye.

After removing all the parts from the lye bath, they should be thoroughly blown off with steam, and a careful examination of them made, to note the wear of the main slide valve on its seat, and the wear on the piston bush, and also to note the general condition.

If the piston bush is worn 1/64-inch the brake valve should be returned to the manufacturer for repairs

If the slide valve seat is badly worn the valve body should be taken to the planer and a cut taken across the seat just sufficient to clean it up. The main slide valve should be gone over in the same manner. This work is done much more quickly in this way than it could be by filing the valve seat and valve face down to a smooth even surface.

The main slide valve is made of hard metal, and care should be taken when machining not to allow the tool to break off the sharp edges at the ports or on the ends of the valve. This would enlarge the ports and would probably cause trouble in handling the train.

The slide valve seat should then be scraped down to a perfect bearing.

It is much better to scrape than to grind these parts to a bearing, as the valve will handle much better; the lubricating oil has a chance to lodge in the small scratches left by the scraper in the cast iron seat, making the lubrication more efficient and assisting in making a tight joint.

The graduating slide valve should be fitted in the same manner as the main slide valve; and when assembling, care should be taken to see that it can be pressed below the slide valve seat. This is an important point that should not be overlooked.

The front and back edges of the slide valve and of the graduating valve should be kept perfectly square. When these edges are worn off it allows dirt to work between the faces, which makes it necessary, on account of the extra wear, to reface them oftener; while if the edges are kept perfectly sharp, the dirt is pushed ahead of the slide valve and off the seat, preventing possibility of leakage, and of undue wear.

If a small shoulder is found in the piston bush, it should be scraped out, and the cylinder finished up extra smooth.

If, upon examination, the piston stem should be found bent, it should be straightened perfectly or a new piston and stem should be applied.

A new packing ring QT 3 should be applied to the graduating piston, care being taken to have it fit perfectly free in the piston groove, tight enough to prevent leakage, and yet not get follower bound. The packing ring should also be fitted to the cylinder so as to have a perfect bearing all around, and yet be able to move perfectly free in the cylinder.

If the vent valve EV 180, on the end of the piston, is badly worn it should be renewed, and if the ball check valve seat is worn it should be reseated, and a new ball EV 184 applied, grinding it a little to make it tight.

A new packing leather EV 107 should be applied to the piston, placing the flesh, or rough, side next to the wall of the cylinder. The expander EV 108 should be renewed, if it is worn. If one of the small coils of the expander is higher than the other, it is likely to cut through the leather. In placing it in the cylinder be careful not to spring the coils out of place.

The feed valve EV 97 should be ground in carefully, and the lip on this valve should clear the top of the seat about 1/64 of an inch. If this lip is too close to the seat, it will soon wear down so that it will seat on it; if it has too much clearance, it will not be sufficiently sensitive. The feed valve spring EV 90 should be examined to ascertain its condition, and to see if it has the proper height. If the spring is worn, a new one should be applied. These springs should have a free height of 1½ inch, and eight coils.

The link EV 116A, pins EV 117A, main slide valve lever EV 118, graduating slide valve lever EV 112, and fulcrum pin EV 113, if worn sufficiently to produce any lost motion, should be renewed. There should never be any lost motion in the slide valve connections, if there is, the valve will not automatically reduce the brake pipe pressure the desired amount in the service graduating notches.

Assembling.—Before assembling the valve the cylinder surface should be well covered with valve oil or with high grade machine oil, and the packing leather and the packing ring, on the piston, should also be well lubricated. After the piston EV 104A is replaced in the cylinder a new back cap gasket EV 167 should be applied; then the back cap EV 102A may be replaced, using plumbago on the head screws EV 129. After the head screws are first drawn up tight, the cap should be tapped lightly between the screws with a hammer; then the screws may be tightened up solid, and this will insure a perfect joint.

The lever shaft EV 120 may now be put in, using a new leather shaft washer EV 121, well oiled. The slide valve lever EV 118 should be well tightened on the lever shaft, and the taper lever shaft pin EV 95 driven in tight. The ½-inch nut should be drawn up tight after the taper pin is driven in, and the small cotter pin driven through the end of the lever shaft pin.

Before putting on the handle EV 123, drop a little oil around the latch pin EV 172. This will prevent the latch from sticking in the quadrant notches.

The lever EV 112, lever pin EV 113, the graduating valve EV 110, with its spring EV 111 should be put in, then the main slide valve EV 114A placed on its seat and connected to the handle lever shaft by the link EV 116, and link pins EV 117. A heavy-bodied oil should then be used on the slide valve and its seat. A new cover gasket made of heavy oiled paper should be put on, care being taken to see that the small port holes are cut properly in this gasket, and that they register with the corresponding ports in its valve seat. After the valve cover EV 115A is put on and properly secured the valve is ready for testing.

TESTING OF BRAKE VALVE.

The brake valve should be tested with a reservoir volume of about 20,000 cubic inches, corresponding to, or the equivalent of, at least 25 cars. This volume is desirable in order to test satisfactorily the equalizing feature of the valve, to make sure that it will operate satisfactorily on a long train.

The method of testing should be as follows:

Empty the brake pipe by placing the handle in emergency position, then place handle in lap position, this will empty the supplementary reservoir; close the cut-out cock under the brake valve, and place the brake valve handle on positive lap position. Maintain 90 pounds pressure in the main reservoir.

If the slide valve leaks the main reservoir air will pass into the brake pipe above the cut-out cock, and an increase of pressure will be indicated by the black hand of the air gauge.

Feed Valve Test.—With the brake pipe charged to 70 pounds, and a brake pipe volume the equivalent of the engine and tender, and 85 pounds main reservoir pressure, the black hand should stand at 70 pounds. If there is any leakage by the excess pressure valve it will increase the brake pipe pressure, and this increase will be indicated by the black hand on the air gauge. Where the duplex pump governor is used, 15 pounds excess pressure is recommended, and the excess pressure valve should maintain this

Equalizing Piston Test.—With the brake pipe pressure at 70 pounds, and the brake valve handle placed in the first service graduating notch, the brake pipe pressure should reduce five pounds If the valve fails to cut off it is an indication of a leak past the packing leather, or past the ball check valve EV 184; or a leak past both, allowing the air to pass from chamber D and supplementary reservoir into the brake pipe; or there is a leak from the back of piston EV 104A to the atmosphere past a defective back head gasket EV 167, from a supplementary reservoir connection, or there is a leak at the small port O in the slide valve seat.

The reductions from the brake pipe pressure at 70 pounds in the service graduating positions should be 5; 5; 3; 3 and 7 pounds respectively.

Care should be taken to have the brake pipe pressure just at 70 pounds when making these reductions. If the valve fails to lap automatically after the brake pipe pressure has reduced 5 pounds, in the first service graduating notch, there being no leak in the supplementary reservoir chamber or any of its connections, it is an indication that there is too much lost motion in the connections to the main slide valve.

Tightness of Cut-Off Valve—To test this valve, place the handle in the first service graduating notch, with only the volume of the engine and tender piping attached. If a continuous blow occurs at the exhaust port, after making the required reduction in brake pipe pressure, accompanied by a falling of the black hand of the gauge, this valve is leaking.

Before commencing test be sure the air gauge is accurate.

NEW YORK DUPLEX AIR PUMP.

QUESTIONS AND ANSWERS.

Q. How many sizes are there of the New York Duplex Air Pump?

A. Four; known as Nos. 1, 2, 5 and 6.

Q. How many cylinders has the duplex air pump?

A. Four; two steam and two air cylinders.

Q. Give the dimensions of each size pump

A. The No. 1 pump has both steam cylinders 5 inches each in diameter; one air cylinder, known as the high pressure air cylinder, 5 inches in diameter, and one air cylinder, known as the low pressure air cylinder, 7 inches in diameter.

The No. 2 pump has both steam cylinders, 7 inches each in diameter; one high pressure air cylinder 7 inches in diameter, and one low pressure air cylinder 10 inches in diameter.

The No. 5 pump has both steam cylinders 8 inches each in diameter, one high pressure air cylinder 8 inches in diameter, and one low pressure air cylinder 12 inches in diameter. The stroke of the Nos 1 and 2 pumps is 9 inches; that of the No. 5 is 12 inches.

The No. 6 pump has both steam cylinders 7 inches in diameter, one high pressure air cylinder 7 inches in diameter, and one low pressure air cylinder 11 inches in diameter. The stroke of the No. 6 pump is 10 inches.

Q. What is the relative position of the steam and the

air cylinders with respect to each other when the pump is in position on the locomotive?

A. The air cylinders are above the steam cylinders.

Q. What are the relative volumes, or capacities, of the high pressure and the low pressure air cylinders of each pump?

A. The low pressure air cylinder of each size of air pump has a volume, or capacity, about double that of the high pressure air cylinder.

Q. Are the steam cylinders of each of these pumps always the same size as the high pressure air cylinder?

A. Yes.

Q. Describe the steam end of the pump.

A. The steam end of the pump consists of two steam cylinders of equal diameter, and a steam head, having in it two reversing valve chambers and two reversing slide valves, one of each for each steam cylinder. The steam pipe connection, from the boiler, is made to this steam head, and the exhaust connection, for the exhaust steam from the cylinders, is also made to this steam head at the opposite end.

Q. How is the steam distributed in the duplex pump?

A. The piston in each steam cylinder operates the reversing slide valve that controls the flow of steam into the other steam cylinder, and from that cylinder to the atmosphere.

Q. How is this accomplished?

A. By locating the slide valve for the right steam cylinder in the valve chamber under the left steam cylinder, and the slide valve for the left steam cylinder in the valve chamber under the right steam cylinder; and by crossing the steam ports as shown in the drawings.

Q. Describe the steam valves and the seats.

A. They are ordinary D slide valves, such as are used in locomotives; they admit steam to the cylinder by the outside edge, and exhaust it from the cylinder through a cavity in the center; and the seats have three ports, two steam and one exhaust, the exhaust port being between the two steam ports.

Q. Which piston will start first when steam is admitted to the pump?

A. The right, or what is commonly known as the low pressure piston. On account of the arrangement of the steam ports, and design of the reversing valve gear, the low pressure piston will always be the first to start from rest, and will lead the other or high pressure piston.

Q. What actuates the steam valves?

A. Valve stems, familiarly known as reversing valve stems or tappet rods, which are attached to the steam valves, and extend into the hollow piston rods.

Q. How are the tappet rods moved?

A. The piston rod is made hollow on the steam end for a distance sufficient to clear this valve stem; a plate is bolted on to the steam piston head in such a manner as alternately to strike a button head, and a shoulder, on the tappet rod, just before the stroke of the piston in either direction is completed, and thus moves this rod up and down a distance equal to the travel of the valve, changing the steam valve from one position to the other in the steam chest.

Q. Does the upper steam port in each steam chest lead to the upper end of its respective steam cylinder?

A. No; the upper port in the left steam chest leads to the lower end of the right cylinder, while the upper port in the right chest leads to the upper end of the left cylinder.

Q. Do both pistons of the duplex pump move at the same time?

A. No; after one piston makes a stroke, it waits until the other makes a stroke.

Q. Explain the movement of the pistons.

A. Both pistons and steam valves being at rest in the lower end of the cylinders, when steam is turned on, the right piston makes a stroke up; at the completion of this stroke, the piston changes the position of its reversing slide valve, causing the left piston to take steam and make a stroke up. At the completion of the up-stroke of the left piston, this piston changes the position of its reversing slide valve, causing the right piston to take steam and move down.

When the low pressure piston completes its down stroke it shifts its reversing slide valve so as to admit steam to the upper end of the opposite cylinder, so that the high pressure piston makes its down stroke

Q. Describe the air end of the duplex pump.

A. It consists of two air cylinders, one larger than the other, and of six (the No. 5 pump has 8) air valves, with their seats and cages. The larger air cylinder has a capacity about double that of the smaller air cylinder. Two of the air valves, upper and lower, are known as the air inlet valves, simply; two, upper and lower, located just above, are called the intermediate air inlet and discharge valves; and two, located in the final discharge passage of the high pressure cylinder, are known as the final discharge valves. The No. 5 pump has independent air inlet and air discharge valves.

Q. Where are the air valves located?

A. The air inlet valves are located in the air passages leading from the atmosphere to the low pressure air cylinder; the intermediate air inlet and discharge valves in air passages leading from low pressure cylinder to high pressure cylinder; the high pressure and the final discharge valves in passages leading from high pressure cylinder to the main reservoir.

Q. Explain how free air is taken into the air cylinders.

A. The low pressure piston moves up first to the end of its stroke, creating a vacuum behind it, and free air from the atmosphere follows it into the low pressure air cylinder through the lower air inlet valve; the high pressure piston then moves up to the end of its stroke, the air from the atmosphere follows it through the lower air inlet valve and lower intermediate air inlet and discharge valve into the high pressure cylinder; on the down stroke of the low pressure piston air is taken into the low pressure cylinder at the upper end from the atmosphere through the upper air inlet valve in the same manner as it was taken in at the lower end on the previous up stroke; on the down stroke of the high pressure piston, air is taken into the high pressure air cylinder through the upper air inlet valve and intermediate air inlet and discharge valve in the same manner as on the previous up stroke.

Q. Explain how the air is discharged from the air cylinders.

A. The low pressure piston moving up compresses the air in front of it and discharges it past the upper intermediate air inlet valve and discharge valve into the high pressure air cylinder; the high pressure piston then moves upward, compressing the air in front of it to a pressure equalling that in the main reservoir, and then discharges it past the upper final discharge valve into the discharge pipe and main reservoir. This operation is repeated through the lower air valves on the down strokes of the air pistons.

Q. What air pressure does the low pressure piston always work against?

A. About 40 pounds, after the pressure in the main reservoir has reached this amount.

Q. How much pressure does the high pressure piston work against?

A. When about 30 or 40 pounds pressure has accumulated in the main reservoir the high pressure piston always starts on its stroke against the pressure accumulated in its cylinder by the low pressure piston, and must compress the air it contains to a pressure slightly above that in the main reservoir in order to raise the final discharge valve, and discharge the air to the reservoir.

Q. What should be known about the air pump before leaving the round-house?

A. That the piston rod packing does not leak; that there are no unusual knocks or pounds; that the steam exhausts are regular; and that the air-compressing capacity is normal.

DISORDERS AND REMEDIES.

Q. What will be the result if the rod packing blows out?

A. It will blow the oil from the rod and swabs. If it is the air end high pressure rod packing that is blowing, it will lower the capacity of the pump very materially, and the cushion which the pump should have to prevent the piston from striking the head will be lost.

If it is the rod packing on the steam end that is blowing, it will permit a waste of steam from the steam cylinders, and a large portion of this waste steam will be taken in at the lower air receiving valves, helping to increase the quantity of water which gathers in the main reservoir.

Q. Give the common causes for pounding of pump.

A. The loss of air cushion to stop the pistons at the completion of the stroke, due to air piston packing or air cylinder packing leaking, and on modern engines, high pressure steam and racing the pumps.

Q. What are the other causes for pump pounding?

A. Loose reversing plates on the steam piston heads; badly worn button head on the end of valve stem; pump loose on its bracket fastenings to boiler; back leakage through the final discharge valve, and racing the pump against low main reservoir pressure.

Q. Suppose either of these troubles had existed and had been remedied and the pump still pounds, what is wrong?

A. It will probably be found that either the steam or the air piston head is loose on the rod, which is probably the result of loss of cushion and of permitting the piston to strike the head.

Q. What are the causes for the steam exhausts to sound irregular?

A. Air leakage from the main reservoir back into the high pressure cylinder, from the high pressure cylinder into the low pressure cylinder, or an air valve stuck to its seat.

Q. What is wrong if the steam exhausts sound in two pairs, one pair spaced well apart, and the other pair very close together?

A. An intermediate air valve, or a cylinder-head gasket is leaking at a point between the two cylinders.

Q. How could this cause it?

A. By permitting the air from the high pressure cylinder to pass over into the low pressure cylinder, thus forcing the low pressure piston away from its cylinder end, instead of forcing the air into the main reservoir. As a result, when the low pressure piston takes steam, it has both steam and air pressure to cause it to make a quick stroke, which brings two steam exhausts very close together.

Q. What is wrong with the pump when the spaces between three exhausts are about equal and the space between the third and fourth exhaust is very long?

A. A discharge valve is probably broken, or the upper air cylinder gasket is leaking badly between the final discharge valve cavity and air cylinder; or the lower intermediate valve seat is loose and has worked up sufficiently to raise the intermediate air valve against its stop post.

Q What will be the result if the upper intermediate valve seat works loose?

A. As it forms the lift stop for the upper air inlet valve, the seat will work down and prevent the opening of the receiving valve.

Q. When an air pump stops of its own accord, what should be done to correct the trouble?

A. First examine the pump governor carefully to see that the relief ports are open, that is, the small relief port above the governor piston, or in the diaphragm body (see pump governor) and also the one in the spring case. If a constant blow of air is found at the little port above the governor piston it is an indication that the governor is at fault, and it should be examined and repaired.

If it is found that the governor is in perfect order, then jar the steam head lightly. If this does not start the pump close the air pump throttle, open the waste cock on the steam chest of the pump, and allow all steam to drain away, then open the pump throttle.

Q. If, after making the throttle test, the low pressure piston moves up and stops at the upper end of the stroke, and the high pressure piston refuses to move, where should the trouble be looked for?

A. In the steam reversing gear on the right, or low pressure, side. Probably the valve-stem has broken, or the reversing plate has worn through.

Q. After the throttle test, suppose the low pressure piston moves up, then the high pressure, too, but the low pressure piston fails to move down, what is the probable cause of the trouble?

A. The valve stem is probably broken, or the reversing plate worn through on the high pressure side.

Q. How should you test for back leakage from the low pressure air cylinder through air inlet valves?

A. By holding the hand on, or close to either of these valves while the low pressure piston is moving toward it, if they leak, air will be felt blowing past them.

Q. How can leakage past intermediate valves be detected?

A. By the earlier movement of the low pressure piston away from the defective valve, and the weak intake of air at the inlet valves, upper or lower, as the case may be, and also by the heating of the pump.

Q. How can leakage past the final discharge valves in high pressure cylinder be detected?

A. By the slower movement of both the low and the high pressure pistons toward the leaky valve, and the quicker movement of the high pressure piston away from it.

Q. What will be the result if either of the steam piston heads pulls off the rod?

A. The pump will stop.

Q. How could you tell that a steam piston head had pulled off?

A. A hard steam blow at the exhaust will be noticed, the same as though a blower was turned on full.

Q. Should the pump stop on account of a piston rod nut working off, how could the loose nut be located?

A. The piston will strike hard on the air end. By removing the oil cups it can be located by running a piece of wire through the oil cup hole.

Q. Could this defect be remedied on the road?

A. If the top air head is removed, the nut can be put back on the rod, or removed entirely from the cylinder, with very little trouble. Usually, however, but little can be done on the road in the way of extensive repairs.

Q. What usually causes the intermediate air inlet valves to stick open?

A. If the low pressure cylinder is given too much oil it will collect on the intermediate discharge valve, and probably cause it to stick open.

Q. What are the probable causes for the air pump running hot?

A. Leaks by the piston rod packing; also a leaky intermediate discharge valve; leaky receiving valves or badly worn packing rings in the air end, and racing under high pressure steam.

Q If the pump runs hot what should be done to cool it off?

A. If the air valves are clean, and the piston rod packing tight a small quantity of valve oil should be used in the high pressure air cylinder, and the pump run as slow as possible, for a short period of time, to give it a chance to cool.

Q How should an air pump be started?

A. The pump drain cock should be opened until all water is drained off, and then the pump started very slowly, running it slowly until 35 or 40 pounds air pressure is accumulated in the main reservoir. This pressure is needed to form a cushion for the air piston.

Q. Why should the pump be started slowly?

A. Because all locomotive air pumps depend more or less on the air pressure in the main reservoir cushioning the air pistons to prevent them from striking the heads, and starting them up rapidly causes the pistons to pound and get loose.

Q. How fast should the pump be run, and how should the steam cylinders be lubricated?

A. Just fast enough to maintain the maximum pressure and the train pipe leakage, and oil should be fed continuously to the steam cylinders, according to the work it is doing.

Q. If this pump is run at a high rate of speed would any more air be compressed than at a moderate speed?

A. As the air valves must have time to seat, the pump will do better at a reasonable speed, not over 60 double strokes per minute.

THE NO. 5 DUPLEX AIR PUMP.

Q. Is there any difference in principle of operation between the No. 5 Duplex Air Pump and the Nos. 1 and 2 Duplex Pumps.

A. No; the principle of operation is the same.

Q. In what particulars does the No. 5 pump differ from the others?

A. Principally in design and proportions of parts, and in having larger pumping capacity.

Q. In what ways is the design of the No. 5 pump an improvement over the others?

A. In the air end an independent set of air inlet valves is provided for the high pressure air cylinder, and each air valve for the air cylinders is in a cage by itself, where it is easily accessible for repairs and renewals, and air inlet passages of large capacity are provided for the air inlet valves.

In the steam end the reversing slide valves are provided with flat seats and the reversing valve chamber caps are bolted to the steam head with tap bolts, instead of being screwed in, as in the other pumps.

The stroke of the pump is considerably increased, the ratio of clearance space to cylinder volume is materially reduced.

Q. What benefit is derived from reducing the clearance spaces of the pump cylinders?

A. It increases the efficiency of the pump in both the air and steam ends, and materially reduces the chances of heating and damage due to working the pump too fast.

Q. What size pipe is used with the No. 5 pump for the various connections?

A. For the air discharge to the main reservoir and for the steam exhaust, 1½-inch pipe is used. For the steam supply 1¼-inch pipe is used, although 1-inch pipe may be used with good results.

LUBRICATION OF AIR CYLINDERS.

Q. How many styles of automatic oil cups are there?

A. Two, one known as style A, and the other style B.

Q. What is the difference between the two styles of automatic oil cups?

A. Style A has a fixed feed, while style B has an adjustable feed.

Q. What can render the operation of the cup defective?

A. Should scale or dirt get into the small feed port in the cap or adjustable needle feed on top of the center post, blocking it up, then the cup would not feed properly.

Q. In filling up the cup with oil, should care be taken to see that the oil is clean?

A. Yes; since the feed port through the oil cup must be very small, care should be taken to see that the oil is perfectly clean before being put into the cup.

Q. Should the automatic oil cup be filled level full?

A. No; in filling the cup leave a little space in the top so that as the cylinder warms up, a little room will be left for expansion of the oil, and so that there will be no waste.

Q. How often should these cups be filled with oil?

A. That will depend upon the service in which the pump is employed and the amount of work it is required to do.

Q. What kind of oil should be used in the automatic oil cup?

A. Good valve oil always; never use engine oil.

Q. Why should engine oil never be used to lubricate the air cylinder?

A. As the temperature in the air cylinders, due to the compression of the air, is usually higher than the flashing point of engine oil, this oil cannot lubricate them properly. Good valve oil should always be used for lubricating the air cylinders, because it remains oil instead of gas at a higher temperature than the air cylinders usually reach.

Q. When the governor causes the pump to run very slowly or stop momentarily, will the automatic oil cup feed oil at the same rate as when the pump is running at its normal rate?

A No; the automatic oil cup can feed oil only when the pistons are moving. When the pump is stopped the automatic oil cups cease to supply oil to the air cylinders, and retain what remains in the cup until the time when the pump is again started.

Q. Can the cup be filled without stopping the pump?

A. Yes; as easily as when the pump is stopped.

Q Why is automatic lubrication of the air cylinders more necessary now than formerly?

A. Because of the much harder work the air pump is required to do, and the inability of the engineman to lubricate it frequently enough by hand to prevent groaning and cutting.

PUMP GOVERNORS.

Note.—As the construction and action of the single styles of the New York pump governors are practically the same as the Westinghouse single governors, the questions and answers pertaining to the Westinghouse will also apply to the New York type of single governor.

DUPLEX PUMP GOVERNOR—HIGH PRESSURE CONTROL.

Q. When the duplex pump governor is used for the "double pressure" system, how is it piped?

A. Both tops are connected to chamber E at the brake valve, or the brake valve governor connection proper, in front of the feed valve, and a tee for dividing the connecting pipe is put in at a convenient point; a stop cock is placed between the tee and the low pressure governor top.

Q. How are these governor tops adjusted?

A. One is adjusted to operate when the ordinary brake pipe pressure of 70 pounds has accumulated, and the other, when using the high pressure control, is usually adjusted at 90 pounds, and sometimes 100, to operate when this pressure has accumulated in the brake pipe.

Q. When it is desired to use the higher brake pipe pressure, what is it necessary to do?

A. To cut out the low pressure governor top. This is done by closing the stop cock in the branch pipe to this top, thus placing the control of the pump under the high pressure top.

Q. For what class of service is the high pressure control used?

A. It is used on coal and mineral roads and in places where the majority of the trains are hauled with the cars empty in one direction, and with them loaded in the other; the light or ordinary pressure is used on trains when running with the cars empty, and the higher pressure is used on them when they are loaded.

Q. In addition to the duplex pump governor, properly piped, what other apparatus is necessary?

A. Safety valves, such as are used with the combined automatic and straight air brake, are necessary for the driver brakes, tender brakes, and for the engine trucks if it has a brake.

Q. Why are safety valves necessary for the brake cylinders named?

A. Because the braking force upon the locomotive is

calculated from a brake pipe pressure of 70 pounds to give all the wheels will stand ordinarily, and the weight of the locomotive hardly ever varies much; so that if a higher braking force were employed one time than another it would probably tend to slide the wheels.

Q. When using the "high pressure control" how much excess pressure is carried?

A. Just the same as with the ordinary pressure, about 20 pounds.

TRIPLEX GOVERNOR.

Q. In what service is the triplex governor used?

A. It is used in place of the duplex with the "high pressure control" system, in freight service on both level and mountainous roads, and also for high speed passenger service.

Q. How is the triplex governor piped up?

A. One top is piped direct to the brake pipe connection at the brake valve, and sometimes to the brake pipe direct, below the cut-out cock, and this top is adjusted for the higher brake pipe pressure; in this pipe a tee is placed, and connection from this tee is made to another governor top, which is adjusted for the lower brake pipe pressure; the third top is piped to the main reservoir pressure direct, either at the brake valve, or at the main reservoir, as convenience requires.

Q. With the triplex governor, how can the change be made from the lower brake pipe pressure to the higher, when desired?

A. By closing the stop cock in the branch pipe leading from the main governor pipe connection to the low pressure governor top, just as in the "duplex high pressure control."

Q. Where is the advantage in having the third pressure top?

A. It permits of any desired excess pressure being accumulated in the main reservoir while the brakes are applied; and while brakes are released requires the pump to operate against the ordinary main reservoir pressure only.

Q. What are the advantages to be had from the use of the triplex governor when using "single pressure" system and with the triplex governor when using the "double pressure" system?

A. In a main reservoir of ordinary size a high pressure may be accumulated while brakes are applied, and when releasing brakes this pressure is very effective in causing the prompt and certain release of all brakes. Also, on account of the smaller main reservoir capacity and higher pressure, a much quicker recharging of all the auxiliary reservoirs in the train may be effected, which is a very desirable feature, especially in mountainous service.

NEW YORK AUTOMATIC BRAKE VALVE.

Q. What are the principal parts of the engineer's automatic brake valve?

A. The main slide valve and its seat, controlling the ports between the main reservoir and the brake pipe, and between the brake pipe and the atmosphere; the quadrant, the handle, handle shaft, and link for moving the main slide valve; the equalizing piston with valves and lever, and small cut-off valve for regulating the brake pipe reduction in service applications and for automatically closing the service opening; the excess pressure valve and spring for maintaining excess pressure in the main reservoir; the body, and cover for enclosing these parts, and the supplementary reservoir.

Q. What are the air pipe connections to the brake valve and how many?

A. There is a main reservoir, brake pipe, pump governor, air gauge, red hand, and air gauge, black hand, connection, five in all.

Q. How many positions are there on the automatic brake valve for the handle?

A. Five.

Q. Name them.

A. Release, running, positive lap, service graduating, sub-divided into five notches, and emergency.

Q. How does the brake valve reduce the brake pipe pressure when it is desired to apply the brakes in service applications? In emergency applications?

A. The service exhaust port in main slide valve between the brake pipe and the atmosphere, is opened, by placing the handle in the service graduating notch, corresponding to the amount of reduction it is desired to make. Air from the brake pipe and chamber A can now escape through port F and G in slide valve and exhaust port C, in its seat, to the atmosphere. The graduating slide valve, operated by the equalizing piston and lever, gradually reduces the service port opening as the reduction in brake pipe pressure is being made, until it entirely closes or automatically laps port F. In emergency applications the main slide valve opens the brake pipe wide through the large ports J and K, making a quick, heavy reduction in pressure.

Q In emergency application does the valve automatically lap itself?

A. No; when the handle of the brake valve is placed

in the emergency position a large direct opening is made between the brake pipe and the atmosphere, which will be closed only when the handle is moved to any one of the other positions.

Q. When making any kind of a brake application, is communication between the brake pipe and the main reservoir closed?

A. Yes; always by the main slide valve.

Q. In positive lap position are all ports closed?

A. Yes; all except port O.

Q. Where is main reservoir pressure found in the valve?

A. In chamber B on top of the main slide valve under the excess pressure valve, and in the pipe to the red hand of the air gauge.

Q. Where is brake pipe pressure found?

A. In chamber A; on the face of the main slide valve; on the brake pipe (chamber A) side of the equalizing piston; in the pipe to the black hand of the air gauge, and the pump governor cavity.

Q. Where is the supplementary reservoir pressure found?

A. In chamber D, between the equalizing piston and the back cap, in passages H to the supplementary reservoir and in the supplementary reservoir.

Q. How does air pass from the main reservoir through the engineer's brake valve into the brake pipe?

A. In full release position, it flows through a large, free opening in the valve seat, past the end of the main slide valve, and in running position, this direct passage being closed, it flows past the excess pressure valve which holds a definite amount of pressure in the main reservoir above that contained in the brake pipe, and through a small opening or passage in the slide valve seat, and a cavity in the main slide valve into chamber A and the brake pipe.

Q. What takes place when the handle is placed in full release position, after a brake application?

A. Main reservoir air, as already explained, flows in large volume direct into the brake pipe, releasing the brakes and recharging the auxiliary reservoirs. At the same time a portion of the air in the supplementary reservoir and chamber D is discharged to the atmosphere. Main reservoir air also flows into passage E and the pump governor cavity, thence direct to the pump governor.

Q. Why is it necessary to discharge a small quantity of air from the supplementary reservoir and chamber D when the handle is moved to release position?

A. In order to permit brake pipe pressure in chamber A to force the piston to its normal position, where it should always be at the commencement of a service reduction.

Q. What takes place when the brake valve handle is placed in running position?

A. The large, free opening from the main reservoir to the brake pipe, past the end of the main slide valve, is closed, and governor cavity E is connected direct to the brake pipe through cavity M in the main slide valve. Main reservoir air then flows past the excess pressure valve, as already explained, into pump governor cavity E and brake pipe.

Q. What is the function of the excess pressure valve?

A. To maintain in the main reservoir, with the handle in running position, a predetermined pressure above that in the brake pipe. After this pressure has been accumulated in the main reservoir, the excess pressure valve will unseat and permit air to flow into the brake pipe

Q. What is excess pressure used for?

A. For releasing brakes promptly, and for quickly recharging auxiliary reservoirs.

Q. What is the positive lap position used for?

A. To blank all ports, excepting port O, between the atmosphere and the supplementary reservoir, and to prevent the flow of air in any direction through the valve

Q. What valve controls or closes passage and port O, when the handle is in any position except service and emergency?

A. The vent valve.

Q. What occurs when the handle of the brake valve is placed in any one of the service graduating notches?

A. Communication is cut off between the main reservoir and the brake pipe; port O (the end in the main slide valve seat) is closed by the main slide valve; the brake pipe exhaust port F, in the main slide valve, is moved past the edge of the graduating slide valve so as to open this port. Brake pipe air then passes into ports and passage F and G, in the main slide valve and out through exhaust port C, in the slide valve seat, to the atmosphere. This reduction of brake pipe pressure in chamber A, on the brake pipe side of the equalizing piston allows the supplementary reservoir pressure in chamber D (equal to the initial brake pipe pressure before service brake pipe reduction began) to expand, and move the equalizing piston forward. This piston, by means of the connecting lever, then moves the graduating slide valve backward, on the face of the main slide valve until it gradually closes exhaust port F.

Q. After exhaust port F is thus closed, what occurs

if the brake handle is moved to the next graduating service notch?

A. The same as explained in the preceding answer.

Q. Why is port F, with the handle of the brake valve in the first service graduating notch, only half uncovered?

A. So that on trains consisting of four cars or less the initial reduction in brake pipe pressure, which should be made in this notch, will not be heavy enough to cause quick action of the triple valves. But with five or more cars any service graduating notch except the first may be used in making the initial reduction.

Q. How much pressure will be drawn from the brake pipe if all the service notches have been used?

A. From 23 to 25 pounds, the initial brake pipe pressure being 70 pounds.

Q. If all the service graduating notches on the engineer's brake valve are used, will the brakes be set in full service?

A. Yes; as a total service reduction of from 23 to 25 pounds will apply the brakes in full.

Q. If, after a service application has been made, either partial or full, an emergency should arise, where should the handle be placed?

A. In emergency position always.

Q. Of what benefit would this be?

A. If any brakes on the train had partially leaked off, thereby reducing their holding power, the additional reduction in brake pipe pressure would increase brake cylinder pressure and set them harder; those that were only partly set would be set in full.

Q. How does air escape from the brake pipe when the handle is placed in the emergency position?

A. The air is discharged direct from the brake pipe

through large exhaust ports J and K in the main slide valve, and exhaust port C, in the seat, to the atmosphere.

Q. Why are exhaust ports J and K made large?

A. So that in emergencies the reduction in brake pipe pressure may be made sufficiently quick and heavy to produce serial action of the triple valves.

Q. If upon making service application the graduating valve fails to lap automatically, what should be done?

A. Move the handle gradually back until brake pipe exhaust ceases, or to positive lap position, after the desired reduction in brake pipe pressure has been made.

Q. What is usually the cause of the graduating valve failing to lap automatically?

A. Leakage from the supplementary reservoir and its connections; also from chamber D through the back head gasket. Leakage past the piston packing leather and the packing ring will also cause the valve to fail to lap automatically.

Q. How can this leakage from chamber D and the supplementary reservoir be located?

A. If the leakage is to the atmosphere it may be found by coating the joints with soapsuds. If it is in the piston packing leather or ball check valve, after ascertaining that there is no leak in the main slide valve, move engineer's valve handle to emergency position, letting all air out of the brake pipe. If now the cut-out cock in the brake pipe beneath the brake valve be closed, and the handle placed in any service notch, a leak by the packing leather or the ball check valve from supplementary reservoir and chamber D will be manifest by the rising of the black hand of the duplex air gauge. With the handle left in emergency position it will be manifested by a blow at the exhaust port C.

Q. Should a more exacting test be desired, how should it be made?

A. By increasing brake pipe volume, making it equivalent to the volume found with a long train. Then operate the valve to be tested, in service application position, to ascertain if the valve will automatically close off. If the brake pipe discharge fails to close off entirely there is leakage at some point from the supplementary reservoir, its connections or chamber D, probably past the packing leather of the equalizing piston.

Q. What would cause leakage past the piston packing leather?

A. Packing leather improperly fitting the cylinder, being worn through by the expanding spring, or bottom of the cylinder cut by dirt accumulating there from the brake pipe.

Q. How could you test the main slide valve for leakage?

A. With the engine alone, by first moving the handle to emergency position and exhausting the brake pipe air, then returning the handle to positive lap position, exhausting the supplementary reservoir air, then closing the stop cock under the brake valve. With the reduced brake pipe volume any leak through the main slide valve will be quickly manifested by an increase of pressure in the brake pipe and chamber A, indicated by the rising of the black hand on the air gauge, or by a blow at the exhaust port C, or by both.

Q. How could you test the small cut-off valve for leakage?

A. Place the handle in the second service graduating notch, and after the automatic cut-off has taken place, close the cut-out cock under the brake valve. If a blow is heard at the exhaust port, accompanied by a falling of the black hand on the air gauge, the cut-off valve is leaking.

CLEANING AND OILING.

Q. What parts of the valve require lubrication?

A. The main slide valve, the graduating slide valve, the equalizing piston, and the handle shaft.

Q. What is likely to be wrong if, after applying brakes on a train or while the brake valve handle is on lap, the governor stops the pump (where the single governor is used) and prevents the accumulation of excess pressure

A. Leakage past the excess pressure valve will most likely be the cause, provided the small relief port in the pump governor is plugged up. With this relief port open excessive leakage past the excess pressure valve would prevent the pump from accumulating the excess pressure

Q. How would you proceed to clean the excess pressure valve?

A. After closing the stop cock in the brake pipe below the brake valve, and drawing off all the main reservoir air, remove the cap of the excess pressure valve, take out the valve and rub it clean with a little kerosene oil, replacing it perfectly dry.

Q. When is the best time to clean the excess pressure valve?

A. Before starting the pump and before any pressure has accumulated in the main reservoir. All then that is necessary to do is simply unscrew the cap, clean the valve, and replace it dry.

Q. If with a long train and the brake valve handle in release position brake pipe pressure increases slowly, where should the trouble be looked for?

A. Lost motion on the inner end of the handle shaft, or in the link and pins in the main slide valve.

Q. What provision has been made to assist the engineer in finding the running position on the older style of valves, when the sharp point of the handle latch has been worn off?

A. A pin is set on the inside face of the quadrant, just below the running notch, by which the engineer may be guided to running position. On the later form, however, the quadrant has been modified so as to contain deeper notches.

Q. For what purpose are the two brass plugs in the cover of the automatic brake valve?

A. To enable the engineer or air brake inspectors to oil the main slide valve without taking the brake valve apart.

Q. When and how should the main slide valve be oiled?

A. The best time to oil the valve is before starting the air pump, and when there is no pressure in the main reservoir; when this is the case remove both brass plugs, place the handle in full release position and pour a few drops of good oil through the hole back of the main slide valve, then place the handle in emergency position, and pour a few drops through the hole in front of the main slide valve, replace the brass plugs and work the handle back and forth a few times to spread the oil over the seat. The slide valve should receive a little oil through the oil plugs only when it commences to work harder than usual. Don't pour in too much oil; it will only serve to gum up the working parts.

Q. Suppose there is pressure in the main reservoir and it is desired to oil the main slide valve?

A. Then take the same steps as would be necessary to clean the excess pressure valve. Close the stop cock in the brake pipe, under the brake valve, stop the pump and exhaust the air from the main reservoir, when the oil plugs may be removed for oiling the slide valve, and the excess pressure valve may be removed for cleaning. However, the best time to do this work is before the pump has been started and before commencing the trip.

LEAKS AND OTHER DISORDERS.

Q. Will an ordinary leak in the main slide valve release the brakes?

A. No; with an ordinary leak from the main reservoir through the main slide valve during the time of application of the brakes, air will be going out to the atmosphere along with the brake pipe air and, as the main reservoir leak will augment the brake pipe pressure in front of the equalizing discharge piston somewhat, the graduating slide valve will hold the service port in the main slide valve open sufficiently to accommodate the main reservoir leak, and thus prevent increase of brake pipe pressure sufficient to release brakes.

Q. Suppose such a leak exists and the handle is moved back to positive lap position, after a service reduction, what will be the effect?

A. The brake will probably release, especially if the train is a short one.

Q. If a continuous blow of air is heard at the main exhaust port when the handle is in release, running or positive lap position, where would the trouble likely be found?

A. The vent valve on the end of the graduating valve is probably leaking.

Q In applying new leathers to the equalizing pistion what precautions should be taken?

A. The piston should be removed from the cylinder and all parts cleaned with kerosene. Care should be taken not to bend or kink the coil spring expander as, if this is done, the tendency will be for the expander on account of being distorted, to cut the leather.

Q. If the copper pipe between the brake valve and the supplementary reservoir be broken off on the road, could the train be handled satisfactorily with the brake valve?

A. Yes; it could be handled satisfactorily.

Q. In what manner?

A. By plugging the connection at the brake valve of this pipe, and by making the required brake pipe reduction in the first or second graduating notch, depending on the length of the train, and moving the handle slowly to positive lap position when this is done. As the brake pipe and gauge is connected to chamber A, it shows the actual brake pipe pressure in all positions of the brake valve handle, and the engineer will have no difficulty in controlling the flow of air from the brake pipe without danger of an emergency, or of making an insufficient reduction.

Q. Will the brake valve reduce pressure in service applications and automatically lap the valve, as it should, if any other initial brake pipe pressure than 70 pounds be used?

A. Yes; if the brake pipe pressure be carried to 90 or 110 pounds and the handle of the brake valve be placed in the last service graduating notch, a reduction in pressure sufficient to equalize the auxiliary reservoir, and brake cylinder pressure will be had before the valve automatically laps.

Q. What are the reductions made at the brake valve corresponding to the different notches when the brake pipe pressure is 90 pounds? When 110 pounds?

A.	70 lbs.	90 lbs.	110 lbs.
1st Service Graduating Notch	5-5	5-5	6-6
2nd " " "	8-3	9-4	10-4
3rd " " "	11-3	13-4	14-4
4th " " "	16-5	19-6	21-7
5th " " "	23-7	27-8	30-9

Q. Will these reductions in each case fully equalize the auxiliary and the brake cylinder pressures?

A. Yes, from 70 pounds a reduction of 23 pounds will allow the brake to set in full; from 90 pounds a reduction of 27 pounds will allow it to be set in full, and from 110 pounds, provided there are no reducing valves on the brake cylinder, a brake pipe reduction of 30 pounds will set the brake in full.

Q. When the handle of the brake valve is moved to any one of the service graduating notches, is air allowed to escape direct from the brake pipe?

A. Yes; brake pipe reductions are always made direct from the brake pipe with this valve

Q In making water tank stops, and in fact all station stops, with high speed trains how should the brake valve be handled?

A. By the two application method.

NEW YORK TRIPLE VALVE.

PLAIN TRIPLE STYLE A.

Figure 27 illustrates this valve which is intended for use only on engines and tenders, in conjunction with 6-inch and 8-inch brake cylinders. The essential parts

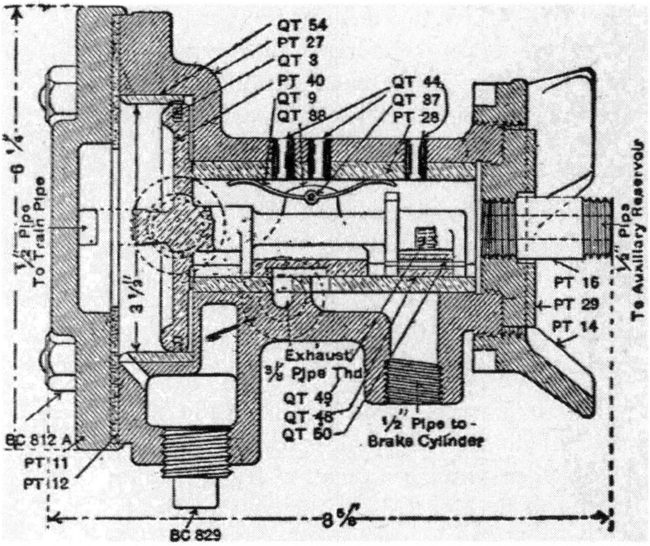

Fig. 27—Style A, Plain Triple Valve.

are, the triple piston valve PT-40, the exhaust slide valve QT-38, and the graduating slide valve QT-48, operating in a suitable casing or body, PT-27. The pipe connections are, brake pipe, auxiliary reservoir, and brake cylinder. The functions of the operating parts are as follows:

Exhaust slide valve QT-38 controls the exhaust of air from the brake cylinder to the atmosphere, to release brakes; and the graduating valve QT-48 controls the admission of air from the auxiliary reservoir to the brake cylinder, to apply the brakes. The triple piston PT-40 moves the exhaust valve QT-38 and the graduating valve QT-48, when brake pipe pressure is reduced below auxiliary reservoir pressure, so that the exhaust valve will close the exhaust port, in its seat, before the graduating valve QT-48 opens the service port, in its seat, leading to the brake cylinder. The slide valve QT-38 remains stationary after once reaching application position, while the piston PT-40, in partial service applications (brake pipe reductions of less than 20 pounds), returns part way, and causes graduating valve QT-48 to cover, or lap, the service port. The abutments on the triple piston stem that move valve QT-38 are about one-quarter inch farther apart than the length of the valve, so as to permit the triple piston to move graduating valve QT-48 this limited distance without disturbing the exhaust valve.

To charge the auxiliary reservoir, air from the brake pipe passes to the cylinder and chamber on the plain side of piston PT-40, then through a small charging groove shown in the top of bushing QT-54 and passage on the shoulder of piston PT-40 to the chamber on the slide valve side of piston PT-40, thence into the auxiliary reservoir, until the latter is charged up equal to the brake pipe.

The operation of this valve in an application of the brakes is as follows:

When the brake pipe pressure is reduced below that in the auxiliary, the piston PT-40 moves its full stroke,

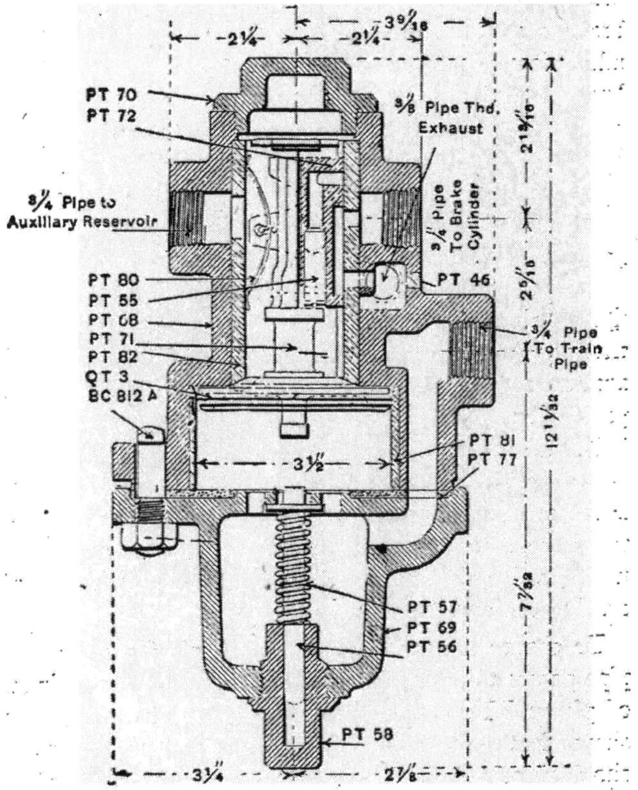

Fig. 28—Style C, Plain Triple Valve.

first cutting off the communication between the auxiliary reservoir and the brake pipe through the charging grooves in the top of its bushing QT-54, then moving the exhaust valve QT-38 and the graduating valve QT-48 to application position, covering the exhaust port and opening the service, or graduating, port. This move-

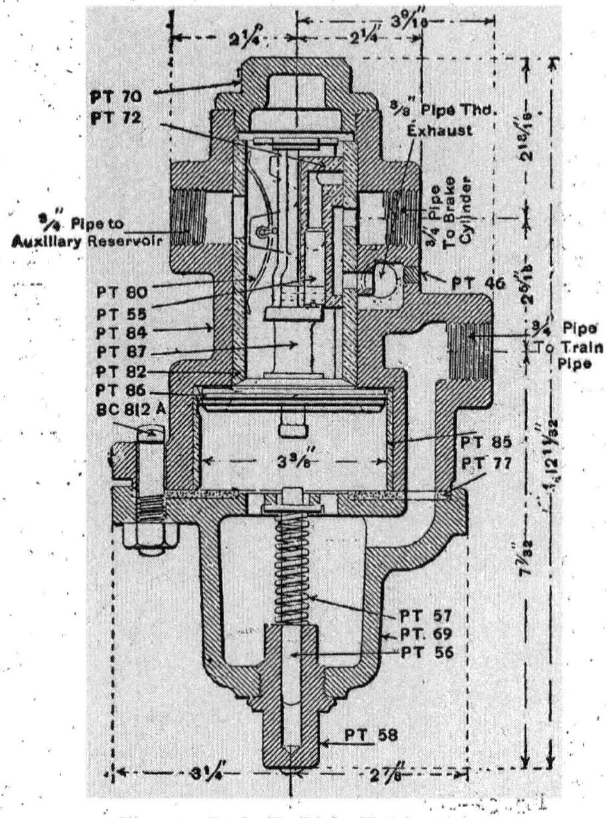

Fig. 29—Style E, Plain Triple Valve.

ment of the triple piston, and the position of the slide valves allows reservoir air to enter the brake cylinder, the quantity admitted being in proportion to the brake pipe reduction. If the brake pipe pressure is reduced but little, the pressure in the reservoir is soon reduced, by expansion, into the brake cylinder, to slightly less than

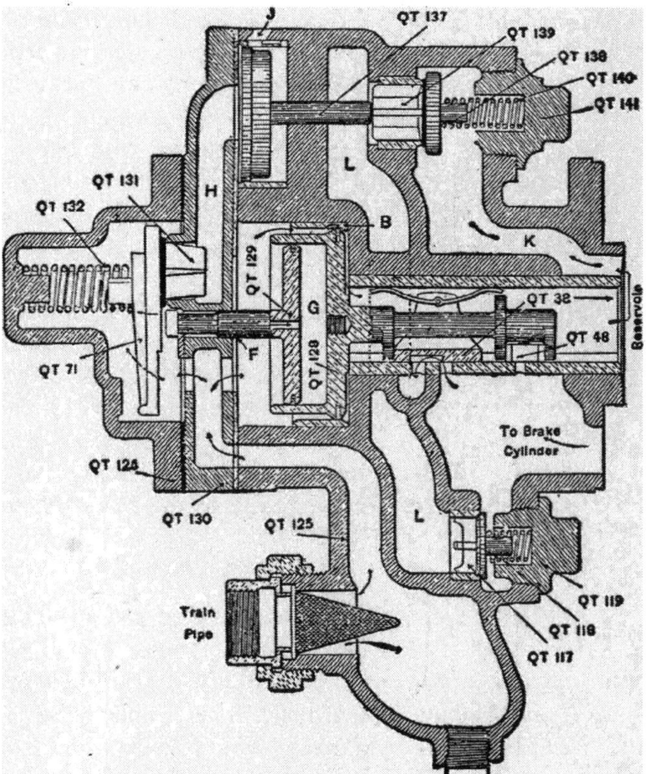

Fig. 30—New York Quick Action Triple Valve, Release Position.

that in the brake pipe, when the piston PT-40 starts back and carries graduating valve QT-48 to lap position, closing the service port, without disturbing the exhaust valve QT-38, and cutting off further flow of auxiliary air to the brake cylinder. The exhaust valve is held to its seat with some force by the air pressure on top of it, aided by spring QT-9, and checks the return stroke when graduating valve QT-48 has closed the service port.

A further reduction of brake pipe pressure repeats the same action of the triple piston, and the graduating valve, and applies the brake a little harder. A reduction of 5 to 8 pounds applies the brake with but moderate force, and a reduction of 20 pounds or a trifle more causes the graduating valve QT-48 to remain open, and the brake to apply with full force, as the auxiliary will then continue to flow into the brake cylinder until both pressures are equalized. The brakes are released by increasing the pressure in the brake pipe over that in the auxiliary. This will cause the triple piston and slide valves to move back to normal position as shown in Fig. 27, where exhaust valve QT-38 uncovers the port leading to the atmosphere, thus releasing the brakes, and permitting the recharging of the auxiliary reservoir.

PLAIN TRIPLE, STYLE C.

This triple valve, shown in Fig. 28, is intended for use with 12-inch and 14-inch tender brake cylinders; also 12-inch, 14-inch and 16-inch driver brake cylinders, operated either separately, or in combination with the engine truck cylinders. The principal difference between the interior construction of Style C and Style E triple valves is that the triple piston in Style C is larger in diameter than that in Style E.

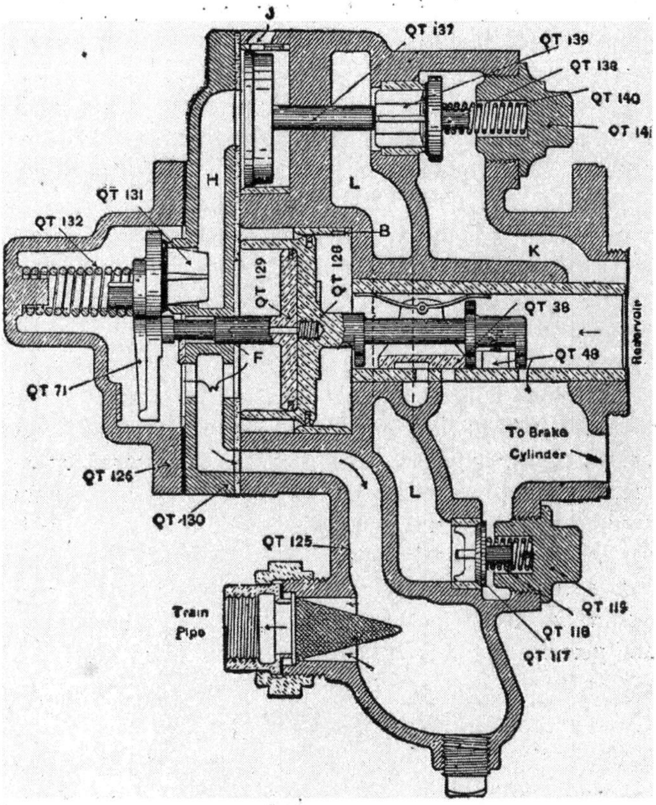

Fig. 31—New York Quick Action Triple, Service Application Position.

PLAIN TRIPLE, STYLE E.

Figure 29 shows this valve which is intended for use with 6-inch, 8-inch and 10-inch tender brake cylinders, and driver brake cylinders, operated either separately, or in conjunction with engine truck brake cylinder.

Three-quarter-inch pipe is required for the connections of this valve, the same as with the Style C plain triple.

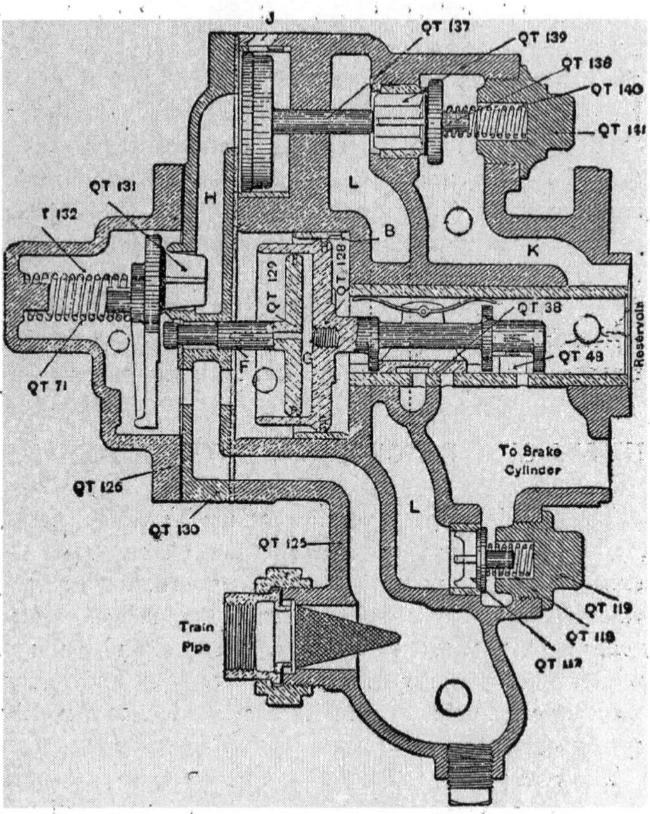

Fig. 32—New York Quick Action Triple Valve, Automatic Lap Position.

The operation of the Styles E and C plain triples is similar to that of Style A. The method of charging the auxiliary reservoir is the same also. However, the construction of the triples is different in that the graduating valves PT-55, in styles C and E, Figs. 28 and 29, are of the poppet or check valve type, instead of the slide valve type, and the triple pistons PT-71 and PT-87 have a double stroke, for the reason that in service applications the triple piston moves over only a portion of its stroke, bringing the small service port in the slide valve PT-72 opposite the port in its seat leading to the brake cylinder. In emergency applications it moves its full stroke, and the slide valve uncovers the whole of the brake cylinder port, thus permitting a quick and full equalization of pressure between the auxiliaries and brake cylinders. The graduating spring PT-57 prevents the triple piston from moving too far, and applying the brakes in emergency when such an application is not required.

NEW YORK QUICK ACTION TRIPLE VALVE.

The principal operative parts of the New York Quick Action Triple are the main triple piston, 128, the exhaust slide valve, 38, the graduating sliding valve, 48, the vent piston, 129, the rubber seated vent-valve, 131, and spring, 132, emergency piston, 137, with rubber seated quick action valve, 139, and spring, 140, non-return brake cylinder check valve, 117, and its spring, 118.

The vent piston, 129, has a port F, which leads through the center of it into chamber G of the main triple piston. This allows train pipe pressure to get in between the pistons, forming a cushion which does away with the graduating spring as used in the Westinghouse triple.

RELEASE AND CHARGING POSITION.

The passage of the air through the New York quick action triple is as follows: referring to Fig. 30, train pipe pressure passes through the strainer, fills the cavity back

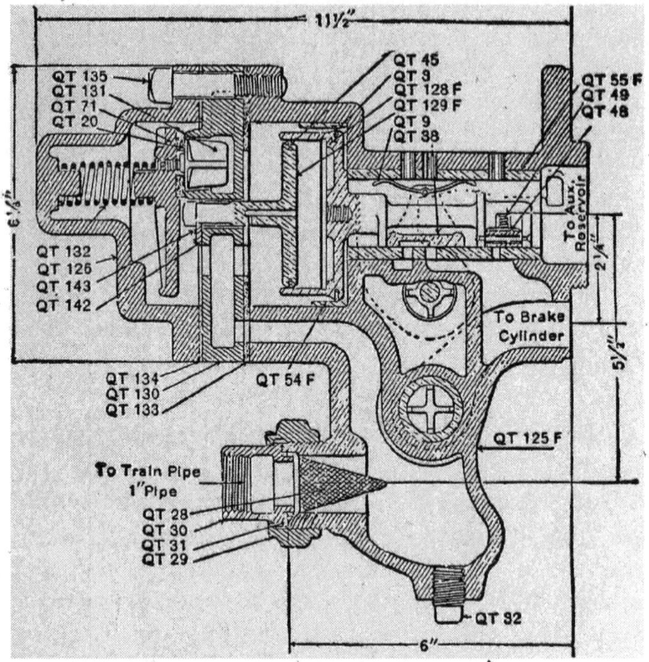

Fig. 33—New York Quick Action Triple Valve.

of tne rubber seated vent-valve, 131, thereby holding that valve to its seat, and also passes through a large opening into the main piston chamber causing the main piston to be forced to charging position, which allows the train pipe pressure to pass through feed groove B into the slide-valve chamber and on into the auxiliary reservoir;

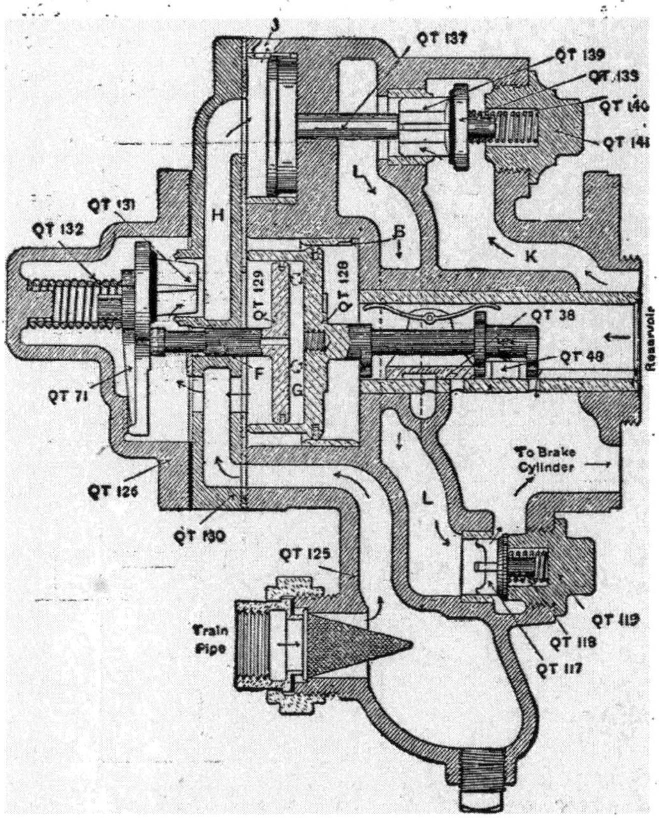

Fig. 34—New York Quick Action Triple Valve, Emergency Position (Special View for Showing Emergency Valve).

at the same time that this action is taking place, train pipe air is feeding through port F in the stem of the vent-piston, 129, thereby charging chamber G between the pistons.

SERVICE APPLICATION.

Figure 31 shows the quick action triple in service application. The main triple piston has moved back until

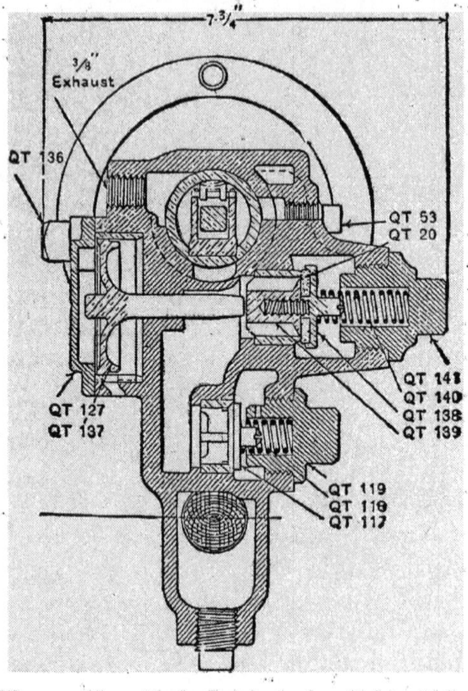

Fig. 35—New York Quick Action Triple Valve.

it has touched the vent piston, 129, and moved it back far enough so that port F is just closed; as the train pipe pressure is reduced, the pressure in chamber G is also reduced, but as it reduces slower than the train pipe pressure it graduates the movement of the main triple piston, so that when the main piston has made its full stroke it has not disturbed the rubber-seated vent-valve, 131, but has moved the graduating slide valve, 48, to a position which opens the supply port from the auxiliary reservoir to the brake cylinder, and at the same time has moved the exhaust slide-valve, 138, forward and closed the exhaust port from the brake cylinder to the atmosphere. When the main piston moves forward it gradually closes port F before all the pressure from chamber G has exhausted, consequently when the auxiliary pressure has reduced to a degree slightly less than train-pipe pressure the air which is confined in chamber G expands and forces the main piston back just sufficient to cause the graduating slide-valve to close the port from the auxiliary reservoir to the brake cylinder without disturbing the exhaust slide-valve that controls the exhaust port from the brake cylinder to the atmosphere. The triple is now in lap position as shown by Fig. 32.

EMERGENCY POSITION.

The emergency action of this triple valve is brought about as follows, referring to Fig. 34:

The air cushion in chamber G cannot be reduced through port F as quickly as the train pipe pressure is reduced, consequently when a sudden reduction is made on the train pipe pressure it causes the auxiliary pressure to drive the main piston back so quickly that port F is closed before chamber G can empty itself, and with an air cushion between the two pistons, the stem of the vent-piston strikes the rubber seated vent valve and drives it from its seat, which allows train pipe pressure to pass into pas-

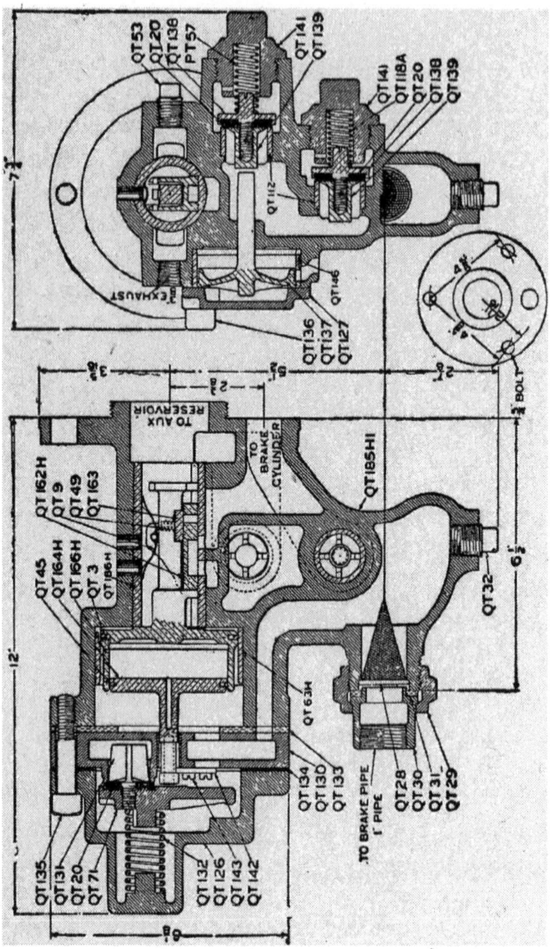

Fig. 36—Quick Action Triple Valve Style H 1

sage H and thereby forces the emergency piston, 137, forward, which action not only opens port J to the atmosphere for the purpose of still further reducing the train-pipe pressure, but it also unseats the rubber seated emergency valve, 139, which allows the auxiliary pressure to flow from chamber K by the rubber seated valve into chamber L, and unseat the non-return check-valve, thereby causing the auxiliary reservoir pressure to quickly equalize with the brake cylinder. When the train pipe pressure has reduced less than the auxiliary reservoir pressure, the emergency valve, 139, is forced to its seat and the brake cylinder pressure equalizes with the pressure in chamber L, causing the non-return check-valve to go to its seat, and it is held thereby both by the brake cylinder pressure and the spring, 118.

The venting of the train pipe air at the first quick action triple on the train causes an equally quick reduction in train pipe pressure at the next quick action triple of the next car, throwing it into quick action; that in turn operates the next one, and so on throughout the whole train, no matter how many cars it may consist of.

Venting train pipe air in this way provides for the almost instantaneous application of all the brakes throughout a train of fifty or more cars in a little over two seconds.

After an emergency application of the brakes is made the release is accomplished in the same manner as in service applications; that is, by restoring the train pipe pressure, or, in other words, by making train pipe pressure greater than the auxiliary reservoir pressure.

While the foregoing description covers more specifically the F1 and P1 valves, it will be seen by reference to the H1 and S1 styles shown in Figs. 36 and 37 that the

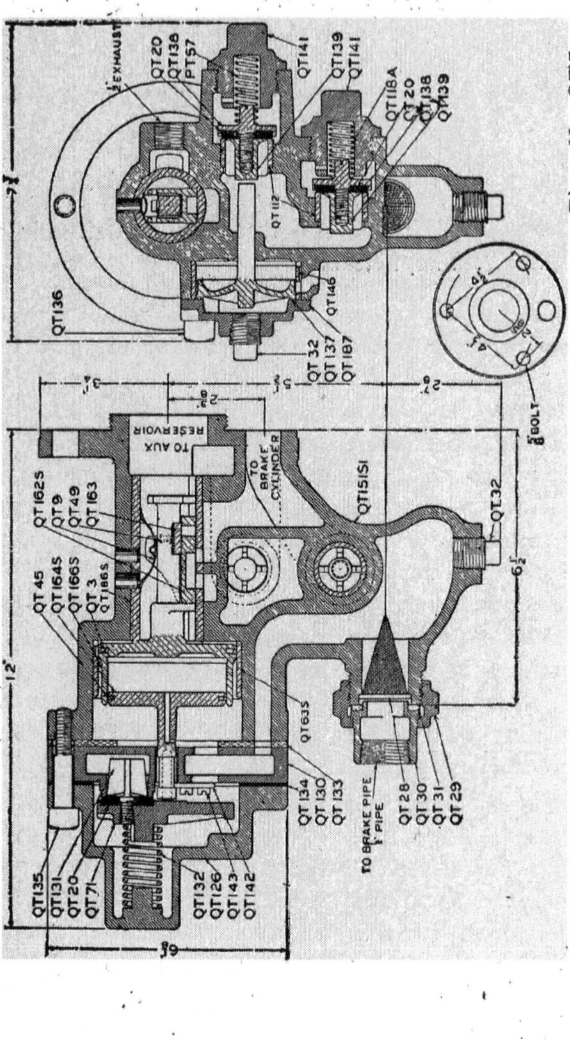

Fig. 37—Quick Action Triple Valve Style S 1.

Piece No. QTS 1.

graduating slide valve is mounted on the exhaust slide valve. This changes the description, inasmuch as when the triple piston moves to close the feed groove, the graduating slide valve is moved with it, uncovering the service port in the exhaust slide valve, and by further movement of the piston the service port is connected with the brake cylinder.

In order to make the triple valve perform its functions satisfactorily, it is necessary that it be maintained in good condition and kept clean.

QUESTIONS AND ANSWERS—NEW YORK TRIPLE VALVE.

PLAIN TRIPLE—STYLES A, C, AND E.

Q. What are the essential parts of the plain triple valve?

A. The triple piston valve, the exhaust slide valve, and the graduating slide valve.

Q. What are the pipe connections to the plain triple valve?

A. Brake pipe, auxiliary reservoir, and brake cylinder.

Q. What are the functions of the operating parts?

A. The exhaust slide valve controls the exhaust of air from the brake cylinder to the atmosphere, to release brakes; and the graduating valve controls the admission of air from the auxiliary reservoir to the brake cylinder, to apply the brakes. The triple piston moves the exhaust valve and the graduating valve, when brake pipe pressure is reduced below auxiliary reservoir pressure, so that the exhaust valve will close the exhaust port, in its seat, before the graduating valve opens the service port, in its seat, leading to the brake cylinder. The slide valve remains stationary after once reaching application position, while the piston in partial service applications (brake pipe reductions of less than 20 pounds), returns part way, and causes graduating valve to cover, or lap, the service port

Q. How does the air pass through the triple to charge the auxiliary reservoir?

A. Air from the brake pipe passes to the cylinder and chamber on the plain side of the piston, then through a small charging groove shown in the top of bushing and passage on the shoulder of the piston, to the chamber on the slide valve side of piston, thence into the auxiliary reservoir, until the latter is charged up equal to the brake pipe.

Q. What causes a brake application with the plain triple?

A. A reduction of brake pipe pressure which makes that pressure less than the auxiliary reservoir pressure.

Q. Explain the operation of the plain triple in a brake application

A. When the brake pipe pressure is reduced below that in the auxiliary, the piston moves its full stroke, first cutting off the communication between the auxiliary reservoir and the brake pipe through the charging grooves in the top of its bushing, then moving the exhaust valve and the graduating valve to application position, covering the exhaust port and opening the service, or graduating, port. This movement of the triple piston, and the position of the slide valves allow reservoir air to enter the brake cylinder, the quantity admitted being in proportion to the brake pipe reduction If the brake pipe pressure is reduced but little, the pressure in the reservoir is soon reduced, by expansion, into the brake cylinder, to slightly less than that in the brake pipe, when the piston starts back and carries graduating valve to lap position, closing the service port, without disturbing the exhaust valve and cutting off further flow of auxiliary air to the brake cylinder. The exhaust valve is held to its seat with some force by the air pressure on top of it, aided by the spring, and checks the return stroke when graduating valve has closed the service port.

Q. Should an increased or full application of the brake be desired, how could it be had?

A. A further reduction of brake pipe pressure repeats the same action of the triple piston and the graduating valve, and applies the brakes a little harder. If the brake pipe pressure is reduced 5 to 8 pounds, the brakes will be applied with but moderate force; if, however, the brake pipe pressure is reduced 20 pounds or a trifle more, the graduating valve will remain open and the brakes go full on, as the auxiliary reservoir pressure will then continue to flow into the brake cylinder until the pressure in both is equalized.

Q. How is the brake released?

A. An increase in brake pipe pressure, over that in the auxiliary, will cause the triple piston and the slide valves to move back to normal position, where the exhaust valve uncovers the exhaust port to the atmosphere, releasing the brakes, and allowing the reservoir to be recharged.

Q. For what purpose is the small chamber?

A. To allow moisture from the brake pipe to collect in this chamber, where it can be readily drained away by unscrewing the plug.

Q. What oil is recommended for lubricating the plain triple?

A. After cleaning, the triple valve requires hardly any oil, just enough to dim the surface of the slide valves and seats, and the piston and the cylinder surrounding it. Vaseline is excellent when used in this way. The oil used, however, should be one that will not gum.

Q Why is there no graduating spring in this triple valve?

A. The piston and the slide valves have the same stroke

for both service and emergency applications, thus making a graduating spring unnecessary.

Q. Suppose the triple valve while in use on an engine or tender should become defective, how could it be cut out?

A. By closing the stop-cock in the branch or cross-over pipe put there for that purpose.

Q. Is the plain triple valve, style A, intended for use on cars?

A. No; it is intended for use only on engines and tenders in conjunction with 6-inch and 8-inch brake cylinders.

Q. If the exhaust valve should leak how can it be detected?

A. By a blow from the exhaust port of the triple, both while the valve is in release and in application positions.

Q. Should graduating valve leak how can it be detected?

A. By a blow from the exhaust port of the triple while the valve is in release position, which ceases when it is in application position; and in partial service applications possibly by the brake releasing without increase of brake pipe pressure.

Q. What size auxiliary reservoir should be used with style A triple valve?

A. A 10-inch by 24-inch auxiliary reservoir should be used with this triple in connection with 6-inch driver brake cylinders, and 6-inch and 8-inch tender and engine truck brake cylinders.

Q. For what is the style C plain triple valve intended?

A. For use with 12-inch and 14-inch tender brake cylinders, and for use with 12-inch, 14-inch and 16-inch driver brake cylinders, operated either separately or in combination with the engine truck cylinders.

Q. How may the style C plain triple valve be distinguished from the earlier plain triples?

A. A three-quarter inch pipe is necessary to use with this triple to allow the air to flow freely enough to the larger brake cylinders with which it is used. One-half-inch pipe is not large enough.

Q. What is the principal difference in the interior construction of style C and style E triple valves?

A. The triple piston in style C triple is larger in diameter than that in style E.

Q. For what service is the plain triple valve style E intended?

A. For use with 6-inch, 8-inch and 10-inch tender cylinders and driver brake cylinders, operated either separately or in conjunction with engine truck brake cylinder.

Q. What size of pipe is necessary with this triple valve?

A. Three-quarter-inch pipe is necessary, the same as with the style C plain triple.

Q. Is the operation of the plain triple valves, styles C and E, the same as that of style A?

A. The method of charging the auxiliary reservoir is the same, and the principle of operation is the same. However, the construction of the triples is different, in that the graduating valves are of the poppet or check valve variety instead of the slide valve type, and the triple pistons have a double stroke.

Q. Why do these triple valves have a double stroke?

A. In service applications the triple piston moves over only a portion of its stroke, bringing the small service port in the slide valve opposite the port in its seat leading to the brake cylinder. In emergency applications it moves its full stroke, and the slide valve uncovers the whole of the brake cylinder port, thus permitting a very quick and full equalization of pressure to take place between the auxiliaries and the brake cylinders.

Q. For what purpose is the graduating spring?

A. In service applications it prevents the triple piston from moving too far, and applying the brakes in emergency.

NEW YORK QUICK ACTION TRIPLE VALVE.

Q. Name the principal operative parts of the New York quick action triple.

A. Main triple piston, exhaust slide valve, graduating slide valve, the vent piston, emergency piston, a rubber seated vent valve, a rubber seated quick action valve, and a non-return brake cylinder check valve.

Q. The plain triple valves have the triple piston, the exhaust valve and the graduating valve. Why are the additional valves placed in the quick action valves?

A. So that in emergency applications the triple may vent the brake pipe locally and at the same time cause quick equalization of auxiliary and brake cylinder pressures.

Q. Why is it necessary to vent brake pipe air to the atmosphere?

A. To produce a quick, serial action of all the quick action triple valves throughout the train, thus getting the brakes on the whole train quickly.

Q. Is any greater pressure obtained in the brake cylinder in an emergency application than in a full service?

A. No; as this triple valve uses auxiliary reservoir air

alone in both service and emergency applications, no higher maximum brake cylinder pressure is obtained in one kind of application than in the other. In service the brakes apply gradually; in emergency they apply almost instantly with the full cylinder pressure.

Q. Why is this triple valve called a quick action triple?

A. For the reason that in emergency applications it carries the auxiliary air to the brake cylinder almost instantly to the full equalized pressure.

Q. How does venting of brake pipe air at the triple produce quick serial action throughout the train?

A. Brake pipe pressure, in an emergency application, is first quickly vented at the engineer's brake valve, this sudden venting actuates the quick action parts in the quick action triple valve on the car next to the engine This quick action triple then vents brake pipe air to the atmosphere, and the venting at this triple actuates the quick action parts in the quick action triple on the next car, causing it to vent brake pipe air to the atmosphere, and so on throughout the train.

Q. Explain the operation of this quick action triple.

A. The exhaust valve and graduating slide valve cover the exhaust and the service graduating ports, and these valves are moved by the main piston to apply and to release the brakes in the usual manner. (See Plain Triple C and A.) Thus it will be seen that in the quick action triple valve, piston, exhaust valve and graduating slide valve alone are used in making service applications, and its operation in these applications is precisely the same as that of the plain triple valve.

Q. Name the quick action parts of the triple valve.

A. They are the vent valve piston, the vent valve, the

plain (quick action) piston, the quick action valve, and the brake cylinder check valve.

Q. Do these parts operate in a service application?

A. No; in service applications these parts remain inoperative, but in emergency applications they are called into action. Vent valve is held to its seat by spring, assisted by brake pipe pressure, and is opened by piston when that piston is forced to the left. Quick action valve is held to its seat by spring, assisted by auxiliary reservoir pressure, and can only be opened when quick action piston moves to the right.

Q. How does the quick action triple operate in service applications? How in energency applications?

A. Main piston has the same stroke for both service and emergency applications, and is extended to form a cylinder in which the vent piston is fitted.

Q. Will the vent valve stand open and exhaust all brake pipe air?

A. No; since port F is always open the momentary excess pressure exerted on the piston will quickly equalize with the brake pipe pressure, and the spring, together with the brake pipe pressure, will return the vent valve to its seat, thus stopping the escape of air when brake pipe pressure is sufficiently reduced to apply the brakes with full force. As the vent valve closes it returns the piston to its normal position, its travel in that direction being limited by the stop. Valve and piston, after equalization has been effected in the brake cylinder, will return to their normal positions.

Q. How does the valve release the brakes?

A. Increasing the brake pipe pressure until it is greater than that in the auxiliary reservoir causes the main piston and with it the slide valves, to return to their normal (release) positions, closing the service port and allowing the auxiliary reservoir to recharge through the feed groove, and at the same time the air in the brake cylinder to escape into the atmosphere through the exhaust cavity in slide valve, and the exhaust port in its seat.

DISORDERS AND REMEDIES.

Q. What would happen if the cap nut were not securely tightened, or the emergency valve leaked?

A. It would leak away auxiliary reservoir air the same as a slightly opened release valve, and if fast enough, cause the brake to release.

Q. Suppose the check valve leaked or the cap nut were not securely tightened and leaked?

A. Brake cylinder air would leak away and the braking force would reduce the same as with a leaky piston packing leather.

Q. Although it is not necessary to disconnect the brake pipe to clean the operative parts of the triple, is it not advisable to disconnect, inspect and clean the triple valve strainer?

A. Yes; the improved drain cup and brake pipe strainer has largely reduced the amount of dirt that usually finds its way to the triple valve but does not entirely exclude it.

Q. Describe this improved brake pipe strainer.

A. The strainer is mounted on a removable spider and may be removed without breaking the pipe joints, for the purpose of examination. The strainer is placed at the top where no water or dirt rolling along in the pipe can reach it. The drainage pocket may be emptied by unscrewing the plug.

Q. Is it not highly essential that dirt should be excluded as far as possible from the triple?

A. Yes; dirt causes the packing rings to stick in their cylinders, and sometimes lodges on the vent valve, causing it to stick. To prevent these troubles as far as possible the strainer should be taken out and cleaned occasionally, and also the strainer in the brake pipe drain cup.

Q. Where would you look for trouble if there was a constant flow of air out of port J in the side of the triple valve?

A. A blow at port J indicates that the vent valve is leaking, or accompanied sometimes by a blow at the exhaust port of the triple valve indicates that the quick action or emergency valve is leaking. Occasionally the quick action valve is held from its seat by the quick action piston cylinder, which prevents that piston from returning properly. If it is the vent valve that is leaking it will be indicated by the application of the brake when the cut-out cock in the branch pipe is closed.

Q. If, while the air pump labored hard, brake pipe pressure continued to fall and brakes could not be properly released, indicating that there was a bad leak in the brake pipe somewhere, where would you look for the trouble?

A. Examine hose connections and brake pipe connections proper and listen for leaks at port J of the triple valve.

Q. How could the particular triple or triples giving the trouble be located?

A. By blowing or leakage of pressure at port J.

Q. Where would this leakage be coming from, and what defective parts would cause it?

A. The leakage would be coming direct from the

brake pipe, through vent valve on account of it not being seated properly, or the rubber seat being defective.

Q. What causes would prevent the vent valve from seating properly and securely?

A. First, there might be some dirt or other foreign matter lodged between the valve and its seat. Second, a too tight fit of the packing ring in vent piston due to poor repair work, or dirty and gummy cylinder. Third, bent vent piston stem, caused by repairman or cleaner wrenching the valve apart or forcing it together, which holds the vent valve off its seat. Fourth, stop plate taken off during cleaning and put back out of line, binding the piston and holding the vent valve partly open. Fifth, in the older triples, the rubber seat of the vent valve, becoming worn at the bottom, will allow the lever arm of the vent valve and the stem of the vent piston to come in contact, thus leaving an opening past the worn seat for brake pipe pressure to escape. This does not occur with the improved vent valve.

Q. Suppose the pump labors hard and brakes refuse to release, and while search is being made to locate the cause of the trouble, it corrects itself and disappears. Where should we look for the trouble?

A. The vent piston is probably gummed up and for this reason is allowing vent valve to return to its seat gradually, and while doing so to discharge brake pipe air to the atmosphere via passage H and port J, the leakage ceasing when the vent valve finally seats. When this disorder is located the triple should be put in order, or should be cut out.

Q. If a quick reduction be made in brake pipe pressure and the quick action parts of the triple do not respond properly, where should the trouble be looked for?

A. Port F should be examined to determine whether it has been enlarged in size or not, and the packing ring in the vent valve piston should be examined for leakage. Port F enlarged beyond standard size and excessive leakage past the piston ring would permit chamber G pressure to reduce almost uniformly with that in the brake pipe and possibly prevent the operation of the quick action parts.

Q. Are the New York and the Westinghouse quick action triples interchangeable?

A. The one will fit on the cylinder and auxiliary reservoir of the other, but the internal working parts of one will not fit into the body of the other.

Q. If, in a train of mixed New York and Westinghouse triples, a brake works in quick action with a service application, can it be told whether the defective triple valve is a New York or a Westinghouse?

A. It can in many cases; a New York triple that works in quick action, when making a service application, usually does so with less than a five-pound reduction; while a Westinghouse in same condition, usually requires a five-pound service reduction to apply it in quick action, and sometimes more.

Q. How can a defective triple valve be located?

A. By stationing the trainmen along the train and noting which valve, in a service application, vents air to the atmosphere. If the ground is dry the defective triple can be located by the dust that will be stirred up by the vented air. Another method is to close an angle cock about the middle of the train and have an application made to determine whether it is in front, or back of this point, proceeding in this manner until located. In cases where quick action occurs during a service reduction, the length of service reduction had at the brake valve before it suddenly terminates the service reduction, is an indication of the location of the point in the train at which the defective triple is located.

Q. What is the object of the small plug in vent piston?

A. To permit of easily grinding in the vent piston ring; a ¼-inch hole is drilled through the piston, which gives a free passage of air to and from chamber G during the process of grinding. After the ring has been fitted the plug referred to is inserted.

Q. Formerly port F was located in the vent piston. What improvement in the action of the triple is had from the present location of port F in the piston stem?

A. In emergency applications the vent valve piston stem is carried to the left, and port F in this stem is carried into the bushing in the vent valve seat, the bushing being made a close fit around the stem, so that the escape of air from chamber G is considerably retarded. This prolonged retardation of the escape of air from chamber G causes the vent piston to hold the vent valve from its seat longer, and thus to vent more of the brake pipe air to chamber H. The increased quantity of brake pipe air vented to chamber H has the effect, after forcing over the quick action piston, of holding it there longer, which results in holding the quick action valve off its seat longer; and the effect of the combined action is to cause an almost instantaneous equalization of pressure between the brake cylinder and the auxiliary reservoir, and a quicker serial application.

Q. What other effect is produced in the operation of the triple valves by the present form of port F?

A. It enables quick action to jump a greater number of plain triple valves placed together in succession or a greater number of cut-out quick action triple valves in succession than formerly. Also it provides for a sufficient venting of air from the longer train pipes found on modern cars, and insures a sufficient reduction to produce serial quick action throughout the whole train.

Q. What is the function of the port and passage leading from port J in front of the piston to the rear of this piston, then back under the bushing to port J again?

A. To relieve the cushioning effect which would be had due to the quick movement of this piston, and to enable the vented train pipe to hold it over the required period of time

Q. Can the present vent piston, having port F drilled through the stem, be substituted in the older triples and produce the same effect in quick action as is had in the modified triple?

A. Yes; and this is done when the older triples come in for cleaning and repairs.

Q. With the exception of the above, is the operation of the present quick action triple and the older triples the same?

A. Yes; and all the answers given to the questions relative to the present form, with the exception of those given below, apply to the older style.

IMPROVED QUICK ACTION PASSENGER TRIPLE, STYLE S-1.

Q. In what does the style S-1 passenger quick action triple differ from the standard quick action triple?

A. It is larger, has a larger service graduating port for the air to pass through to the brake cylinder, also a larger exhaust port; the exhaust valve has a service graduating port drilled through it, and carries the graduating valve mounted on top

Q. What advantage is there in placing the graduating valve on top of the exhaust valve?

A. It reduces the friction of the moving parts. When the triple piston begins to move, the graduating valve is moved first to uncover the service port in the exhaust valve; then the exhaust valve is moved until the graduating ports in the exhaust valve and its seat come in register. In this style of triple but one slide valve is moved at a time.

Q. Should the graduating valve in the style S-1 quick action passenger triple leak, how could it be detected?

A. By making a partial service application, and then noting whether the brake released of its own accord or not.

Q. If the graduating valve in this triple leaks will it allow air to escape through the exhaust port while in release position?

A. No; when the exhaust valve is in release position it controls the opening from the auxiliary to the brake cylinder and atmosphere, and no air leaking by the graduating valve can escape through this port.

Q. With what size brake cylinders are the style S-1 quick action triple valves used?

A. With 12, 14 and 16-inch brake cylinders.

Q. How may this triple valve be distinguished from the freight and 10-inch passenger triple valve?

A. The letter S is cast on the triple valve and it fastens to the brake cylinder with three studs.

Q How may the parts of this triple that are not interchangeable with similar ones of the other triples be distinguished?

A. The letter S is stamped on the parts that are not interchangeable.

Q. Is there any difference in the side cap of the style S-1 and P-1 and the freight triple valves?

A. Yes; the side cap of the triples S-1 and P-1 are tapped out for ½-inch pipe and a pipe plug inserted.

Q. Why is this side cap tapped out for ½-inch pipe?

A. To permit of the attachment of the compensating valve for high speed braking.

Q. The drawings show the brake cylinder check valve made of metal (brass). What is the latest practice in connection with this valve?

A. The brake cylinder check valve is now made with a rubber seat in all styles of quick action triples, and will interchange with quick action valves.

QUICK ACTION TRIPLE, STYLE H-1.

Q. For what is style H-1 triple valve intended?

A. For use on 10-inch freight car equipment.

Q. How may this triple valve be distinguished from other forms of triple valves?

A. The letter H is cast on the side of the triple, and it fastens to the auxiliary reservoir with three studs.

Q. What triple is the style H-1 similar to in appearance and construction?

A. The appearance and construction of this triple is similar in many respects to the style S-1.

Q. As the style S-1 triple fastens to the auxiliary reservoir with the same number of studs as the style H-1, is it possible to get these triples on the wrong size brake cylinder?

A. No; while both these triples fasten with three studs the spacing of the holes is different.

Q. How can the parts of this triple that are not interchangeable be distinguished?

A. The letter H is stamped on the parts that are not interchangeable.

QUICK ACTION TRIPLE, STYLE P-1.

Q. For what use is the style P-1 triple valve intended?

A. For use on 10-inch passenger and tender cylinders.

Q. How can this triple valve be distinguished from style F triple valve which is for freight car use?

A. The letter P is cast on the side of this triple valve.

Q. In what points does this triple valve differ from the freight triple valve?

A. The feed grooves in the main piston bushing, and in the piston are larger. The vent port F in the vent piston stem is also larger.

Q. What parts of this triple valve are not interchangeable with the freight triple valve?

A. The main piston and the vent piston.

Q. How may the parts of this triple valve that are not interchangeable with the freight triple valve be distinguished?

A. The parts that are not interchangeable have the letter P stamped on them.

Q. Is there any difference in the operation of this triple from that of the others?

A. No; its operation is the same as that of the others.

Q. Is its side cap tapped out for the piping of the compensating valve?

A. Yes; compensating valves are used on all sizes of passenger triples.

NEW YORK COMBINED AUTOMATIC AND STRAIGHT AIR BRAKE.

The New York straight air equipment consists of a straight air brake valve, a reducing valve, a double check-

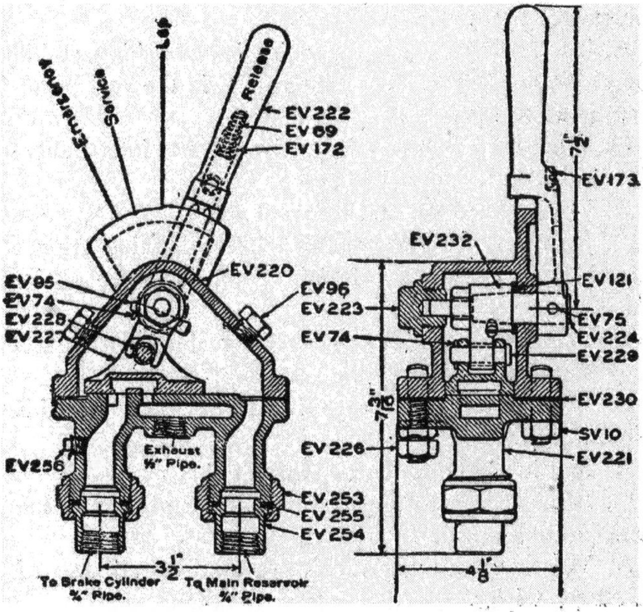

Fig. 38—New York Straight Air Brake Valve.

valve, a brake cylinder gauge and a safety valve on the brake cylinder, the same as is used in the Westinghouse system, but the New York straight air valve is modeled after their automatic engineer's brake valve. It will be seen by reference to Fig. 38, illustrating the straight air brake valve that the essential parts of this valve (aside from the case) is a slide-valve operated by a handle working over a quadrant. There are two oil plugs for the purpose of oiling the slide-valve seat, the same as with the automatic brake valve There are two pipe connections and one exhaust. One pipe connection admits main reservoir pressure into the brake valve and the other pipe connection allows the pressure to pass into the brake cylinder.

STRAIGHT AIR BRAKE VALVE.

The New York Straight Air Brake Valve performs the same functions as the Westinghouse, that is it applies the engine and tender brakes independent of the triple valve when the triple is in release position.

There are four positions on the New York straight air brake valve as follows: Release, Lap, Service, and Emergency.

Referring to Fig 38 it will be seen that the handle is in full release position, and brake cylinder pressure can pass under the slide-valve and out at the exhaust cavity. Should the handle be moved to lap position the slide-valve will close the passage leading to the brake cylinder, thereby preventing main reservoir pressure from getting into the cylinder and also preventing the cylinder pressure from escaping to the atmosphere. Now should the handle be moved to the next notch, or service position, the slide-valve will be moved further back, thereby creating a small opening to the brake cylinder and allowing the engine brakes to be set gradually, but should the handle be thrown to emergency position the slide-valve will be moved still further back, so that the passage to the brake cylinder is wide open, which permits a quick rush of air into the cylinders. Between the main reser-

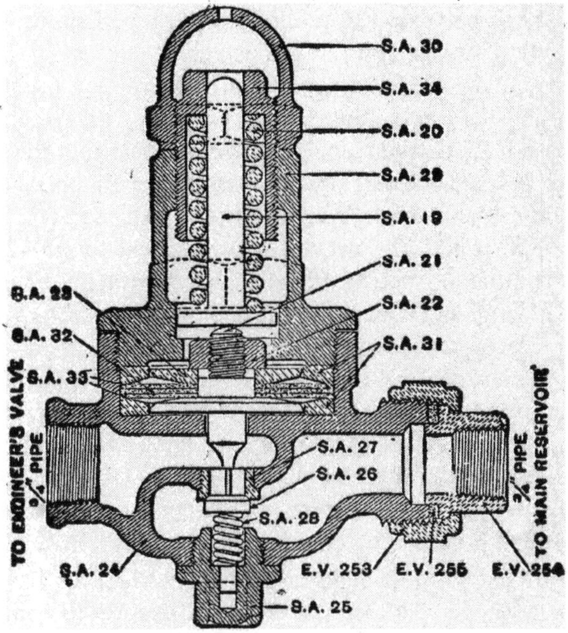

Fig. 39—New York Straight Air Pressure Reducing Valve.

voir and the straight air brake valve there is a reducing valve, Fig. 39, for the purpose of keeping the main reservoir pressure down to a predetermined standard, which is usually 45 pounds.

The straight air reducing valve is connected at one end to the main reservoir and at the other end to the straight air brake valve, and as the regulating spring is supposed to be screwed down to 45 pounds, the force of the regulating spring will drive the diaphragm down so that it unseats the check-valve, 26, therefore when no air is in the brake cylinder the main reservoir pressure can pass by the check-valve and flow through the pipe connection leading to the straight air brake valve, and when the pressure under the diaphragm becomes a fraction greater than what the regulating spring 20 is set at, the diaphragm will be moved up, thereby allowing the check-valve to reseat and shut off the main reservoir pressure, but should the brake cylinder leathers leak, as soon as the leakage brings the pressure down below the tension of the graduating spring the diaphragm will be forced down and again unseat the check-valve to admit main reservoir pressure.

This action enables the engineer to place the straight air brake valve in service position and work under his engine with perfect safety, because he knows that as long as the pump works the straight air brake valve will automatically supply main reservoir pressure to the brake cylinders, and keep the engine from moving.

One of the greatest benefits that the straight air brake valve confers in road service is that it enables the engineer to set the engine brakes independently of the train brakes, so that in slowing down or in making a stop he can keep the train bunched, and thereby prevent a break-in-two.

The safety valve Fig. 40, on the brake cylinders is for the purpose of taking care of any leakage in the reducing valve, for, should the check-valve of the reducing valve leak the main reservoir pressure would of course equalize with the brake cylinder pressure, and in order to prevent this the safety valve is placed on the brake cylinder to allow any extra pressure that might get into the cylinders to automatically blow down.

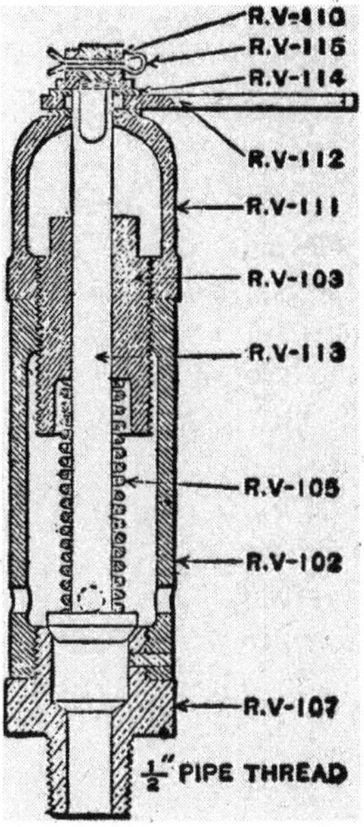

Fig. 40—New York Safety Valve, with Hand Release.

The diagram which illustrates the general arrangement and method of piping the New York Combined Automatic and Straight Air Brake Valve, Fig. 41, will show the relative positions of the several parts.

Referring to Fig. 40, the pipe shown in dotted lines leading from the brake pipe, and having a cock on it is for the purpose of opening the cylinders when descend-

reby
ded.
own
pipe.

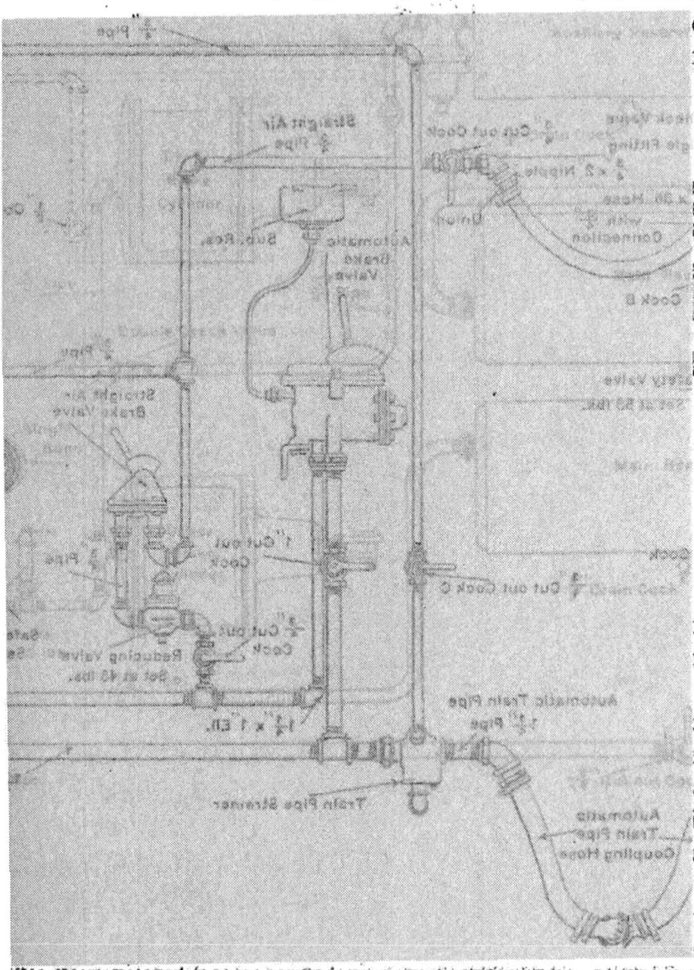

and
nding
have
cylin-
elease
hows
ich is
e and
being
the
n the
f this

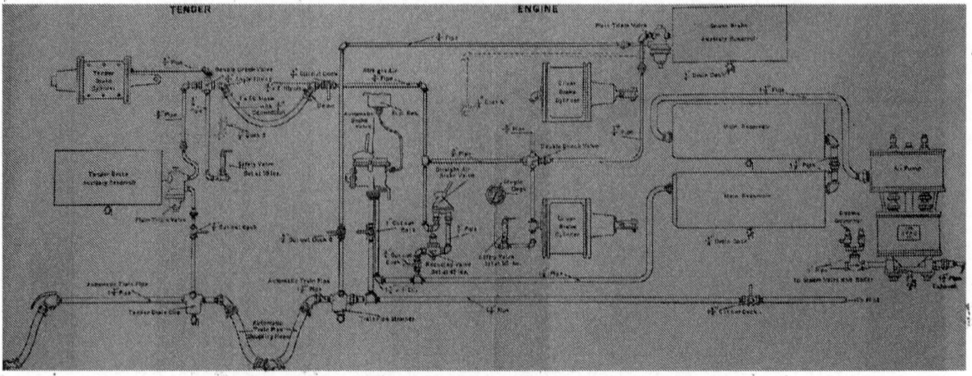

FIG. 41 GENERAL ARRANGEMENT AND METHOD OF PIPING THE NEW YORK COMBINED AUTOMATIC AND STRAIGHT AIR BRAKE.

to TENDER
cyli
the

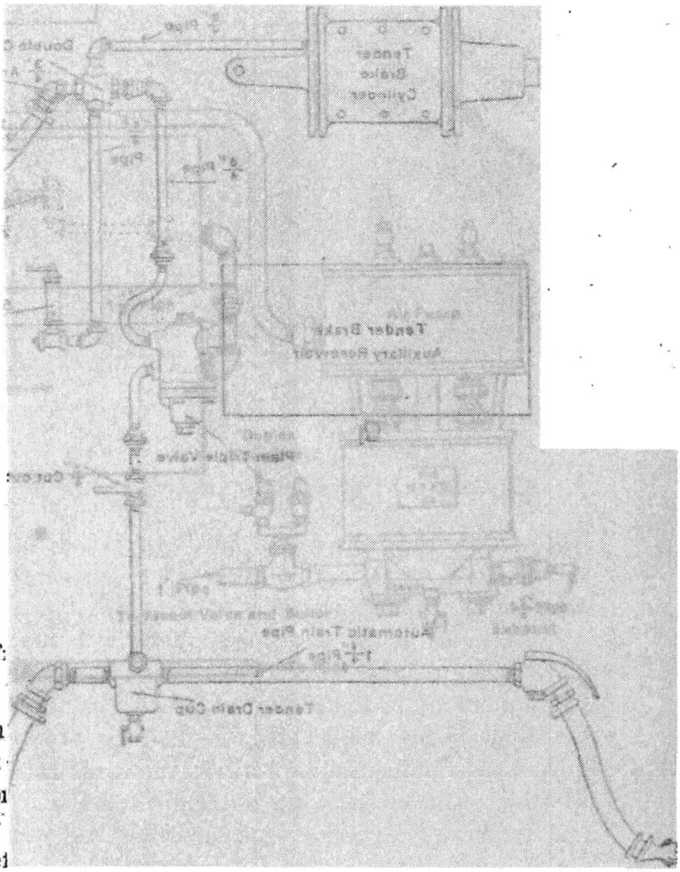

F:

Th
ment
Autor
show
Rei
leadin FIG. 41
for th

ing heavy grades or in case of a hose bursting, thereby saving the engine tires from being loosened or skidded.

There is also another pipe with a release cock shown in dotted lines, connected with the tender brake pipe.

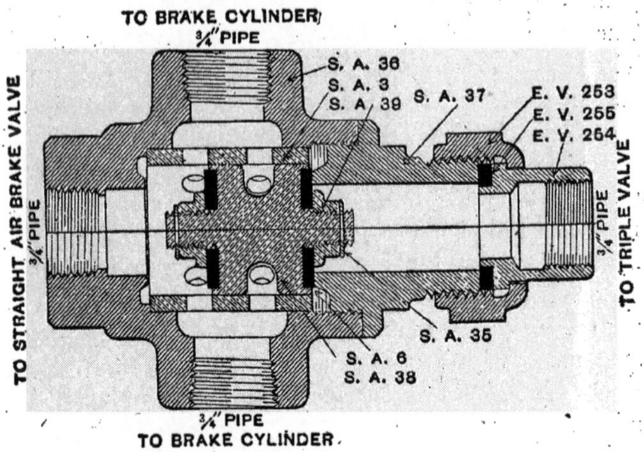

Fig. 42—¾-inch Straight Air Double Check Valve.

These release cocks are placed one in the engine cab and the other in the gangway on the tender. The descending of long heavy grades makes it absolutely essential to have some means by which the engine and tender brake cylinder pressure can be reduced without having to release the train brakes, or in case a hose bursts. Fig. 42 shows the double throw check valve, the function of which is to close the communication between the triple valve and the brake cylinder when the straight air brake is being used, and also to close communication between the straight air brake pipe and the brake cylinder when the automatic brake is being used. The construction of this valve is plainly shown in Fig. 42.

NEW YORK HIGH SPEED BRAKE.

The New York high speed brake consists essentially of a compensating valve for each brake cylinder, a triplex pump governor and the ordinary quick action mechanism. The brake pipe pressure is carried at 100 to 110 pounds. The high speed brake is used in modern heavy, fast passenger service. With the high speed brake a train can be stopped in about thirty per cent less distance than it can with a quick-action brake. For instance, a train running forty-five miles an hour can be stopped in 560 feet with the high-speed brake, as against 710 feet with the quick-action brake. Consequently a train running sixty miles an hour can be stopped in 1,060 feet with the high-speed brake, making a net gain of 300 feet over a stop made with the quick-action brake, which requires 1,360 feet within which to stop a train running sixty miles an hour.

Two applications should always be made with the high-speed brake in making a stop, but the initial reduction can be fifteen pounds instead of ten pounds, as would be proper when using the automatic brake. In making a ten or fifteen-pound reduction with the high-speed brake from 110-pound train pipe pressure, the same cylinder pressure is produced as there would be if the same reduction were made with the automatic brake from seventy-pound train pipe pressure, provided the piston-travel is the same. But, after the brake cylinder pressure has been raised with the high-speed brake to the point at which equalization would take place with the automatic brake, then any further reduction of the train pipe pressure with the high-speed brake would raise the brake cylinder pressure accordingly. For example, an emergency applica-

ould
the

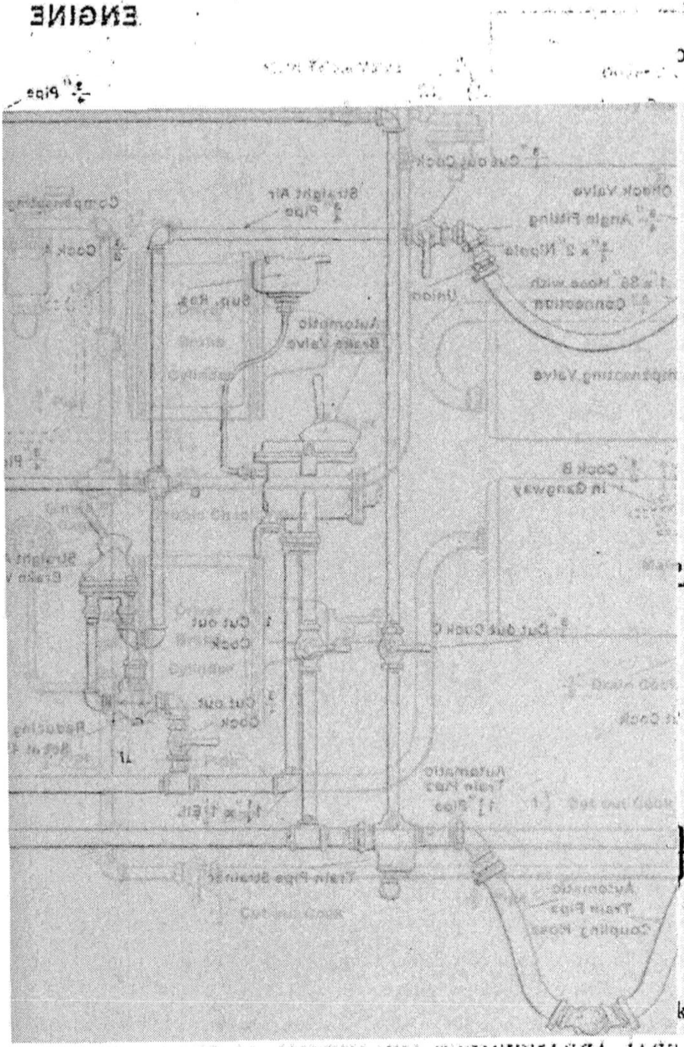

ke.

duce
nds.

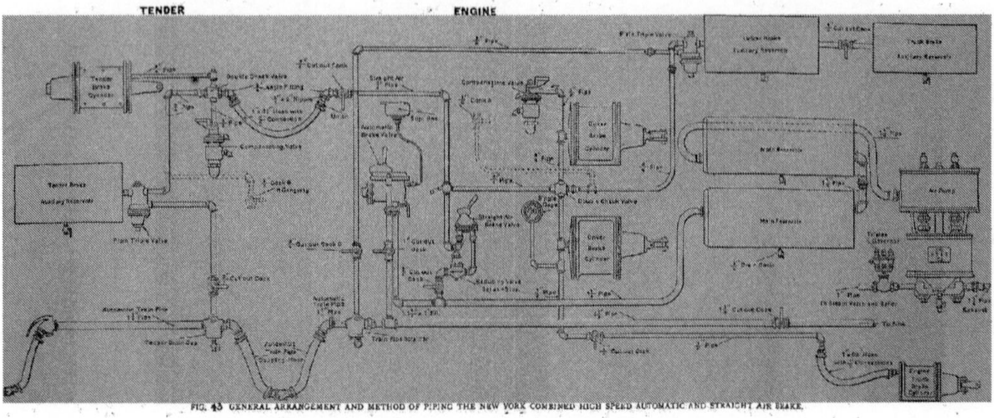

FIG. 43 GENERAL ARRANGEMENT AND METHOD OF PIPING THE NEW YORK COMBINED HIGH SPEED AUTOMATIC AND STRAIGHT AIR BRAKE.

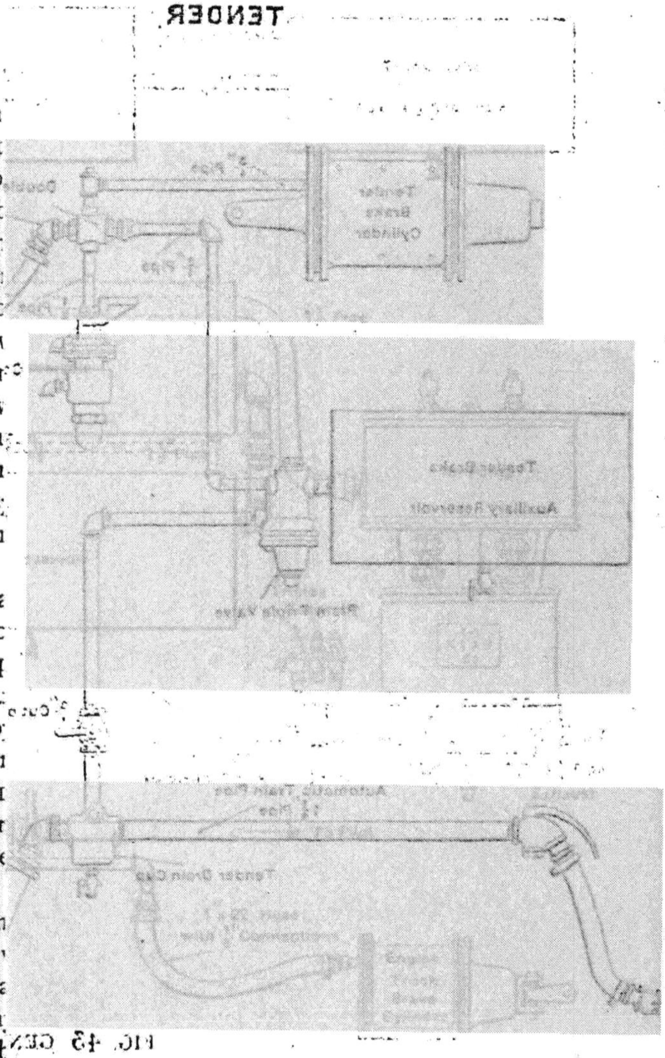

Th
of a c
pump
The b
The h
senge
be sto
can w
runnin
feet w
the qu
sixty n
high-s
stop n
1,360
miles a
Two
high-sp
tion ca
be pro
a ten or
from 1
pressur
tion we
pound
the sam
raised
equaliza
then an
the high
sure ac

tion of the automatic brake with an 8-inch cylinder would produce a cylinder pressure of sixty pounds, but with the

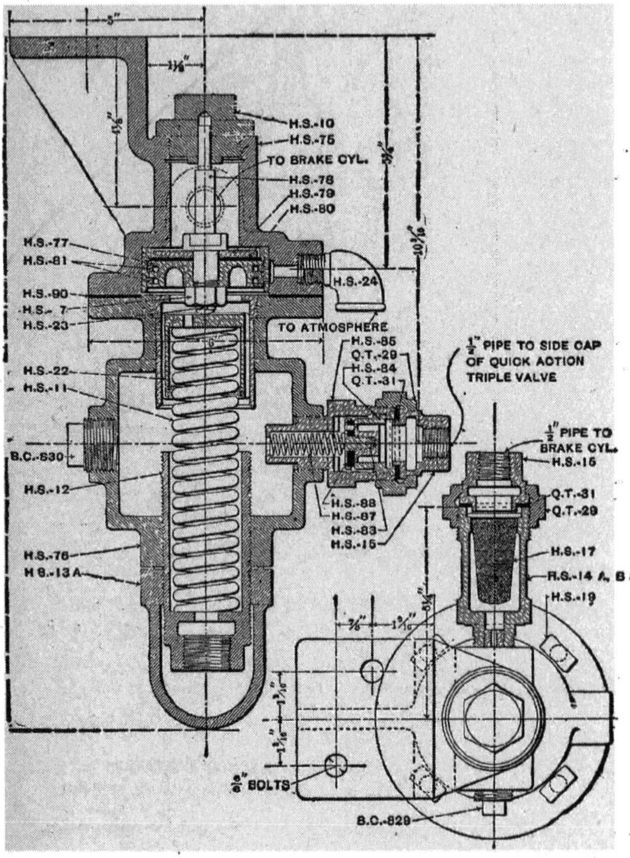

Fig. 44—Style A, Compensating Valve, High Speed Brake.

high-speed brake an emergency application will produce a brake cylinder pressure of about eighty-eight pounds.

P

This fo [illegible]

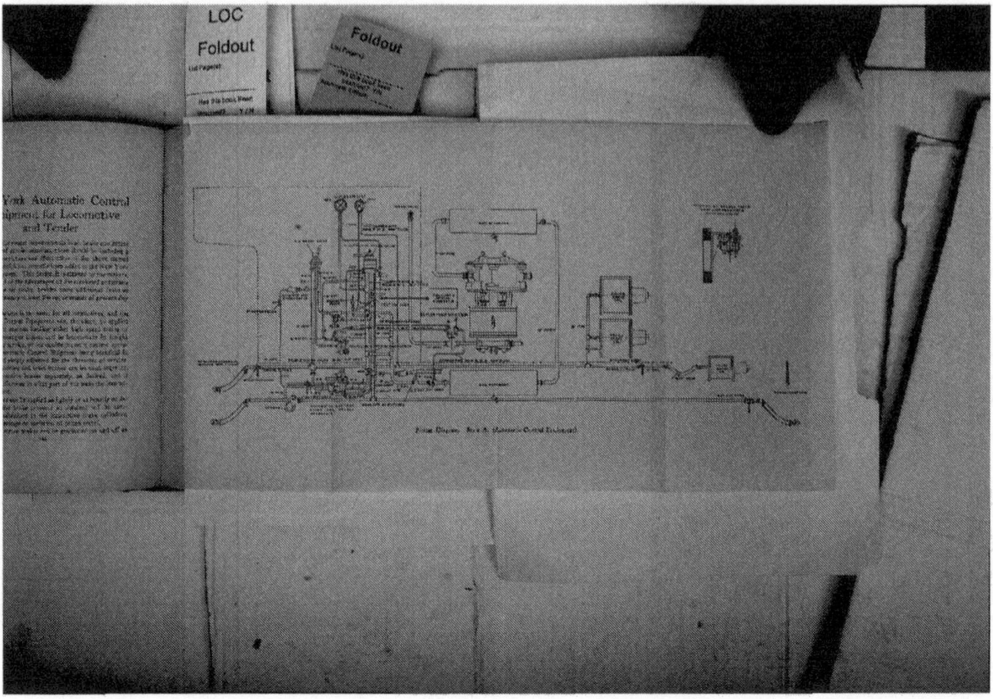
LOC
Foldout
Foldout
York Automatic Control
and Tender

The diagram, Fig. 43, shows a general view of the arrangement and method of piping of the New York

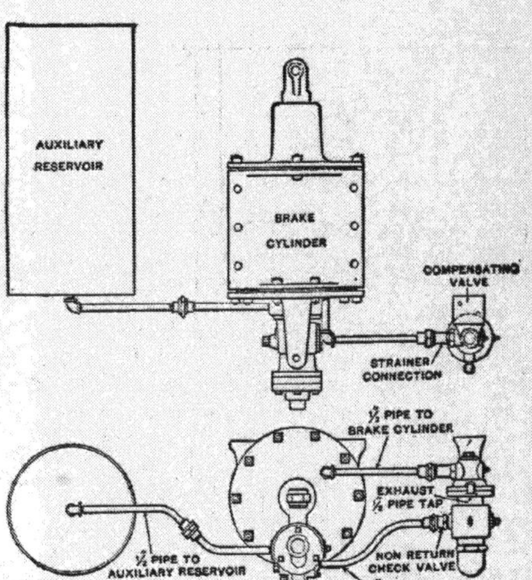

Diagram Showing Method of Piping Style A and A-1 Compensating Valve.

Fig. 45—New York High Speed Brake.

combined high speed automatic and straight air brake. The high speed reducing valve or compensating valve as it is termed, consists essentially of a piston valve H S-77 (see Fig. 44) working in a bushing or cylinder; two packing rings H S-81, that act as valves for the relief and leakage ports; a regulating spring H S-11, by which the piston is held in its normal position against the brake cylinder pressure; a regulating nut or screw H S-12, by which the tension of the regulating spring may be adjusted; a body H S-75; a spring case H S-76; a spring box H S-22; a cap nut H S-10, and a non-return check valve H S-83, with casing complete. Fig. 45 shows the method of piping the style A and A-1 compensating valve, the operation of which in an emergency application is as follows: A portion of the brake pipe air vented at the side cap of the quick action triple valve, passes through the pipe leading to the non-return check valve and spring box air chamber, charging the spring box chamber, under the piston, with air pressure. This air pressure augments, or reinforces, the regulating spring pressure under the piston, and permits the full equalized pressure from the auxiliary reservoir to be had in the brake cylinder, and to be retained therein for several seconds before the piston H S-77, can descend and open the relief ports. The air vented into, and trapped in, the the spring box air chamber requires several seconds to pass back to the atmosphere through the small port in the non-return check valve H S-83. When the air pressure in the spring box air chamber has reduced sufficiently the piston will be forced down by the brake cylinder pressure above it, the relief ports controlled by packing rings H S-81 will be opened, and brake cylinder pressure will be gradually reduced to the point of adjustment of the valve.

In service applications, there being no air vented into

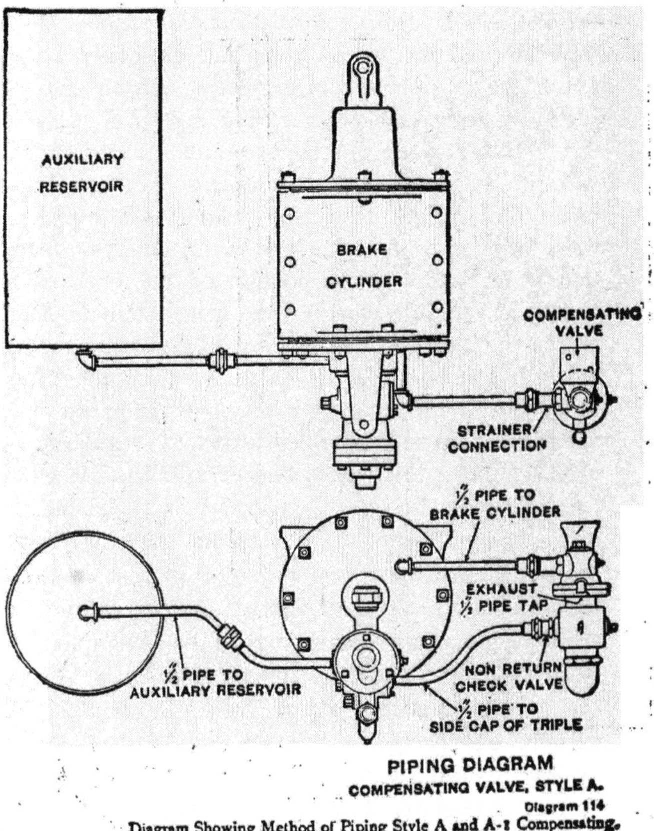

the spring box air chamber, the only pressure which the piston has to overcome is that of the regulating spring; therefore, when the brake cylinder pressure is sufficient to overcome the spring pressure the piston will descend promptly and open the relief ports.

The function of the non-return check valve H S-83

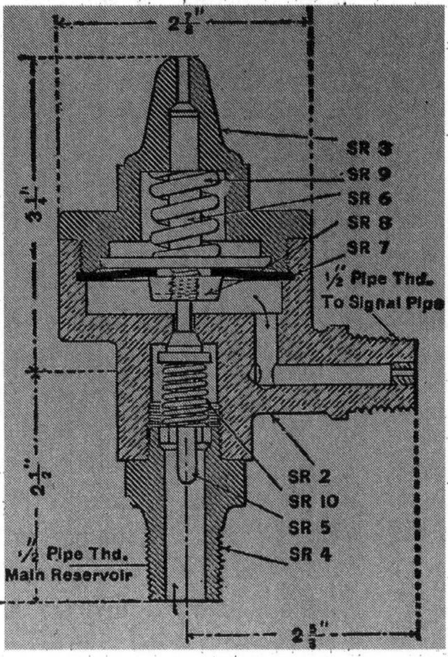

Fig. 46—New York Air Signal Pressure Reducing Valve.

which is screwed into the spring box (see Fig. 44) is as follows:

In emergency applications the air which is vented from the brake pipe into the spring box H S-76 must pass the non-return check valve, which then seats, and prevents the air thus trapped in the spring box from escaping or backing out, except as it passes out slowly through the small port drilled through this check valve. (See Piping Diagram, Fig. 45).

NEW YORK SIGNAL EQUIPMENT.

The number of parts constituting the equipment of the New York Signal is the same as the Westinghouse,

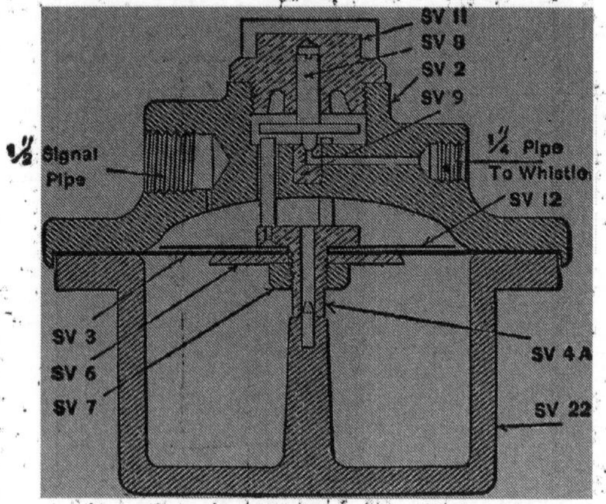

(a)

Plate 117—Fig. 47—Style B, New York Air Signal Valve.

but the construction of the parts is somewhat different. The essential parts are a pressure reducing valve, Fig. 46, and air signal valve, Fig. 47, the car discharge valve, Fig. 48, and the signal whistle, Fig. 49.

The operation of the reducing valve is as follows: When the regulating spring 6 is screwed down to 40 pounds it causes the diaphragm 8 to force the check-valve 5 from its seat, which allows the main reservoir pressure to flow by the check-valve into the diaphragm chamber and out at the pipe connection leading to the signal pipe, and when the signal pipe is charged up to a fraction over 40 pounds it causes the diaphragm to be

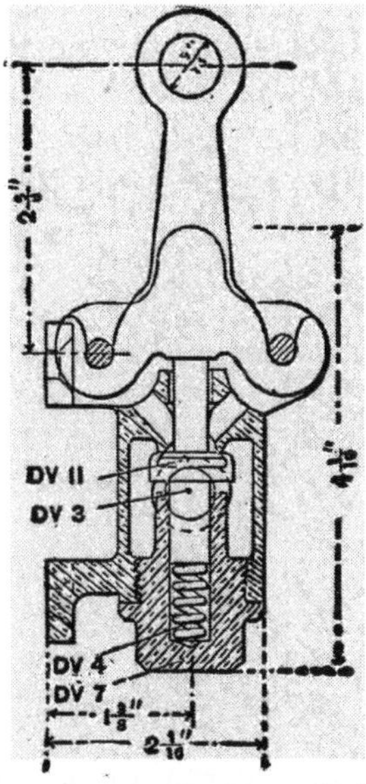

Fig. 48—Car Discharge Valve.

forced away from the check-valve, and thereby enables the check-valve to reseat and shut off main reservoir pressure. As soon as the signal pipe pressure is again reduced below the tension of the graduating spring, the diaphragm again unseats the check-valve and allows the main reservoir pressure to again flow into the signal pipe.

The air signal valve, Fig. 47, is connected to the signal pipe and to the signal whistle, and when the pressure from the signal pipe enters the signal valve it passes down through the port in the diaphragm stem into the lower air chamber, and equalizes on both sides of the diaphragm, and at the same time passes up into the air valve chamber and equalizes on both sides of that valve. When a sudden reduction is made from the signal pipe the air on the top side of the diaphragm is also reduced so that the pressure in the lower air chamber lifts the

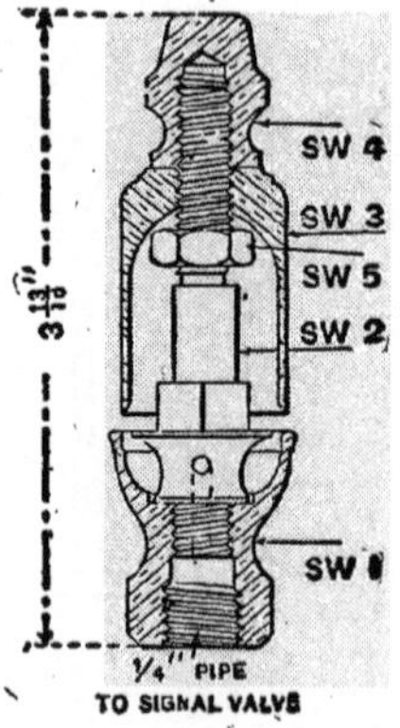

Fig. 49—Signal Whistle.

diaphragm and causes the upright pins which are fastened to the diaphragm stem to force the air valve 8 from its seat, and thereby permit the air from the lower chamber to blow into the whistle. As soon as the signal pipe pressure has stopped exhausting, the diaphragm is forced back to its seat, which allows the air valve to again drop to its seat. The same instructions regarding the manner of operating the air signal that governs the Westinghouse system apply equally as well to the New York Air Signal.

QUESTIONS AND ANSWERS.

THE NEW YORK COMBINED AUTOMATIC AND STRAIGHT AIR BRAKE.

Q. What is the combined automatic and straight air brake?

A. It is a combination, upon the engine and the tender, of an automatic and a straight air brake, so that either of them may be operated separately at the desire of the engineer.

Q. Why was it necessary to combine the straight air brake with the automatic air brake on engines and tenders?

A. Because it was found that in switching service the straight air brake was more satisfactory than the automatic, and would give much better results; that in road service, in slowing up long freight trains, bunching the slack preparatory to a stop with the automatic, and holding trains bunched when releasing the automatic brake, as well as in controlling the speed of trains down long grades, it was an efficient aid.

Q. In addition to the usual automatic air brake parts on the engine and tender, what straight air brake parts are necessary to produce the combined apparatus?

A. There is required one ¾-inch straight air brake valve, style C; one straight air pressure reducing valve, two double throw check valves, and two safety valves with hand release; one each for the driver and the tender brake cylinder; one hose connection and union, with angle fittings, and the necessary stop cocks, cut-out cocks and piping.

Q. What are the functions of the straight air brake valve?

A. With this valve, air is admitted to and exhausted from the brake cylinders in applying and in releasing the brakes.

Q. How many positions are there on the straight air brake valve for the handle?

A Four; the release, lap, service and emergency application positions.

Q. How can these positions be told?

A. By means of the notches made upon the quadrant and the stops at each end.

Q. What is the type of air valve, in the engineer's straight air brake valve, that controls the flow of air between the main reservoir, brake cylinder and atmosphere?

A. It is an ordinary D slide valve.

Q. Should this valve ever become dry and hard to operate, how could it be lubricated?

A. By first closing stop cock in the main reservoir pipe and working the handle back and forth a few times to exhaust the air from the brake valve; then by removing the oil plugs in the cover; the slide valve and its seat may then be lubricated.

Q. What is the function of the straight air brake pressure reducing valve?

A. The straight air brake pressure reducing valve, limits the pressure obtainable in the straight air brake pipe and in the brake cylinder to the desired amount.

Q. At what pressure does the reducing valve usually limit the air for the straight air brake?

A. Usually at 45 pounds, but this may be varied to suit special conditions, and the valve may be set to furnish either more or less.

Q. How is the straight air pressure reducing valve adjusted?

A. By removing the cap nut and screwing the regulating screw to increase the pressure, and by unscrewing it to reduce the pressure.

Q. Why are the spring case, the regulating spring, and regulating nut located above the supply valve?

A. To prevent moisture, dirt and oil coming from the main reservoir from lodging upon the rubber diaphragm, which constitutes the wall between the straight air brake pipe pressure and the regulating spring.

Q. What is the duty of the regulating spring?

A. Its duty is to keep diaphragm stem in position to hold the supply valve away from its seat until the brake cylinder pressure reaches the limit of its adjustment

Q. Should the reducing valve leak, what would be the result?

A. Main reservoir pressure would then be had in the main reservoir pipe as far as the straight air brake valve, and in case of a straight air brake application, the leak would continue to raise the pressure in the brake cylinders until the relief valves opened.

Q. How can the supply valves be cleaned?

A. By closing the cut-out cock between the main reservoir and the pressure reducing valve and unscrewing the cap nut. The supply valve may then be removed and cleaned.

Q. How should the supply valve be cleaned?

A. By softening up the gum or dirt with a little kerosene or other light oil that will cut it, then wiping it perfectly clean.

Q. Should the supply valve be oiled when placed back in position?

A. No; it should be replaced perfectly dry.

Q. Should care be used about screwing up the spring case against the body?

A. Yes; care should be taken, when renewing the diaphragms and in replacing the spring case, not to screw the latter up so tight as to crush the diaphragms. A little space should always be left between the spring case and the body.

Q. How many sizes of double throw check valves are there?

A. Two.

Q. What are the sizes and why are two needed?

A. One is for ½-inch pipe connections and is for use with the smaller plain triples; the other is for ¾-inch pipe connections and is for use with quick action triple valves and the larger plain triples.

Q. Describe the double throw check valve.

A. It is a check valve of the piston variety with two faces, each having a leather washer or seat.

Q. What are the duties of the double throw check valves?

A. To close the communication between the triple valve and the brake cylinder, when the straight air brake is being used; and to close the communication between the straight air brake pipe and the brake cylinder, when the automatic brake is being used.

Q. How does the double throw check valve operate to close the communication between the triple valve, or the straight-air brake pipe, and the brake cylinder, when either brake is being operated?

A. If the straight air brake is being used, air is admitted to the straight air brake pipe, and the pressure will force the double check valve to the right, provided there be no pressure other than atmospheric on the other side of it, causing the leather seat on the triple connection end to seat air tight against the cap; the check valve will thus close the communication between the triple and the brake cylinder, and at the same time will open the ports in the check valve bush leading from the straight air brake pipe to the brake cylinder, in this manner establishing a communication between the straight air brake valve and the brake cylinder.

If it is the automatic brake that is being used, when air passes from the triple valve to the pipe leading to the brake cylinder the air pressure will force the double throw check to the left, and close the communication between the straight air brake pipe and the brake cylinder, and open the communication between the triple valve and the brake cylinder.

Q. Why are safety valves placed in the brake cylinders?

A. For the purpose of relieving the cylinders of any overpressure that might accumulate in them because of leaks from the straight air pressure reducing valve, the double throw check valve, or from an emergency application of the automatic brake while the straight air brake is applied.

Q. Why are these safety valves supplied with a hand release?

A. In order that there may be a double protection against wheel sliding, and so that on slippery or bad rail, should the wheels slide, the engineer may quickly relieve the pressure sufficiently to start them rotating again. Also to prevent overheating of tires on long down grades.

Q. Should both the automatic and the straight air brake ordinarily be kept cut in ready for use at all times?

A. Yes; unless failure of some part requires cutting one or the other out.

Q. Should an excess pressure always be kept in the main reservoir?

A. Yes; to insure the satisfactory operation of the brake and a certain release at all times, an excess pressure of 10 or more pounds should be maintained in the main reservoir.

Q. In what position should the handle of the straight air brake valve be kept while the automatic brake is being used?

A. When using the automatic brake be sure that the handle of the straight air brake valve is in release position.

Q. What might happen if the handle of the straight air brake was in lap position while the automatic brake was being released?

A. There would be a likelihood of the driver and the tender brakes sticking.

Q. Should the automatic brake be used while the straight air brake is applied?

A. Ordinarily the straight air brake should be released before the automatic brake is applied, but in cases of emergency occurring after the straight air is applied no attention should be paid to this instruction, but apply the automatic brake in emergency immediately.

Q. Where should the handle of the automatic brake

valve be carried while the straight air brake is being used?

A. In the running position.

Q. Why should the handle of the automatic brake valve be carried in the running position while the straight air brake is being used?

A. For the same reason that the straight air brake valve handle should be carried in full release while the automatic brake valve is being used; that is, to avoid sticking of the driver and the tender brakes when it is desired to release them.

Q. Why are the driver and the tender brakes likely to stick unless the brake valve handles are carried as directed above?

A. In the case of using the automatic brake, while the straight air brake valve handle is on lap, leakage of air from the brake cylinder, or past the seat of the straight air brake valve as far as the seat of the double throw check valve will charge the straight air brake pipe with pressure; then. when releasing the automatic brake, as soon as the cylinder pressure has reduced below that the straight air brake pipe contains, the double throw check will shift its position and open communication between the straight air brake valve and the brake cylinder, and thus hold the brake applied with the remaining cylinder pressure, augmented somewhat by the higher pressure in the straight air brake pipe.

Q. Should care be used in handling the straight air brake?

A. Yes; as the straight air brake is nearly as powerful as the automatic on the engine and tender, it should be handled with judgment and skill. Care should be taken to avoid rough handling of trains with it, as it must be remembered that the braking power is all on the engine and tender.

When using the straight air brake to steady trains on long down grades care should be taken to avoid loosening the tires on the drivers, from overheating them. This can be done by alternating the straight air on the drivers and the automatic on the train.

Q. When the safety valves that are placed in the brake cylinders operate in a full application of the straight air brake, what does it indicate?

A. Either the safety valves or the special straight air brake pressure reducing valve is out of adjustment or is leaking, and that these parts should be tested and adjusted at once.

Q. What is the best location for the brake cylinder safety valves?

A. It is better to have them piped up to the cab so that the hand release with which they are provided can be operated by the engine crew, whenever it is desirable to do so, to avoid wheel sliding or overheating of tires

Q. How should the double throw check valve be tested for leakage?

A. With the handle of the automatic brake valve in running position, and the triple valve in release position, apply the straight air brake; should there be any leakage past the double throw check valve from the brake cylinder it will appear at the exhaust port of the triple valve in the form of a blow.

Having tested with the straight air brake valve in this way for leakage past one seat, next place the handle of the straight air brake valve in full release position and apply the automatic brake; any leakage past the other seat will appear at the exhaust port of the straight air brake valve. When making this latter test, however, it should be known that the slide valve itself, of the straight air brake valve, is tight.

Q. If the automatic brake is partially applied, and straight air is then used, what will be the result?

A. In this case brake cylinder pressure will not be raised above that at which the pressure reducing valve is set.

Q. Where is the straight air brake valve located?

A. In the cab; usually on the side, in the most convenient place for operating.

Q. Whereabouts on the engine is the straight air brake pressure reducing valve usually located?

A. At some convenient point in the cab, where there is little or no danger of its freezing, and not too close to the boiler head, where it might possibly become overheated.

Q. How may errors in piping the straight air brake valve be avoided?

A. By noting that the main reservoir connection be made at that part of the brake valve that is marked in raised letters "Front." The brake pipe connection is made to the other connection, and in this brake pipe connection there is a hole drilled and tapped for the air gauge pipe.

Q. How would you test for a leaky slide valve in the straight air valve?

A. With the brake released, and the handle in full release position; if a blow is heard at the exhaust port the slide valve is leaking.

Q. What effect does a leak through the slide valve of the brake valve have upon the operation of the straight air brake?

A. Ordinarily during the time that a straight air brake application is held applied, if the leak is from the main reservoir pressure, the brake cylinder pressure will increase to the limit of the pressure reducing valve; but it might happen that the leak be from the brake cylinder to the atmosphere, in which event it would reduce the brake cylinder pressure.

NEW YORK HIGH SPEED BRAKE.

Q. Of what does the high speed brake consist essentially?

A. A brake pipe pressure of from 100 to 110 pounds, a compensating valve for each brake cylinder, a triplex pump governor, and the ordinary quick action mechanism.

Q. In what class of passenger service is the high speed brake used?

A. In modern, heavy, fast passenger service.

Q. Why is the high speed reducing valve called a compensating valve?

A. Because while operating in service applications as an ordinary safety, or pressure, reducing valve, in emergency applications they hold the maximum cylinder pressure for a limited period of time before commencing to relieve the brake cylinder. This period of time of holding the maximum cylinder pressure is automatically lengthened or shortened according to the variations had in the maximum brake cylinder pressure, or in the piston travel, or in both combined. As the valve makes allowance or "compensates" in time of hold of maximum brake cylinder pressure on account of these variations, the closure of all the valves upon a train will be practically uniform.

Q. Of what does the compensating valve consist essentially?

A. Of a piston valve working in a bushing or cylinder; two packing rings that act as valves for the relief and leakage ports; a regulating spring by which the piston is held in its normal position against the brake cylinder pressure; a regulating nut or screw by which the tension of the regulating spring may be adjusted; a body; spring case; a spring box; a cap nut, and a non-return check valve, with casing complete.

Q. What is the duty of the non-return check valve, which is screwed into spring box?

A. In emergency applications the air which is vented from the brake pipe into the spring box must pass the non-return check valve, which then seats and prevents the air thus trapped in the spring box from escaping or backing out, except as it passes out slowly through the small port drilled through this check valve.

Q. How is the compensating valve piped to the brake cylinder and to the triple valve?

A. A ½-inch pipe connection is made from the chamber above the piston in style A to the brake cylinder; and another is made from the side cap of the quick action triple valve to the spring box and air chamber below piston. In style B but one pipe connection is necessary, that from chamber B to the brake cylinder.

Q. Should these pipe connections be absolutely air tight?

A. The pipe connection from the brake cylinder to the chamber above the piston should be absolutely air tight; the pipe connection from the side cap of the triple to the non-return check valve and spring box air chamber should be securely tight.

Q. Describe the operation of the compensating valve, style A.

A. During an emergency application a portion of the brake pipe air vented at the side cap of the quick action triple valve, passes through the pipe leading to the non-return check valve and spring box air chamber, charging the spring box chamber, under the piston, with air pressure. This air pressure augments, or reinforces, the regulating spring pressure under the piston, and permits the full equalized pressure from the auxiliary reservoir to be had in the brake cylinder, and to be retained therein for several seconds before the piston can descend and open the relief ports. The air vented into, and trapped in, the spring box air chamber requires several seconds to pass back to the atmosphere through the small port in the non-return check valve. When the air pressure in the spring box chamber has reduced sufficiently the piston will be forced down by the brake cylinder pressure above it, the relief ports controlled by packing rings will be opened, and brake cylinder pressure will be gradually reduced to the point of adjustment of the valve.

In service applications, there being no air vented into the spring box air chamber, the only pressure which the piston has to overcome is that of the regulating spring; therefore, when the brake cylinder pressure is sufficient to overcome the spring pressure the piston will descend promptly and open the relief ports.

Q. Should all joints around the spring box air chamber be made air tight?

A. Yes; in bolting the spring box to the body of the valve care should be taken to see that the gasket is in good condition and bolted up tight; next the plug that is screwed into the hole that is not used for the non-return check valve, in the spring box, should have a little lead rubbed upon it and be screwed so as to make an air tight joint. The same rule should be observed when screwing the non-return check valve into the other hole. After adjusting the regulating spring the cap nut should be screwed up tight so that no leakage will be had past it.

Q. Why is it necessary to have the spring box air chamber air tight?

A. So that air trapped in there by the non-return check valve will find no means of escape except through the small port in this check valve.

Q. What is the duty of the leather washer on top of the piston?

A. It forms an air tight joint between the brake cylinder and the atmosphere.

Q. What is the function of the upper packing ring of the piston?

A. It makes an air tight joint all around in the cylinder, preventing brake cylinder pressure from leaking past it into the spring box chamber, and it also seals, or closes, the relief ports when in normal position.

Q. What is the function of the lower ports controlled by the lower packing ring?

A. The lower ports are leakage ports, and their function is to carry away to the atmosphere what air may possibly leak by the upper packing ring, thus preventing any leakage down into the spring box air chamber. Leakage from above the piston into the spring box chamber would form a pressure there which might tend to balance the piston, and retard the escape of air from the brake cylinder.

Q. What is the function of the lower packing ring in the piston?

A. The lower packing ring when the piston is in its normal position, seals the leakage ports, and prevents the spring box air leaking by this ring to the atmosphere in emergency applications.

Q. When the piston has moved to the lower end of its stroke, what is the position of the leakage ports relative to the upper and lower packing ring?

A. When the piston moves down its full stroke these ports are about midway between the upper and the lower packing rings; from this it may be seen that the leakage by the upper packing ring would pass out through these ports.

Q. What is the advantage of holding the maximum cylinder pressure obtainable from a reservoir pressure of 110 pounds in emergency applications?

A. At speeds of 60 miles per hour and higher, usually considered high speed, an emergency application is more effective in retarding the motion of the train if the maximum cylinder pressure is retained until the speed of the train has reduced to 15 or 10 miles per hour.

Q. At what pressure is the compensating valve usually adjusted?

A. About 60 pounds, although for driver brakes, tender brakes, and such cars as have not standard foundation brake gear, the adjustment is sometimes varied from this.

Q. Aside from the advantages had in an emergency application with the use of the compensating valve and the brake pipe pressure of 110 pounds, what other advantages are had?

A. In service two or more powerful applications can be made, without recharging the auxiliary reservoirs, and still have sufficient pressure left to make an ordinary emergency application, such as would be had from a 70-pound brake pipe pressure.

Q. Suppose a service application were made, reducing the brake pipe pressure 15 pounds, then a release was made, and then suddenly an emergency application was required, what would the result be?

A. The reservoirs would probably contain about 95 pounds pressure; this would equalize in the brake cylinder at about 75 pounds or a little over with 7-inch piston travel, and the spring box chamber would be charged with the vented brake pipe air to about the same pressure as from 110 pounds. The effect, therefore, would be to maintain the lower maximum cylinder pressure of 75 pounds for several seconds longer than the higher maximum of 85 pounds, had in an emergency application from 110 pounds pressure.

Q. Why is this?

A. Because the spring box chamber air pressure would have to reduce to a lower point before the cylinder pressure could force the piston down to open the ports.

Q. Can the compensating valve be used on any size of cylinder?

A. Yes; the compensating valve can be used on any size of cylinder—6, 8, 10, 12, 14 or 16-inch.

Q. Will the rate of reduction in brake cylinder pressure be about the same when the compensating valve is used on the 16-inch cylinder as it is on the 10-inch?

A. Yes.

NEW YORK AIR SIGNAL EQUIPMENT.

Q. What are the essential parts of the train air signal equipment?

A. They consist of a signal pressure reducing valve, a signal valve, a signal whistle, a car discharge valve, a signal hose and coupling, with the necessary signal piping, stop cocks, cut-out cocks and signal pipe strainers.

Q. What is the function of the signal pressure reducing valve?

A. To maintain the required signal pipe pressure regardless of what the main reservoir pressure may be.

Q. What is the recommended amount of pressure for use with the air signal?

A. About 40 pounds; practice having demonstrated that under average conditions the best results are obtained with this amount of pressure.

Q. How does the pressure reducing valve operate?

A. The tension of the regulating spring on the diaphragm holds the supply valve off its seat to allow main reservoir air to flow into the signal pipe. As soon as the pressure in the signal pipe and the chamber under the diaphragm is sufficient to overcome the tension of the regulating spring (usually about 40 pounds) the diaphragm rises, and the supply valve spring, assisted by main reservoir pressure, forces the supply valve to its seat, thus closing the communication between the main reservoir and the signal pipe.

When the signal pipe pressure reduces below 40 pounds, or whatever the adjustment may be of the valve regulating spring, this spring forces the diaphragm down, unseating the supply valve and establishes communication again between the main reservoir and the signal pipe.

Q. What parts are contained in the signal valve?

A. The upper case, the rubber diaphragm, the diaphragm stem complete, the lower diaphragm plate, the diaphragm nut, the air valve, four ½-inch tee head bolts, the cap, the upper diaphragm washer and the lower case.

Q. What is the function of the signal valve diaphragm?

A. When a reduction is made in signal pipe pressure, to raise the air valve and cause the whistle to sound a blast.

Q. What is the function of the air valve?

A. To control the flow of air from the signal valve to the signal whistle.

Q. How does the signal valve operate?

A. When the signal pipe pressure is reduced suddenly, as when the car discharge valve is opened, the air flows from the chamber above the signal valve diaphragm faster than it can come back through the equalizing port in the diaphragm stem from the lower air chamber. As a consequence, the diaphragm is then forced upward, and the three prongs, or uprights, of the diaphragm stem force the air valve from its seat. Air then flows to the whistle, causing it to make a blast. As soon as the diaphragm rises, the pressure on both sides of it, above and below, equalize quickly through the passage in the diaphragm stem, and it drops back to its normal position, the air valve is seated, and the flow of air to the whistle is cut off.

Q. How should the car discharge valve be operated to obtain the best results?

A. It should be operated quickly so as to produce a short, quick reduction of the signal pipe pressure.

Q. How much of an opening should be made at the car discharge valve when the cord is pulled?

A. The cord should be pulled hard enough to insure the full opening of the car discharge valve.

Q. How long should the cord be held when giving a signal?

A. About one second.

Q. How long should the car discharge valve remain closed before giving the next blast?

A. About three seconds.

Q. Should more time be given between the blasts on long trains?

A. Yes; better results will be obtained if for every six additional cars placed in a train originally of eight cars, a second is added to the time between the blasts.

Q. Why is the opening in the signal pressure reducing valve at the signal pipe connection made small, or restricted?

A. In order to make the main reservoir air feed gently into the signal pipe.

Q. Where would you look for trouble if, when you release brakes, the signal whistle were to blow?

A. In the signal pressure reducing valve.

Q. What would be the probable trouble?

A. The supply valve would probably be stuck open or be leaking, and as a consequence the signal pipe would have main reservoir pressure in it.

Q. With this condition prevailing, how could releasing the brakes cause the signal to operate?

A. When brakes are released the main reservoir pressure is reduced and the signal pipe pressure being equal to main reservoir pressure before the release, signal pipe air will flow back through the signal pressure reducing valve into the main reservoir. The reduction of pressure in the signal pipe thus made will cause the whistle to blow.

Q. If no air can be had in the signal pipe, where would you look for the trouble?

A The reducing valve is probably cut out or stopped up, so that no air can pass through it.

Q. If the signal whistle gives the proper blasts from a short train, but it is impossible to get more than one blast from the rear of a long train, where would you look for the trouble?

A. Examine the signal valve diaphragm; it is probably stretched or distorted.

Q. Why will a distorted diaphragm in the signal valve cause this action?

A. When the pressures are all perfectly equalized, as when the cord is pulled for the first time, the signal valve will probably work with a poor diaphragm, but as the air wave from the second reduction will not flow so perfect to the signal valve, the diaphragm that is in poor shape will operate weakly without moving the diaphragm stem and the air valve.

Q. If the whistle keeps blowing constantly, where would you look for the trouble?

A. Dirt on the seat of the air valve, allowing air to flow constantly to the whistle. If a piece of dirt gets between the diaphragm stem and the center post in the signal valve lower chamber, that is large enough, it will raise the diaphragm up so that the whistle valve will be held off its seat.

Q. If the signal pipe is charged up to the proper pressure, and the whistle does not blow when the cord is pulled from the first car, where would you look for the trouble?

A. The whistle or the pipe leading from the signal valve

to the whistle may be stopped up. A bad leak in this pipe would prevent the whistle blowing.

Q. How would you ascertain if the trouble was in the whistle?

A. Remove the whistle from the pipe to see if any air comes through the pipe when the cord is pulled.

Q. If on pulling the signal cord on one car it is found that air does not escape at the car discharge valves ahead and back of this one, where will the trouble be?

A. If the cut-out cock is open to the discharge valve it is likely the leather seat is loose in the discharge valve stem, or what is more likely, the pipe strainer is blocked up with dirt.

Q. How will this prevent the escape?

A. If the leather seat is loose the pressure will get in behind the seat and the stem will be operated without forcing it off its seat. If the strainer is blocked with dirt no air can get through it.

Q. If the car discharge valve leaks, what should be done?

A. The cut-out cock in the branch pipe should be closed, if it leaks badly, and the valve removed for inspection and repairs.

Q. Where and in what position should the signal pressure reducing valve be located?

A. In the cab, in an upright position, to prevent freezing.

New York Automatic Control Equipment for Locomotive and Tender

Among the recent improvements in air brake equipment deserving of special mention, there should be included a detailed description and illustration of the above named apparatus which has recently been added to the New York air brake system. This device, it is claimed by the makers, possesses all of the advantages of the combined automatic and straight air brake, besides some additional features that are necessary to meet the requirements of present day service.

The apparatus is the same for all locomotives, and the Automatic Control Equipment can, therefore, be applied to passenger engines hauling either high speed trains or ordinary passenger trains, and to locomotives in freight or switching service, or for double pressure control operation, the Automatic Control Euipment being identical in all cases and simply adjusted for the character of service.

The locomotive and train brakes can be used together, or the locomotive brakes separately, as desired, and it makes no difference in what part of the train the locomotive is located.

The brakes can be applied as lightly or as heavily as desired, and the brake pressure so obtained will be automatically maintained in the locomotive brake cylinders, in spite of leakage or variation of piston travel.

The locomotive brakes can be graduated on and off as

ssur-

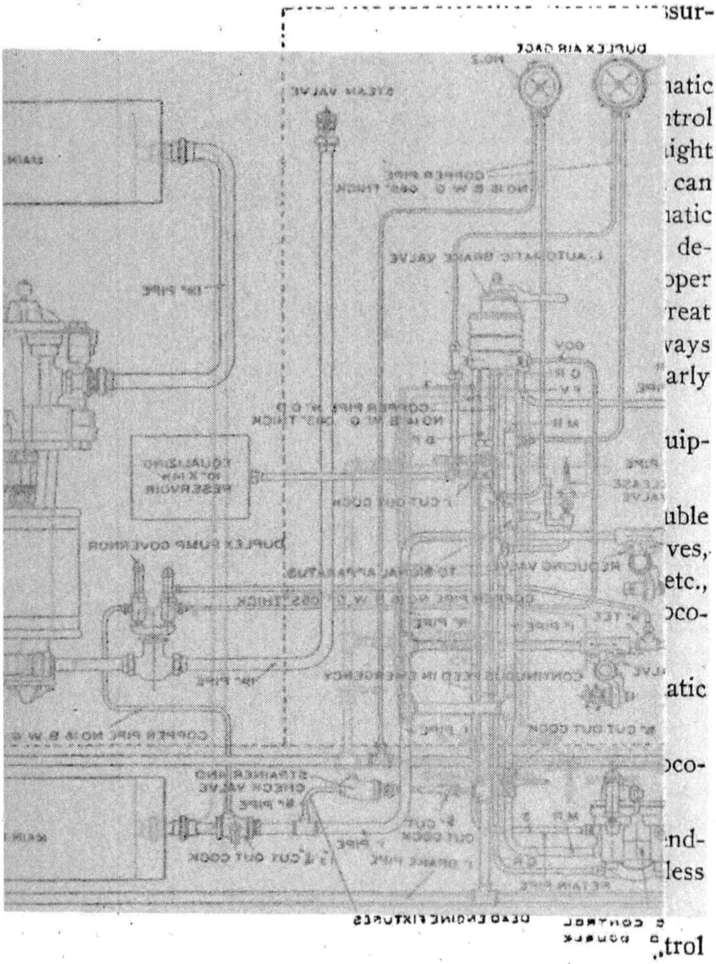

natic
ntrol
right
can
natic
de-
oper
reat
vays
arly

uip-

uble
ves,
etc.,
oco-

atic

oco-

nd-
less

trol

nich
lso

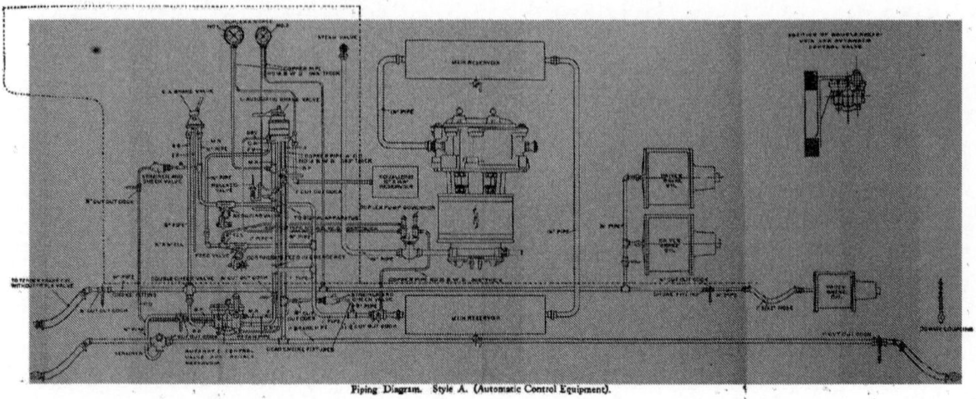

Piping Diagram. Style A. (Automatic Control Equipment).

Nev
E

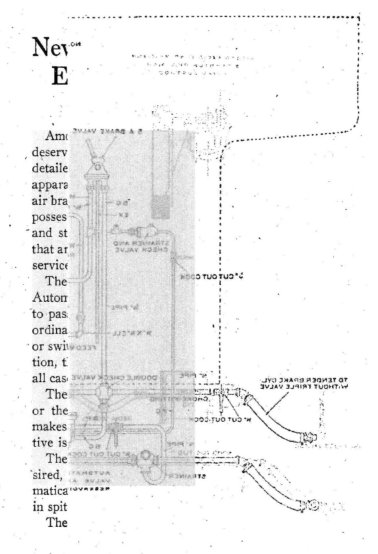

Amc
deserv
detaile
appara
air bra
posses
and st
that ar
service
The
Autom
to pas
ordina
or swi
tion, t
all cas
The
or the
makes
tive is
The
sired,
matica
in spit
The

desired,—thus enabling better stops to be made, and assuring smooth handling of trains.

One very important feature of the former automatic and straight air brake is part of the Automatic Control Equipment, viz:—maintaining the automatic and straight air brakes as two separate units, so that their operation can be independent of one another. If either the automatic or straight air brake should become inoperative, the defective brake will therefore not interfere with the proper operation of the other brake. This is a feature of great value, as it is very necessary that a good brake shall always be available on the locomotive and tender, particularly when the locomotive is detached from the train.

The following parts of the Automatic Control Equipment are of special interest, viz:

1—Automatic Control Valve complete with double chamber reservoir, and taking the place of triple valves, auxiliary reservoirs, high speed reducing valves, etc., heretofore required in the automatic brake system for locomotive and tender.

2—Automatic Brake Valve, for operating the automatic brakes on engine and train as usual.

3—Independent Brake Valve, for operating the locomotive brakes only.

4—Double Throw Check Valve, to insure the independent brake operation under all conditions, and regardless of the Automatic Control Valve.

5—Double Pressure Feed Valve, for supply and control of brake pipe pressure.

6—Reducing Valve, for obtaining the pressure which the independent locomotive brake is designed to use; also for obtaining the required air signal pressure on passenger engines, when so desired.

7—5-inch Duplex Air Gauge, one hand of which shows main reservoir pressure; the other hand showing pressure in the equalizing reservoir.

8—3½-inch Duplex Air Gauge, one hand of which shows brake pipe pressure; the other hand showing brake cylinder pressure on the locomotive.

9—Special Release Valve, to keep the brakes released on locomotive while remaining applied on the train, when so desired.

When repair or replacement of the valves is necessary, they can be removed without breaking pipe joints.

OPERATION

For operating the Automatic Control Equipment the instructions are about the same as issued for the combined automatic and straight air brake, viz:—

When not in use, keep handle of automatic brake valve in Running position, and handle of straight air brake valve in Release position.

For Service Application, move handle of the automatic brake valve to the Service position until the required brake pipe reduction is made, then back to Lap position, which is the position used to keep brakes on.

To release the train brakes, move handle of the automatic brake valve to the Release position and hold it there until all triple valves are released; if the locomotive brakes are to be released at once, use Running position, but if they are to be held on for a time, move to Holding position, and then graduate off as desired, by short movements between Running and Holding positions.

ase
ain
ich

to-
ere
een

er-
ip-
rst
een
osi-
ich
in-
the

to-
ase
of

ent
nd
ing

ent
to-
ake

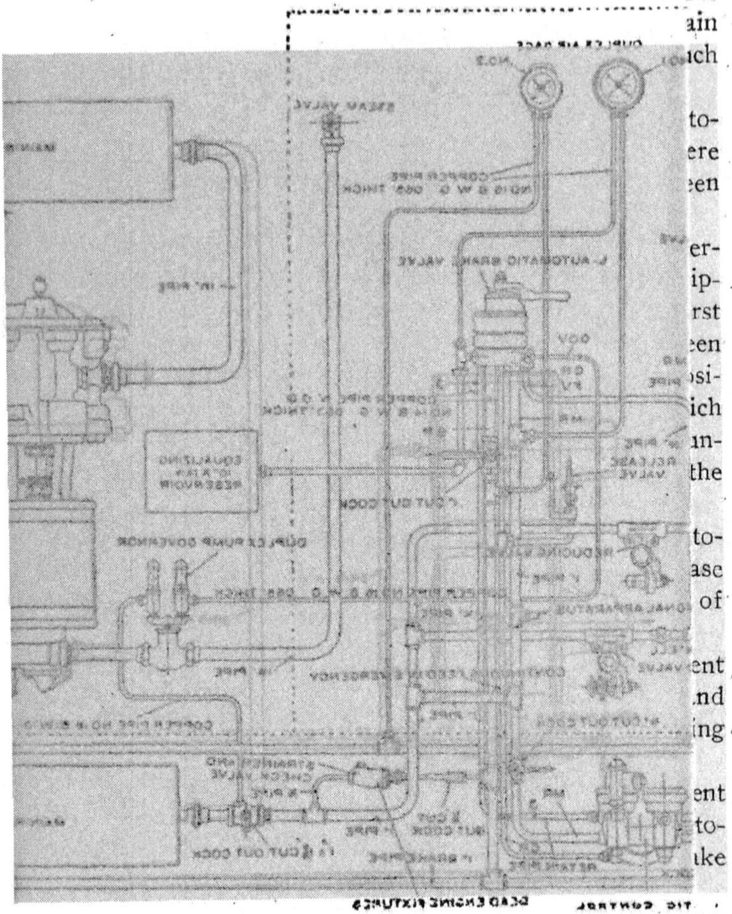

ces
not
ves
the

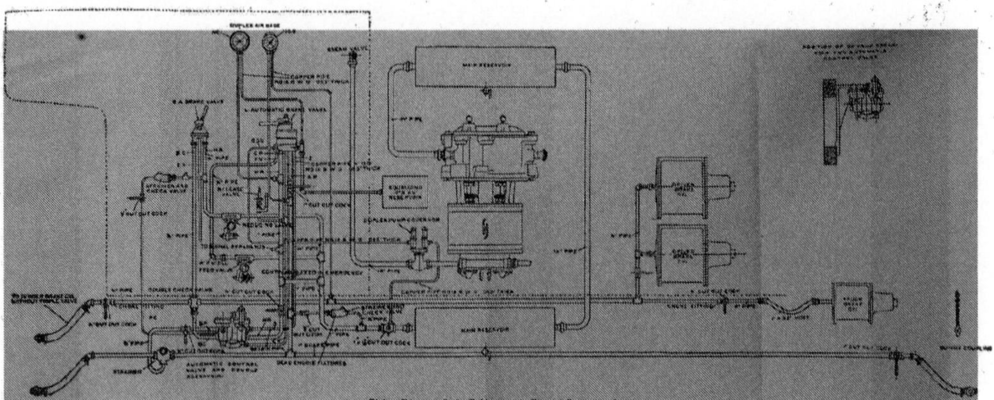

Piping Diagram Style B (Automatic Control Equipment).

for c
ger e

7–
main
in th

8–
show
cylin

9–
on lo
so de

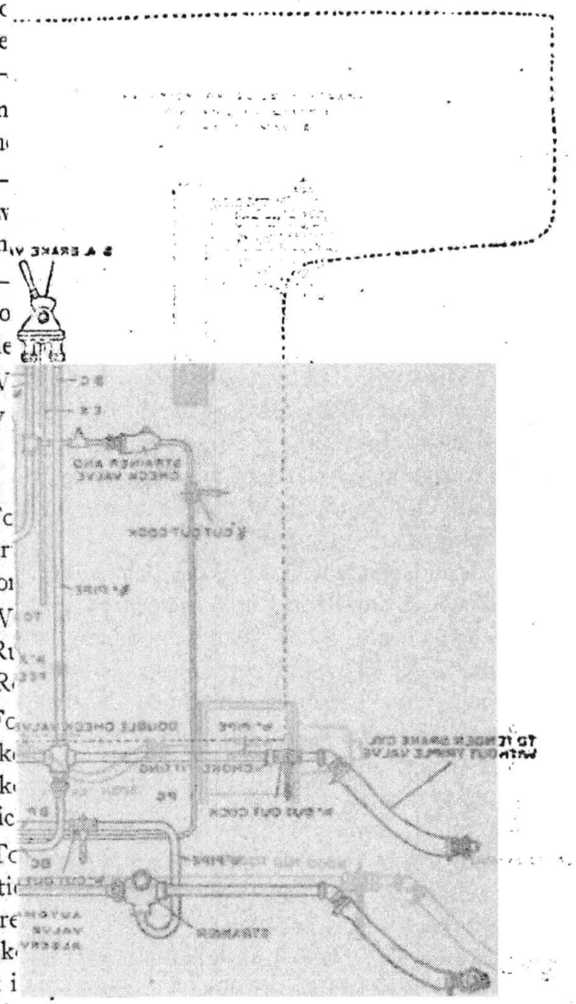

W
they

Fc
instr
autor

W
in Ru
in R

Fc
brak
brak
whic

Tc
matic
there
brak
but i
posit
ment

How long to hold the automatic brake valve in Release and Holding positions depends upon the length of train and other conditions that would affect the matter, such as speed, grade, etc.

For Emergency Application, move the handle of automatic brake valve to Emergency position and leave it there until the train is brought to a stop or the danger has been avoided.

The desirable two application stop for passenger service is very easily made with the Automatic Control Equipment. Use the automatic brake valve and make the first application strong enough to reduce speed to about fifteen (15) miles an hour; then move handle into Release position in order to release only the train brakes, after which release the locomotive brakes, by moving handle into Running position for two or three seconds before making the second application of the brakes.

When the independent brake is used alone, carry automatic brake valve handle in Running position, and release the independent brake, when desired, by moving handle of independent brake valve into the Release position.

With long trains, careful operation of the independent locomotive brake is necessary to avoid injury to cars and contents, by bunching the train too suddenly, or letting the slack run out with a jerk.

If emergency conditions occur while the independent locomotive brake is already on, immediately set the automatic brake also, and the safety valve will keep the brake cylinder pressure within safe limits.

On heavy grades, use the locomotive and train brakes alternately, so that the tires of the driving wheels will not become over-heated and that the pressure retaining valves may have assistance in controlling the train while the auxiliary reservoirs are being recharged. To use the locomotive and train brakes alternately in this manner, proceed as follows: When train brakes are set, use the special release valve to keep the locomotive brakes off; then apply locomotive brakes and immediately release the train brakes. After again applying brakes on the train, immediately release the locomotive brakes with the special release valve, as described above.

If all brakes have been automatically applied in the usual manner, and it is desired to only release the locomotive brakes, either wholly or gradually, this can be done by means of the special release valve.

In operating the Automatic Control Equipment, observe the pressure obtained in the locomotive brake cylinders, as shown by red hand of the gauge connected to them.

Never detach a locomotive without first releasing air brakes upon the train, and setting hand brakes when necessary to hold the train. This is of vital importance on grades, as the automatic brakes should never be relied upon to hold cars or locomotives that are to stand on a grade, whether the locomotive is attached to the train or not, as if anything caused the air brakes to leak off, the locomotive, or cars would start down the grade.

Hand brakes should always be used to hold any locomotive or cars that are to stand more than a few minutes on grades, and also keep the auxiliary reservoirs fully charged, so that full brake power could be used at once if a start down grade occurs.

If, with the automatic brake applied, it happens that the brake pipe and chamber pressures leak so much as to get below the adjustment for which the straight air reducing valve is set, the full power of the straight air brake will still be available, as this is constantly maintained by the Automatic Control valve.

The independent or straight air brake is a very effective and desirable safety provision, and is capable of holding, on ordinary grades, a train of the usual tonnage handled on such grades, after the train has been brought to a stop and the slack is all in. It is always advisable, however, to have the automatic brake in condition to apply also, should anything occur to make this necessary, and to set hand brakes whenever it seems advisable.

When the engine is standing at a water crane, or coal chute, or when the engineer is working about it, the straight air brake valve should be left in the applied position.

If the brakes are automatically applied by parting of train or burst hose, or if the brakes have been set with the conductor's valve, the automatic brake valve handle must be placed in Lap position.

If more than one locomotive is attached to a train, all except the one from which the brakes are being operated, must have the cut-out cock closed in the brake pipe under the automatic brake valve, and the handles of the automatic brake valves carried in Running position.

Always try both brake valves before leaving the round house, and make sure that there are no leaks of importance. The pipes must be perfectly tight that connect the Automatic Control Valve to the automatic brake valve.

PIPING ARRANGEMENTS

The piping diagrams show the parts of this equipment and the method of piping it correctly. Parts to be connected are designated by duplicate Letters and Numbers on Brake Valve and Divided Reservoir.

CONTROL RESERVOIR PIPE: This connects the Control

reservoir of the Automatic Control Valve to the automat.c brake valve. The release valve is attached to this pipe.

BRAKE PIPE: This connects the automatic brake valve to the Automatic Control valve and all triple valves.

BRAKE CYLINDER PIPE: This connects the Automatic Control Valve to the driver, tender and truck brake cylinders, through the double check valve.

CONTINUOUS FEED PIPE: This connects the reducing valve pipe to the auxiliary reservoir of Automatic Control valve.

DISCHARGE PIPE: This connects the air pump to first main reservoir.

AUTOMATIC CONTROL VALVE RELEASE PIPE: This connects the control reservoir exhaust port of the Automatic Control Valve to the automatic brake valve.

EQUALIZING PIPE: Connects the two main reservoirs.

EXCESS PRESSURE GOVERNOR PIPE: This connects feed valve pipe to the excess-pressure head of pump governor.

FEED VALVE PIPES: This leads from feed valve to the automatic brake valve.

MAIN RESERVOIR PIPE: This leads from the second main reservoir to pump governor, reducing valve, feed valve, Automatic Control valve and automatic brake valve.

REDUCING VALVE PIPE: This connects the reducing valve to straight air brake valve; also to the signal system when desired.

STRAIGHT AIR PIPE: This leads from straight air brake valve to the double check valve.

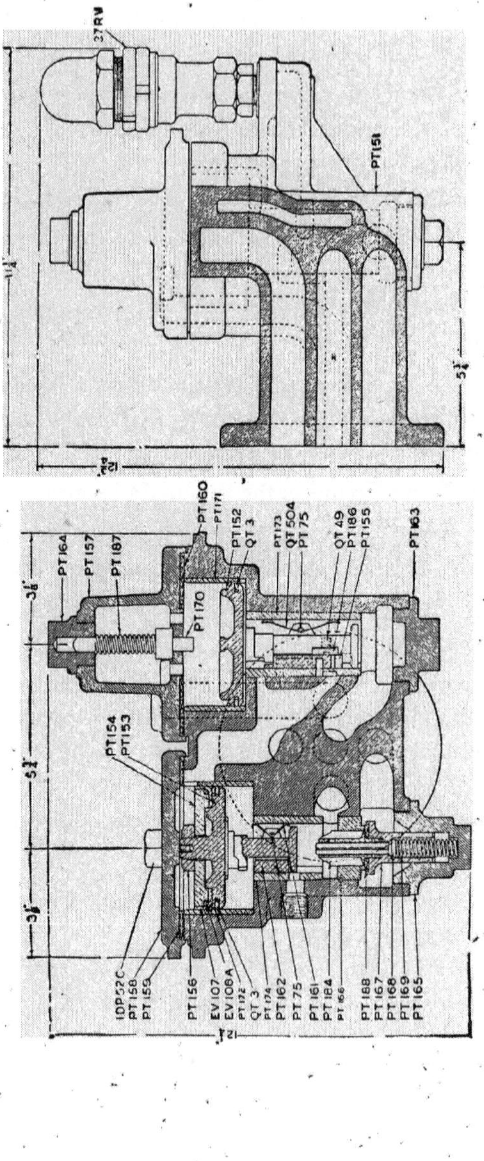

Fig. 50—Automatic Control Valve.

THE AUTOMATIC CONTROL VALVE.

The main functions of this valve have been briefly mentioned in the foregoing description, and its operation in detail is shown on following pages. The names and piece numbers of parts, as shown by figures 50 and 51, are as follows:

PT 75, Pin; PT 151, Body; PT 152, Triple Valve Piston; PT 153, Control Piston; PT 154, Piston Follower; PT 155, Slide Valve; PT 156, Piston Nut; PT 157, Triple Cylinder Cap; PT 158, Control Cylinder Cap; PT 159, Control Cylinder Gasket; PT 160, Triple Cylinder Gasket; PT 161, Exhaust Valve Spring; PT 162, Exhaust Valve; PT 163, Auxiliary Reservoir Cap; PT 164, Graduating Stem Nut; PT 165, Main Reservoir Chamber Cap; PT 167, Check Valve; PT 168, Check Valve Stem; PT 169, Check Valve Spring; PT 170, Graduating Stem; PT 184, Check Valve Guide; PT 186, Graduating Valve; PT 187, Graduating Spring; PT 188, Valve Seat; QT 3, Packing Ring; QT 49, Service Valve Spring; QT 504, Slide Valve Spring; EV 107, Packing Leather; EV 108A, Expander; 1DP 52 C, Bolt; 37 RV, Safety Valve.

Referring to Fig. 51, the names of the parts of the Quick Action Cylinder Cap are as follows: PT 177, Emergency Head; PT 179, Emergency Graduating Stem; PT 180, Emergency Slide Valve; PT 182, Cap Nut; PT 183, Emergency Head Plug; PT 187, Graduating Spring; QT 20, Rubber Seat; QT 49, Service Valve Spring; QT 118A, Check Valve Spring; QT 138, Quick Action Valve; QT 139, Guide; QT 141, Cap.

Fig. 52 shows the exact location of the ports in the graduating valve, slide valve and seat of the slide valve.

To enable the ports and connections of the Automatic Control valve to be more easily followed and understood,

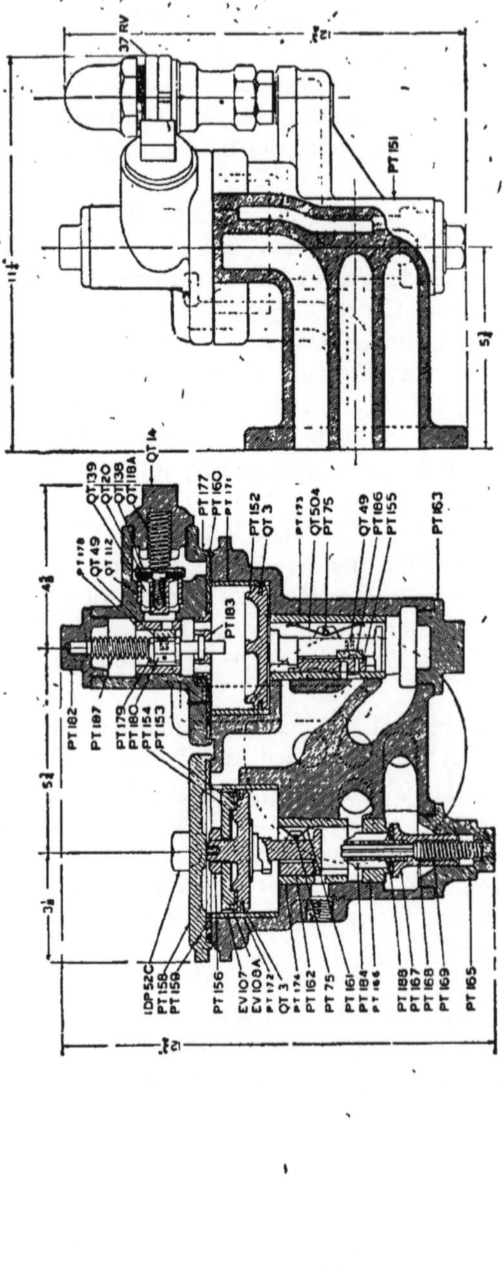

Fig. 51—Automatic Control Valve.

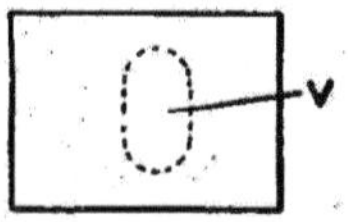

Plan of Graduating Valve.

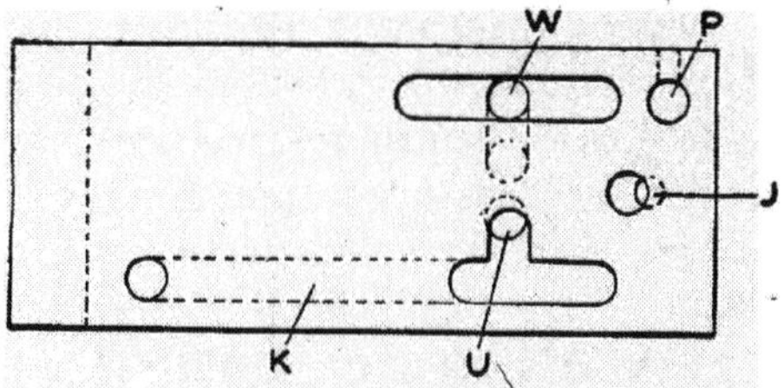

Face of Slide Valve.

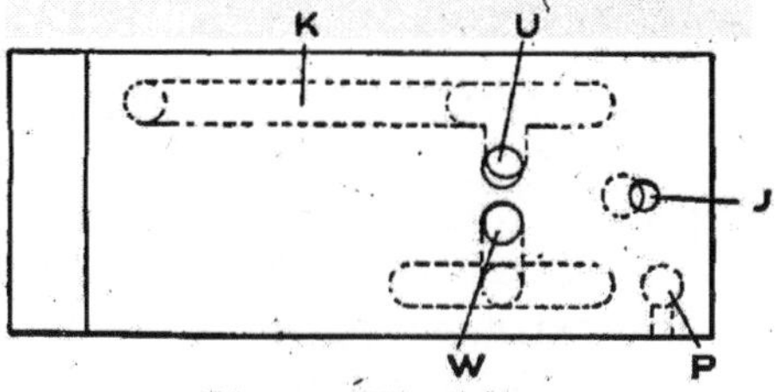

Plan of Slide Valve.

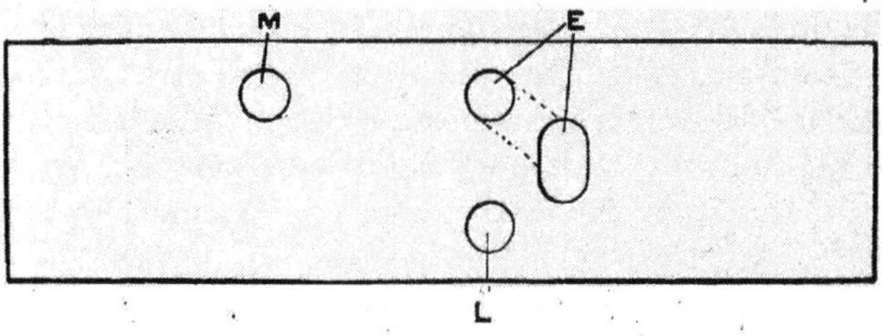

Slide Valve Seat.

Fig. 52.

the actual construction has been disregarded in the diagrammatic views. Nos. 54-60 inclusive, that show the different positions of this valve in the most convenient way to understand the matter. For this reason, the reservoir chambers are shown at bottom of these drawings.

Ports E lead to the control reservoir, and are connected by a cored passage underneath; port L leads to the safety valve and port M to the Automatic Control valve release pipe.

Figure 53 shows a plan view of the exhaust valve and seat. Port N is the brake cylinder exhaust port.

AUTOMATIC RELEASE POSITION.

Figure 54 shows what occurs when the automatic brake valve is put in release position, the increase of brake pipe pressure in chamber F moving piston 3, graduating valve 10 and slide valve 4, to the positions shown, allowing brake pipe pressure to flow through feed groove G until the pressure is the same on both sides of the piston

The train brakes are released in this way, but the locomotive brakes remain on because the pressure is retained in the control cylinder, and the release pipe is closed, in this position, by the rotary valve of the automatic brake valve.

For releasing locomotive brakes, put automatic brake valve into Running position. The rotary valve then connects the release pipe to the atmosphere, allowing control reservoir pressure to be discharged through exhaust cavity K in valve 4, and passages E and M. Pressure in chamber B and the brake cylinder, will now force piston 2 upward, carrying with it exhaust valve 7, uncovering exhaust port N, and allowing the pressure in the brake cylinder and chamber B to escape to the atmosphere, and thus release the brakes.

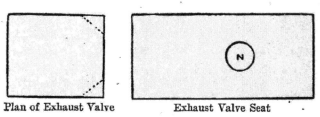

Plan of Exhaust Valve   Exhaust Valve Seat

Fig. 53.

FULL RELEASE OR NORMAL POSITION.

Figure 54 shows the parts in their normal position, of full release. In the chamber about control valve 1 and 1A there is always main reservoir pressure, which has free communication through A. On the under side of control piston 2, the chamber B is always connected to the brake cylinders through passage C and the brake cylinder pipe.

Control cylinder D, above piston 2, is connected by passage E to the slide valve seat, and through passage K in slide valve 4, which registers with port M, to the automatic brake valve through the control cylinder release pipe at IV.

CHARGING POSITION.

As shown by Figure 54 the chamber F is connected to the brake pipe at the place marked BP. When the parts are in release position, as shown, air from the brake pipe passes around piston 3, through charging groove G at the top of piston, into the chamber around slide valve 4, and thence through port H to the Auxiliary reservoir, until the air pressure is equalized on both sides of piston 3.

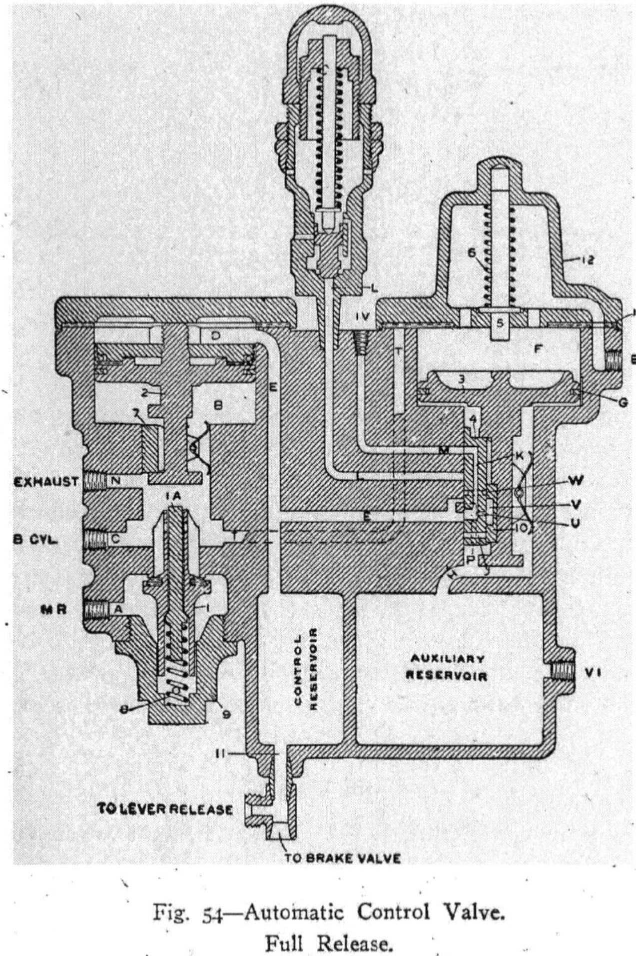

Fig. 54—Automatic Control Valve.
Full Release.

SERVICE POSITION

A service application, caused with the automatic brake valve, reduces the brake pipe pressure in chamber F, and piston 3 is accordingly moved upward by the higher pressure that remains below it. This movement of the piston immediately closes feed groove G, and moves graduating valve 10 far enough to cause port J, in slide valve 4, to register with port E in the seat. Next, a shoulder on the end of the piston stem, moves slide valve 4 upward until the piston reaches stem 5, and further movement is prevented by spring 6 In this position the graduating valve, through cavity V, connects the control reservoir and safety valve through ports U and W in the slide valve, and ports E and L in the seat, while exhaust port M of the control reservoir is closed.

The slide valve chamber and the auxiliary reservoir being connected together at all times, this position allows air to flow from the auxiliary reservoir to the control cylinder D, and to the control reservoir also. The pressure on control piston 2, therefore, moves the piston down, as shown in Fig. 55, the exhaust valve 7 closing exhaust port N and moving the preliminary admission valve 1A from its seat, against the tension of spring 8 and the pressure in chamber O. As the valve 1A has a small area compared with the admission valve 1, it is opened by a very light pressure in chamber D.

Valve 1 is extended so as to form a guide in cap nut 9, thus forming a chamber O When the preliminary admission valve 1A is forced from its seat, the air in chamber O passes by valve 1A to the brake cylinders. The air from chamber O can be discharged to the brake cylinders more rapidly than it can be supplied around the close fitting extension of admission valve 1, thus creating a balanc-

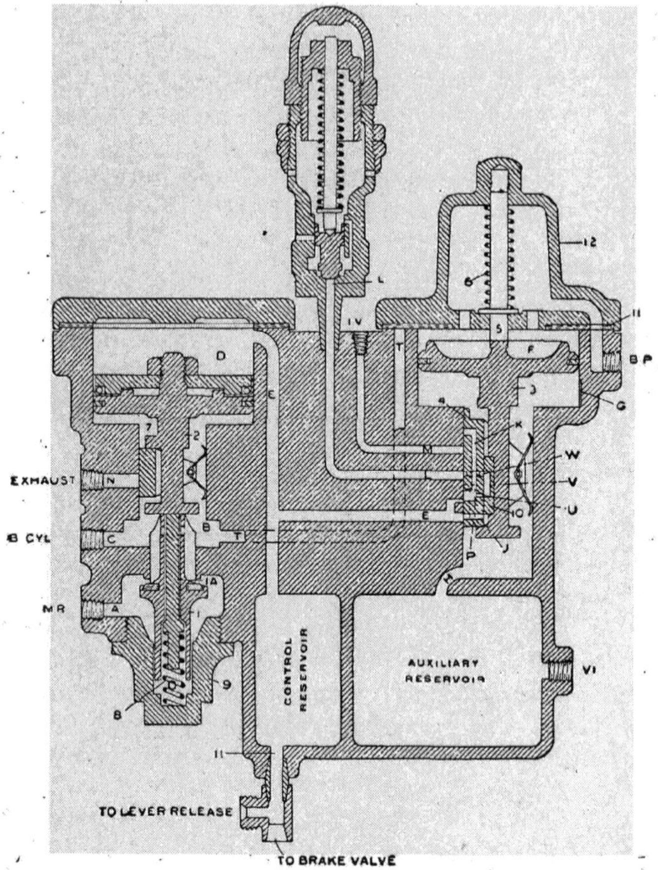

Fig. 55—Automatic Control Valve.
Service Position.

ing effect on valve 1, which allows it to be opened against main reservoir pressure with a slight increase of pressure in chamber D. Air from the auxiliary reservoir will flow

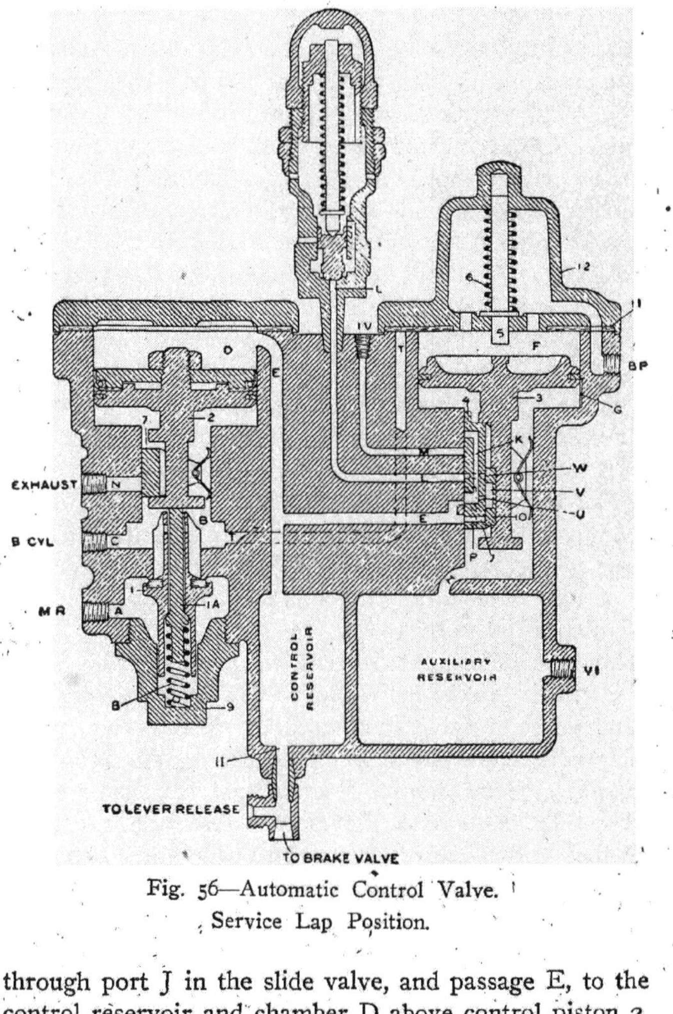

Fig. 56—Automatic Control Valve.
Service Lap Position.

through port J in the slide valve, and passage E, to the control reservoir and chamber D above control piston 2, until the pressure in the auxiliary reservoir has been reduced slightly below the pressure in chamber F and the brake pipe, when piston 3 and graduating valve 10 move down to the position shown in Fig. 56. The pressure admitted to the control reservoir will hold piston 2 down, in the position shown in Fig. 55, admitting air from chamber A and the main reservoir, to chamber B and the brake cylinders. Air will continue to flow from chamber A to chamber B and the brake cylinders, until the pressure in chamber B is slightly greater than that in chamber D, when piston 2 will move up and allow valves 1 and 1A to be seated, as shown in Fig. 56. Should any leakage occur in the brake cylinders from any cause, the pressure in chamber B will be reduced, and the pressure in chamber D, remaining constant while the triple piston and graduating valve are in Lap position, piston 2 will be forced down, unseating valves 1 and 1A and replenishing the loss of air in the brake cylinders. Thus the brake cylinder pressure is automatically maintained against leakage and regardless of piston travel.

Should it be desired to increase the brake cylinder pressure, further brake pipe reduction can be made with the automatic brake valve, thus repeating the operation hereinbefore described, until the pressures in the auxiliary reservoir, and the control reservoir become equalized.

The relative volumes of these two reservoirs are such that they will equalize at a pressure of about 50 pounds with a full service application from 70 pounds brake pipe pressure.

SERVICE LAP POSITION.

This position, shown by Fig. 56, is called Service Lap, and occurs when the reduction of brake pipe pressure is not enough to cause a full service application. The parts remain as in the foregoing description until the pressure in auxiliary reservoir has fallen sufficiently to allow brake pipe pressure, on the other side of piston 3, to move the piston down until further movement is prevented by slide valve 4, when a shoulder on the piston comes in contact with the upper part of this valve. The downward movement of the piston carries graduating valve 10 along, closing port J, and stopping the flow of air from auxiliary reservoir into control cylinder and reservoir The pressure in chamber B and brake cylinder, having equalized with chamber D and the control reservoir, valves 1 and 1A have become seated by the greater pressure in chamber A. The safety valve is cut off from the control reservoir in this position, port W being closed by the graduating valve, so that any possible leak in the former cannot affect the pressure in the control reservoir and brake cylinders.

EMERGENCY POSITION

Fig 57 shows the position that the parts assume when the brakes are applied with emergency suddenness and force. The rapid reduction of brake pipe pressure causes the air in auxiliary reservoir to move piston 3 upward with such force as to overcome the resistance of spring 6 and strike against leather gasket 11, causing the full opening of large port E to be uncovered by valve 4, and thereby allowing air from the auxiliary reservoir to flow to the control reservoir much more rapidly than in a service application, thus forcing piston 2 down and unseating valves 1 and 1A to their full capacity, admitting air from chamber A and the main reservoir to chamber B and the brake cylinders very rapidly. Port P now registers with port L to the safety valve, permitting the pressure in the auxiliary reservoir, and control reservoir to be governed

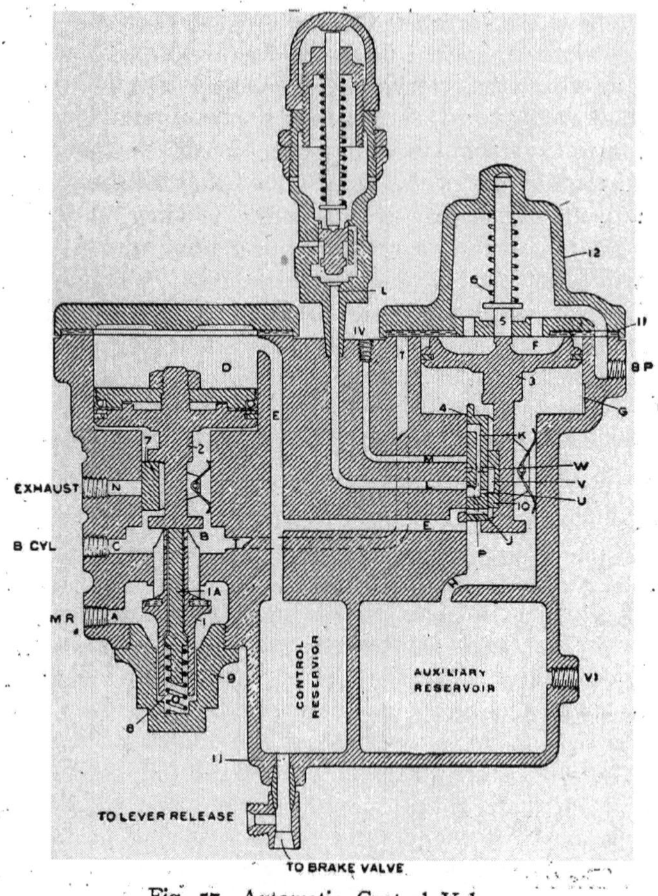

Fig. 57—Automatic Control Valve.
Emergency Position.
Standard Plain Cylinder Cap.

by the adjustment of the safety valve. At the same time a small port provided for that purpose in the rotary valve of the automatic brake valve, allows main reservoir air to feed into the control reservoir and to control cylinder D. The port in the rotary valve of the automatic brake valve is of such size that the air from the main reservoir, feeding to the control reservoir, supplies this reservoir at a faster rate than port P can carry it off at the safety valve adjustment, consequently there is a building up of pressure in the control reservoir to a point where port P will carry it off through the safety valve, as rapidly as it is being supplied from the main reservoir, thus giving a higher brake cylinder pressure in emergency than in a service application.

EMERGENCY LAP POSITION

Figure 58 shows the valve in this position. The parts remain in the position shown by Fig. 57 until pressure in the brake cylinder is a little higher than pressure in the control cylinder, when the control piston accordingly moves upward and allows valves 1 and 1A to seat.

For releasing brakes after an emergency application, proceed the same as previously described for releasing brakes after service application.

THE QUICK ACTION CYLINDER CAP

(Only Supplied when Specially Ordered.)

The triple valve portion of the Automatic Control valve takes the place of the plain triple valve in former locomotive brake apparatus, and this is standard Automatic Control Equipment.

Figure 59, however, illustrates a quick action cylinder cap to take the place of cylinder cap 12, Fig. 54, when it is desired to have this portion of the Automatic Control

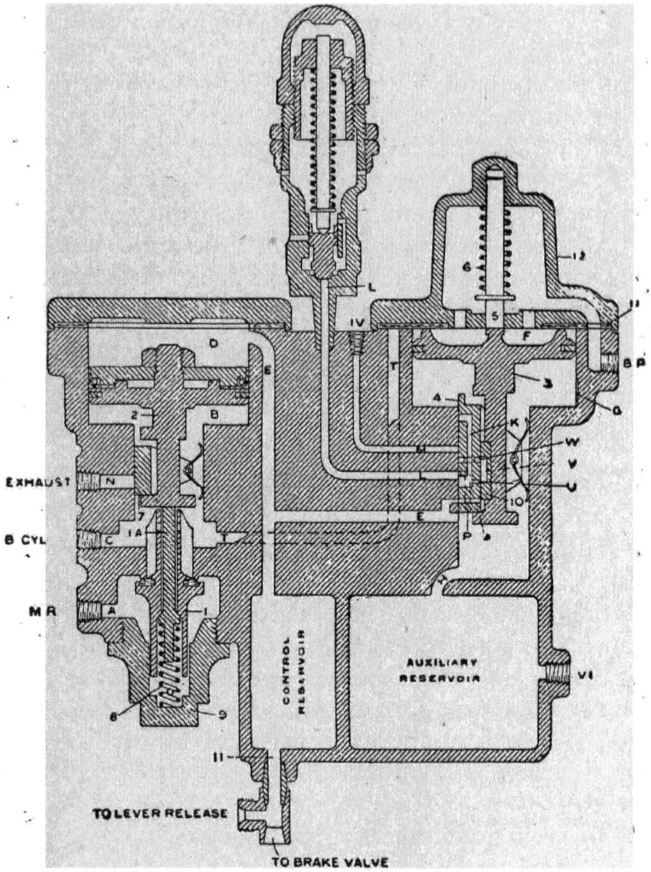

Fig. 58—Automatic Control Valve.
Emergency Lap Position.

valve correspond to a quick action triple valve, by venting brake pipe air into brake cylinder on emergency application of the brakes.

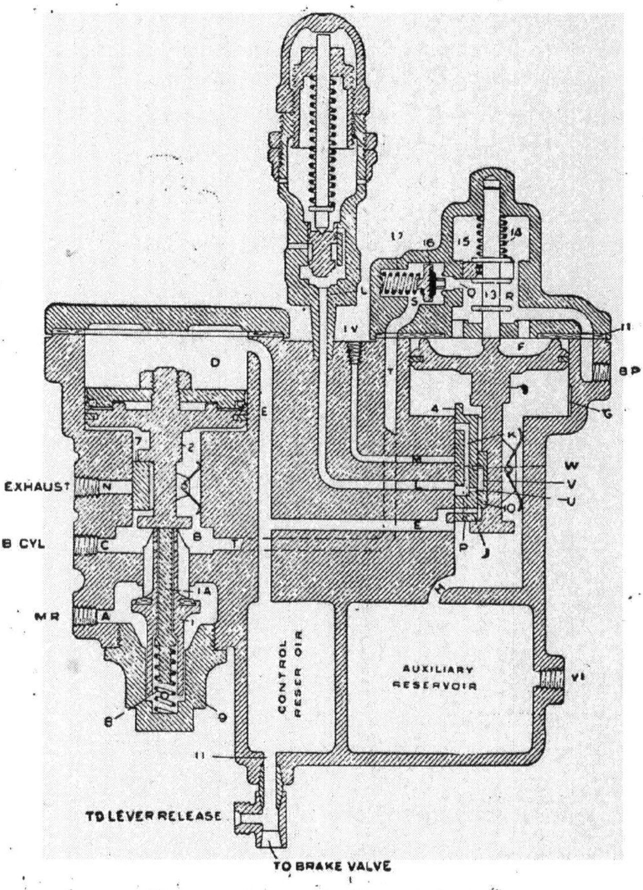

Fig. 59—Automatic Control Valve.
Emergency Position, with Quick Action Cylinder Cap.

When a quick action cylinder cap is substituted and an emergency application is made, piston 3 is moved upward to seat against gasket 11, and the piston button, coming in contact with graduating stem 13, causes it to overcome the resistance of graduating spring 14 and move slide valve 15 upward, thus opening port Q. Check valve 16 is moved from its seat by brake pipe pressure in chamber R, which flows into chamber S, connecting with passage T to chamber B, and thence into the brake cylinders.

When pressure is equalized between brake cylinder and brake pipe, the spring 17 moves valve 16 to its seat, so that air from the brake cylinder cannot flow back into the brake pipe.

When brakes are released, piston 3 returns to its normal position, as in Fig. 54, and spring 14 returns graduating stem 13 and slide valve 15 to their normal position again, as shown in Fig. 51.

INDEPENDENT RELEASE

After making an application of the brakes, should it be desired to release the engine brakes independently of the train brakes, the engineer will discharge air from the control reservoir through the release valve, provided for this purpose, attached to connection II and located conveniently in the cab. By discharging a small amount of air from the control reservoir through the above mentioned release valve, the pressure in the control reservoir will be less than the pressure in chamber B and the brake cylinders, causing piston 2 to move upward, carrying with it exhaust valve 7, and assume the position shown in Fig. 60, allowing the air to escape from chamber B and the brake cylinders through port N to the atmosphere, until the pressure in the brake cylinders and chamber B has been reduced slightly below the pressure remaining in the

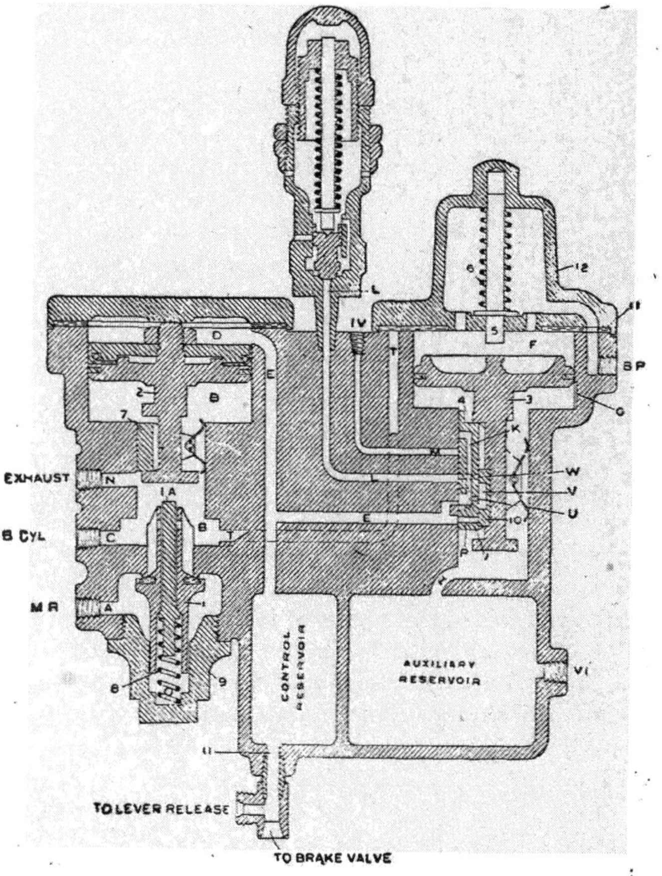

Fig. 60—Automatic Control Valve.
Locomotive Release Position.

control reservoir when piston 2 will move down, carrying with it the exhaust valve 7, closing the exhaust port N. This operation can be repeated until the brake cylinder pressure has been entirely exhausted, or the locomotive brakes can be entirely released at once by holding the release valve open until the pressure is wholly exhausted from the control reservoir and chamber D.

Should it be desired to again apply the locomotive brakes, without making a further reduction of brake pipe pressure, and thereby increase the braking force on the train, they can be applied and released by the Straight Air Brake Valve, without disturbing the Automatic Control valve. Should this be done, the Automatic Control valve will remain in the position shown in Fig. 60, until returned to its normal position by the usual movements of the automatic brake valve for releasing brakes, or a further reduction is made in brake pipe pressure. If a further reduction of brake pipe pressure is made to increase the braking force on the train, the triple piston and valve and control valve will again assume the piston shown in Fig. 55.

Should only a partial release of the automatic brakes on the locomotive be made with the release valve, and the straight air brake applied, and it is desired to again release the locomotive brakes without releasing the train brakes, it will be necessary to use the release valve in addition to placing the straight air brake valve in release position.

INDEPENDENT STRAIGHT AIR BRAKE

The Independent brake operation is accomplished by the use of the Straight Air Brake Valve, and is entirely independent of the automatic brake, a double throw check valve being inserted in the piping between the straight air brake valve and the Automatic Control valve. See piping diagrams.

AUTOMATIC MAINTENANCE OF CYLINDER PRESSURE

With this equipment there is provided a pipe connection, between the reducing valve pipe and connection VI. to the auxiliary reservoir.

In this pipe there is a combined non-return check valve and strainer. Should it so happen from any cause that the pressure in the brake system becomes depleted, unknown to the engineer, it would not be possible to lose the braking power on the engine, for when the pressure is reduced in the brake system (including auxiliary reservoir), below the adjustment of the straight air reducing valve, air will flow through the straight air reducing valve and combined strainer and check valve into the auxiliary reservoir, forcing piston 3 upward, carrying with it the graduating valve 10 and slide valve 4, and apply the locomotive brakes to a pressure equal to the adjustment of the straight air reducing valve, and maintain this pressure as long as there is sufficient air in the main reservoir, thereby notifying the engineer, by the application of the locomotive and tender brakes, that the brake system is dangerously depleted, caused either by stoppage of pump or the automatic brake valve being inadvertently left in Lap position.

TYPE "L" AUTOMATIC BRAKE VALVE

Fig. 61 illustrates the type "L" automatic brake valve, showing a vertical plan, a cross section, and also a plan view of the rotary valve. It is of the construction required to operate the Automatic Control Equipment, providing the functions of former brake valves and the new ones now required.

Reading from left to right, the six positions of the

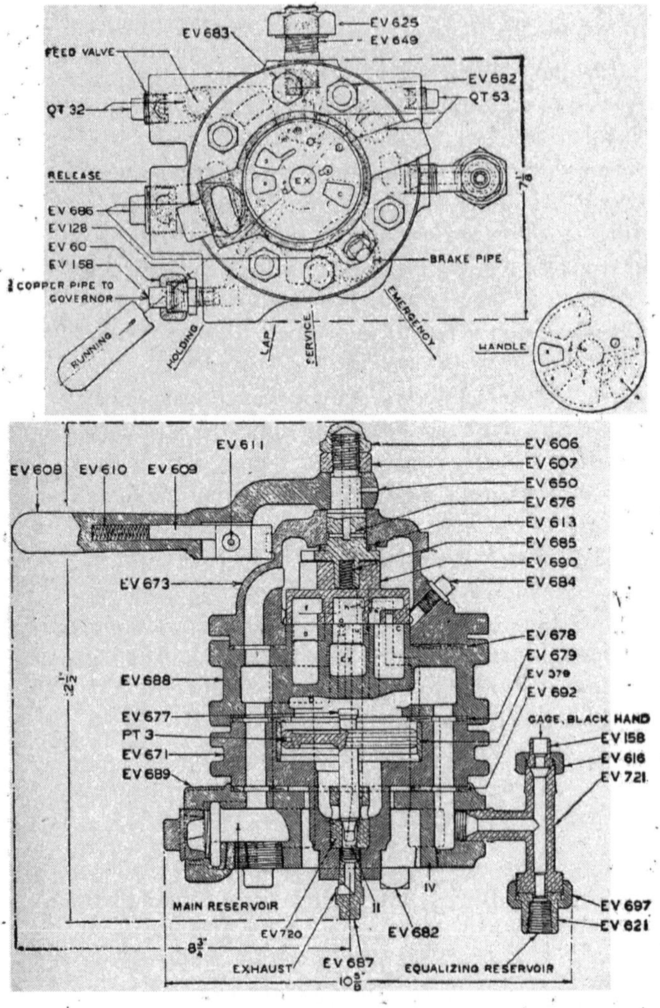

Fig. 61—Type L. Automatic Brake Valve.

handle are—Release, Running, Holding, Lap, Service and Emergency.

The parts are designated as follows:

EV-60, Union Nut; EV-128, Union Stud; EV-158, Small Union Swivel; EV-606, Handle Lock Nut; EV-607, Handle Nut; EV-608, Handle; EV-609, Handle Latch; EV-610, Handle Latch Spring; EV-611, Handle Latch Screw; EV-613, Key Washer; EV-616, Union Nut; EV-621, Large Union Swivel; EV-625, Bracket Stud Nut; EV-649, Bracket Stud; EV-650, Handle Pin; EV-671, Bottom Case; EV-673, Top Case; EV-676, Rotary Valve Key; EV-677, Equalizing Piston; EV-678, Valve Seat Upper Gasket; EV-679, Valve Seat Lower Gasket; EV-682, Bolt & Nut; EV-683, Cap Screw; EV-684, Oil Plug; EV-685, Rotary Valve Spring; EV-686, 1" Pipe Plug; EV-687, Service Exhaust Fitting; EV-688, Rotary Valve Seat; EV-689, Pipe Bracket; EV-690, Rotary Valve; EV-692, Pipe Bracket Gasket; EV-697, Large Union Nut; EV-721, Brake Valve Tee; QT-32, ½" Pipe Plug; QT-53, ⅜" Pipe Plug; PT-3, Equalizing Piston Packing Ring.

In the rotary valve, Fig. 61, ports a, j and s go through it, port s connecting to a groove in the face; f and k are cavities in the face; o is the exhaust cavity; x and t are ports in the face of the valve, connected to o by cored passages; h is a port in the face above cavity k connecting with exhaust cavity o; n is a groove in the face and having a small port that connects with cavity k through a cavity in the valve Port d in the seat leads to the feed valve pipe; b and c go to the brake pipe and g to chamber D. The exhaust port EX leads to an opening at the back of the valve; e is the preliminary exhaust port connecting with chamber D; r is a warning port leading to the exhaust; p connects to the pump governor; l to the distributing valve release pipe and n to the application chamber pipe.

CHARGING AND RELEASE POSITION

This position provides a direct passage of large size from main reservoir to brake pipe, for quick release and recharge of the brakes; and, if locomotive brakes are applied, to prevent their release.

Air from the main reservoir goes to the brake pipe through port a of the rotary valve, and port b in the valve seat. Chamber D, above the equalizing piston, also receives the main reservoir air through port j of the rotary valve and port g in the valve seat.

The brake system would be charged with air at main reservoir pressure, if handle was kept in the Charging and Release position. To prevent this, move handle to Running or Holding position when the desired effect has been obtained. That the engineer may not forget to do this, air from the feed valve pipe escapes to the atmosphere, through a small port, while the handle is in Release position, viz., through cavity f in the rotary valve, connecting warning port r in the seat to port d, thereby causing a small flow of air into EX that makes noise enough to remind the engineer that the handle is in Charging and Release position.

In the face of the rotary valve a small groove, connecting with port s that extends to port p in the valve seat, permits air from the main reservoir to reach the excess pressure head of the pump governor.

RUNNING POSITION

The brake valve handle should be in this position when the brakes are not being operated, and to release the locomotive brakes.

While in this position a direct passage of large size leads from the feed valve pipe to the brake pipe, through ports b and d in the valve seat, connected by cavity f of the rotary valve, and brake pipe pressure will increase to the pressure at which the feed valve is adjusted, as rapidly as the capacity of feed valve permits.

Chamber D and the equalizing reservoir are charged with air at the same rate as the brake pipe, through cavity k of the rotary valve, which connects ports c and g in the valve seat, thus keeping pressure the same on both sides of the equalizing piston.

Air from main reservoir also passes to the pump governor through port s of the rotary valve, port p in the seat, and thence to the lower connection of the excess pressure head of the governor.

The release pipe of the Automatic Control valve is also connected to the atmosphere through exhaust cavity EX, port h of the rotary valve being connected with port I in the valve seat.

If uncharged cars are cut in while the handle of the automatic brake valve is in Running position, or if the handle is moved back into Running position too quickly after releasing brakes following a heavy application, the pump will be stopped by the governor until there is less than 20 lbs. difference showing between the hands on gauge No. 1. Do not move handle into Running position before the brakes have all been released and the system nearly recharged, or some brakes may stick, caused by the slower charging rate that Running position permits.

SERVICE POSITION

This position causes gradual reduction of brake pipe pressure to produce service application, air being discharged to the atmosphere at the proper rate from chamber D and the equalizing reservoir, through port h and cavity o of the rotary valve, connecting with port e and cavity EX in the valve seat. The other ports are all closed in the Service position, and gradual discharge of the air is insured by the size of port e.

As the pressure in chamber D has been reduced, the greater pressure that remains below the equalizing piston causes the piston to rise and unseat its valve, so that brake pipe pressure will discharge to the atmosphere at the opening marked EXHAUST. When the reduction of pressure in chamber D has caused the desired brake pipe reduction, move handle to Lap position in order to stop the loss of air from chamber D. Brake pipe air will continue to discharge, however, until brake pipe pressure gets a little below the pressure that remains in chamber D, when the preponderance of pressure moves equalizing piston slowly downward, gradually cutting off the discharge of air. The amount of brake pipe reduction is regulated by the quantity of air discharged from the equalizing reservoir, whether the train is long or short.

Brake pipe pressure is reduced slowly, so that quick action will not occur. Gradual closure of brake pipe exhaust is to prevent undesired release of the head brakes, which might otherwise occur owing to air from the rear part of train accumulating at the front end.

LAP POSITION

In the Lap position all ports are closed. It is the position for holding brakes applied after service application, until ready to release or re-apply them.

Also use Lap position to prevent loss of main reservoir pressure if the brakes are automatically applied by a break in two or burst hose, or through use of the conductor's valve.

RELEASE POSITION

This is for releasing train brakes only, the locomotive brakes remaining applied. See "Charging and Release."

While handle is in Release position, brake pipe pressure is restored from the main reservoir, through port a of the rotary valve, and port b in the valve seat. This increase of brake pipe pressure moves the triple valves on the cars, and the triple valve piston of the Automatic Control valve, to their normal positions of full release,—thus releasing train brakes and allowing auxiliary reservoirs on the cars and the auxiliary reservoir of the Automatic Control valve, to be recharged.

When the desired effect has been obtained, move handle to Holding position, if locomotive brakes should be kept on, or into Running position to release them.

HOLDING POSITION

This is to keep the locomotive brakes on after the train brakes have been released as above. Port l is closed, but all the other ports remain as in Running position.

EMERGENCY POSITION

This is for applying the brakes as quickly and powerfully as possible. In this position brake pipe pressure is suddenly discharged to the atmosphere, through a large passage that is made when port x, in the rotary valve, connects port c in the valve seat, with cavity o of the rotary valve and cavity EX in the valve seat, the sudden discharge of a large quantity of brake pipe pressure causing emergency action of the triple valves on the cars and the Automatic Control valve, so that the full power of the brakes is instantly applied.

Air pressure is maintained in the control reservoir of the Automatic Control Valve, however, as explained in describing the emergency position of that valve, as air from the main reservoir comes through port j of the rotary valve, connected by a groove in the seat with cavity k, and then goes through port n of the rotary valve and port u in the seat, to the control reservoir.

Air from the equalizing reservoir is all discharged during an emergency application, port t in the rotary valve connecting with port g in the valve seat, and air from the equalizing reservoir will therefore pass to the atmosphere through port o.

THE INDEPENDENT BRAKE VALVE

This is of the slide valve type, and figure 62 shows two sectional views, with pipe connections. Reading from right to left the four positions of the handle are Release, Lap, Service and Emergency. The parts are designated as follows:

EV-69, Handle Spring; EV-74, Cotter; EV-75, Handle Pin; EV-77, Handle Set Screw; EV-95, Lever Shaft Pin; EV-96, Oil Plug; EV-121, Lever Shaft Packing; EV-165, Lever Shaft Nut; EV-172, Quadrant Latch; EV-173, Latch Screw; EV-220, Cover; EV-221, Body; EV-223, Lever Shaft Plug; EV-226, Bracket Stud and Nut; EV-227, Slide Valve; EV-228, Slide Valve Thimble; EV-229, Slide Valve Pin; EV-230, Cover Gasket; EV-253, ¾" Union Nut; EV-254, ¾" Union Swivel; EV-

255, ¾" Union Gasket; EV-256, ¼" Plug; EV-323, Nut Lock Bolt; EV-325, Nut Lock Spring; EV-328, Handle; EV-329, Lever Shaft; EV-330, Slide Valve Lever; SV-10, Bolt and Nut.

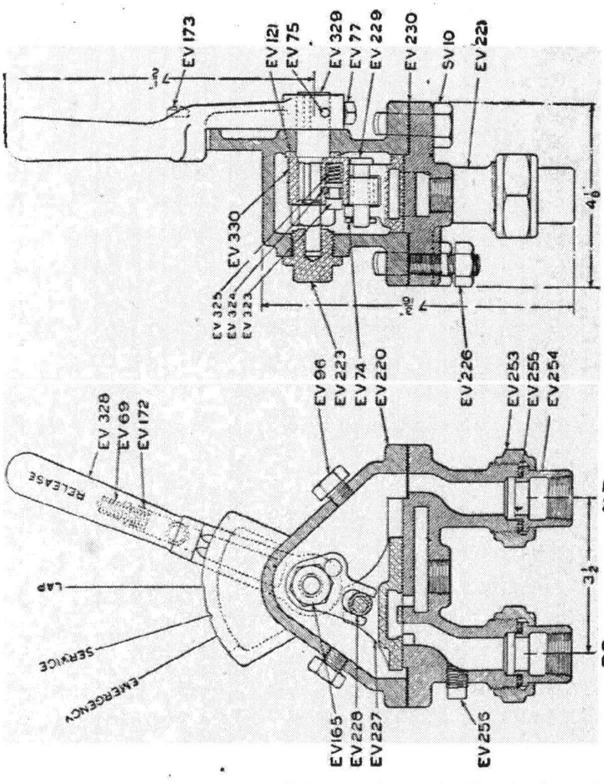

Fig. 62—Independent Brake Valve.

The connection marked MR leads to the Reducing Valve Pipe; BC leads to the brake cylinder pipe through the double check valve; EX is the exhaust. Reducing Valve Pipe pressure (45 pounds) is above the slide valve, EV-227, at all times.

RELEASE POSITION

Always carry the handle of the independent brake valve in Release position, when the independent brake is not in use.

In this position the brake cylinder pipe is in communication with the exhaust, through the cavity in the slide valve.

LAP POSITION

This is the position for keeping the locomotive brakes on after they have been applied at the desired pressure. All ports are closed when the handle is in lap position.

SERVICE POSITION

In this position a small port in the slide valve seat is uncovered by the slide valve, through which air can pass, from the chamber above the slide valve, to the locomotive brake cylinders, applying the brakes gradually.

EMERGENCY POSITION

This is for quick application of the independent locomotive brakes at full power.

In this position the slide valve fully uncovers the large port leading to the brake cylinder pipe, allowing the air to flow rapidly from the reducing valve pipe to the locomotive brake cylinders until the maximum pressure of 45 pounds is obtained. This supply is governed by the adjustment of the reducing valve.

THE 37 RV SAFETY VALVE

Figure 63 is a sectional view of the special safety valve that is really part of the Automatic Control valve,—being a necessary attachment of same. Its functions will be readily understood from the description of how the brakes are manipulated. The parts are designated as follows:

RV-162, Cap nut; RV-163, Valve; RV-164, Valve stem; RV-166, Spring; RV-176, Exhaust regulating ring; RV-177, Lock ring; RV-179, Regulating nut; RV-180, Body; RV-185, Body bush; RV-186, Valve seat; RV-203, Reducer.

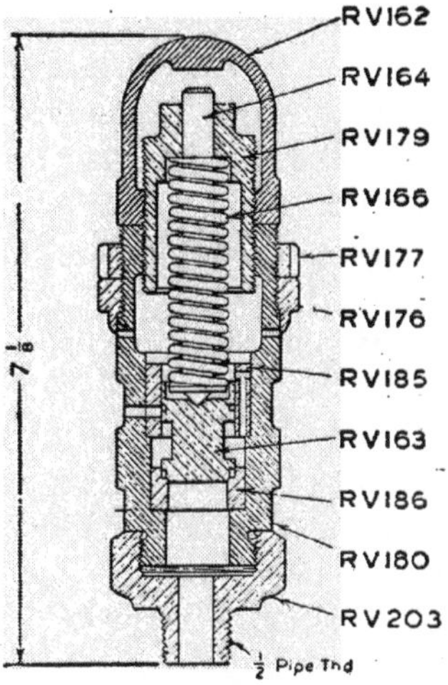

Fig. 63—The 37 RV Safety Valve.

It is constructed to close quickly and seat firmly. Valve RV-163 is held to its seat by spring RV-166. If the air pressure under valve RV-163 rises sufficiently to overcome the resistance of the spring, it will raise the valve and escape to the atmosphere through the lower ports.

As the air pressure reduces under valve RV-163, the spring moves the valve down far enough to partially close the lower ports to the atmosphere, and also open ports in the bushing RV-185 that allow air to pass into the spring chamber, where it will assist the spring to close the valve quickly and firmly, by accumulating above the valve faster than it can escape through the two small holes with which the spring chamber is provided.

THE DOUBLE PRESSURE FEED VALVE

Fig. 64 shows two sectional views of the Double Pressure Feed Valve used with the Automatic Control Equipment, located between the main reservoir and the automatic brake valve. It provides high and low brake pressure control, and the pressure in feed valve pipe and brake pipe is regulated by this valve, when the handle of the Automatic Brake Valve is in Running and in Holding positions.

This Feed Valve has one set of parts for supply purposes, viz: EV-705, Supply Valve; EV-656, Supply Valve Spring; EV-704, Supply Valve Piston; EV-706, Piston Spring; and another set of parts for regulating purposes, viz: EV-707, Regulating Valve; EV-660, Regulating Valve Spring; EV-657, Diaphragm; EV-710, Diaphragm Spindle; PG-141, Regulating Spring; EV-711, Adjusting Handle.

The other parts are as follows: EV-661, Regulating Valve Cap; EV-663, Diaphragm Ring; EV-668, Piston Spring Tip; EV-701, Valve Body; EV-702, Flush Nut; EV-703, Cap Nut; EV-709, Spring Box; EV-712, Upper Stop; EV-713, Lower Stop; EV-714, Stop Screw.

Main reservoir air, entering chamber surrounding the supply valve, moves piston EV-704 towards the left against the resistance of spring EV-656, until the port of supply valve connects with the port that leads to the

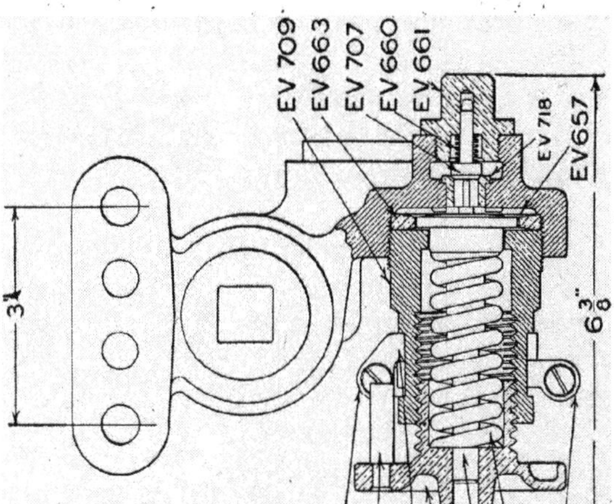

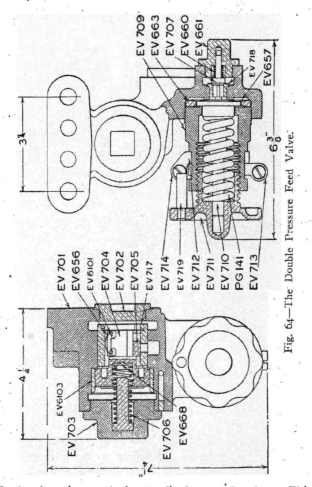

Fig. 64—The Double Pressure Feed Valve.

feed valve pipe, and also to diaphragm chamber. This movement of the piston opens regulating valve EV-707, thus connecting diaphragm chamber to the feed valve pipe. When the pressure in the feed valve pipe and diaphragm chamber is just sufficient to overcome the compression of the regulating spring, the diaphragm allows the regulating valve to close. The air feeding by the piston now builds up to main reservoir pressure and the piston spring moves the piston to the right causing the supply valve to close the port admitting air to the feed valve pipe.

When the pressure of the regulating spring is greater than the feed valve pipe pressure in the diaphragm chamber, it opens the regulating valve. This allows the supply valve to admit air to the feed valve pipe, until the pressure for which the feed valve is adjusted is obtained, when the operation described in the preceding paragraph stops the flow to the feed valve pipe.

The stops EV-712 and EV-713 may be secured in any position on the spring box by the screw EV-714, and limit the movement of the adjusting handle, to the distance between them, by means of the pin which is part of the handle.

By turning the handle EV-711 until its pin strikes either one of the stops, increasing or decreasing the compression of the regulating spring, the regulation of the feed valve is changed from the high pressure to the low or the opposite, as desired.

The duplex adjusting arrangement of this feed valve avoids the necessity of using two feed valves in high and low pressure service

To adjust the double pressure feed valve loosen the screws EV-714 and turn the adjusting handle until the valve closes at the lower brake pipe pressure that is desired. Then move stop EV-712 into contact with the handle pin, and fasten it securely there with screw EV-

714. Next turn adjusting handle until the high pressure adjustment is obtained, moving Stop EV-713 into contact with the handle pin and fasten it securely in that position with the screw. We advise adjustment for high brake pipe pressure at 110 pounds, and for low brake pipe pressure at 80 pounds.

Care should be taken when replacing the feed valve on its pipe bracket, that the gasket is in place, and in condition to insure a tight joint.

THE REDUCING VALVE OR SINGLE PRESSURE FEED VALVE

Fig. 65 illustrates the Single Pressure Feed Valve, which is used in connection with the Automatic Control Equipment to control the pressure for operating the independent brake (and signal system when desired). When used for this purpose it is called a reducing valve, that it may be readily distinguished from the double pressure feed valve used for the automatic brake.

It is the same as the double pressure feed valve excepting the adjustment feature, which is used for reducing main reservoir pressure to the 45 pounds that the independent brake is designed to use. To adjust this valve, remove the cap nut EV-666 and by the use of the adjusting screw EV-665, increase or decrease the compression of spring EV-667, as desired.

Two styles of feed valve brackets are illustrated herein (Figs 66 and 67). Unless otherwise specified the one into which the main reservoir pressure enters at the right, will be furnished with the equipment. However, there may be cabs in which it would be more convenient to use the other style in which the main reservoir pressure enters the bracket at the left, to prevent crossing the pipes.

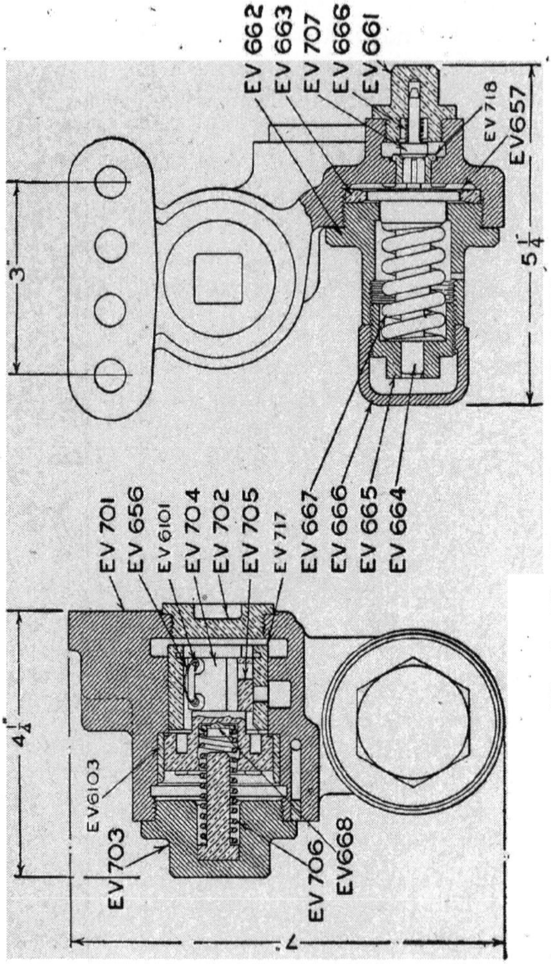

Fig. 65—The Single Pressure Feed Valve.

THE DUPLEX PUMP GOVERNOR

Fig. 68 and piping diagram, Style A, shows the "Excess Pressure" type of pump governor, used with the

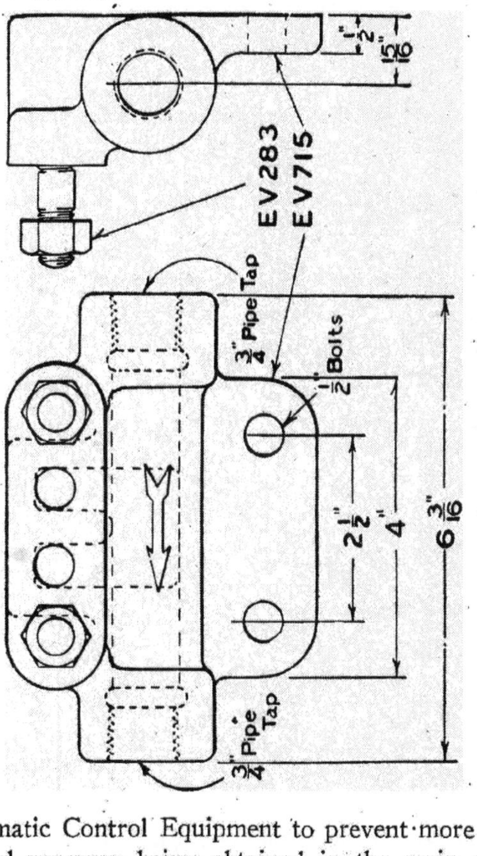

Fig. 66—Feed Valve Bracket. Cross Passage.

Automatic Control Equipment to prevent more than the desired pressure being obtained in the main reservoir. While the brakes are not in use, the automatic brave valve should be in Running position, keeping the brakes charged. As little excess is then needed, the governor regulates the main reservoir pressure to about 20 pounds above the brake pipe pressure. When an application of

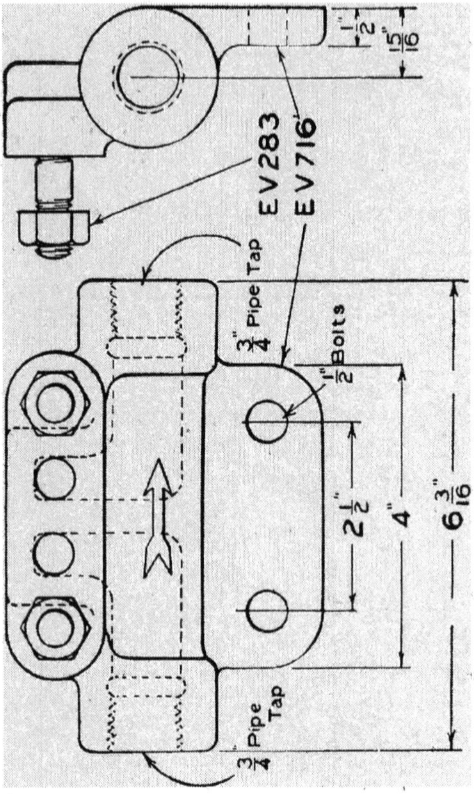

Fig. 67—Feed Valve Bracket. Straight Passage.

the brakes has been made, a higher main reservoir pressure is needed to effect a prompt release and recharge. When the handle of Automatic Brake Valve is moved into Lap, Service or Emergency position, this Governor lets the pump run without interference until maximum main reservoir pressure is again obtained.

The governor changes the main reservoir pressure

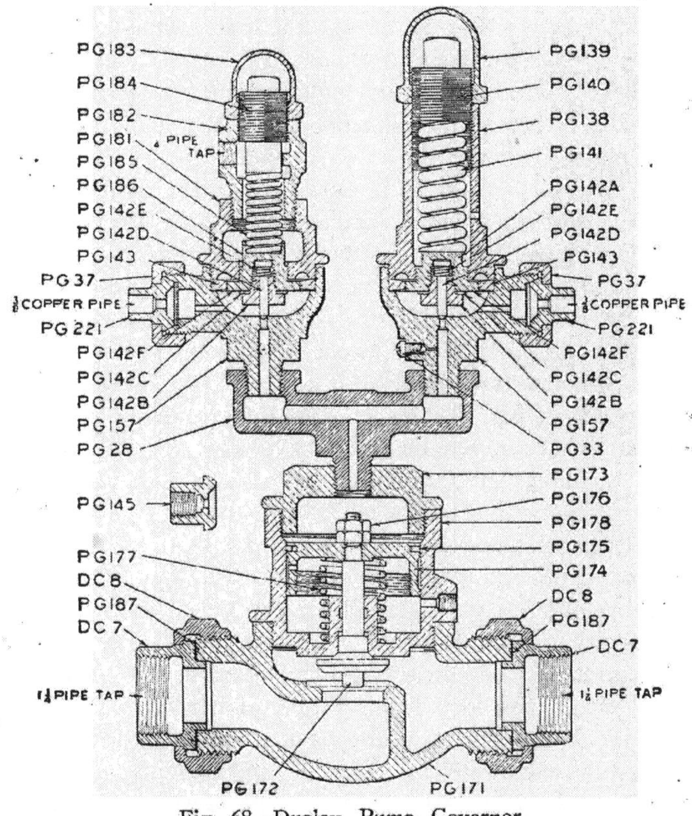

Fig. 68—Duplex Pump Governor.

automatically, when the brake pipe pressure is changed from one pressure to another by the feed valve, and governs the pump as described just the same.

Fig. 68 illustrates this Governor with the steam valve open. When handle of Automatic Brake Valve is in either Release, Running or Holding positions, air from the main reservoir passes through the brake valve to the connection marked ABV and into the chamber below the diaphragm. The feed valve pipe is connected to FVP, and air pressure in the chamber above the diaphragm will therefore increase the pressure exerted by the regulating spring. The spring is adjusted for a pressure of about 20 pounds and the diaphragm will therefore be kept down until the main reservoir pressure under it becomes a little higher than the spring and air pressure together on top. The diaphragm will then rise and by unseating the pin valve allow air to pass to the top of the Governor piston and move it downward to lessen the flow of steam past the steam valve until there is only enough to run the pump sufficiently to offset any loss of air in the brake system caused by leakage. Reduction of main reservoir pressure under the diaphragm allows the spring and air pressure on the other side to move the diaphragm down and thereby seat the pin valve. The air above the piston will escape through the small vent port, which is always open to the atmosphere, when the steam pressure and piston spring will raise the steam valve to the position shown in the illustration. This governor top is cut out in all positions of the automatic brake valve except Release, Running and Holding.

The maximum pressure head of the Governor must always have direct communication with the main reservoir, so that this head will control the pump when the other or excess pressure head is cut out by the brake valve, or the main reservoir cut-out cock is closed. Therefore connect the Governor head marked MR to the main reservoir cut-out cock, or so that it will be directly connected to the main reservoir at all times. When the main reservoir pressure overcomes the resistance of the regulating spring, and the diaphragm lifts the pin valve, air will flow to the top of the Governor piston and control the pump as described above. While the handle of the Automatic Brake Valve is in either Lap, Service or Emergency positions, the maximum reservoir pressure will be what the maximum pressure head of the Governor has been adjusted for.

Each governor head has a small vent port to the atmosphere, through which air escapes whenever there is pressure above the governor piston, and one of these should be plugged, to prevent unnecessary waste of air.

Adjustment of the maximum pressure head is made by placing the handle of Automatic Brake Valve into Lap position, removing the cap nut of Governor, and changing the tension of the spring, by means of the regulating nut, until the adjustment is such as to stop the pump when the desired maximum main reservoir pressure is obtained. This head should be adjusted for a pressure of from 120 to 140 pounds, according to the service.

Adjustment of the excess pressure head is made by placing the handle of Automatic Brake Valve in Running position, removing the cap nut and altering the tension of the spring, by means of the regulating nut, until the desired difference is obtained between main reservoir and brake pipe pressure. Adjust this head to give 20 pounds excess pressure in main reservoir.

The piping diagram, Style B, shows the Automatic Control Equipment with the ordinary style of duplex Governor instead of the "Excess Pressure Governor" previously described. Both regulating heads are the same as the maximum pressure head just described. One is adjusted to control the pump at the maximum and the other at a lower main reservoir pressure. The low pressure head is connected to the brake valve at the governor connection, and the high pressure top is connected with the main reservoir as explained for the "Excess Pressure Governor." Main reservoir pressure flows through the automatic brake valve to the diaphragm chamber of the low pressure top and controls the pump when the brake valve is in Release, Running and Holding positions. It should be adjusted to allow 20 pounds excess pressure, and is cut out in Lap, Service and Emergency positions, at which time the high or maximum pressure head controls the pump. The latter head should be adjusted to control the pump when the highest main reservoir pressure necessary for the service, is obtained. These heads are adjusted in the same manner as those on the "Excess Pressure Governor" previously described.

THE COMBINED AIR STRAINER AND CHECK VALVE

Fig. 69 illustrates the combined air strainer and check valve, having one end arranged to restrict the flow of air, which can only pass through a small bushing shown in the center at the end marked MR.

Two of these are used with the Automatic Control Equipment, as shown by the piping diagrams. One being in the Continuous Feed Pipe, to prevent back leakage from the auxiliary reservoir of the Automatic Control valve, and the other being part of the Dead Engine Fixtures. The latter consists of a pipe leading from the brake pipe to the main reservoir pipe, a cut-out cock, and the combined check valve and strainer. When, from any cause the air pump on a locomotive becomes inoperative, the air for operating the brakes on such locomotive must then be supplied through the brake pipe from the locomotive that is operating the train brakes.

With the cut-out cock open, air from the brake pipe enters at the union connection, passes through the curled hair strainer, and, lifting the check valve that is held to its seat by a spring, flows through the small hole in the

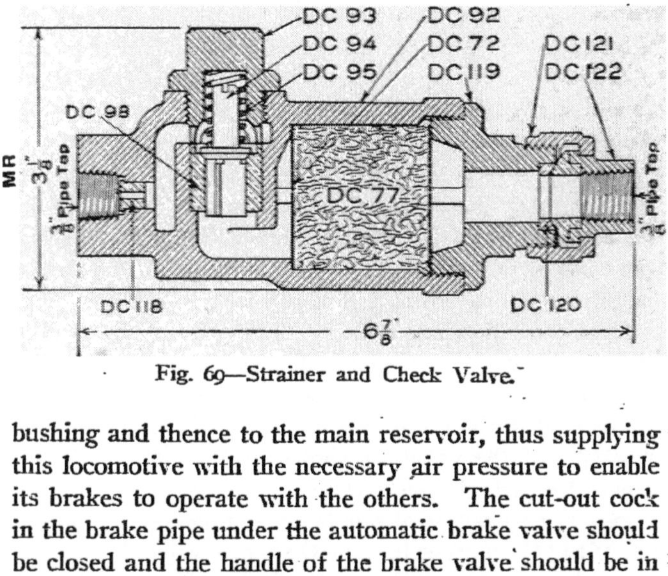

Fig. 69—Strainer and Check Valve.

bushing and thence to the main reservoir, thus supplying this locomotive with the necessary air pressure to enable its brakes to operate with the others. The cut-out cock in the brake pipe under the automatic brake valve should be closed and the handle of the brake valve should be in Running position. Should it be necessary to keep the maximum braking power of a "dead engine" below the standard, it can be done by suitably changing the adjustment of the safety valve of the Automatic Control valve. It can also be reduced at will by using the Release valve, as previously explained, under heading "Independent Release.":

The check valve and the choked passage are protected from dirt by the strainer. The spring insures seating of the check valve, allows ample pressure, for operating the brakes and keeps main reservoir pressure below that of the brake pipe, thus reducing any leakage from the reservoir pressure. The restricted passage or choke is provided so that flow of air from brake pipe will not be too rapid and cause an application of the train brakes if an undercharged reservoir is connected up with brake pipe fully charged.

STYLE "L" AUTOMATIC BRAKE VALVE NEW YORK AIR BRAKE SYSTEM.

This valve has already been alluded to, and partly described in the section on the "Automatic Control Equipment," and its construction shown by Fig. 61. Its functions, and operations will be further illustrated, and described in detail in the following pages.

It is of the rotary valve type, having a detachable pipe bracket for convenience in removing the valve for repairs or cleaning, without disturbing the pipe joints.

The six positions of the valve are shown in Fig. 61, which represents the actual construction of the valve, but the positions are shown in detail by diagrammatic drawing, Figs. 71 to 76. In order to show the rotary valve and seat in one plane, it was necessary to disregard the actual construction of the valve and the position of the mechanism, ports, passages and cavities, the arrangement being such that the air can be easily traced in all positions and the results readily understood.

PIPE BRACKET

Fig. 70 illustrates the pipe bracket in detail, showing the ports and pipe connections. The connections having two outlets, one at the side, and one at the bottom of the bracket for convenience in piping. The outlet not being used must be plugged. The letters which appear on the bracket are explained as follows: BP connects with the brake pipe; CR connects with control reservoir continuous feed pipe; ER connects with the equalizing reservoir; FV connects with the feed valve; GOV connects with excess pressure top of pump governor; MR connects with the main reservoir and 3 connects with the control reservoir retain or release pipe.

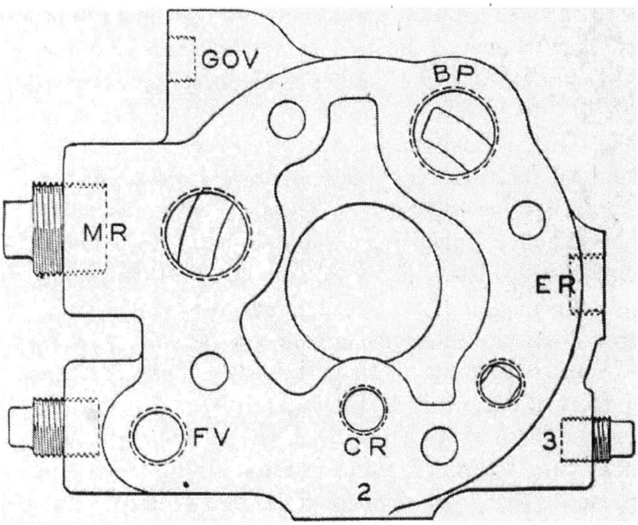

Fig. 70—Pipe Bracket.

RELEASE POSITION

Fig. 71 shows the Release Position, in which the train brakes are released and the engine brakes held on. Air from the main reservoir enters at the connection marked MR and passes to the top of the rotary valve, this being true for all positions, passing from the top of the rotary valve, down through port a in the rotary valve to port b in the seat which also connects with port c, and then to the brake pipe at the connection marked BP, to charge the brakes or to release and recharge them in case the brakes have been previously applied.

In the Release Position, main reservoir air also passes from the top of the rotary valve, down through port j in the rotary valve to port g in the seat, which leads to chamber D above Equalizing Piston, EV-677, thus moving Equalizing Piston, EV-677, down, until its stem seats on Bushing, EV-720, closing the port which leads from the train or brake pipe to the atmosphere by way of the Service Exhaust Fitting, EV-687. The air then passes from Chamber D to the Equalizing Reservoir at the connection marked ER. Air from the main reservoir also passes through port s in the rotary valve to port p in the seat, and then to the excess pressure top of pump governor by way of the connection marked GOV.

Air from the Feed Valve, at reduced pressure or the pressure which the train or brake pipe is to carry, enters the Brake Valve at the connection marked FV, passes through port d in the seat to cavity f in the rotary valve, then through warning port i in the seat, which leads to the exhaust port EX and the atmosphere, to warn the engineer that to prevent overcharging the auxiliary reservoirs, the handle of the brake valve should be moved from Release to Running Position, as soon as all brakes

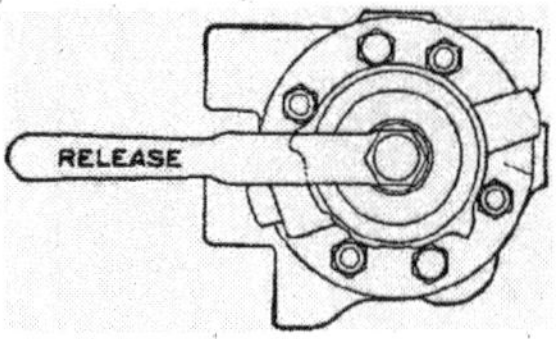

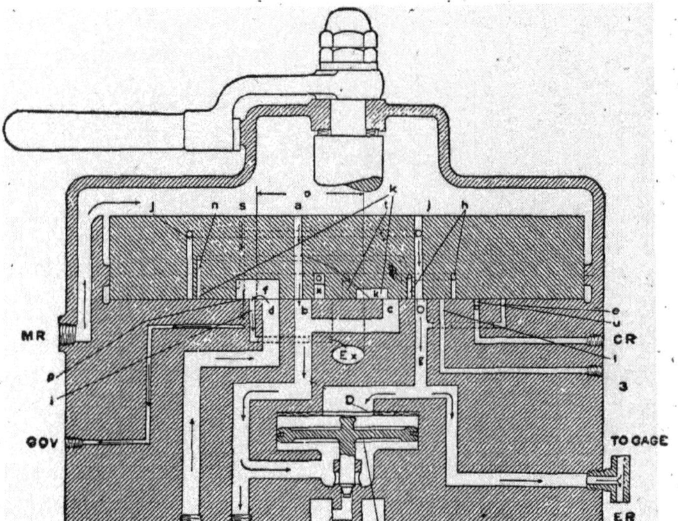

Fig. 71—Release Position.

are released and auxiliary reservoirs nearly recharged; the time varying according to length of train.

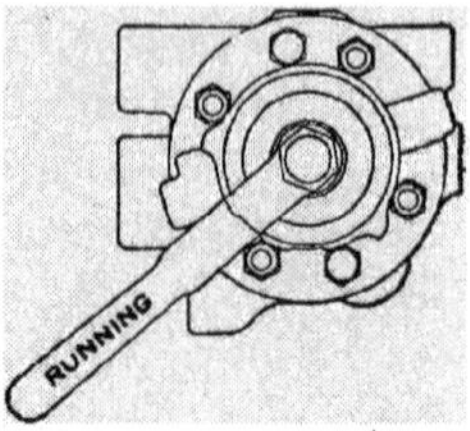

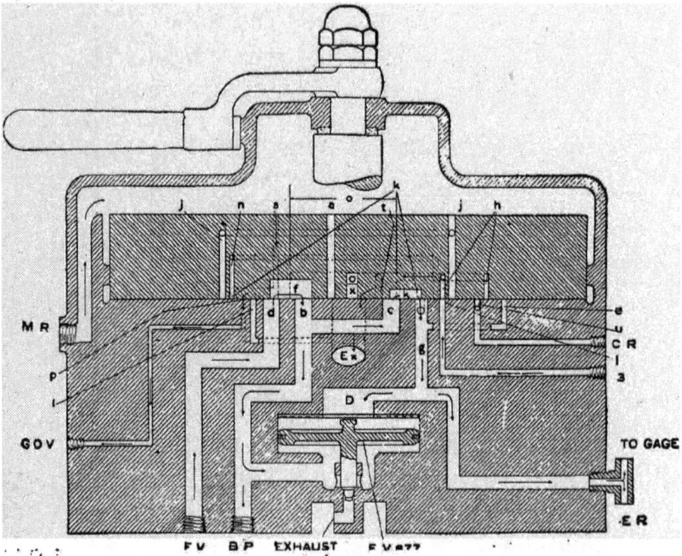

Fig. 72—Running Position.

RUNNING POSITION

In this position, air from the main reservoir reaches the top of the rotary valve by way of the connection marked MR, the same as described in Release Position, passes through port s in the rotary valve to port p in the seat, then to the excess pressure top of the pump governor, by way of the connection marked GOV.

In the Running Position main reservoir air is supplied to the train pipe at a pressure corresponding to the adjustment of the feed valve, which is connected to the main reservoir pipe. The air from the feed valve enters the Brake Valve at the connection marked FV, the same as described in Release Position, passes through port d in the seat, cavity f in the rotary valve, then through port b in the seat and enters the train pipe at the connection marked BP; also at the same time, air passes from port b in the seat, through port c in the seat, cavity k, in the rotary valve port g, in the seat to chamber D, above the equalizing piston, EV-677, and then to the equalizing reservoir by way of the connection marked ER.

In the Running Position, the locomotive or automatic control brakes are released by reason of the air contained in the control reservoir of the automatic control valve, flowing into the brake valve at the connection marked 3. passing through port l in the seat, ports h and o in the rotary valve and flowing through exhaust port EX in the seat to the atmosphere.

HOLDING POSITION

Holding position is for the purpose of holding the locomotive brakes on and not overcharging the train line, after the train brakes have been released.

This is accomplished by moving the handle of the brake valve to Holding Position, in which the rotary valve closes port l in the seat; thus retaining or holding the air in the control chamber of the automatic control valve. When desired, the locomotive brakes can be graduated off by short movements of the brake valve

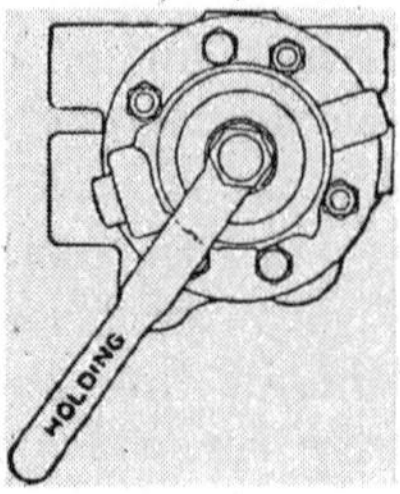

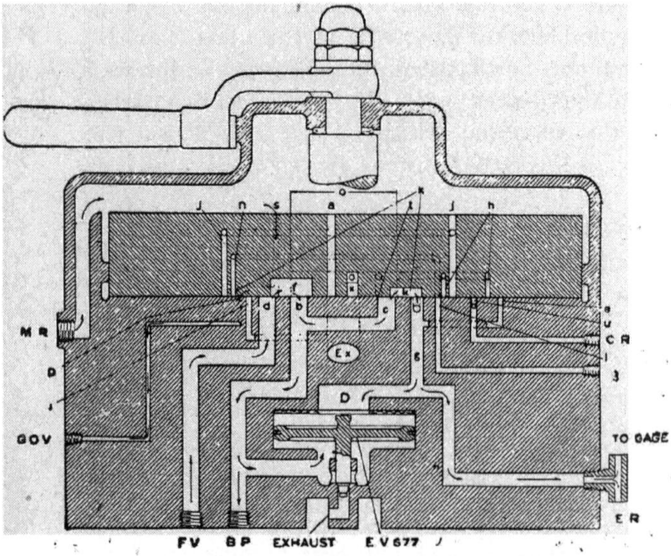

Fig. 73—Holding Position.

handle from Holding to Running position, or released entirely by leaving it in Running Position.

In the Holding Position, main reservoir air from the connection marked MR and the top of the rotary valve, passes down through port s in the rotary valve, port p in the seat to the connection marked GOV and the excess pressure top of the pump governor, the same as described in Release Position.

The air from the Feed Valve, in Holding Position, enters the brake valve at the connection marked FV, the same as described in Release and Running Positions, passes through port d in the seat, cavity f in the rotary valve and port b in the seat to the train pipe, at the connection marked BP, and also at the same time, passes from port b in the seat, through port c in the seat, cavity k in the rotary valve, port g in the seat, to chamber D above the equalizing piston, EV-677, and then to the equalizing reservoir at the connection marked ER, the same as described in Running Position.

LAP POSITION

In the Lap Position, all ports are closed. It is the position used in connection with service applications for graduating the service reductions and holding the brakes when applied. It is also used to prevent the loss of main reservoir air, when brakes are applied from the conductors valve, bursted or parted hose or from any cause outside of the brake valve itself.

SERVICE POSITION

This position causes gradual reduction of brake pipe pressure to produce service application. Air is discharged from chamber D and the equalizing reservoir, through preliminary exhaust port e in the seat, ports **h** and o in the rotary valve, and EX in the seat to the atmosphere. The other ports are all closed in Service

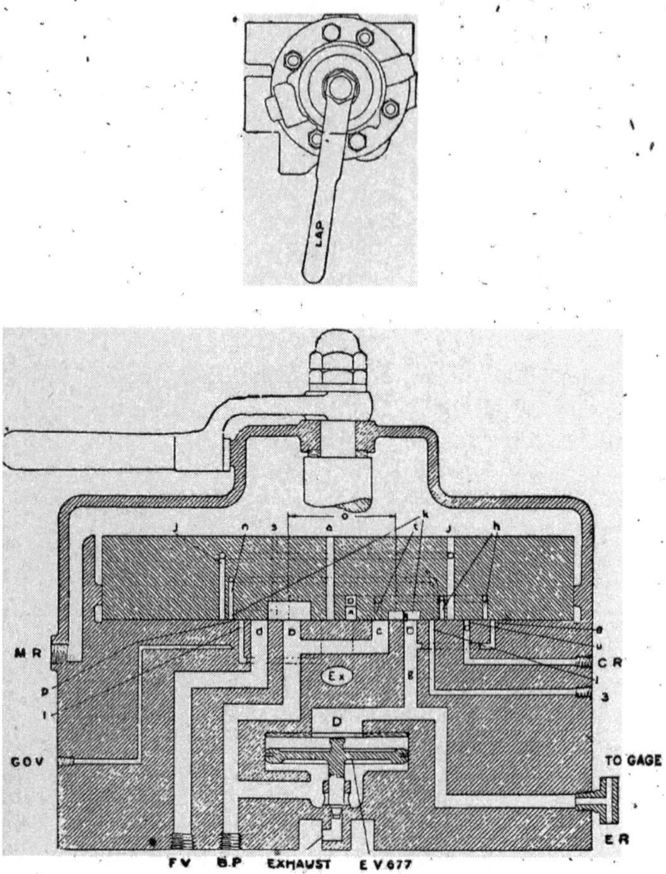

Fig. 74—Lap Position.

Position, and gradual discharge of the air is insured by the size of port e. As the pressure in chamber D and the equalizing reservoir, which is above the equalizing piston, EV-677, has been reduced, the train pipe pres-

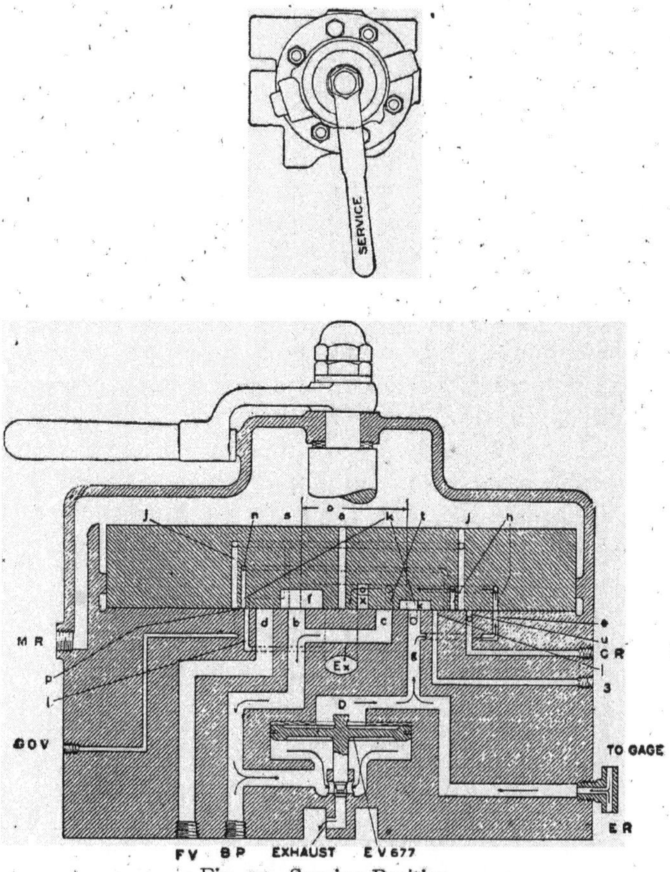

Fig. 75—Service Position.

sure or pressure below equalizing piston EV-677, is greater and causes the piston to rise, unseating its stem or valve, and discharging train pipe pressure through service exhaust fitting, EV-687, to the atmosphere at the point marked "EXHAUST."

The operation just described, may be repeated a number of times, during a service application, if desired or necessary, by returning the handle to Lap Position after each preliminary reduction. The first reduction, however, should be sufficient to insure all brakes going on, and the following reductions according to necessity, all of which will vary, according to condition of brakes, train, gradient, atmospheric and other conditions met with in train operation.

When desired, or necessary, a continuous or complete service application can be made by placing the valve in Service Position, and leaving it there until a full service reduction has been made, when the valve should be placed in Lap Position to prevent waste of air. When the valve has been placed in Lap Position, after all service reductions, the train pipe pressure continues to flow to the atmosphere as described above, until the pressure of chamber D and the equalizing reservoir, above equalizing piston EV-677, is slightly greater than train pipe pressure below the equalizing piston, when the piston will gradually move down to its seat, closing the service or train line exhaust. After a service application, the brakes are released, as described in the Release and Running Positions.

EMERGENCY POSITION

In Emergency Position, the brakes are applied suddenly and with full force throughout the train. Train pipe pressure flows rapidly through ports x and o in the rotary valve, and port EX in the seat, to the atmosphere.

The pressure in chamber D and the equalizing reservoir is discharged through port g in the seat, ports t

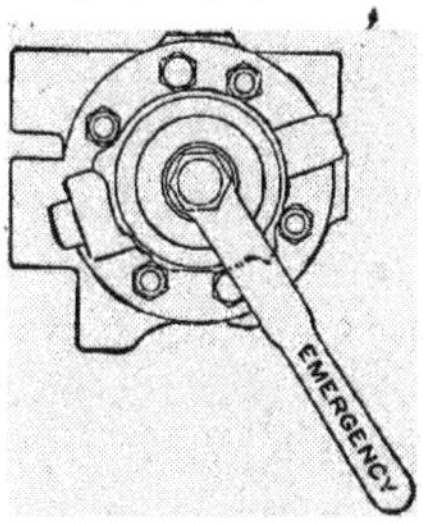

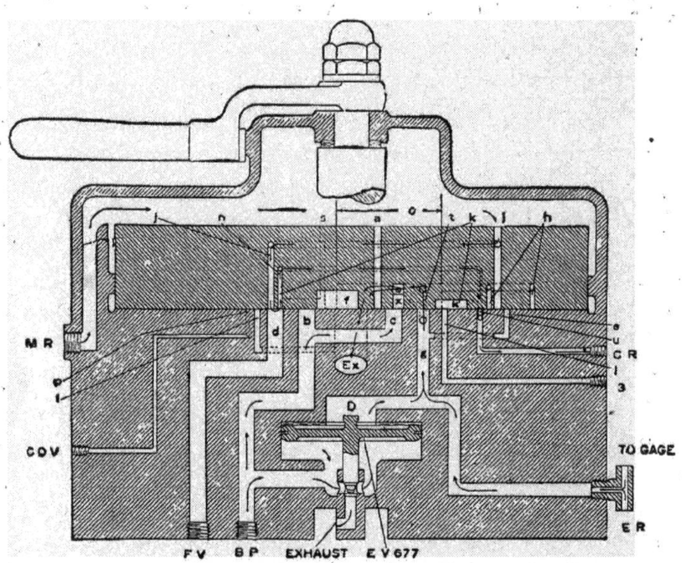

Fig. 76—Emergency Position.

and o in the rotary valve, and port EX in the seat to the atmosphere. This causes equalizing piston, EV-677, to rise and a portion of the train pipe pressure to be discharged through service exhaust fitting, EV-687.

In the Emergency Position, main reservoir air flows from the connection marked MR and the top of the rotary valve, down through port j in the rotary valve, port d and groove in the seat, cavity k in the rotary valve, groove and port n in the rotary valve and port u in the seat to the connection marked CR and the control reservoir of the automatic control valve, thus insuring the automatic maintenance of cylinder pressure in the Automatic Control Equipment.

After an Emergency application, the train brakes are released in Release Position, and the locomotive brakes are released in Running Position, the same as described for releasing after a service application.

OILING

Use good heavy oil, such as valve oil, that will not gum or harden. The valve should be taken apart occasionally for cleaning and oiling, the necessity for which will vary according to conditions of service and location of the valve. However, for ordinary purposes, the key washer EV-613 can be oiled by removing the handle lock nut, EV-606, and filling the hole in Rotary Valve Key EV-676, and the rotary valve EV-690 can be oiled by removing the plug EV-684, and filling the hole which leads to a groove in the top case, EV-673, around the edge of the rotary valve and seat.

VARIETY OF SERVICE

Although the Style "L" Brake Valve is for use in connection with the Automatic Control Equipment, it will successfully operate the brakes on locomotives which are equipped with triple valves, if the connections for Automatic Control Equipment in the pipe bracket are plugged and the feed valve properly connected.

QUESTIONS AND ANSWERS

NEW YORK AUTOMATIC CONTROL EQUIPMENT

Q. What advantages are claimed for the automatic control equipment?

A. It posses all the advantages of the combined automatic and straight air system, besides being adapted for use on all locomotives, whether high speed or ordinary passenger service, freight or switching service.

Q. Mention three prominent characteristics of this equipment.

A. With it the locomotive or train brakes can be used together or separately as desired. The brakes can be applied as lightly, or as heavily as desired.

The locomotive brakes may be graduated on and off as desired.

Q. What is one very important feature of the automatic control equipment?

A. The automatic and straight air brakes are maintained as two separate units. If either should become inoperative it will not interfere with the proper operation of the other.

Q. Name the different parts of the automatic control equipment.

A. 1, Automatic control valve; 2, automatic brake valve; 3, independent brake valve; 4, double throw check valve; 5, double pressure feed valve; 6, reducing valve; 7, 8, two duplex air gauges; 9, special release valve.

Q. What rules should be observed in the operation of this equipment?

A. Practically the same as those given for the combined automatic and straight air equipment.

Q. When the independent brake alone is used where should the handle of the automatic brake valve be carried?

A. In running position.

Q. What method should be pursued when descending heavy grades?

A. Use the locomotive and train brakes alternately.

AUTOMATIC CONTROL VALVE.

Q. What are the main functions of the automatic control valve?

A. The automatic control valve with double chamber reservoir takes the place of triple valves, auxiliary reservoirs, high-speed reducing valves, etc., heretofore required in the automatic brake system for locomotive and tender.

Q. What is the function of the quick action cylinder cap?

A. It enables the automatic control valve to vent brake pipe air into brake cylinder in emergency applications, in the same manner as does the quick action triple valve.

Q. After an application, how may the engine brakes be released independently of the train brakes?

A. By allowing air to discharge from the control reservoir through the release valve located in the cab.

Q. Should it be desired to again apply the engine brakes without making a further reduction of brake pipe pressure, how may it be done?

A. By means of the straight air brake valve.

Q. If a partial release of the automatic brakes on the engine is made with the release valve, and straight air is then applied, how can the engine brakes be released without releasing train brakes?

A. By using the release valve in addition to placing the straight air brake valve in release position.

TYPE L AUTOMATIC BRAKE VALVE.

Q. What brake valve is used with the automatic control equipment?

A. The type L automatic brake valve.

A. How many and what are the positions of the type L brake valve handle?

A. Six; as follows: release, running, holding, lap, service and emergency.

Q. What occurs when the handle is in release position?

A. A large direct passage is provided for the air from main reservoir to brake pipe, for quick release and recharge of the brakes; and, if locomotive brakes are applied, to prevent their release.

Q What would occur if handle was kept in release and charging position?

A. The entire brake system would be charged with air at main reservoir pressure.

Q. How is this prevented?

A. By moving the handle to running or holding position when the desired effect has been obtained.

Q How is the engineer warned that the handle is in release and charging position?

A. By the escape of air to the atmosphere through a small warning port.

Q. In what position should the handle be when the brakes are not being operated, and to release the locomotive brakes?

A. Running position.

Q What occurs during the time that the brake valve is in running position?

A. A direct air passage of large size leads from the feed valve pipe to brake pipe, and brake pipe pressure will increase to the pressure at which the feed valve is adjusted. Chamber D and the equalizing reservoir are charged with air at the same rate as the brake pipe. Air from main reservoir also passes to the pump governor through ports in the rotary valve and seat, and thence to the lower connection of the excess pressure head of the governor.

Q. If uncharged cars are cut in while the handle of the automatic brake valve is in running position, or if the handle is moved back into running position too quickly after releasing brakes, what will happen?

A. The pump will be stopped by the governor until there is less than 20 pounds difference showing between the hands on gauge No. 1.

Q. What pressures are indicated by gauge No. 1?

A. One hand shows main reservoir pressure, the other shows the pressure in the equalizing reservoir.

Q. What pressures are indicated by gauge No. 2?

A. One hand shows brake pipe pressure, and the other shows locomotive brake cylinder pressure.

Q. What rule should be observed when releasing brakes after a heavy application?

A. Do not move the handle into running position before all brakes have been released and the system nearly recharged.

Q. What results when the handle is placed in service position?

A. A gradual reduction of brake pipe pressure, air being discharged to the atmosphere at the proper rate from chamber D, and equalizing reservoirs.

Q. What are the functions of lap position?

A. It holds the brakes applied until it is time to release, or re-apply them. It is also used to prevent loss of main reservoir pressure in case the train breaks in two, or burst hose, or the use of conductor's valve.

Q. What is release position for?

A. For releasing train brakes only, the engine brakes remaining applied.

Q. When the desired effect has been obtained with the handle in release, where should it then be placed?

A. In holding position if the engine brakes are to be kept on; or running position to release them.

Q. What is the purpose of holding position?

A. To keep the locomotive brakes on after train brakes have been released.

Q. What occurs when the handle is moved to emergency position?

A. Brake pipe pressure is suddenly discharged to the atmosphere through a large passage by way of the rotary valve and seat thus causing emergency action of the triple valves, and instantaneous application of the brakes at full power.

Q. Is air pressure maintained in the control reservoir of the automatic control valve during an emergency application?

A. Yes.

Q. What becomes of the air in the equalizing reservoir during emergency?

A. It is all discharged through the rotary valve and passes to the atmosphere.

INDEPENDENT BRAKE VALVE.

Q. Of what type is the independent brake valve?

A. It is a slide valve operated by a lever.

Q. How many, and what are the positions of this valve?

A. Four; release, lap, service and emergency.

Q. In what position should the handle of the independent brake valve be carried when this brake is not in use?

A. Release position, always.

Q. What is the purpose of lap position with this valve?

A. To keep the engine brakes on after they have been applied at the desired pressure.

Q. What occurs when the independent brake valve is placed in service position?

A. A small port in the slide valve seat is uncovered through which air can pass from the chamber above the slide valve to the locomotive brake cylinders, applying the brakes gradually.

Q. What is the result when the handle of the independent brake valve is placed in emergency position?

A. The slide valve fully uncovers the large port leading to the brake cylinder pipe, allowing the air to pass rapidly from the reducing valve pipe to the engine brake cylinders.

Q. What is usually the maximum pressure obtained in the engine brake cylinders?

A. Forty-five pounds. This supply is controlled by the adjustment of the reducing valve.

DOUBLE PRESSURE FEED VALVE.

Q. What is the purpose of the double pressure feed valve?

A. To provide high and low brake pipe pressure control.

Q. What pressures are regulated by this valve?

A. Brake pipe pressure, and feed valve pipe pressure, when the handle of the automatic brake valve is in either running or holding position.

Q. What is the advantage of having the duplex adjusting arrangement of this feed valve?

A. It avoids the necessity of using two feed valves in high and low pressure service.

Q. How is the regulation of the valve accomplished?

A. By turning the handle until its pin strikes either one of the stops, thus increasing or decreasing the compression of the regulating spring.

SINGLE PRESSURE FEED VALVE.

Q. What is the purpose of the single pressure feed valve?

A. It is used to control the pressure for operating the independent brake; also the signal system when desired; in which case it is called a reducing valve.

Q. In what way does it differ from the double pressure feed valve?

A. In the adjustment feature which is used for reducing main reservoir pressure to the 45 pounds required for the independent brake.

Q. How is this valve adjusted?

A. Remove the cap nut, and adjust the tension of the spring by means of the adjusting screw.

DUPLEX PUMP GOVERNOR.

Q. Describe the function of the duplex pump governor used with the automatic control.

A. It changes the main reservoir pressure automatically when the brake pipe pressure is changed from low to high by the feed valve; and controls the speed of the pump accordingly.

Q. In what positions of the automatic brake valve is this governor in action?

A. Release, running and holding positions.

Q. Is it cut out in all the other positions of the automatic brake valve?

A. It is.

Q. With what is the maximum pressure head of the duplex governor always in direct communication?

A. The main reservoir.

Q. Why? Explain.

A. So that this head will control the pump when the other or excess pressure head is cut out by the brake valve; or the main reservoir cut-out cock is closed.

Q. How is the maximum pressure head adjusted?

A. Place the handle of the automatic brake valve in lap position, remove cap nut of governor and change tension of the spring with regulating nut until it is adjusted so as to stop the pump when the desired maximum main reservoir pressure is obtained.

Q. For what pressure should this head be adjusted?

A. A pressure of from 120 to 140 pounds, according to the service.

Q. How is the excess pressure head of this governor adjusted?

A. Place the handle of automatic brake valve in running position, remove cap nut, and change tension of the spring by means of the regulating nut, until the desired difference between main reservoir and brake pipe pressure is obtained.

Q. How much excess pressure should this head be adjusted for?

A. Twenty pounds excess pressure in main reservoir.

COMBINED AIR STRAINER AND CHECK VALVE.

Q. Describe the location and purpose of the combined air strainer and check valve.

A. Two of these are used with the automatic control equipment; one being in the continuous feed pipe to prevent back leakage from the auxiliary reservoir of the automatic control valve, and the other being part of the dead engine fixture.

Q. Of what does the dead engine fixture consist?

A. A pipe leading from brake pipe to main reservoir, a cut-out cock and the combined check valve and strainer.

Q. When two or more locomotives are operating together on one train and the air pump on one engine becomes inoperative, how may the air for operating the brakes on such locomotive be supplied to it?

A. With the cut-out cock open, air from the brake pipe enters and passes through the strainer, lifts the check valve and flows on into the main reservoir thus supplying this engine with the air pressure necessary to operate its brakes.

Q. What precautions should be observed when operating engine brakes in this way?

A. The cut-out cock in the brake pipe under the automatic brake valve should be closed, and the handle of the brake valve placed in running position.

Q. If it becomes necessary to keep the maximum braking power of a dead engine below standard how may it be done?

A. By changing the adjustment of the safety valve of the automatic control valve. The pressure can also be reduced by using the release valve.

Q. How is the seating of the check valve assured?

A. By means of the spring.

B2 H. S. EQUIPMENT—NEW YORK AIR BRAKE.

The locomotive brake equipment described and illustrated herewith is known as the B2-HS equipment and is arranged in three different schedules to cover the requirements of railroad service in general.

Schedule B2 covers the single pressure system, B2-HP the double pressure system, and B2-HS the double pressure system with high speed attachment such as shown herewith.

The equipment differs materially from any schedule heretofore furnished. As with the Combined Automatic and Straight Air Brake, the independent brake valve has been dispensed with, and by the addition of the Duplex Pressure Controller and Accelerator Valve, more has been accomplished than was heretofore possible, and with less apparatus.

With this equipment the train brakes can be released, and the locomotive brakes held on. The locomotive brakes can then be released when desired, or can be applied and released independently of the train brakes, or together with same at the option of the engineer.

The locomotive brakes can be operated at all times by automatic or independent application, and without regard to position of the locomotive in a train, whether used as a helper, coupled to another or assigned to any other part of train. They can be applied and released at will, and can be graduated off after an application of the train brakes; therefore, in all kinds of service the train brakes can be handled without shock to the train.

The accelerator valve will be found a valuable addition to these equipments when operating long trains, for, with the use of same, shorter stops will be effected, and a more uniform application of the train brakes obtained.

All excess pressure is confined to the main reservoir, and in no position of the brake valve handle can the brake pipe pressure increase above its maximum. This will prevent over-charging of auxiliary reservoirs on the head end of trains, and also reduce the strain on air brake hose.

B2 EQUIPMENT.

This equipment is designed for passenger or freight service where but one brake pipe pressure is used.

Both pump governor and pressure controller have single regulating heads. The pressure head for the pressure controller should be adjusted to 70 lbs. for brake pipe pressure, and the pump governor head adjusted to 90 lbs. for main reservoir pressure.

B2-S EQUIPMENT.

This equipment is for use with switch engines as before stated. A single pump governor is provided, also a single pressure controller for brake pipe pressure regulation. In the pipe connecting the regulating and supply portions of the pressure controller is located cut-out cock No. 2. When this cock is open the controller should give a maximum brake pipe pressure of 70 lbs. and the pump governor adjusted to 110 lbs. for main reservoir pressure. This will give the necessary air pressure for freight service. By closing the cut-out cock the pressure controller will become inoperative, allowing the main reservoir pressure of 110 lbs. to pass to the brake valve, and brake pipe for high speed service.

B2-HP EQUIPMENT.

This equipment is for use in freight service only. Both regulating portions of the pump governor and pressure controller are duplex, so that pressures of 70 and 90 lbs. can be carried in the brake pipe and 90 and 110 lbs. in the main reservoir for the ordinary brake pipe pressure and the high pressure control.

For the operation of these duplex regulating portions, three way cocks are provided, being connected as shown in the piping diagram.

To operate these cocks turn the handle in line with the pipe leading to the regulating head to be used, high or low pressure as desired. This will cut in the head to regulate the supply portion, and cut off the one not in use.

B2-HS EQUIPMENT.

High speed locomotive brake equipment. The system of regulation of pressure for the high speed equipment is the same as with the B2-HP except that the regulating heads of the pressure controller should be adjusted to 70 and 110 lbs. for brake pipe pressure, and the pump governor heads adjusted to 90 and 120 or 130 lbs. as desired for main reservoir pressure.

MANIPULATION.

On the folded sheet (Insert) will be found piping diagrams of the several B-2 equipments, and it should be referred to in connection with the following instructions:

GENERAL.

To apply the locomotive and train brakes (automatic), move the handle of the brake valve to the graduating notch necessary to make the required brake pipe reduction.

To release both locomotive and train brakes, move the handle to Running and Straight Air release position.

To release the train brakes and hold the locomotive brakes set (Straight Air), move the handle to Full Automatic release and Straight Air application position.

To release the locomotive brakes, move the handle to Running and Straight Air release position.

To apply the locomotive brakes (Straight Air), move the handle to Full Automatic release and Straight Air application position.

To apply the brakes in an emergency, move the handle quickly to Emergency position, and leave it there until the train stops, or the danger has passed

In case the automatic brakes are applied by the bursting of a hose, the train parts, or a conductor's valve is opened, place the handle in Lap position to retain the main reservoir pressure.

To graduate off or entirely release the locomotive brakes after an application of the train brakes, use the lever safety valve to make the required reduction.

The handle of the brake valve will be found to work freely and easily at all times, as the pressure on the main slide valve does not exceed the maximum brake pipe pressure.

The cylinder gauge will show at all times the pressure in the locomotive brake cylinders, and should be observed in all brake manipulations.

Where there are two or more locomotives in a train cut-out cock No 1, shown in plate 36, should be turned to close the brake pipe, and the brake valve handle carried in Running and Straight Air release position on all locomotives, except the one from which the brakes are operated.

In case it becomes necessary to cut out the Straight Air brake, close cut-out cock No. 3 which is located in the straight air pipe between the Brake Valve and the Reducing Valve.

To cut out the Automatic Brake, close cut-out cock No. 6 located in the pipe connecting the Triple Valve with the Double Check Valve.

By locating the cut-out cock between the Triple and Double Check Valves, the auxiliary reservoirs will remain charged, while the brake is cut out, and can be alternated with the train brakes in descending long grades to prevent overheating of the locomotive tires.

Cut-out cocks Nos. 3 and 6 are special, they are of the three-way pattern, and when turned off drain the pipes leading to the double check valve to keep the latter seated in the direction of the closed cock.

The main reservoir cock No. 4 is to cut off the supply of air when removing any of the apparatus except the governor.

The straight air controller is to limit the pressure in

the driver, truck and tender brake cylinders for the straight air brake, and should be adjusted to 40 pounds pressure.

Cut-out cocks Nos. 5, 6 and 7 are recommended when truck brake is used, their purpose being fully understood. Nos. 9 and 10 can be added, if desired, so that the driver brake cylinders and reservoir can be cut out, and engine truck brake operated by truck brake reservoir.

THE B2 BRAKE VALVE.

This brake valve, although modeled somewhat upon the principles of the B and B1 valves, is necessarily different in detail so as to embody the features of the pressure controller and those of the united straight air. Fig. 77 is a photographic view of the valve. Fig. 78 is a

Fig. 77—B-2 Brake Valve.

longitudinal side section showing travel of main slide valve EV 194 and how the graduating valve EV 110 is controlled by the piston EV 193. This view also shows the different positions of the brake valve handle. Fig. 79 is a top view of the valve with the cover, slide valve and handle removed, showing seat and connections for the straight air and divided reservoir pipes. Fig. 80 is a cross section through the valve (rear view). Fig. 81 is a cross section through the main slide valve. Fig. 82 shows the face of the main slide valve.

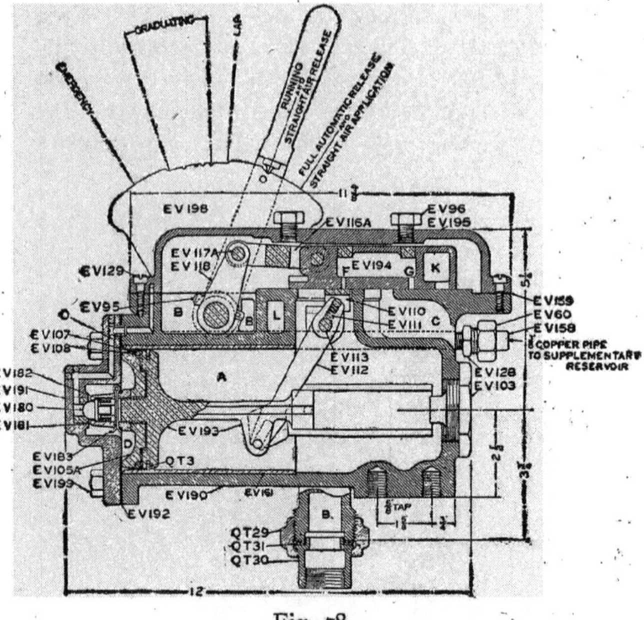

Fig. 78.

The main reservoir pipe is connected from the pressure controller to chamber B (Fig. 78) in the top of the valve. The brake pipe is connected to chamber A. Discharge of brake pipe air to the atmosphere for service applications occurs through ports F and G in the main slide valve and exhaust passages C in the valve body and for emergency applications through ports J and K in

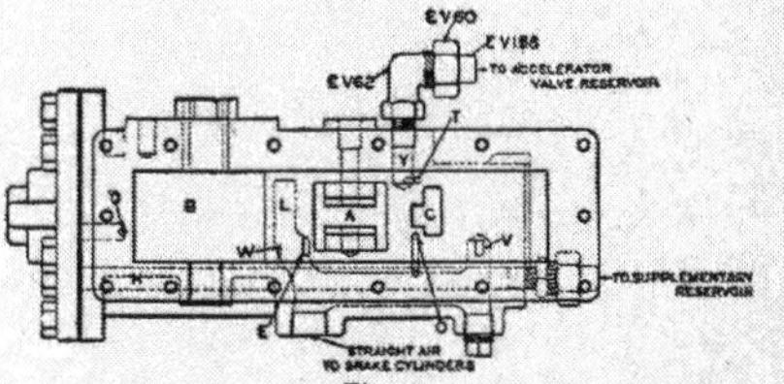

Fig. 79.

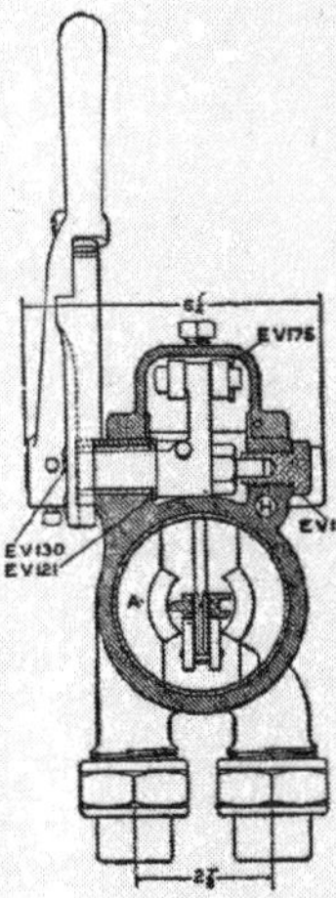

Fig. 80.

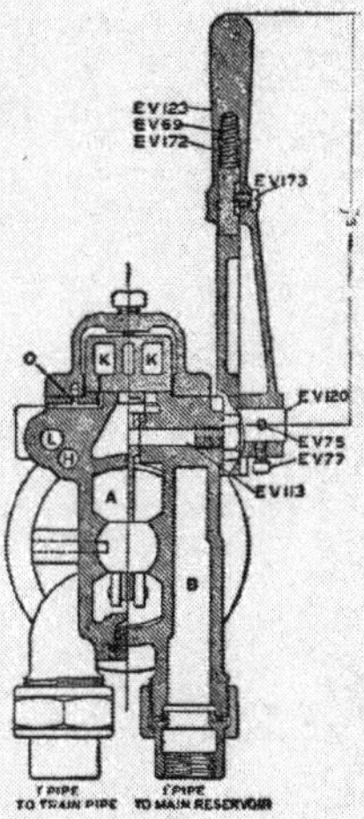

Fig. 81.

the slide valve (Fig. 82) and exhaust passage C. The main slide valve also controls the flow of air from the main reservoir to the brake pipe. In Full automatic release position air is free to pass from the main reservoir to the brake pipe through ports M and also around the slide valve, as in this position the slide valve is moved forward, uncovering a portion of the passage. (See Fig. 83.) When the handle is in Running position only ports M are open but are of a size to promptly release all train brakes. (See Fig. 84.)

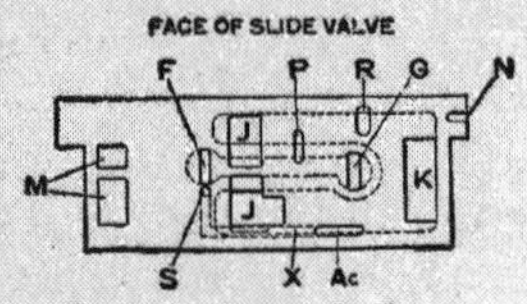

Fig. 82.

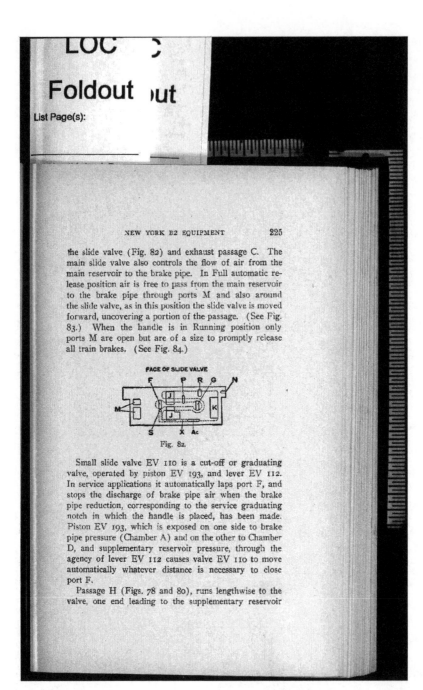

Small slide valve EV 110 is a cut-off or graduating valve, operated by piston EV 193, and lever EV 112. In service applications it automatically laps port F, and stops the discharge of brake pipe air when the brake pipe reduction, corresponding to the service graduating notch in which the handle is placed, has been made. Piston EV 193, which is exposed on one side to brake pipe pressure (Chamber A) and on the other to Chamber D, and supplementary reservoir pressure, through the agency of lever EV 112 causes valve EV 110 to move automatically whatever distance is necessary to close port F.

Passage H (Figs. 78 and 80), runs lengthwise to the valve, one end leading to the supplementary reservoir

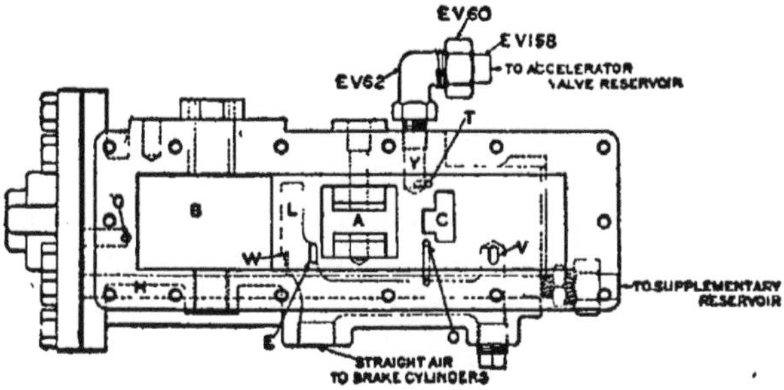

Fig 79.

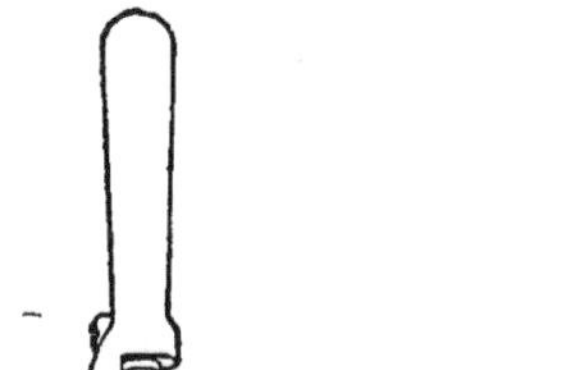

Fig. 80.

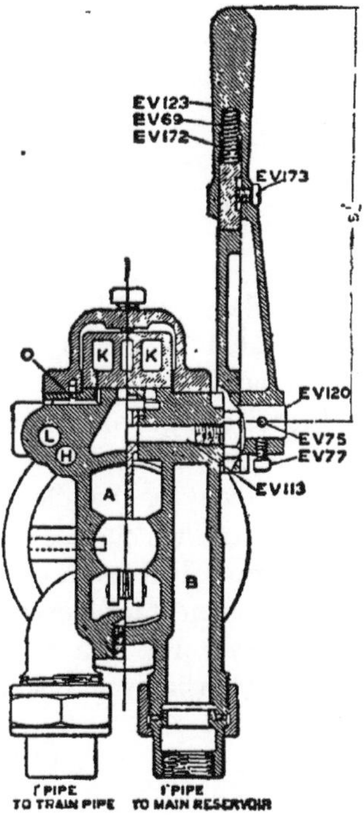

Fig 81.

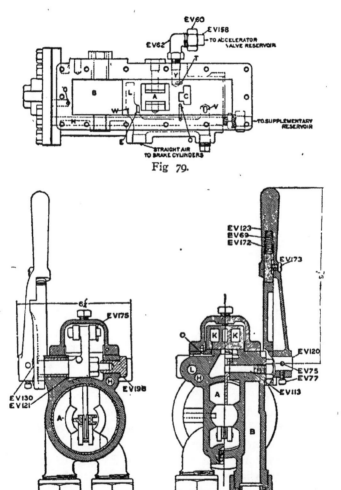

the slide valve (Fig. 82) and exhaust passage C. The main slide valve also controls the flow of air from the main reservoir to the brake pipe. In Full automatic release position air is free to pass from the main reservoir to the brake pipe through ports M and also around the slide valve, as in this position the slide valve is moved forward, uncovering a portion of the passage. (See Fig. 83.) When the handle is in Running position only ports M are open but are of a size to promptly release all train brakes. (See Fig. 84.)

FACE OF SLIDE VALVE

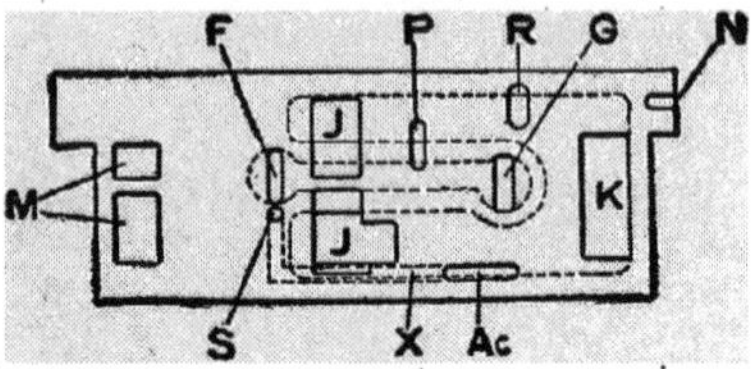

Fig. 82.

Small slide valve EV 110 is a cut-off or graduating valve, operated by piston EV 193, and lever EV 112. In service applications it automatically laps port F, and stops the discharge of brake pipe air when the brake pipe reduction, corresponding to the service graduating notch in which the handle is placed, has been made. Piston EV 193, which is exposed on one side to brake pipe pressure (Chamber A) and on the other to Chamber D, and supplementary reservoir pressure, through the agency of lever EV 112 causes valve EV 110 to move automatically whatever distance is necessary to close port F.

Passage H (Figs. 78 and 80), runs lengthwise to the valve, one end leading to the supplementary reservoir as indicated in Fig. 78, while the other end leads to the space D, back of the piston EV 193. In Full automatic release, and in Running and Straight Air release positions, air from chamber B, Fig. 79, passes through port W to passage H and supplementary reservoir, until there is equal pressure on both sides of the piston EV 193 and the supplementary reservoir pressure is equal to the brake pipe pressure.

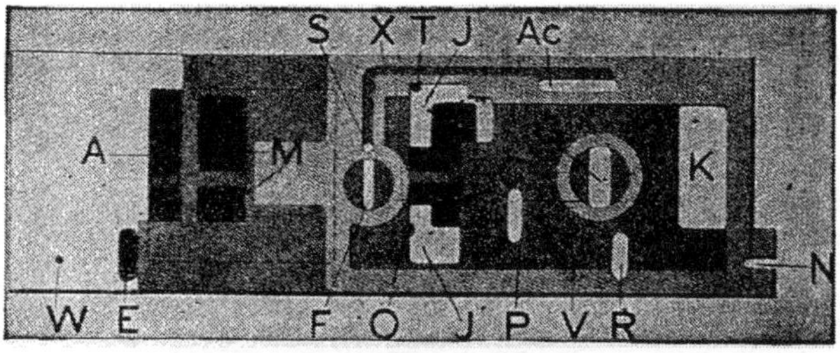

Fig. 83—Release Position.

Port O (Fig. 78), is used to return the piston EV 193 to its normal position when releasing the brakes, and is open to the exhaust passage C when the handle of the brake valve is in Full Automatic Release, Running, and Lap positions, and closes just before the handle is brought to the first graduating notch. During the time the brake valve handle is in any of these positions, port O is open through passage C to the atmosphere, as stated, and if it were not for the vent valve EV 180 the function of piston EV 193 would be destroyed, as a continual blow from chamber D would result while the piston EV 193 is in operation the vent valve EV 180 is away from its seat, thus opening port O to the slide valve seat, to be opened when the handle is again returned to release position.

Connection is made with the straight air pipe through passage L (See Figs. 79 and 83) to which ports E and V connect from the main slide valve seat. Port E is the admission port and is open to receive pressure from chamber B when the handle of the brake valve is in Full automatic release and Straight Air application position. Port V is the exhaust port and is used to exhaust the pressure from the driver brake cylinders in releasing the straight air brake, the release being accomplished through ports R and J in the main slide valve, and passage C in the valve body. (See Fig. 84.)

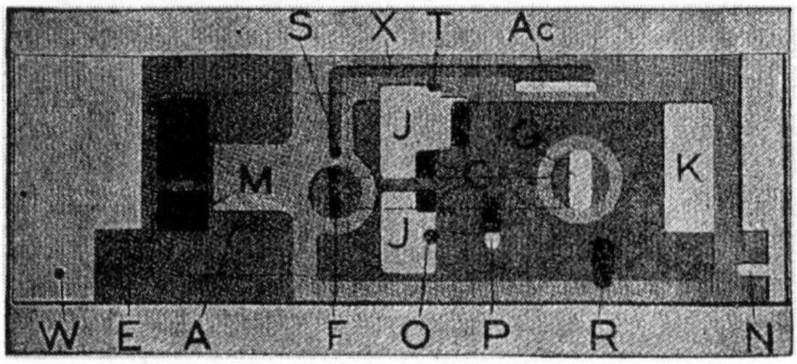

Fig. 84—Running Position.

Port V is also used to pass pressure from chamber B to the straight air brake when the handle is in the Fifth graduating notch and Emergency position. This is done so that if there is cylinder leakage or excessive piston travel, the Straight Air brake will hold the pressure in these cylinders to the adjustment of the Reducing Valve.

In all graduating positions of the Brake Valve, brake pipe pressure is admitted to the divided reservoir (Large compartment Fig. 90) to operate the Accelerator Valve.

When the Brake Valve handle is moved to any of the graduating notches, brake pipe pressure will flow through port S, passage X, and cavity AC in the main slide valve (Fig. 82) and through port T, and passage Y in the Valve body (Fig 79) to the divided reservoir until the port S is cut off by the Graduating Valve EV 110, when the latter closes the service port F. To guard against possibility of the Accelerator Valve being open while the Brake Valve handle is in a Release position, which might occur if the handle was returned before a service application had been completed, port J in the main slide valve (Fig. 82) has been enlarged so as to open port T to the exhaust passage C, and the atmosphere when the handle is in a release position These ports are large enough to rapidly discharge the air accumulated in the divided reservoir, and thereby permit the accelerator valve to immediately close. By referring to the diagrammatic views of the main slide valve and seat shown in Figs. 83 to 88 inclusive, it will be seen what ports are open and closed in the different positions of the slide valve.

FULL AUTOMATIC RELEASE AND STRAIGHT AIR APPLICATION POSITION (FIG. 83).

The purpose of this position is to promptly release the automatic brakes and to apply the straight air brakes on the Locomotive In this position, air is flowing directly from chamber B (main reservoir) into chamber A (brake pipe) past the end of the slide valve and through ports M. Port O is open to port J and exhaust passage C to return the piston EV 193, and port W is open to charge the supplementary reservoir. Port T, also by means of port J, is open to the exhaust passage C to discharge the pressure from the large compartment of the divided reservoir. Port E is also open for pressure to pass to the driver brake cylinders through the straight air pipe until shut off by the reducing valve.

RUNNING POSITION.

Running and Straight Air Release Position. (Fig. 84.) This is the proper position of the handle when wishing to release both Straight Air and Automatic brakes simultaneously, or to release the Straight Air Brake. Connection from Chamber B into Chamber A

Fig. 85—Lap Position.

is made through the ports M. Port E is lapped. Ports O, T and W remain the same as in Release Position. Ports R and V register with each other, thus connecting the straight air brake with the exhaust passage C as shown, to discharge the pressure from the driver brake cylinders.

Lap Position. (Fig. 85.) This position should be used in case a hose bursts, the train parts or a conductor's valve is opened, to save the main reservoir pressure. In this position all ports are blanked, excepting port O. As in Release and Running Positions, this port is open to the exhaust passage C. In this particular position cavity P in the slide valve seat is made use of to connect the port with passage C.

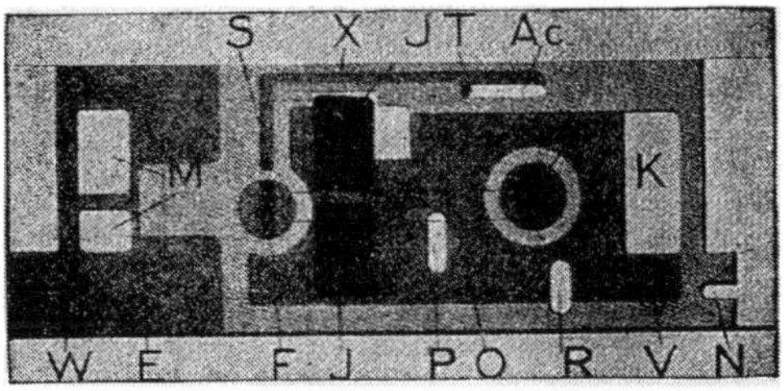

Fig. 86—First Graduating Position.

Graduating Positions. (Figs. 86 and 87.) These positions give a gradual reduction of brake pipe pressure for service applications. In Fig. 86 ports M are

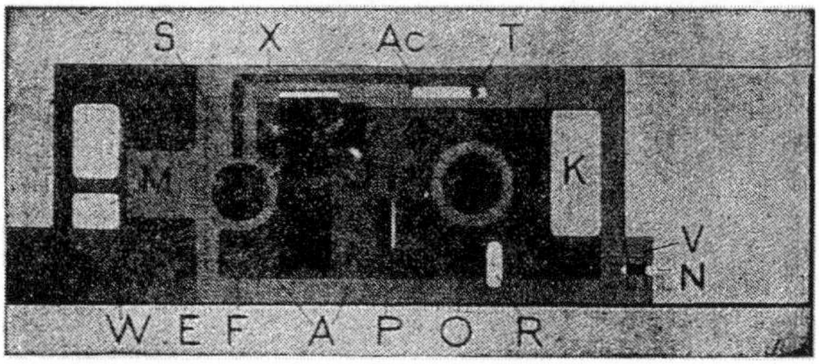

Fig. 87—Last Graduating Position.

blanked and communication from the main reservoir to the brake pipe is cut off. The straight air ports E and V are also blanked, as well as ports O and W, which are cut off just before the handle reaches the First Graduating Notch. Ports F and G are open to the exhaust passage C, and port S is open through passage X to port T to receive pressure from the brake pipe and pass it to the divided reservoir to operate the Accelerator Valve. Ports F and S will remain open to receive brake pipe pressure until cut off by the graduating valve EV 110 when the service reduction has been made.

In the remainder of the Graduating Positions, the relation of ports remains the same with the exception of the restricted passage N (Fig 87) in the end of the slide valve which in the Fifth Graduating notch is over the straight air port V, and should there be excessive piston travel or cylinder leakage the Straight Air equipment will hold the pressure in these cylinders to the adjustment of the reducing valve. The restriction of port N is to prevent the pressure from passing to the driver brake cylinders in advance of pressure from the auxiliary reservoir of the automatic brake.

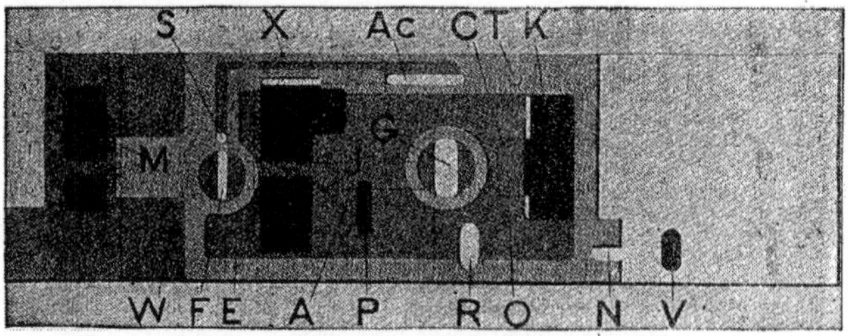

Fig. 88—Emergency Position.

EMERGENCY POSITION (FIG. 88)

This position is to be used when it is desired to apply the brakes to their quickest and fullest capacity. In this position, the active ports are J and K, which are open to exhaust brake pipe pressure from chamber A to the atmosphere. Port V as in the fifth graduating notch is open to maintain the pressure in the driver brake cylinders against leakage, etc. Port E is closed, also ports F, M, O, S, T and W.

To dismantle the Valve, the valve cover EV 195 should first be removed, and then the back cap EV 191. The main slide valve EV 194 should be taken off, and the Graduating valve EV 110 lifted out—also the Graduating valve spring EV 111. Next remove the fulcrum pin EV 113, after which remove the piston EV 193.

Do not attempt to remove the follower cap nut EV 181 from the piston EV 193 while the piston is in the valve body, as to do this would probably result either in springing the groove in the piston stem, or in breaking off the dowel pin in the valve body.

Figs. 78 to 81 show the different parts of the valve, their names being as follows: EV 60, Small union nut; EV 62, Small union ell; EV 69, Handle spring; EV 75, Handle pin; EV 77, Handle set screw; EV 95, Lever shaft pin with cotter; EV 96, ¼″ plug; EV 103, End plug; EV 105-A, Follower; EV 107, Packing Leather; EV 108, Expander; EV 110, Graduating Valve; EV 111, Graduating valve spring; EV 112, Graduating valve lever; EV 113, Fulcrum pin; EV 116-A, Link; EV 117-A Link pin; EV 118, Slide valve lever; EV 120, Lever shaft; EV 121, Lever shaft packing; EV 123, Handle; EV 128, Small union stud; EV 129, Cover screw; EV 130, Quadrant screw; EV 158, Small union swivel; EV 159, Cover gasket; EV 172, Latch; EV 173, Latch screw; EV 175, Link pin cotter; EV 180, Vent valve; EV 181, Follower cap nut; EV 182, Vent valve spring; EV 183, Piston cotter; EV 190, Body; EV 191, Back cap; EV 192, Cap gasket; EV 193, Piston; EV 194, Main slide valve;

EV 195, Valve cover; EV 196, Lever shaft plug; EV 198, Quadrant; EV 199, Back cap stud and nut; QT 3, Piston ring; QT 29, 1" Union nut; QT 30, 1" Union swivel; QT 31, 1" Union gasket.

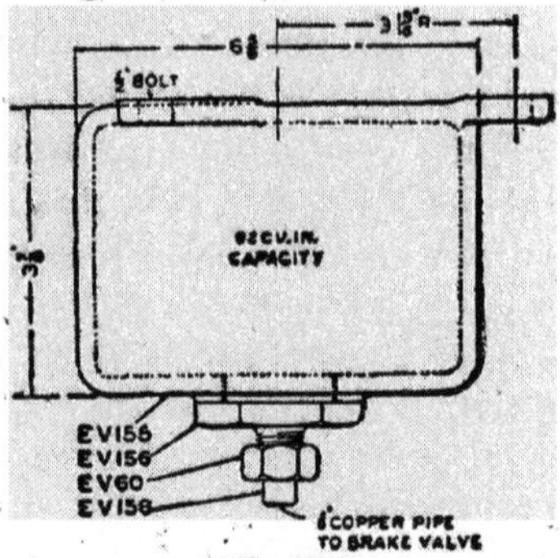

Fig. 89.

SUPPLEMENTARY RESERVOIR USED WITH SWITCH ENGINE EQUIPMENT, SCHEDULE B2-S (FIG. 89).

NAMES OF PARTS.

EV 60, Small union nut; EV 155, Supplementary reservoir; EV 156, Reservoir plug; EV 158, Union swivel (⅜" copper pipe).

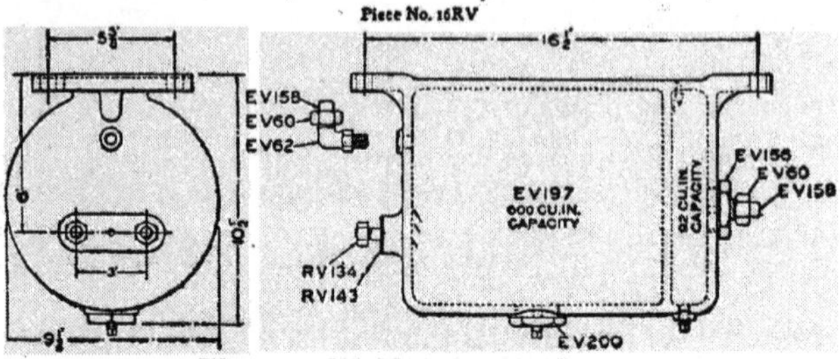

Fig. 90—Divided Reservoir.

E V 60—Small union nut.	E V 197—Divided reservoir.
E V 62—Small union ell.	E V 200—Botton plug.
E V 156—Reservoir plug.	R V 134—½-inch stud and nut.
E V 158—Union swivel.	R V 143—Accelerator valve gasket.

THE DUPLEX PRESSURE CONTROLLER AND DOUBLE PRESSURE SYSTEM.

This valve, in reality, is a part of the Brake Valve, taking place of the excess pressure or feed valve, and is connected in the main reservoir pipe near the Brake Valve, to control the brake pipe pressure. The Con-

Fig. 91—Duplex Regulating Portion of Pressure Controller.

troller is in principle the same as that of a Duplex Pump Governor with the exception of the regulating tops, which connect to the brake pipe. In no position of the Brake Valve handle is there danger of the brake pipe becoming over-charged, or equal to that in the main reservoir.

This equipment is designed so that two pressures may be carried in the brake pipe, and also in the main reservoir. It will be seen by reference to the piping diagram that there is a union three-way cock, from which pipes lead to the regulating tops, and supply which in this case is brake pipe pressure. The same arrange-

Fig. 92—Supply Portion of Pressure Controller.

ment also applies to the pump governor. A sectional view of this cock is shown in Figs. 95 and 96. When one regulating top is cut in the other one is cut out and vice versa. This is done to relieve the strain on the regulating tops when not working. When the cocks are in the position shown in the piping diagram the low pressure regulating tops of the Controller and Duplex Pump

Governor are cut in, giving a pressure of seventy pounds to the brake pipe, and ninety pounds to the main reservoir. When the cocks are reversed, one hundred and ten pounds will then be carried in the brake pipe, and one hundred and thirty pounds in the main reservoir.

Fig. 91 is a photographic view of the Duplex Pressure controller, and Fig. 92 is a view of the supply portion. Figs. 93 and 94 are sectional views of both the

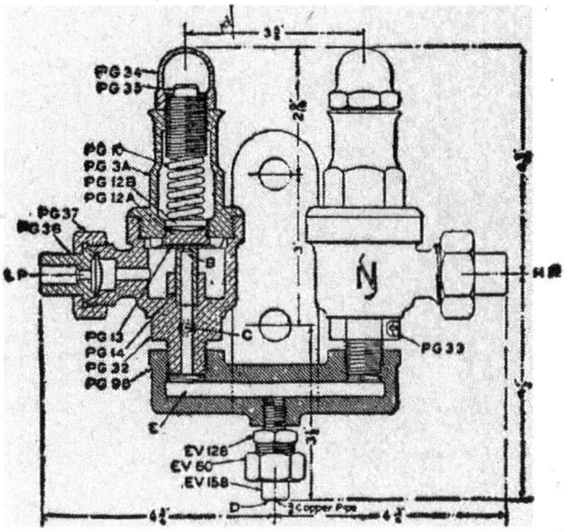

Fig. 93.

duplex and single regulating portions. Fig. 97 shows the supply portion in section. Referring to Fig. 97, connection is made with the main reservoir at M. R. and by means of the cored passage, air is free to pass to the under side of the valve P G 95. Connection BV leads to the brake valve, main reservoir connection, and connection D to the regulating portion (single or duplex) also connecting at D in Figs. 93 and 94.

In operation with either a single or duplex regulating portion, as soon as the pressure in the brake pipe is great enough to overcome the resistance of the spring PG 10 which is holding the diaphragm PG 13 seated over port B, the pressure will pass through passage E to connection D, and by piping to the space E in the supply portion of the controller above the piston PG 4, forcing the piston, and valve PG 95 down until seated, cutting off communication between main-reservoir and brake pipe.

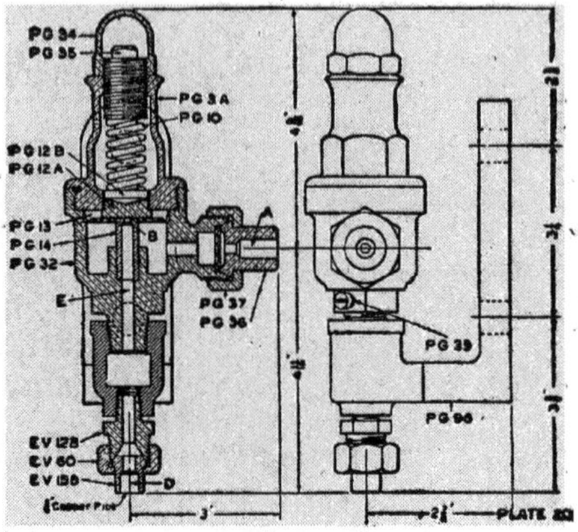

Fig. 94.

As soon as the pressure falls in the brake pipe below the adjustment of spring PG 10, the latter will force diaphragm PG 13 to its seat, closing off port B, whereupon pressure in passage E, and piping connecting supply and regulating portions, and space E above piston PG 4 will immediately escape to the atmosphere through the small port C in the regulating head of the controller, after which main reservoir pressure will lift valve PG 95 off its seat, and again open communication to the brake pipe.

Port X in the supply portion of the controller connects the under side of piston PG 4 with atmosphere, so that it will be free to operate and to discharge any leakage by the ring PG 24 or valve PG 95.

The regulating portions are provided with brackets so that they can be attached to the cab in some convenient place where they will be handy for adjustment. The adjustment of these regulating heads is accomplished by means of nut PG 35 which regulates the tension of spring PG 10.

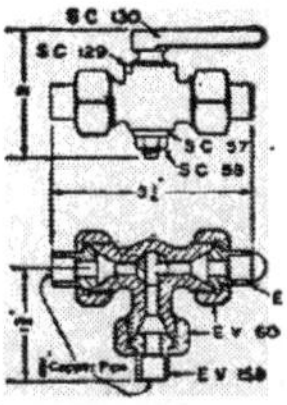

Fig. 95.

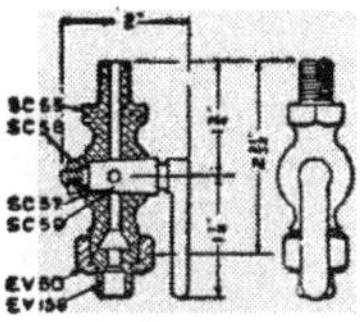

Fig. 96.

Each regulating head has a vent port C, and to avoid any unnecessary waste of air, one of these heads should be plugged with screw PG 33. The cut-out cock shown in Fig. 96 is used with the B2S equipment, between the regulating and supply portions. When this cock is closed the supply portion of the controller is cut off.

The hand wheel PG 45 can be used in descending grades if desired, to increase the brake pipe pressure to that of the main reservoir. By screwing the wheel up, it will lift the valve PG 95 off its seat and thus allow the two pressures to become equal. The Controller will then be inoperative, and main reservoir pressure will be free to pass to the brake pipe until the Controller is again restored to its operative condition.

The names of parts of the regulating portion are: PG 3A Spring Casing; PG 10 Regulating Spring; PG 12A and B Diaphragm button; PG 13 Diaphragm; PG 14 Air valve seat; PG 32 Diaphragm body; PG 33 Vent plug; PG 34 Cap; PG 35 Regulating nut; PG 36 Air union swivel (⅜" copper pipe); PG 37 Air union nut; PG 98 Duplex bracket; EV 60 Small union nut; EV 128 Small union stud; EV 158 small union swivel (⅜" copper pipe). The parts of the three-way cock are: SC 57 Washer; SC 58 Nut; SC 129 Body; SC 130 Plug; EV 60 Small union nut; EV 158 Union Swivel (⅜" copper pipe).

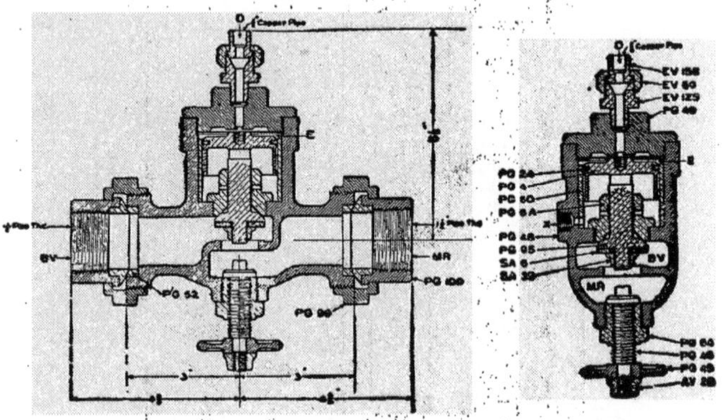

Fig. 97.

The parts of the supply portion are: PG 4 Piston; PG 6A Valve guide; PG 24 Piston ring; PG 45 Hand wheel; PG 46 Lifting Stem; PG 48 Body; PG 49 Cap; PG 94 Guide; PG 95 Valve; PG 99 1¼" union nut; PG 100 1¼" union swivel; EV 60 Small union nut; EV 128 Small union stud; EV 158 Union swivel (⅜" copper pipe); SA 6 Leather seat; SA 39 Valve stem nut; AV 28 Hand wheel nut.

ACCELERATOR VALVE.

This valve is designed to assist the Brake Valve in discharging brake pipe pressure when making service stops on long trains to bring about a more uniform application of the brakes, and to apply them more promptly than heretofore.

Fig. 98—Accelerator Valve.

The Valve is perfectly automatic in its operation, being governed entirely by the volume of air in the brake pipe, operating only when the train is of such a length as to warrant the use of same. The operation is similar to that of the graduating mechanism in the Brake Valve, opening about four seconds after the Brake Valve handle has been moved to a graduating notch, and closing in about the same length of time after the graduating valve has closed.

Figure 98 is an outside view of the Valve showing connection to brake pipe and exhaust which is through the street ell. A sectional view is shown in Fig. 99. The Valve is bolted to the end of the divided reservoir (Fig.

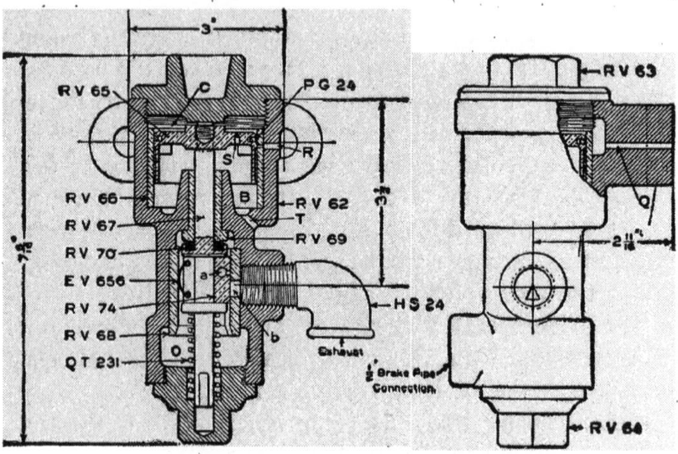

Fig. 99.

90), and receives pressure from same through passage Q which connects to the space C above the piston RV 65. The brake pipe connection leads to the slide valve chamber O.

Chamber B is open to the atmosphere through port T, and in the operation of the Valve, will carry off the discharge of pressure through port S, and any leakage by the piston RV 65 or valve stem RV 67.

The slide valve RV 74, when at rest, laps the port b and exhaust, and is held in this position by the spring QT 231 through the medium of valve stem RV 67, which seats in the manner shown. Port b is triangular, the larger portion being at the bottom, and in operation brake pipe pressure is gradually cut off as the slide valve closes. Port a in the slide valve is oblong being just long enough to uncover the triangular port b, when the slide valve is wide open. To give the slide valve a slow closure port R is provided in the valve body, and port S through the piston RV 65 as shown. When the valve is in operation and brake pipe pressure is being discharged to the atmosphere through ports a and b, ports R and S are open to discharge the pressure above the piston and divided reservoir. As soon as the pressure in the divided reservoir has reduced sufficiently for the spring QT 231 to operate, it will move the valve slowly upward until the port R is cut off, which will then reduce the discharge from the reservoir about one-half, giving the slide valve the slow closure desired.

The valve operates when there are eight or more cars in a train, and requires from fifteen to seventeen pounds pressure in the divided reservoir to operate it. Any pressure passing into this reservoir, as with a shorter train than eight cars, will be discharged to the atmosphere through ports S and T, the slide valve remaining closed.

The proper names of parts of the accelerator valve are as follows: PG 24, Piston ring; RV 62, Body, RV 63, Upper cap; RV 64, Lower cap; RV 65, Piston; RV 67, Valve stem; RV 70, Leather seat; RV 74, Slide valve; QT 231, Spring; EV 656, Slide valve spring; HS 24, ½" Street ell.

STRAIGHT AIR REDUCING VALVE.

The purpose of this valve is to limit the pressure in the driver, and truck brake cylinders, to 40 pounds when using the straight air brake.

Fig. 100—Straight Air Reducing Valve.

Fig. 100 is a photographic view of the reducing valve and Fig. 100 a section showing the valves, passages, etc.

Connection from the brake valve is made to the union fitting A and by means of the passage C pressure is free to pass to the feed valve SA 26. Connection B leads to double check valve and brake cylinders. During the time the tension of the spring against the diaphragm is stronger than the force exerted against it by the brake cylinder pressure, valve SA 26 will be held open, whereupon pressure from the main reservoir will be free to pass to the brake cylinders. As soon as the pressure

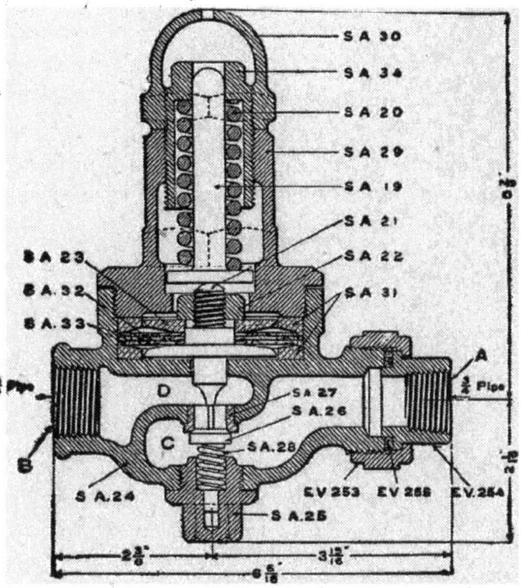

Fig. 101.

against the diaphragm is strong enough to overcome the resistance of the spring, the diaphragm will be moved upward, allowing the feed valve SA 26 to be closed by the spring SA 28, shutting off communication from the supply to the brake cylinders.

The names of the parts of this valve are as follows: SA 19, Regulating stem; SA 20, Regulating spring; SA

21, Diaphragm stem; SA 22, Nut; SA 23, Diaphragm Washer, SA 24, Body; SA 25, Feed valve cap nut; SA 26, Feed Valve; SA 28, Feed valve spring; SA 29, Spring box; SA 30, Check nut; SA 31, Diaphragm ring; SA 32, Diaphragm; SA 33, Diaphragm Shield; SA 34, Regulating nut; EV 253, 3/4" Union nut; EV 254, 3/4" Union swivel; EV 255, 3/4" Union gasket.

HIGH SPEED CONTROLLER WITH LEVER SAFETY VALVE.

This valve is operative when the locomotive equipment is set for high speed service.

Fig. 102—High Speed Controller.

Fig. 102 is an outside view showing the general arrangement. Fig. 103 is a section showing the operative parts.

The Safety Valve is for use at all times to graduate off brake cylinder pressure after an application of the train brakes when same is desired and to regulate the pressure in the brake cylinders during high speed operations. It is set at 53 pounds, and should so be adjusted in service.

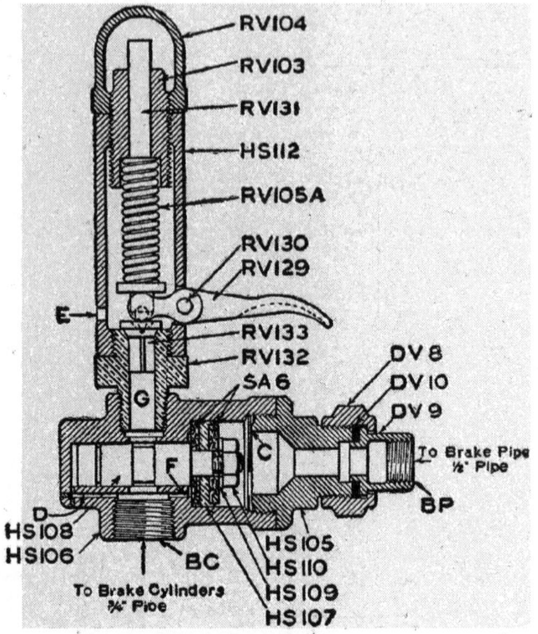

Fig. 103.

The High Speed Valve to which the Safety Valve is fastened connects with the brake cylinder pipe at BC and with brake pipe at BP.

The valve HS 108 with piston HS 107 operates when the brake pipe pressure is less than the pressure in brake cylinders. During all ordinary service applications the valve HS 108 will remain in position shown. In an emergency application when brake pipe pressure is greatly reduced, the brake cylinder pressure will move the piston HS 107, and valve its full traverse to the seat C. This movement will restrict passage G leading to the safety valve, and atmosphere by the circular groove in the valve HS 108 being moved forward, closing a portion of the passage. This will give a gradual blow down from the brake cylinders through passage G until shut off by the Safety Valve. The valve will remain in this position until the brakes are released.

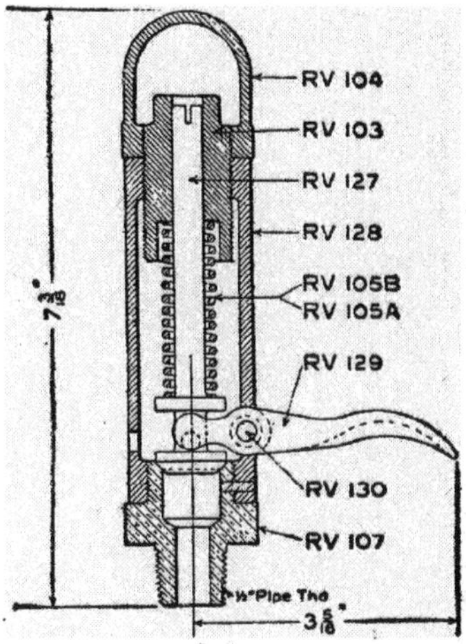

Fig. 104.

Ports F and D allow the brake cylinder pressure around the piston HS 107, and back of the valve HS 108, so that the piston is free to operate at a slight difference of pressure.

Fig. 104 is a sectional view of the lever safety valve, furnished with schedules B2, B2-S and B2-HP.

Fig. 105 shows the quick release valve which is used

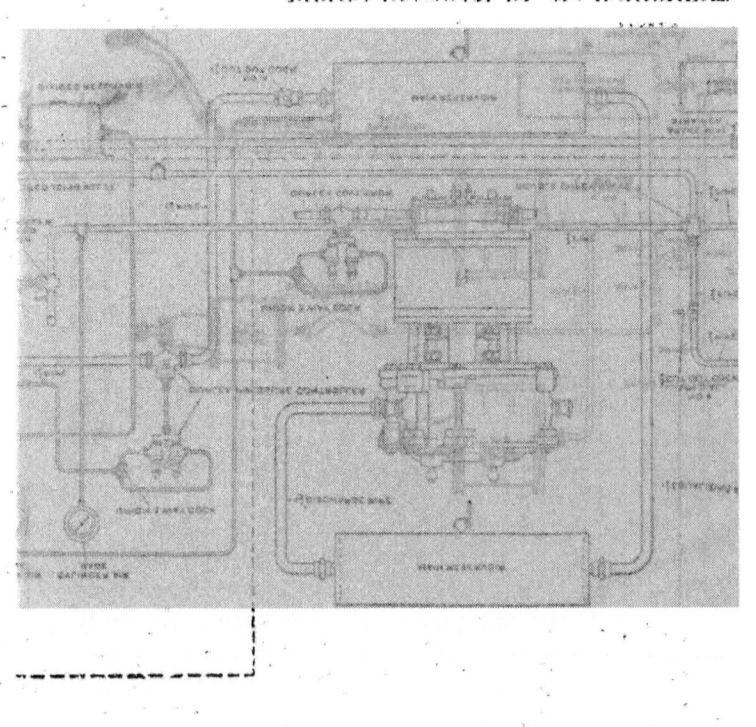

Cut-out cocks 5, 6 and 7 are recommended with this equipment.

NOTE 1—If desired, cut-out cock No. 8 can be substituted for cock No. 6. We recommend the latter, as with this arrangement the brake cylinders can be cut out, and the auxiliary reservoirs will remain charged.

NOTE 2—Cut-out cocks 9 and 10 can be added, if desired, so that the driver brake cylinders and reservoir can be cut out, and the engine truck brake operated by truck brake reservoir.

A triplex gauge is furnished with this equipment if desired, which embodies the two gauges in one case with the pointers on a single dial.

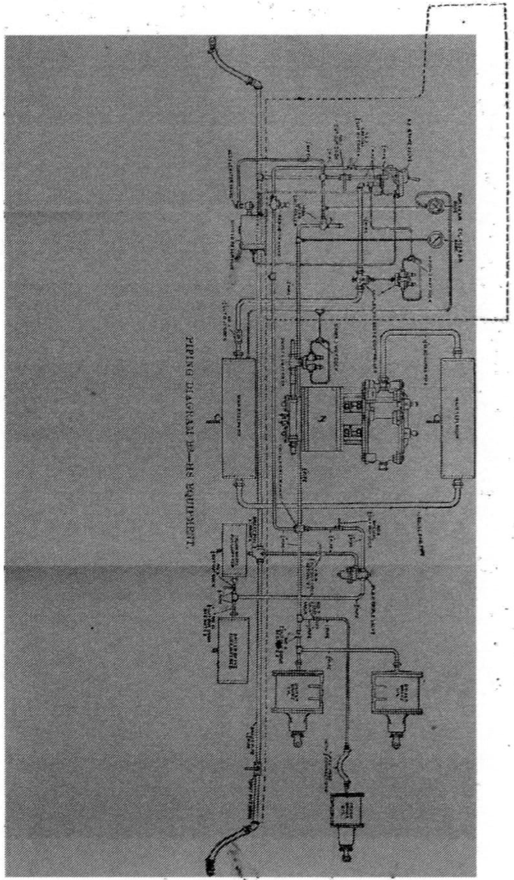

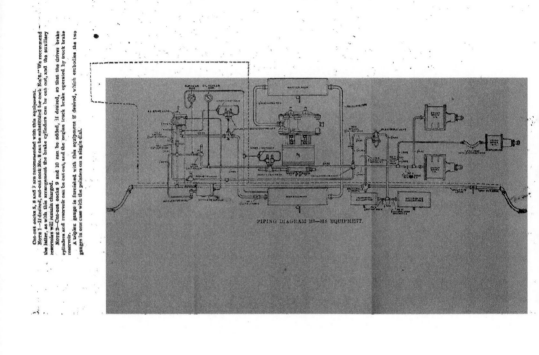

PIPING DIAGRAM B3—HS EQUIPMENT.

Cut-out cocks 5, 6 and 7 are recommended with this equipment.

NOTE 1—If desired, cut-out cock No. 8 can be substituted for cock No. 6. We recommend the latter, as with this arrangement the brake cylinders can be cut out, and the auxiliary reservoirs will remain charged.

NOTE 2—Cut-out cocks 9 and 10 can be added, if desired, so that the driver brake cylinders and reservoir can be cut out, and the engine truck brake operated by truck brake reservoir.

A triplex gauge is furnished with this equipment if desired, which embodies the two gauges in one case with the pointers on a single dial.

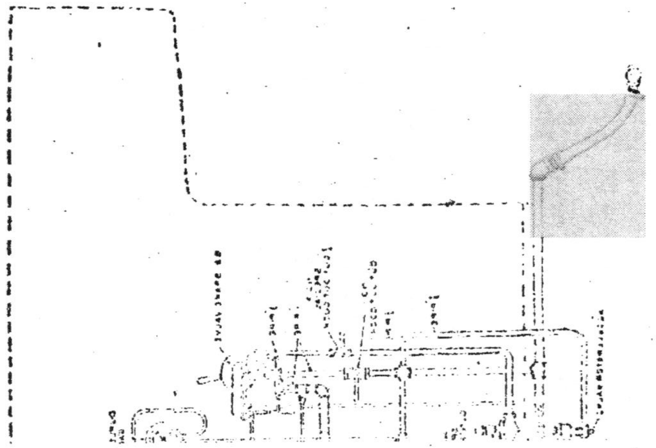

with the B2-S equipment, for switch engine service, to quickly release the pressure from the driver brake cylinders.

The lever safety valves shown in Figs. 103 and 104 are for use at all times to graduate off brake cylinder pressure, after an application of train brakes, when the same is desired. These valves are set at fifty-three pounds, and should be so adjusted in service.

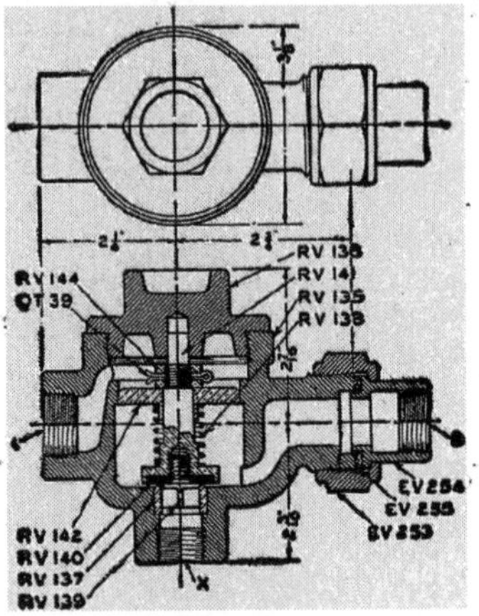

Fig. 105.

The two lever safety valves, although similar in appearance, are different in operation. In Fig. 103 the valve RV 133 is of a pop-safety valve design, and when forced open will remain so until the pressure beneath it has fallen to a trifle less than the force exerted against it by the spring RV 105 A. The safety valve shown in Fig. 104 is an ordinary blow-down pop valve, and while it will operate and reduce brake cylinder pressure to the desired amount, is not as free an operating valve as the one shown in Fig. 103. It is obvious to state that these lever safety valves are also for use to keep the brake cylinder pressure within a certain prescribed limit, as, if they were not used, an application of the straight air brake, followed by one of the automatic, would greatly increase the brake cylinder pressure over the prescribed limit.

The quick release valve shown in Fig. 105, as before stated, is for use with schedule B2-S switch engine equipment. This valve is to hasten the release after an application of the automatic or straight air brakes. Referring to Fig. 105, connection A leads to the double check valve as shown in the piping diagram of this equipment. Connection B leads to the driver brake cylinders and connection X to the exhaust.

E

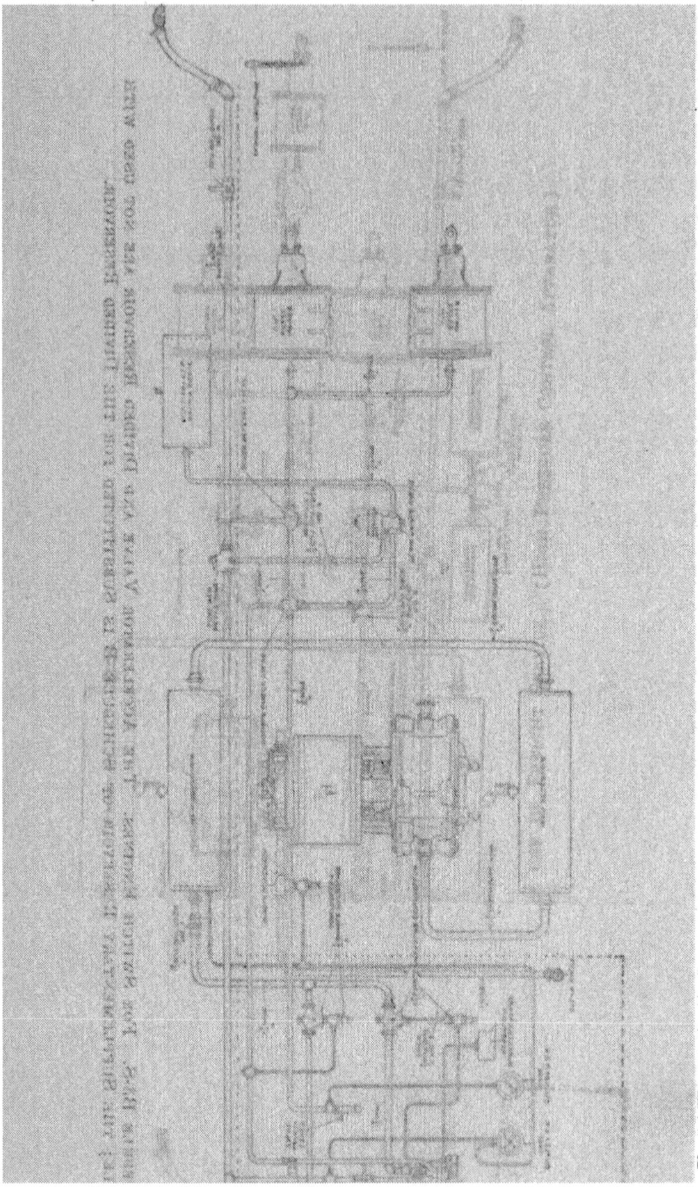

-3
to

ht
th.
u-
rd

gle
ed.
70
in
w-
ng
ds
d-
en
2
n-
ng
he
gh
he
re-

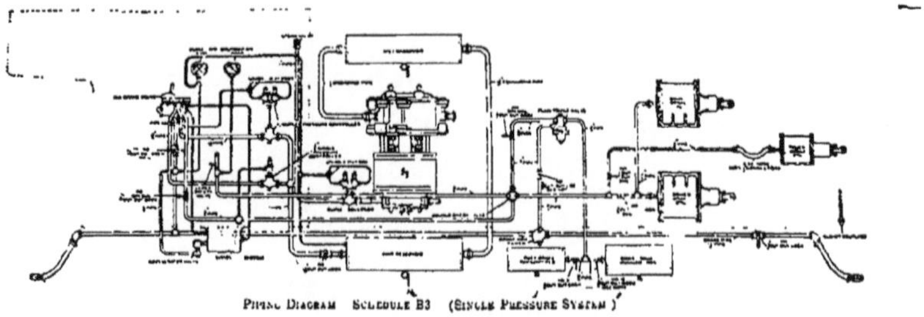

Piping Diagram Schedule B3 (Single Pressure System)

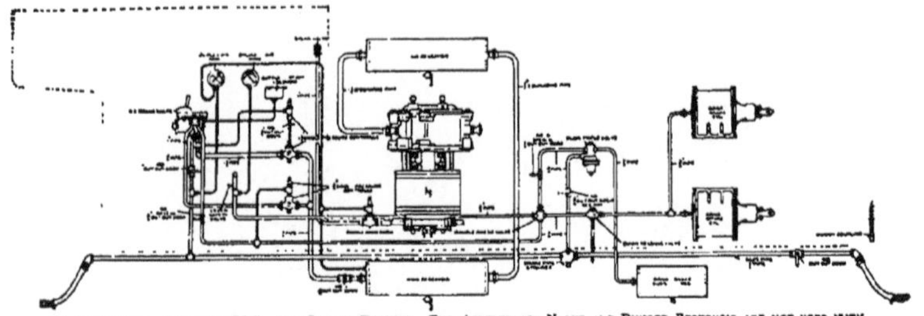

Piping Diagram Schedule B3-S For Switch Engines The Accelerator Valve and Divided Reservoir are not used with this Schedule, the Supplementary Reservoir of Schedule B is Substituted for the Divided Reservoir.

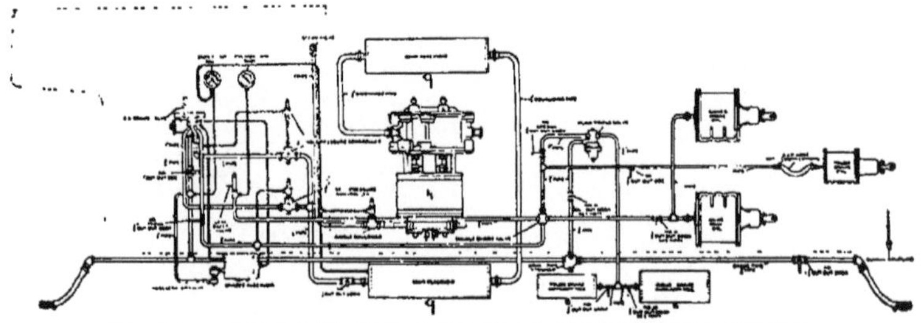

Piping Diagram. Schedule B3 HP For use in Freight Service. (High Pressure Control Apparatus)

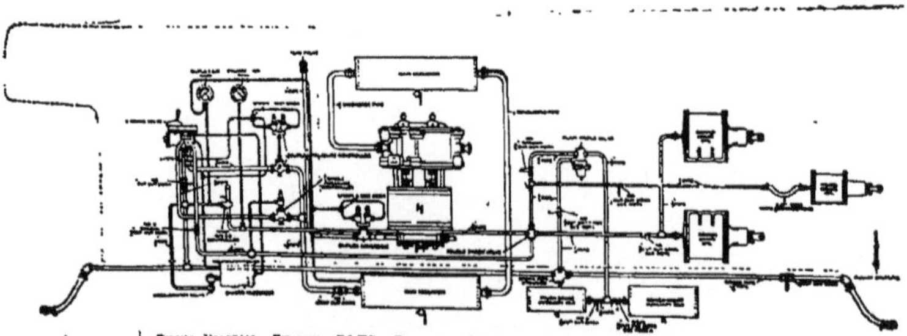

Piping Diagram Schedule B3 HS. For use in Passenger Service. (High Speed Brake.)

th
th
br
as,
air
gr
scr

sta
me
pli
fer
che
equ
ind

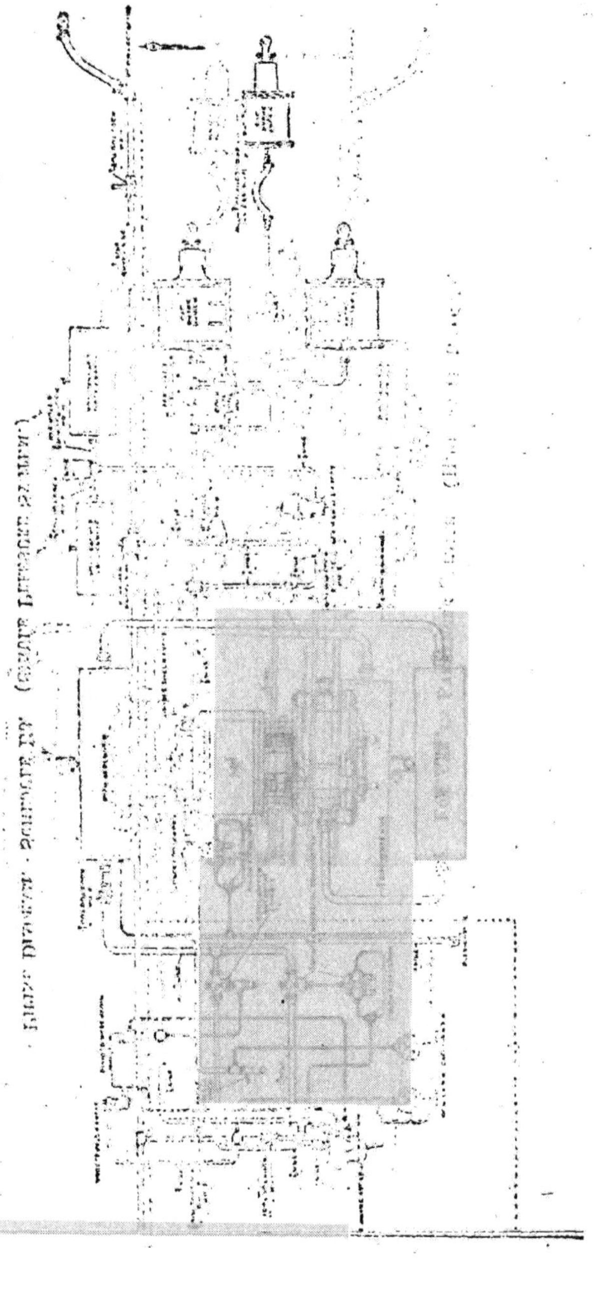

THE NEW YORK B-3 LOCOMOTIVE BRAKE EQUIPMENT.

This locomotive brake equipment is known as the B-3 equipment, and is arranged in four different schedules to cover the general requirements of railroad service.

SCHEDULE B-3 is for engines in passenger or freight service, where but one brake pipe pressure is used. Both pump governor and pressure controller have single regulating heads, which should be adjusted for the standard brake pipe and main reservoir pressure.

SCHEDULE B-3S is for switch engines only. A single pump governor and single pressure controller are used. The controller is set to give a brake pipe pressure of 70 pounds and the pump governor for 90 pounds main reservoir pressure, for ordinary switching service. However, when the engine is used for passenger switching service, and handles trains that are using 110 pounds brake pipe pressure, the pump governor should be adjusted to 110 pounds main reservoir pressure. When handling a train using the high pressure, close cock No. 2 between the regulating and supply portions of the controller. This renders the controller inoperative, allowing the main reservoir pressure of 110 pounds to pass to the brake valve and brake pipe, so that trains using the high speed brake can be handled without delay without the necessity of carrying additional apparatus. A quick release valve is furnished with this schedule, to be placed in the straight air pipe, so that the brakes can be released quickly, permitting quicker movement. The divided reservoir and accelerator valve are not furnished with this schedule. The supplementary reservoir is substituted for the divided reservoir.

SCHEDULE B-3HP is for freight service where heavily loaded trains are handled on heavy grades, or loads handled down grades and empties up Both regulating portions of the pump governor and pressure controller are duplex, so that pressures of 70 and 90 pounds can be carried in the brake pipe and 90 and 110 pounds in the main reservoir for the ordinary brake pipe pressure and the high pressure control.

For the operation of these duplex regulating portions, three-way cocks are provided, being connected as shown in the piping diagram. To operate these cocks, turn the handle in line with the pipe leading to the regulating head to be used, high or low pressure as desired This will cut in the head to regulate the supply portion, and cut off the pressure to the one not in use.

SCHEDULE B3-HS is the high speed brake. It includes the duplex pressure controller and the duplex pump governor. The regulating heads of the pressure controller should be adjusted to 70 pounds and 110 pounds for brake pipe pressure, and the pump governor heads adjusted to 90 pounds and 130 pounds for the main reservoir pressure. A union four-way cock is used with the regulating heads of the pressure controller. This is a special cock with a connection to each regulating top, one to the supply pipe, between the controller and brake valve, and one to the pipe between the brake valve and accelerator reservoir. When the handle of the four-way cock is in the position to operate the regulating head adjusted to 110 pounds brake pipe pressure, a small port in the accelerator reservoir connection is brought into communication with a port to the atmosphere. The object of this port is to prevent more than the usual predetermined reduction of brake pipe air, obtained in the graduating notches, taking place with 110 pounds pressure A union three-way cock connected to the main reservoir and pump governor regulating tops, is used to change the main reservoir pressures

The piping diagrams of the four schedules of the B-3 equipment, inserted at the beginning of this section, show the several parts comprising each schedule, as well as the proper pipe connections. This equipment is an improvement on former equipments. It not only includes all necessary features for the automatic brake, but also a straight air brake for the locomotive and tender, all operated by the automatic brake valve, without any additional positions.

Some of the notable improvements incorporated in the B-3 brake valve, which will be appreciated by those who come in contact with it, are: the use of tap bolts instead of screws to fasten the valve cover to the body. Port O is bored instead of being drilled through the cover. The projection for centering the piston packing leather, EV-107, is on the piston instead of on the follower. A new packing leather can now be applied without removing the piston from the brake valve. It is only necessary to remove the back cap and the follower Other parts of this equipment, such as the pressure controller, the accelerator valve, and the high-speed controller, are each and all fully described and illustrated in the section on the B-2HS equipment.

MANIPULATION.

To apply the automatic brakes on the locomotive and train, move the handle of the brake valve to the graduating notch necessary to make the required brake pipe reduction.

Fig. 106—B-3 Brake Valve.

To release both locomotive and train brakes, move the handle to Running and Straight air release position.

To release the train brakes and hold the locomotive brakes set, move the handle to Automatic release and Straight Air Application position.

To apply the locomotive brakes (Straight Air), move the handle to Full Automatic release and Straight Air Application position.

To release the locomotive brakes move the handle to Running and Straight Air release position

To apply the brakes in an emergency, move the handle quickly to Emergency position and leave it there until the train stops.

In case the automatic brakes are applied by the bursting of a hose, the train parts, or a conductor's valve is opened, place the handle in Lap position to retain the main reservoir pressure.

To graduate off or entirely release the locomotive brakes while holding the train brakes applied, use the lever safety valve to make the required reduction.

The handle of the brake valve will be found to work freely and easily at all times, as the pressure on the main slide valve does not exceed the maximum brake pipe pressure.

The cylinder gauge will show at all times the pressure in the locomotive brake cylinder and should be observed in brake manipulations.

Where there are two or more locomotives in a train, cut-out cock No. 1 should be turned to close the brake pipe and the brake valve handle carried in Running and Straight Air release position on all locomotives except the one from which the brakes are operated.

In case it becomes necessary to cut out the Straight Air brake, close cut-out cock No 3, located in the straight air pipe.

To cut out the automatic brake on the engine, close cut-out cock No. 6, located in the pipe connecting the triple valve with the double check valve. By locating the cut-out cock at this point the auxiliary reservoir will remain charged if the brake is cut out, and can be cut in immediately should it be so desired. This cut-out cock and also cut-out cock No. 3 are special; they are of the three-way pattern and when turned off, drain the pipes leading to the double check valve, which insures the check valve remaining seated in the direction of the closed

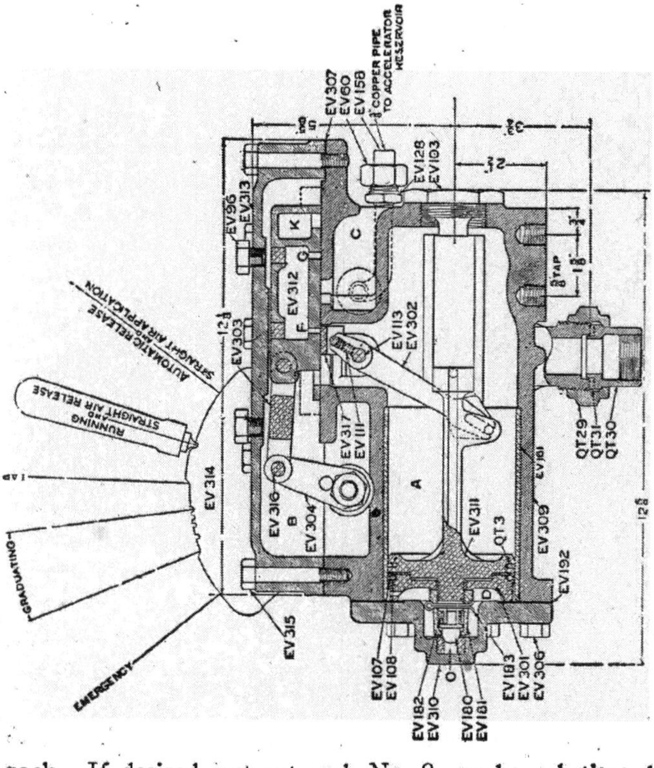

Fig. 107.

cock. If desired, cut-out cock No. 8 can be substituted for cock No. 6; the latter is, however, recommended.

The main reservoir cock No. 4 is to cut off the supply of air when removing any of the apparatus except the governor.

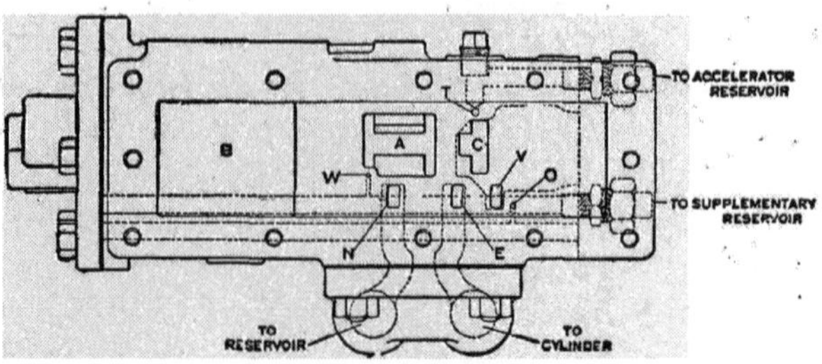

Fig. 108.

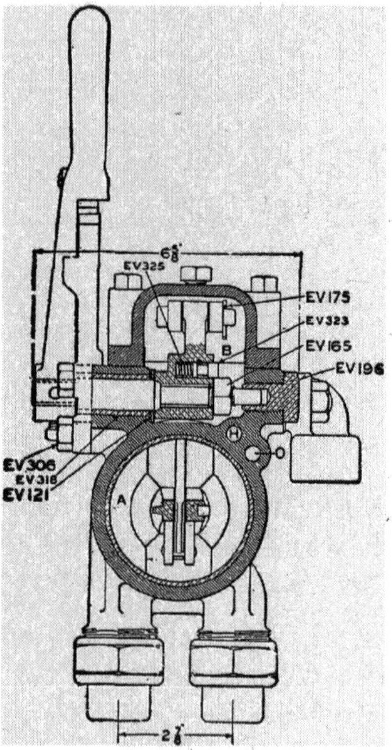

Fig. 109.

The straight air controller is to limit the pressure in the driver, truck and tender brake cylinders for the straight air brake, and should be adjusted to 40 pounds pressure.

Cut-out cocks Nos. 5, 6 and 7 are recommended when truck brake is used, their purpose being fully understood. Nos 9 and 10 can be added, if desired, so that the driver brake cylinders, and reservoir can be cut out, and engine truck brake operated by truck brake reservoir.

B-3 BRAKE VALVE.

Figure 107 is a longitudinal side section of the brake valve (Running position), showing the main slide valve EV 312, and how the graduating valve EV 317 is controlled by the piston EV 311 and lever EV 302, also port O in the back cap closed by the vent valve, EV 180. This view also shows the different positions of the brake valve handle. Fig. 109 is a cross section through the valve (rear view). Fig. 110 is a cross section through the main slide valve, EV 312. This view shows the main reservoir and brake pipe connection. It also shows the location of passage H, which connects the supplementary reservoir and chamber D, back of piston EV 311, also port O drilled to the slide valve seat and cavity R in the slide valve. Fig. 108 is a top view of the valve with the cover, slide valve and handle removed, showing the seat and connections for the straight air and divided reservoir pipes. A' shows the opening through the slide valve seat to the brake valve chamber A, beneath the slide valve. B is a cavity back of the slide valve seat, into which the air flows from the main reservoir pipe, although all the space under the valve cover and above the slide valve is known as chamber B. C is the exhaust passage. V is through to the exhaust passage and is an exhaust port for the straight air brake in running, and straight air release positions,

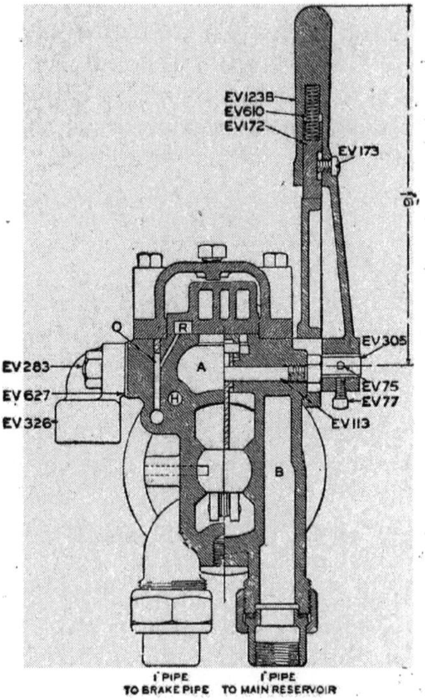

Fig. 110.

and is also an exhaust port for the air from chamber D, through port O in the release, running and lap positions. Port T is to the accelerator reservoir. Port W is to the passage H and the supplementary reservoir. The location of port O in the seat is also shown.

Port O is used for the purpose of venting air from chamber D to the atmosphere, so as to permit piston EV 311 to return to its normal position (Fig. 107), when releasing brakes. It runs from the vent valve seat through the back cap, lengthwise through the body of the brake valve to a point shown in Fig. 110, thence up to the seat of the slide valve. It is connected to the exhaust passage by cavity R in the slide valve, and port V in the seat, in full release, running and lap positions.

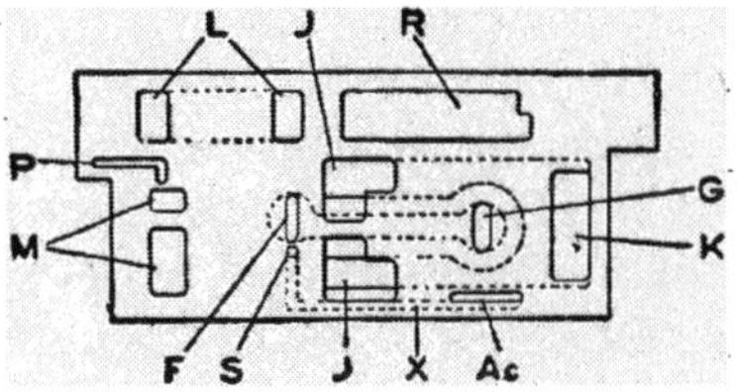

Fig. 111.

Chamber D air is prevented from escaping to the atmosphere in these positions by the vent valve EV 180 on the end of piston EV.311. Just before the slide valve reaches the first graduating notch, it covers port O, so that when the piston moves forward to automatically close the service exhaust port F, and unseats vent valve EV 180, chamber D air only gets to the face of the slide valve. When the brake valve is placed in the full release, running or lap positions, air from chamber D flows through port O, cavity R and port V to the atmosphere until the pressure in chamber D is slightly below that in chamber A (brake pipe), when the brake pipe pressure being the greater it forces piston EV 311 to the position shown in Fig. 107, seating the vent valve, and preventing further escape of chamber D air.

EV 326 is a pipe bracket bolted to the side of the brake valve. It has two pipe connections, one to the main reservoir and the other to the brake cylinders. Dotted lines show the cored passage from the main reservoir connection to port N, and from port E to the cylinder pipe connection.

Figure 111 shows the face of the slide valve. F and G are the service exhaust ports and are connected by a passage through the center of the slide valve. J and K are the emergency exhaust ports connected by passages on each side of the central passage, connecting F and G. S is a small port connected by passage X to the elongated port Ac, which registers with port T in the seat in all the service application positions. P is a groove whose function is to connect port W and the supplementary reservoir with brake pipe pressure in release and running positions. L is a passage through which air passes from the main reservoir pipe to the brake cylinder pipe in straight air application position R is a cavity connecting ports E and V in the running and straight air release positions, to release the straight air brake, and O and V in release, running and lap positions. It also permits the partial opening of port N to E in the last graduating notch and full opening in emergency position. Ports M are through the slide valve and are for charging the brake pipe.

Main reservoir air, reduced to brake pipe pressure by the pressure controller, flows into chamber B. The slide valve EV 312 controls the flow of air from the main reservoir to the brake pipe, and from the brake pipe to the atmosphere. The brake pipe is connected to chamber

A. Discharge of brake pipe air to the atmosphere for service applications occurs through ports F and G, and exhaust passage C, but for emergency applications through ports J and K and exhaust passage C. In full automatic release position air is free to pass from the main reservoir to the brake pipe through ports M, and past the end of the slide valve EV 312. In the running position, ports M only are open between the main reservoir and brake pipe, but they are sufficiently large to permit release of train brakes. Small slide valve EV 317 is a

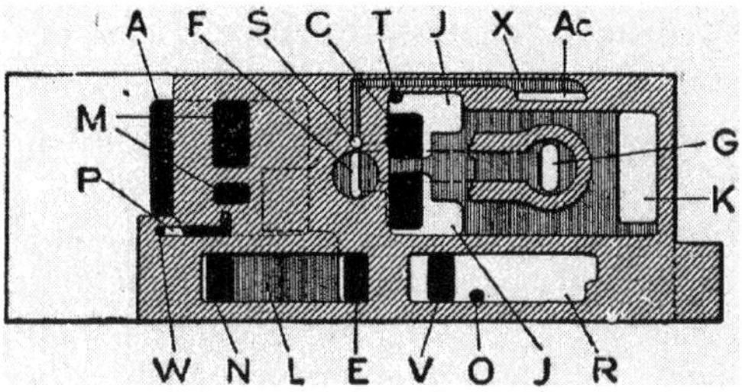

Fig. 112—Release Position.

cut-off or graduating valve operated by piston EV 311 and lever EV 312. In service applications it automatically laps port F and stops the discharge of brake pipe air, when the brake pipe reduction corresponding to the service graduating notch in which the handle is placed has been made. Piston EV 311, which is exposed on one side to brake pipe pressure and on the other to chamber D or supplementary reservoir pressure, through the agency of lever EV 302 causes valve EV 317 to move automatically whatever distance is necessary to close port F.

AUTOMATIC RELEASE AND STRAIGHT AIR APPLICATION POSITION (FIG. 112). The purpose of this position is to promptly release and recharge the automatic brakes and to apply the straight air brakes, or retain the pressure in the locomotive and tender brake cylinders In this position air flows directly from chamber B (main reservoir), into chamber A (brake pipe), past the end of the slide valve and through ports M. Port O is open to the atmosphere through port V to permit piston EV 311 to return to its normal position. Port T is open to the atmosphere through J and C. The supplementary reservoir is being charged to brake pipe pressure through groove P and port W from chamber A. Port E is brought into communication with port N by passage L, permitting air to pass to the locomotive and tender brake cylinders through the straight air pipe and double check valve until shut off by the ¾" pressure controller, the regulating top of which is connected to the straight air pipe and adjusted at 40 pounds. By placing the valve handle about midway between release and running positions the straight air ports can be lapped, making it possible to increase or decrease the brake cylinder pressure as may be necessary.

RUNNING AND STRAIGHT AIR RELEASE POSITION (FIG. 113). This is the proper position in which to place the handle when wishing to release the train and locomotive brakes simultaneously, or to release the straight air brake when it only has been applied. Air passes from the main reservoir to the brake pipe through ports M. Port N is closed. Port E is brought into communication with port V and the atmosphere by cavity R, releasing the straight air brake. Ports O and T are still open to the atmosphere as in full release position. Port T is open to the atmosphere through J and C in release and running positions, so that in case of a release following a partial application, the accelerator reser-

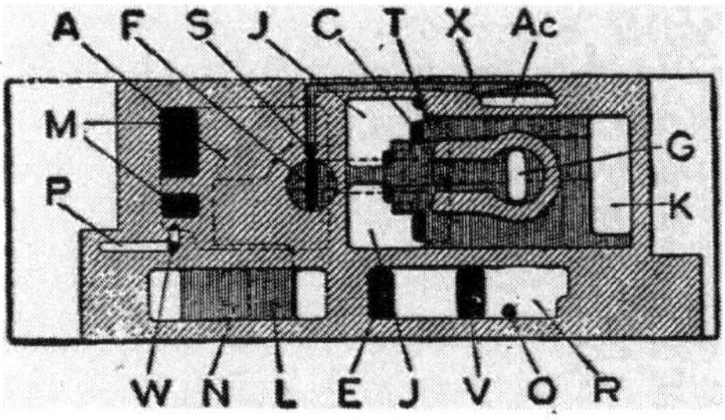

Fig. 113—Running Position.

voir pressure can escape and prevent the operation of the accelerator valve. Groove P still holds port W in communication with the brake pipe pressure in chamber A.

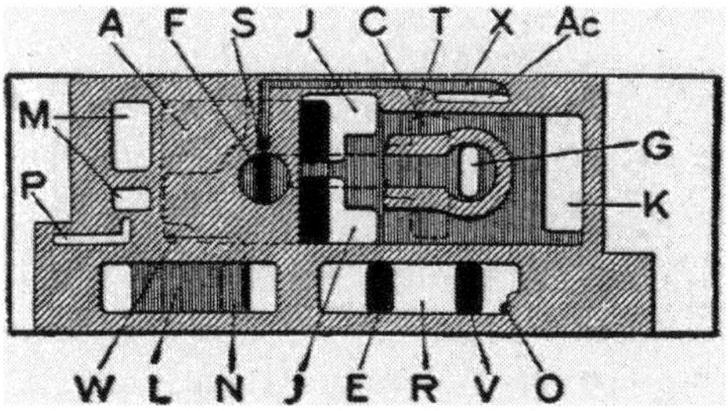

Fig. 114—Lap Position.

LAP POSITION (Fig. 114). The brake valve handle should be placed in this position when a hose bursts, the train parts or a conductor's valve is opened to save the main reservoir air. All ports are closed in this position excepting port O, which is open to the atmosphere through port V and the exhaust passage in release, running and lap positions.

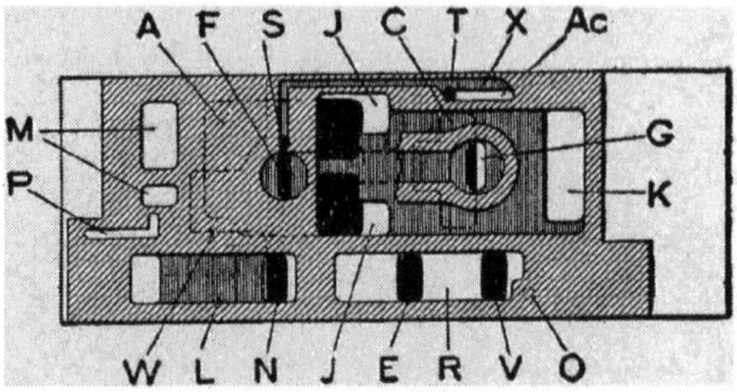

Fig. 115—First Graduating Notch.

SERVICE APPLICATION POSITION (FIGS. 304 and 305). This position is for the purpose of gradually applying the brakes and is divided into five graduating positions designated by notches on the quadrant. The reductions ob-

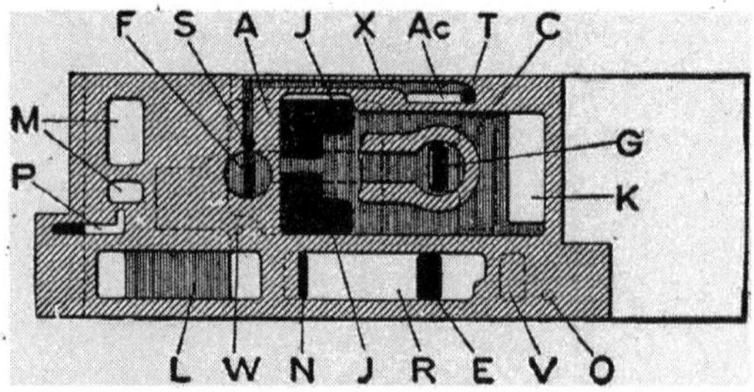

Fig. 116—Last Graduating Notch.

tained in the different notches are respectively, 5, 8, 11, 15 and 23 pounds. The amount of the initial reduction should always be governed by the length of the train, speed, grade, etc. Always place the handle of the brake valve in the notch which will give the required reduction. When the handle of the brake valve is moved to the first graduating notch the slide valve is in the position shown. Port O is closed to prevent the escape of chamber D pressure. Port F is moved back of the graduating valve EV 317 and port G registers with the exhaust port C. Brake pipe air now flows to the atmosphere. It also flows through port S, passage X, and port T to the accelerator valve. As soon as the pressure in the brake pipe reduces, the pressure in chamber D now being greater than brake pipe pressure, it begins to expand to equalize with the brake pipe pressure. In doing so it moves piston EV 311 forward. The piston carries with it the lower end of the graduating valve lever EV 302, which is so proportioned that the graduating valve EV 317 on the other end of it is moved back just far enough to close ports F and S when the pressures in chamber D and the brake pipe have equalized.

This stops the flow of air from the brake pipe to the atmosphere, and to the accelerator reservoir (see accelerator valve). This action is called automatic lap, and it takes place in all of the graduating positions.

A further reduction of the brake pipe pressure is made by moving the handle back to any of the service notches, the piston moving farther forward for each successive reduction. The action of the brake valve is the same, and the ports are in the same relation to each other in all service positions of the brake valve, except the last graduating position. In this position a partial opening of port N admits air slowly to the locomotive and tender brake cylinders through cavity R and port E up to the adjustment of the controller on the straight air pipe. This is to insure full braking pressure on the engine with a full application regardless of piston travel and brake cylinder leakage.

EMERGENCY APPLICATION POSITION (FIG. 117). This position is for the purpose of producing a quick, heavy

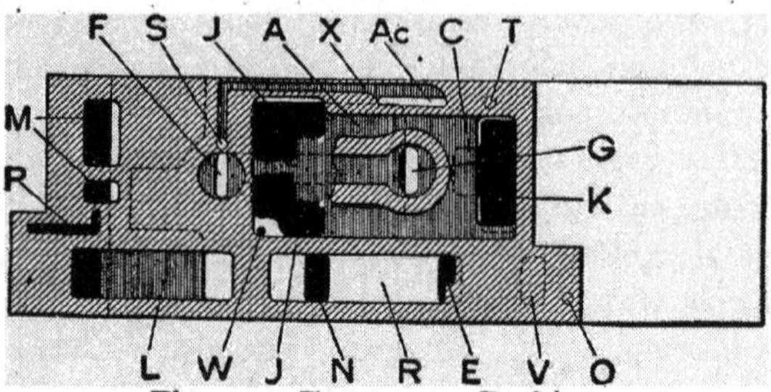

Fig. 117—Emergency Position.

reduction in brake pipe pressure so that all triple valves on the train will operate in quick action and apply the brakes in the shortest possible time.

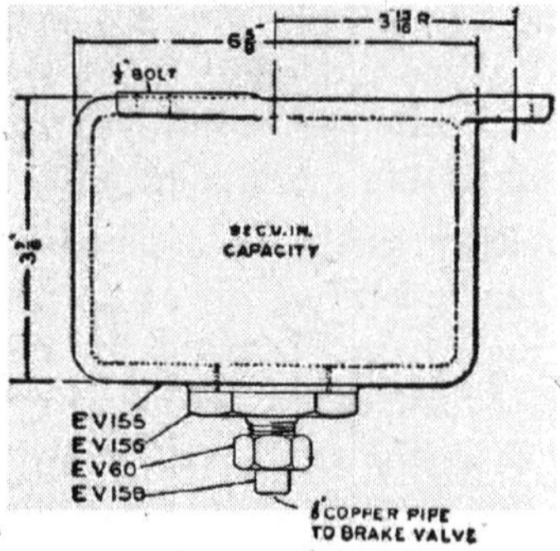

Fig. 118—Supplementary Reservoir.
Used with Switch Engine Equipment, Schedule B3-S.

Ports J register with chamber A and K with the exhaust port C, allowing brake pipe air to escape rapidly to the atmosphere. Cavity R allows air from the main reservoir to pass through ports N and E to the locomotive brake cylinders, and the full pressure of the straight air brake is maintained on the engine.

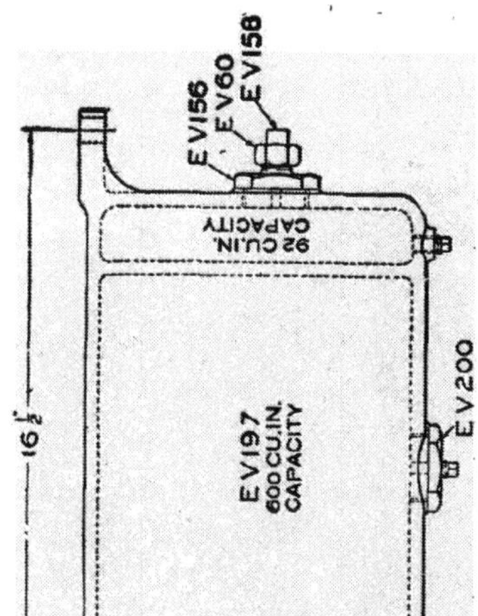

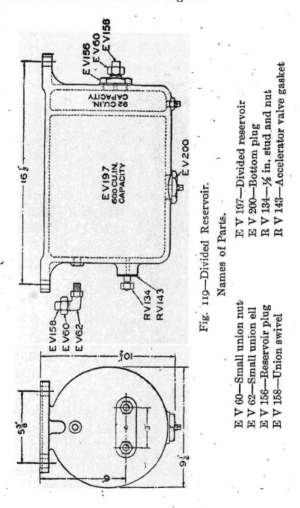

Fig. 119—Divided Reservoir.

Names of Parts.

E V 60—Small union nut	E V 197—Divided reservoir
E V 62—Small union ell	E V 200—Bottom plug
E V 156—Reservoir plug	R V 134—½ in. stud and nut
E V 158—Union swivel	R V 143—Accelerator valve gasket

TYPE J TRIPLE VALVES.

The Type J triple valve of the New York Air Brake Company has been designed to meet the conditions of all classes of passenger train service.

Fig. 120—J-6 Style A Triple Valve.

The valve is made in two styles, Style "A" and Style "B," and both are quick action, automatic and of the pipeless type. Suitable pipe connections are provided for in the type J triple valve, whether it is connected to a bracket or direct to the brake cylinder.

Style "A" is fitted with a high emergency pressure cap, and 32 R. V. safety valve in connection with a supplementary reservoir, and is so constructed as to guard against sliding of wheels when making the slow-speed or ordinary station stops, but retains the maximum pressure throughout in emergency applications, when it is necessary to stop in the shortest possibe distance. Style "B" performs the same functions as Style "A," except those in connection with the high emergency pressure cap, safety valve and supplementary reservoir.

The following are the principal features of the Type J triple valves:

The auxiliary reservoirs are recharged in about the same time required to release the air from the brake cylinders, therefore, the maximum braking pressure is available at all times.

Figure 121 shows a vertical side section, and a vertical cross section of the J-5 triple Style "A." Fig. 122 shows the different ports, and cavities of this valve in their actual positions, and their relation to each other may be readily understood by locating the letters used to designate them in Figs. 122 to 126.

FULL RELEASE AND CHARGING POSITION.

Figure 123 shows the valve in full release and charging position. Air from the brake pipe enters at A, passes to chambers B and C, then through feed groove D to chamber E, and the auxiliary reservoir. Air from passage A also unseats check valve 1, and passes through chamber F and port G to chamber E, and the auxiliary reservoir. In this position auxiliary reservoir pressure flows through port H in graduating valve 2, port I in slide valve 3, and port J in the seat, to the supplementary reservoir, and

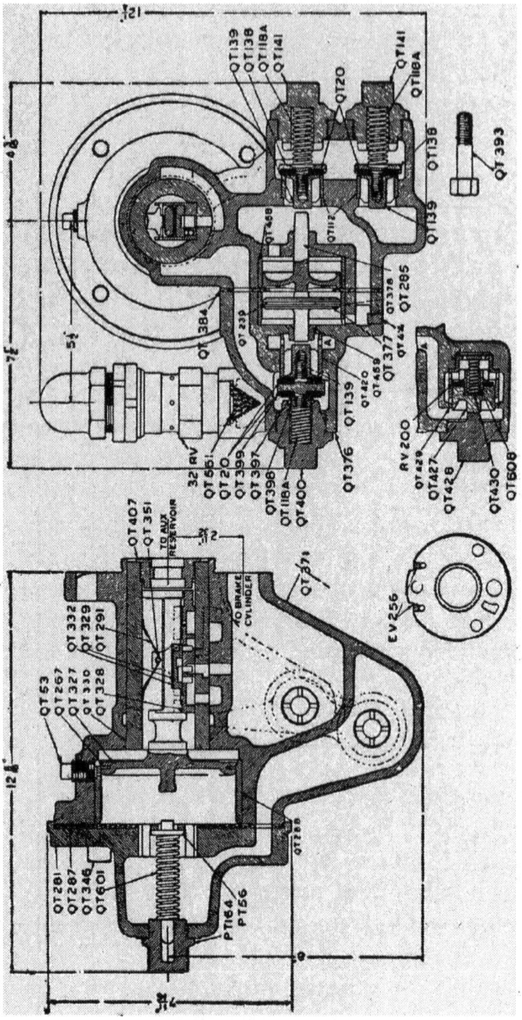

Fig. 121—Sections of J-5 Style A Triple Valve.

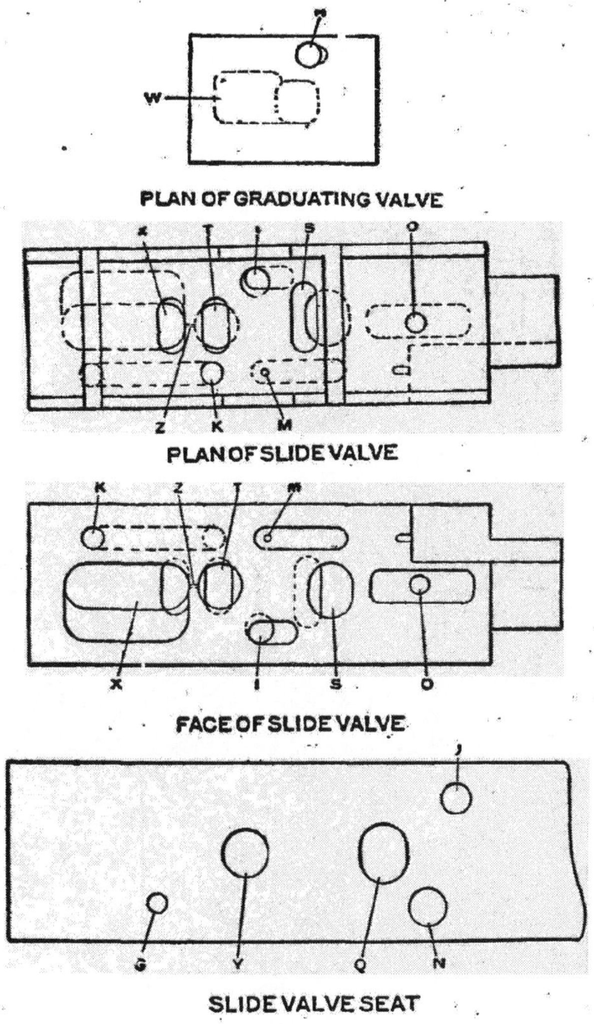
W
PLAN OF GRADUATING VALVE
T
S
O
Z
K
M
PLAN OF SLIDE VALVE
K
Z
T
X
S
O
FACE OF SLIDE VALVE
J
G
Y
Q
N
SLIDE VALVE SEAT

Fig. 122

brake cylinder pressure flows through port Q in the seat, ports T and Z in the slide valve 3, cavity W in graduating valve 2, port X in slide valve 3, and port Y in the seat to the atmosphere, thus recharging the auxiliary and supplementary reservoirs and releasing the brakes.

SERVICE APPLICATION.

Figure 124 shows the valve in service position. A slight reduction of the brake pipe pressure at the brake valve reduces the pressure in chamber C, and piston 10 is

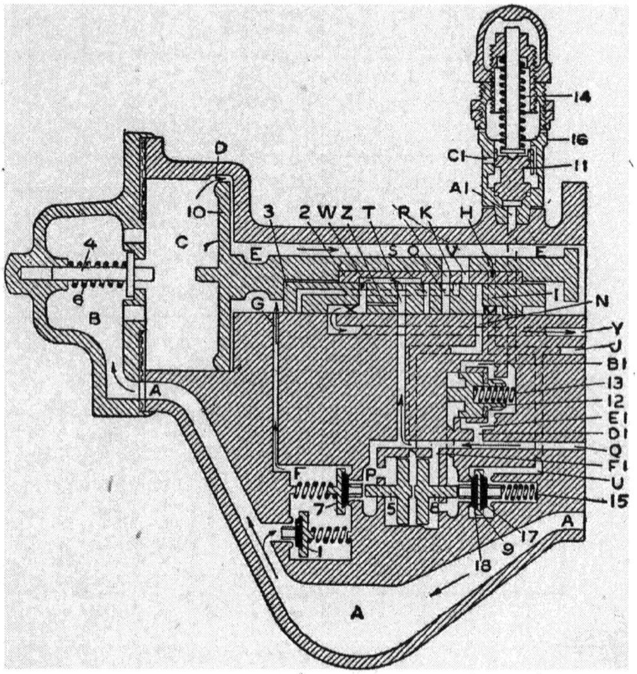

Fig. 123—Full Release and Charging Position.

moved to the left by the greater pressure which is then contained in chamber E, and the auxiliary reservoir, carrying graduating valve 2, and slide valve 3 to the position shown in Fig. 124. Auxiliary reservoir air now flows through ports R, S and Q, to the brake cylinder. The service ports are so proportioned as to insure against obtaining an emergency application when making a service application. In service applications the safety valve which is set to close at 60 pounds, is in communication with the brake cylinders through ports A1, E1, D1, and Q, and the brake cylinder pressure is kept within the adjustment of the safety valve to prevent danger of sliding wheels.

LAP POSITION.

When a light reduction of brake-pipe pressure is made and the auxiliary reservoir pressure becomes slightly less than brake pipe pressure in chamber C, the brake pipe pressure moves piston 10, and graduating valve 2 to lap position, as shown in Fig. 125, closing all ports, and stopping the flow of auxiliary reservoir pressure to the brake cylinder. A slight brake pipe reduction will again move the valve to service position, after which it will again move to light service lap, or full service lap, (according to its previous position) both of which are identical, except that in full service lap, slide valve 3 would occupy the position shown in Fig. 124, while in light service lap it would occupy the position shown in Fig. 125. This operation can be repeated until the auxiliary reservoir and brake pipe pressures become equalized.

RELEASE AND RECHARGE.

When brake pipe pressure is restored after a service application, or when the valve is in lap position, the pis-

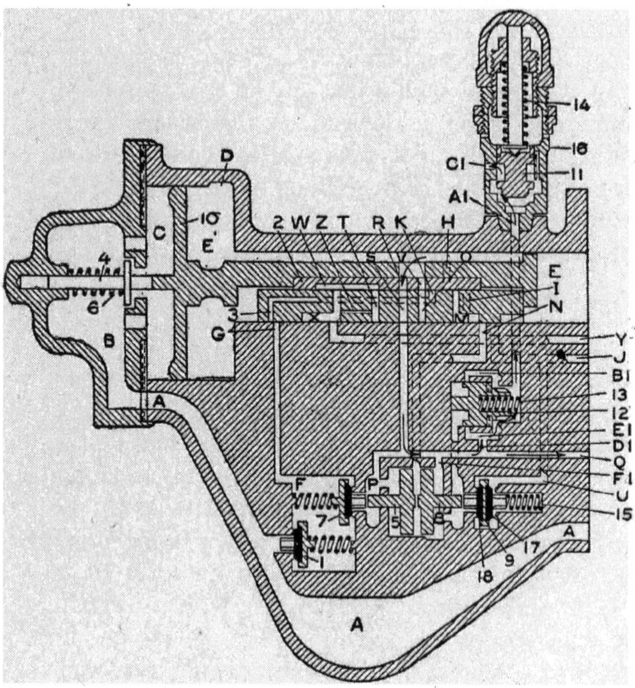

Fig. 124—Full Service Position.

ton, slide valve and graduating valve are returned to the position shown in Fig. 123, and the brakes released, and auxiliary reservoirs recharged as described under full release and charging position.

EMERGENCY POSITION.

Figure 126 shows the valve in emergency position. This position is caused by putting the brake valve handle in emergency position, or from the conductor's valve, or

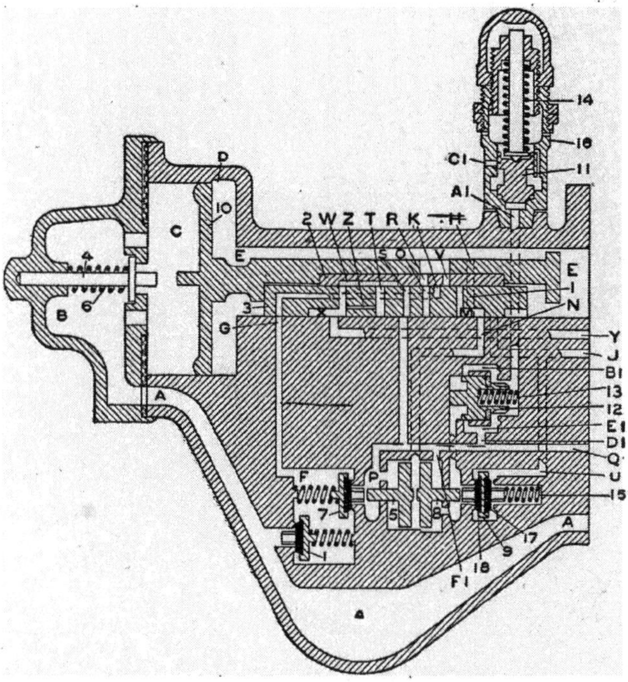

Fig. 125—Light Service Lap Position.

any condition that suddenly reduces the brake pipe pressure. Auxiliary reservoir pressure flows through port N, moving pistons 5 and 8 to the left and right respectively

tively, unseating quick action valve 7, and emergency valve 9, causing check valve 1 to be unseated by brake pipe pressure, which then flows to port Q, and the brake cylinder, while at the same time supplementary reservoir

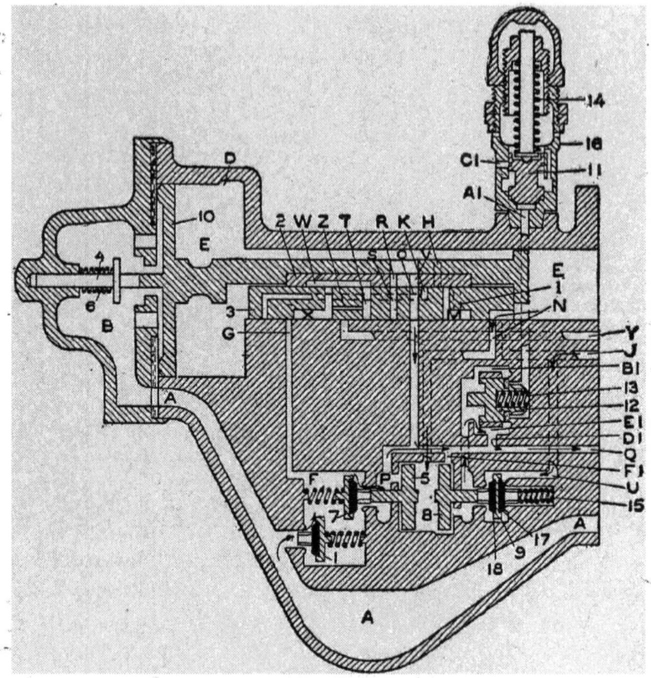

Fig. 126—Emergency Position.

pressure flows from port J around emergency valve 9 to chamber around the face of valve 12, moving this valve to its seat, and closing communication to port A1, and the safety valve, then flowing through passage D1, to port Q and the brake cylinder, thus obtaining the maximum brake cylinder pressure and holding same throughout the stop, or until released in the regular way. During the application and when the brake pipe and brake cylinder pressures become equal, check valve 1 will be returned to its seat, by the spring, preventing brake cylinder pressure from flowing back into the brake pipe. When the brakes are released after an emergency application, spring 13 will move valve 12 to its normal position, as shown in Fig. 123.

SAFETY VALVE.

The action of the safety valve used in connection with the J triple valve is practically the same as with other triples previously described. Therefore it will not be necessary to give a detailed description of it here.

NEW YORK, TYPE K TRIPLE VALVE.

This triple valve is manufactured in two sizes; K-5 to be used with 8-inch brake cylinders, and the K-6 to be used with the 10-inch brake cylinders. Each valve is marked with its designation on the side of the valve body, and the K-6 may also be distinguished from the K-5 by the fact that the K-6 has three bolt holes, whereas the K-5 has two bolt holes in the reservoir bolting flange.

These triple valves perform all the functions of the older type of quick action triple valves, as well as three additional functions, viz.:—quick service, restricted release and uniform recharge. They can be used in the same train with the older type of triples, and they improve the action of the latter when so used. With the exception of the slide valve, all of the moving parts of

K-5 and K-6 are identical. The K-5 and K-6 triples are particularly well adapted for the proper operation of

Fig. 127—The K-6 Triple Valve.

long trains, but give the desired results in any length train.

As the action of the K-5 and K-6 valves is the same, the K-6 will be dealt with in the following pages.

The brake pipe, auxiliary reservoir, and brake cylinder connections are shown in Fig. 128. The brake pipe connects at the union swivel QT-30. The opening marked "To brake cylinder" comes opposite one end of the tube

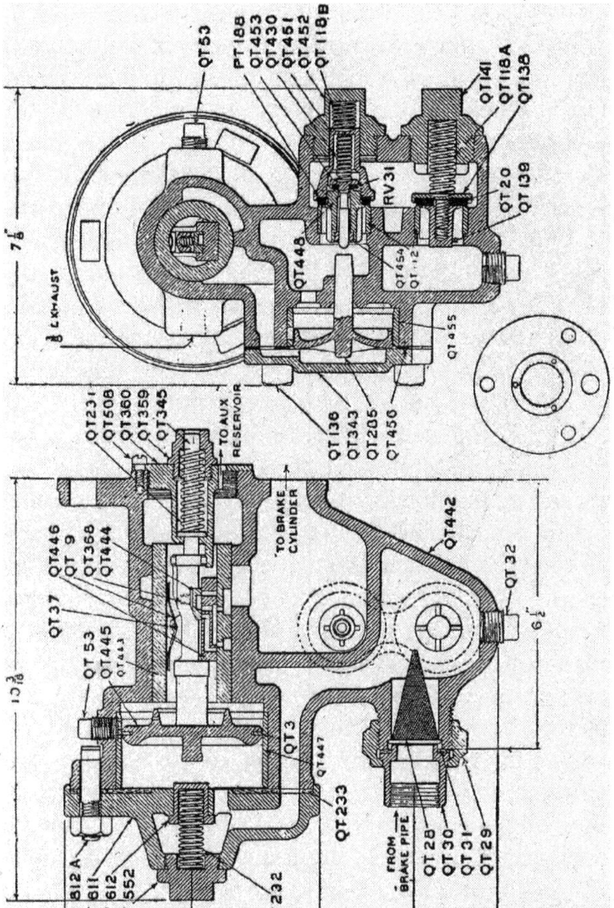

Fig. 128—K-6 Triple Valve.

which leads through the auxiliary reservoir to the brake cylinder when the valve is bolted to the auxiliary reservoir. Provision is made for the free passage of air through piston stop spring box QT-360.

Referring to Fig. 129, port Q in the slide valve seat is the exhaust port to the atmosphere. Ports I and J lead to the brake cylinder. Port W leads to the emergency piston. Exhaust cavity P in the slide valve is used in the normal release of the brake. The lower end of port M in the slide valve is the exhaust port connecting the brake cylinder with the atmosphere in the restricted release position, connecting port J from the brake cylinder with port Q to the atmosphere by means of port S, drilled from cavity P into port M, through the slide valve from bottom to top, and longitudinally above cavity P. The upper end of port M is controlled by the graduating valve and connects the brake cylinder through cavity P and port R by means of graduating valve cavity N, ports M and Q, with the atmosphere in the normal release following restricted release position, to hasten the escape of brake cylinder pressure in case the release of the brake is not entirely completed. Port T which passes directly through the slide valve is controlled at its upper end by the graduating valve, and carries the auxiliary reservoir pressure to the face of the emergency piston QT-285 (Fig. 128), in the quick service position, by means of graduating valve port O, and port W in the slide valve seat. Port U also by the graduating valve at its upper end, its lower end registering with port I to the brake cylinder in service application The graduating valve controls the upper ends of ports M, R, T and U. The face of the graduating valve contains a cavity N, for the purpose of connecting together ports R and M in the normal release, after re-

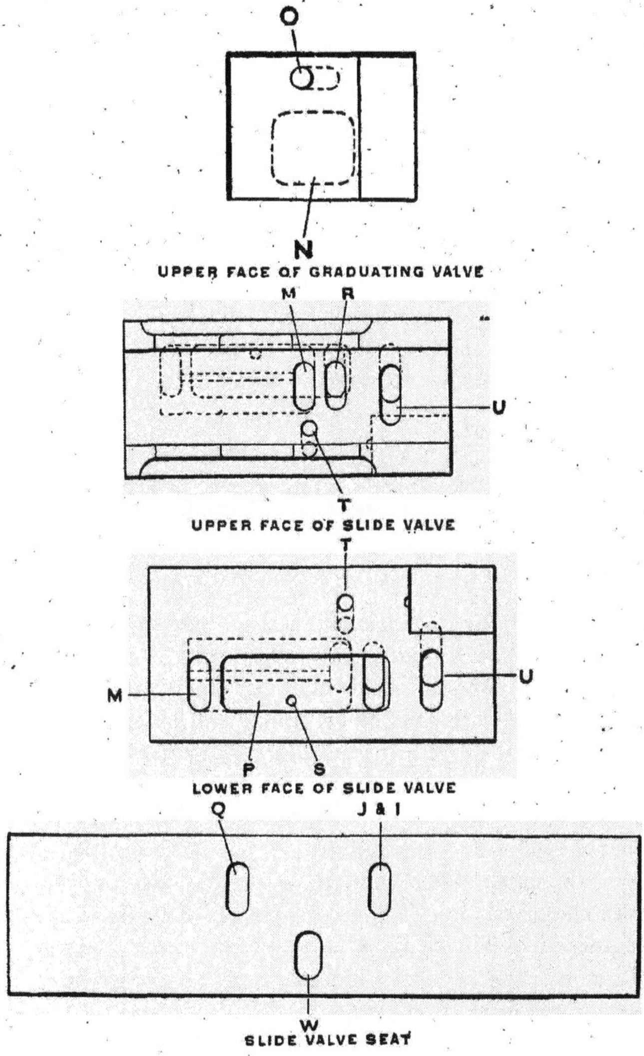
O
N
UPPER FACE OF GRADUATING VALVE
M
R
U
T
UPPER FACE OF SLIDE VALVE
T
M
U
P
S
LOWER FACE OF SLIDE VALVE
Q
J & I
W
SLIDE VALVE SEAT

Fig. 129.

stricted release position, and a combined port and cavity O which controls the flow of auxiliary air through ports T and W to the face of the emergency piston in the "serial service" position.

Figure 129 shows the relative position of the ports and cavities of the slide valve, graduating valve and slide valve seat of the New York K-6 triple valve. As it is difficult to show all of these in their actual positions relative to each other in a single section, the diagrammatic cuts are made to show the principal positions with all ports and passages shown in one plane. In preparing these cuts, the actual proportion, and mechanical construction of the triple valve was disregarded for the purpose of making the connections of the ports and the operation more easily understood. The same designating letters are used for the same ports in all the illustrations.

NORMAL RELEASE AND RECHARGING POSITION.

Referring to Fig 130, air from the brake pipe enters the triple valve at A, passes through passage B to chamber C, through passage D to chamber E, through feed ports F, G and H to chamber K and the auxiliary reservoir The rate of charging the auxiliary reservoir in this position is approximately the same as with the older type of triple valve (H-1) on the same size reservoir. While the piston 6, and slide valve 2, are in this position, cavity P in slide valve 2 connects brake cylinder passage J, and exhaust passage Q, giving a normal exhaust to the atmosphere. When piston 6 is in the position shown in Fig. 130, port F is partly closed so as to reduce to a minimum the back flow from auxiliary to brake pipe, however, when brake pipe pressure at any time is slightly above auxiliary pressure, piston 6 will be moved to the right against the power of spring 10 fully uncovering port F. Brake pipe air can then feed more rapidly to the auxiliary by means of port F, and the combined capacity of ports G and H. As soon as the pressures become practically equalized, the power of spring 10 will again return piston 6 to the position shown in Fig. 130, and air will

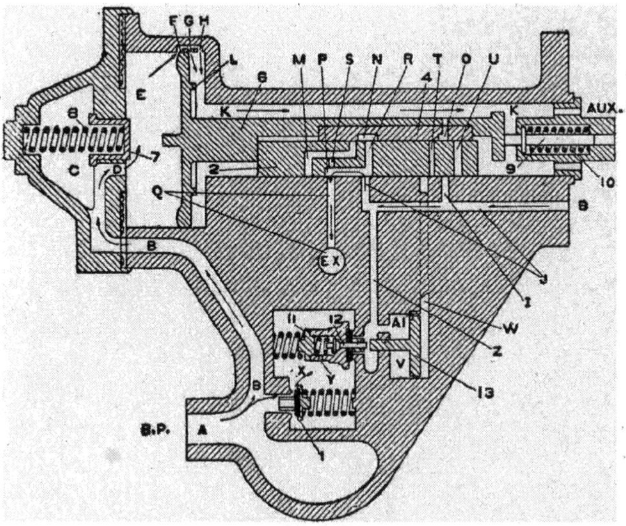

Fig. 130—Normal Release and Recharging Position.

flow from brake pipe to auxiliary until these pressures are equalized. At the same time the auxiliary is being charged, brake pipe pressure unseats check valve 1, and chamber X is charged equal to brake pipe pressure.

SERVICE POSITION.

When it is desired to make a service application, a gradual reduction of brake pipe pressure is made with the brake valve, and this reduction in chamber E causes piston 6 to move to the left until the stem of piston 6 comes in contact with graduating stem 7 which is held in place by spring 8. This movement of the piston carries graduating valve 4 and slide valve 2 to the position shown in

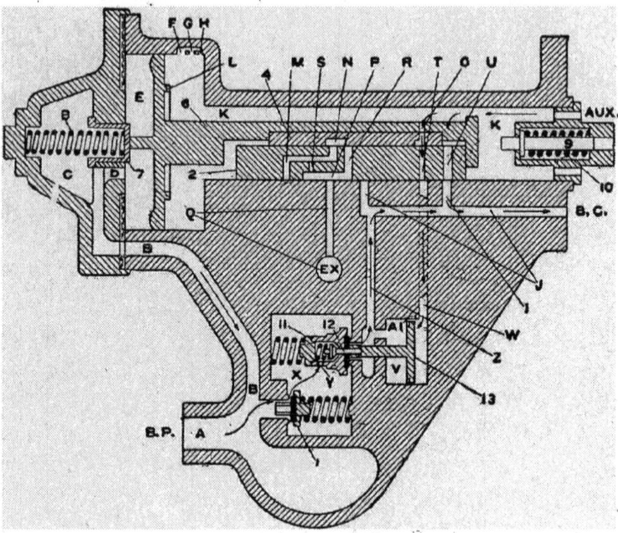

Fig. 131—Service Position.

Fig. 131. Passage J is now cut off from passage Q leading to exhaust port, and auxiliary air passes through port U in slide valve 2 and port J to the brake cylinder, and at the same time auxiliary air feeds through port O in graduating valve 4, and port T in slide valve 2, and passage W leading to the emergency piston, where pressure now builds up sufficient to unseat inner check valve 12, thus reducing the pressure in chamber X. Brake pipe pressure will now unseat check valve 1, allowing brake pipe air to flow past this valve through the small port y, past inner check valve 12 into chamber V, through passages Z and J to the brake cylinder. In this position of emergency piston 13, by pass port A-1 is open to the right of the piston allowing auxiliary pressure which has built up, on the right of emergency piston 13 to equalize with brake cylinder pressure on the left of the piston in chamber V. Any pressure that might accumulate at the right of piston 13 in excess of that sufficient to unseat inner check valve 12 will be relieved through by-pass port A-1. By this means a serial venting is obtained from brake pipe to brake cylinder in service application.

SERVICE LAP POSITION.

When the desired brake pipe reduction has been made, and the brake valve exhaust has closed, as the relative capacity of ports U and O is such that auxiliary pressure will be reduced at a more rapid rate than brake pressure will reduce through port Y, the greater pressure in chamber E will cause piston 6 and graduating valve 4 to move to the right and assume the position shown in Fig. 132, known as service lap position. When brake pipe reduction ceases, and auxiliary pressure, by flowing through ports U, I and J to the brake cylinder becomes slightly less than brake pipe pressure, piston 6 and graduating valve 4 are moved to the right until the shoulder of piston 6 comes in contact with the end of slide valve 2.

This movement closes ports U and T, thus preventing any further flow of air from the auxiliary to brake cylinder. If it is desired to make a heavier application, a further reduction of brake pipe pressure is made, and piston 6 will again be moved to the left, carrying with it graduating valve 4, uncovering feed port U, permitting additional air from the auxiliary to feed to the brake cylinder. As soon as auxiliary pressure is again reduced below that of the brake pipe, piston 6 will again be re-

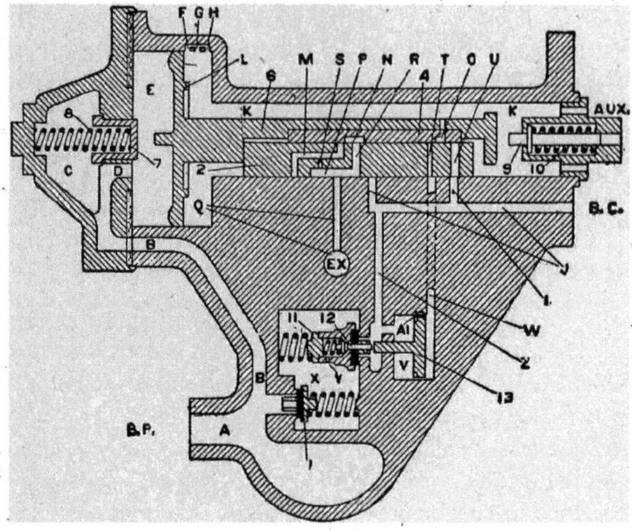

Fig. 132—Service Lap Position.

turned to the right, carrying with it graduating valve 4, and closing port U. This action can be repeated until the auxiliary reservoir and brake cylinder pressures equalize.

RESTRICTED RELEASE.

When it is desired to put the triple valves in restricted release position, air is admitted to the brake pipe in sufficient volume to force piston 6, slide valve 2 and graduating valve 4 to the position shown in Fig. 133. In this position the upper end of port M is closed by graduating valve 4, and air from the brake cylinder will pass through passage J into cavity P, up through small port S into pas-

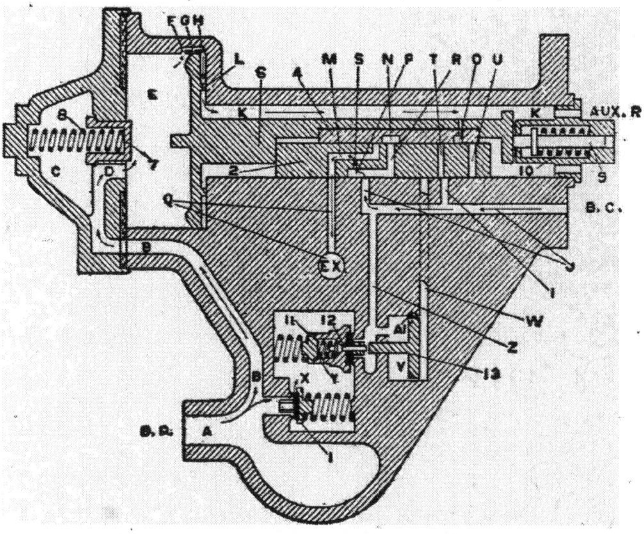

Fig. 133—Restricted Release Position.

sage M to exhaust port Q, thus restricting the release of air from the brake cylinder, the flow of air to the atmosphere being limited to the capacity of small port S. When piston 6 is held in the position shown in Fig. 133, the triple piston packing ring covers port G, limiting recharging of the auxiliary to the capacity of port H in the triple cylinder bushing.

NORMAL RELEASE AFTER RESTRICTED RELEASE.

When piston 6 moves to the position shown in Fig. 133, it moves stem 9 to the right, compressing spring 10 and when auxiliary pressure becomes nearly equal to brake pipe pressure, spring 10 forces stem 9, piston 6 and grad-

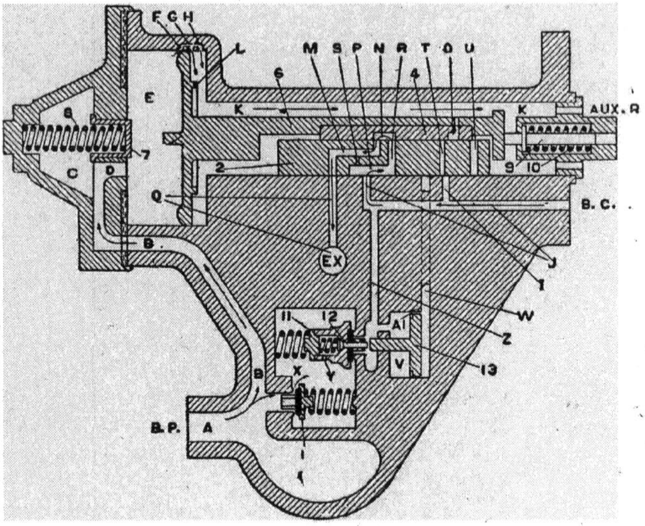

Fig. 134—Normal Release After Restricted Release.

uating valve 4 to the left, to the position shown in Fig. 134. In this position cavity N in the graduating valve connects brake cylinder passage J with passage R, and uncovers the upper end of port M, thus connecting to the exhaust port Q, giving a free exhaust from brake cylinder to atmosphere.

EMERGENCY POSITION.

When an emergency application of the brakes is desired, a quick reduction of the brake pipe pressure is made, causing piston 6, slide valve 2 and graduating valve 4 to move to the position shown in Fig. 135. In this po-

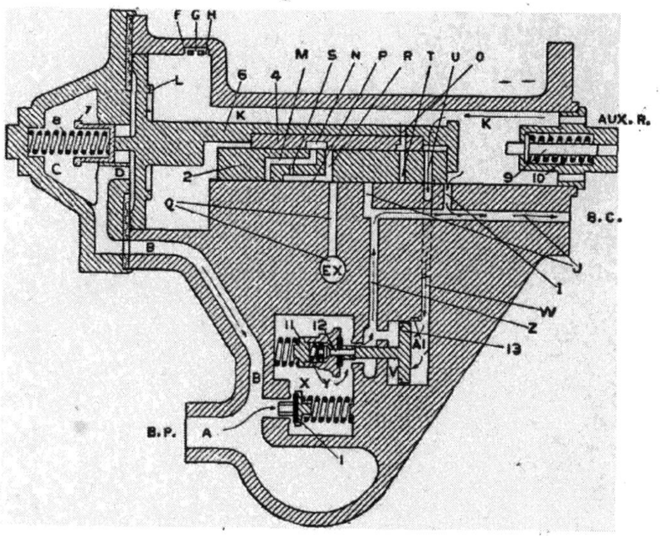

Fig. 135—Emergency Position.

sition piston 6 seats on the leather gasket, forming an air tight joint and prevents leakage of air from the auxiliary reservoir to the brake pipe. With slide valve 2 and graduating valve 4 in the position shown, port U registers with passage W, permitting air from the auxiliary reservoir to flow to emergency piston 13, forcing piston to the extreme left, unseating quick action valve 11, permitting brake pipe air to flow past check valve 1 and quick action valve 11, through passages Z and J to the brake cylinder.

Due to the large opening through ports U and W, auxiliary reservoir pressure is admitted to the right of piston 13 in such quantity as to force the piston beyond by-pass port A-1, thus preventing the power on the right of the piston being destroyed before emergency is completed. At the same time air from the auxiliary reservoir passes through ports I and J to the brake cylinder, causing a quick and full application of the brakes

When the brake pipe and brake cylinder have become nearly equalized, check valve 1 will be returned to its seat by the spring QT-118-A, preventing any back leakage from the brake cylinder to the brake pipe. The release of the brakes, following an emergency application is brought about in the same way as following a service application.

QUESTIONS AND ANSWERS.

NEW YORK B-2 H. S. EQUIPMENT.

Q. What are the principal features of the B 2 H. S. equipment?

A. The engine brakes can be operated at all times, either by automatic or independent application, regardless of the location of the engine in a train. They can be graduated off after an application, thus avoiding all shock. All excess pressure is confined to the main reservoir, thus preventing overcharging of the auxiliary reservoirs.

Q. How many, and what are the schedules into which this equipment is divided?

A. Three; as follows: Schedule B 2, single pressure system; Schedule B 2-H. P., double pressure system, and B 2-H. S. double pressure with high speed attachment

Q. What service is the B 2 equipment designed for?

A. For passenger or freight service where but one brake pipe pressure is used.

Q. For what service is the B 2-S equipment?

A. Switch engines.

Q. What service is the B 2-H. P. equipment used in?

A. Freight service, only.

Q. What is the B 2-H. S. equipment?

A. It is a high speed locomotive equipment.

Q What system of regulation is used with the B 2, and B 2-S equipments?

A Single pump governor and single pressure controller.

Q. What system of regulation is employed with the B 2-H. P. and B 2-H. S. equipments?

A. A duplex pump governor, and duplex pressure controller.

Q In what respect does the B 2 brake valve differ from the B and B 1 brake valves?

A. It is constructed so as to embody the features of the pressure controller, and those of united straight air.

Q. How many, and what are the different positions of this brake valve?

A. Six; as follows: release, running, lap, first graduating, last graduating and emergency.

Q. What are the two graduating positions for?

A To give a gradual reduction of brake pipe pressure for service applications.

NEW YORK B-3 EQUIPMENT.

Q. What is the B 3 locomotive brake equipment?

A. It is the New York Air Brake Company's locomotive air brake equipment which has the automatic and straight air operating features combined in one brake valve.

Q. In how many schedules is this equipment furnished?

A. Four

Q. Why these different schedules?

A. To suit the requirements of the different classes of railroad service. Switch engines, for instance, do not require all the parts necessary for road engines.

Q. What are its principal constructive features?

A. (a) It does away entirely with the separate straight

engineer's brake valve. (b) Combines in one engineer's valve all the operative features of the standard automatic engineer's brake valve, and of the straight air brake engineer's valve.

Q. What are its principal operative advantages?

A. (a) But one engineer's valve, with only the usual positions of former styles of automatic valves to manipulate in using either the locomotive straight air brake or the automatic locomotive and train brakes.

Q. What are the principal new operative parts used with the B 3 equipment?

A. (a) B 3 engineer's brake valve; (b) Pressure controller; (c) Accelerator valve; (d) Divided reservoir; (e) High speed controller; (f) Lever safety valve; (g) Quick release valve; (h) Supplementary reservoir.

Q. What are the principal parts of the B 3 brake valve?

A. (a) The main slide valve; (b) Piston; (c) Graduating valve; (d) Vent valve; (e) Supplementary reservoir.

Q. Into how many chambers is the valve divided?

A. Three.

Q. What are these chambers called?

A. Main reservoir, or chamber "B," brake pipe, or chamber "A" and supplementary reservoir, or chamber "D."

Q What separates chamber "B" from chambers "A" and "D?"

A. The main slide valve.

Q. Is full main reservoir pressure carried in chamber "B?"

A. Not when the main reservoir pressure is above the standard brake pipe pressure.

Q. What is the greatest pressure admitted to chamber "B?"

A. The maximum brake pipe pressure.

Q. Why then is chamber "B" called a main reservoir chamber?

A. Because, while the air in chamber "B" does not exceed maximum brake pipe pressure, it is not brake pipe air, as the slide valve is the actual dividing line between the main reservoir and brake pipe, and controls the flow of air from the main reservoir to the brake pipe for the purpose of releasing the brakes and charging the brake pipe and auxiliary reservoirs, it is obvious that chamber "B" must be considered as part of the main reservoir.

Q. Where then does main reservoir pressure begin, and where does it end?

A. It begins at the air pump and ends at the slide valve in chamber "B."

Q. Of what is chamber "A" really a part?

A. It is a part of the brake pipe.

Q. What pressure is carried in chamber "A" at all times?

A. Brake pipe pressure.

Q. Of what use is chamber "D?"

A. It contains the pressure that operates the automatic cut-off of the brake pipe exhaust in service reductions.

Q. What pressure is the air in chamber "D" equal to?

A. It is equal to brake pipe pressure.

Q. What are the duties of the main slide valve?

A. Generally speaking, to admit air to and discharge it from the various parts of the equipment to which air is to be admitted, and from which it has to be discharged. They can best be described by taking each position separately.

B 3 BRAKE VALVE.

Q. How many positions has the B 3 engineer's brake valve?

A. Five positions.

Q. Name them.

A. Automatic release and straight air application position, running and straight air release position, lap position, service application position and emergency application position.

Q. Why is the usual release position called the automatic release and straight air application position with this type of valve?

A. Because, while it is a position in which the automatic brakes on the train can be released, it is also a position in which the locomotive straight air brake can be applied.

Q. When is it used?

A. It is used at a time when it is desired to release the automatic brakes on the train, and to hold the locomotive brake applied, as in holding the slack bunched on grades at the time when releasing the train brakes to recharge the brake pipe and auxiliary reservoirs.

Q. How is the service position of this brake valve arranged?

A. Like all types of New York brake valves, it is divided into five graduating positions designated by notches on the quadrant.

Q. What is the quadrant?

A. The part over which the brake valve handle travels, and on which the various stops, denoting the different positions into which the brake valve is to be placed, are arranged.

Q. What is the effect of placing the valve handle in any one of the service graduating positions?

A. A certain reduction of brake pipe pressure is made.

Q. Is this reduction the same in any notch that the valve handle is placed in?

A. No; it varies with each notch.

Q. What reduction is obtained in the first notch?

A. About five pounds.

Q. If the valve handle is moved directly to the second notch without stopping at the first, what reduction is obtained?

A. About eight pounds.

Q. If the handle is moved directly to the third notch without stopping at either of the first two, what reduction is obtained?

A. About eleven pounds.

Q. If the handle is moved directly to the fourth notch without stopping at either of the first three, what reduction is obtained?

A. About fifteen pounds.

Q. If the handle is moved directly to the fifth notch, what reduction would be made?

A. About twenty-three pounds.

Q. If, after the valve handle had been placed in the first notch and a five pounds reduction made, it was moved to the second notch, how much more would the brake pipe reduce?

A. About three pounds, or enough to make the total brake pipe reduction eight pounds, as supposed to be drawn off in this notch.

Q. If the handle is then moved to the third notch, how much more would the brake pipe be reduced?

A. About three pounds again, or enough to make the

total reduction eleven pounds, as supposed to be drawn off in this position.

Q. If the handle is then moved to the fourth notch, how much more would the brake pipe be reduced?

A. About four pounds, or in all fifteen pounds.

Q. If the handle is then moved to the fifth notch, how much more would the brake pipe be reduced?

A. About eight pounds, or enough to make the total brake pipe reduction twenty-three pounds.

Q. Has the fifth graduating notch any other effect than that of making a full service reduction?

A. Yes, it also opens a port which permits the main reservoir pressure to flow into the straight air pipe up to the pressure the straight air controller is set at.

Q. What advantage is gained by this?

A. It keeps the locomotive brakes applied with practically full braking pressure, regardless of long piston travel or brake cylinder leakage.

Q. Where is the graduating valve located?

A. In a cavity in the slide valve seat directly below the slide valve.

Q. On what does the graduating valve seat itself?

A. On the bearing face of the slide valve.

Q. What holds the graduating valve in position?

A. The graduating valve lever, and graduating valve spring.

Q. What gives the graduating valve its motion?

A. The piston.

Q. Is the graduating valve fastened directly to the piston?

A. It is connected to it by means of the graduating valve lever,—the long end of which is connected to the piston, and the short end to the graduating valve.

Q. On what is the graduating valve lever fulcrumed?
A. On the fulcrum pin.

Q. Where is the fulcrum pin located?
A. It is screwed into the body of the brake valve from the handle side and passes through the graduating valve lever as the lever projects up through a passage cored between the cylinder of the brake valve and the slide valve seat

Q. Where is the graduating valve spring located?
A. In the jaw of the graduating valve lever and inside of the graduating valve.

Q. Where is the piston located?
A In the cylinder of the brake valve.

Q What are the duties of the piston?
A. It separates chamber "A" from chamber "D," gives motion to the graduating valve by means of the graduating valve lever, and prevents flow of chamber "D" air to the atmosphere, by means of the vent valve, when the piston is in or returns to its normal position with the brake valve handle in release, running or lap position

Q What pressures act on the piston?
A Brake pipe on the side to which the graduating valve lever is connected and chamber "D" pressure on the vent valve side

Q. How do these pressures stand when fully charged?
A Equal.

Q. Does the space between the piston and back cap constitute the volume of chamber "D?"
A No; the supplementary reservoir is connected to and is part of chamber "D."

Q Where is the supplementary reservoir?
A It is generally fastened to the roof of the cab, and

is connected by a pipe to passage "H," which is connected to chamber "D."

Q. Is this reservoir to be considered a part of the engineer's valve?

A. Yes; it is just as much a part of the engineer's valve as the slide valve or piston.

Q. Where does the air come from that supplies chamber "D" and the supplementary reservoir?

A. From chamber "A."

Q. Where does it come from with the B 2 brake valves?

A. From chamber "B."

Q. Why this change?

A. This is simply a structural change, the results obtained being the same with either method.

Q. Is it necessary for the supplementary reservoir to be of a certain size?

A. It is.

Q. What would be the effect if a supplementary reservoir larger than that furnished with the equipment be used?

A. The brake pipe reduction in any particular notch would be less than that intended.

Q. What if a smaller reservoir be used than that furnished?

A. Then the reduction would be greater than that intended.

Q. What is the volume of the supplementary reservoir?

A. About 92 cubic inches.

Q. When the brake valve handle is placed in a service notch is air drawn from the supplementary reservoir?

A. No; only from the brake pipe.

Q. What reduces the pressure in chamber "D" and supplementary reservoir?

A. The movement of the piston to close off brake pipe exhaust increases the space in chamber "D."

Q. What prevents leakage of chamber "D" pressure past the piston into chamber "A?"

A. The piston packing ring, and in addition a packing leather, and expander.

Q. What takes place when the valve handle is placed in a service notch?

A. One of the service application ports is moved away from the graduating valve, and the other is over the exhaust port in slide valve. Brake pipe air is now free to exhaust to the atmosphere, and the pressure in chamber "A" becomes less than that in chamber "D," and the latter pressure now pushes the piston forward causing the graduating valve lever to revolve on the fulcrum and carry the graduating valve toward the open exhaust port in the slide valve to a position where it again covers this port and cuts off further reduction of brake pipe pressure.

Q. If the brake valve handle is moved back to the next notch, what then takes place?

A. The slide valve is moved, carrying the exhaust port away from the graduating valve, and brake pipe air is again free to exhaust to the atmosphere until the expansion of air in chamber "D" once more moves the piston, and it in turn carries the graduating valve to the point where it once more covers the slide valve exhaust port and again cuts off the flow of brake pipe air. This operation is repeated in each of the graduating notches that the brake valve handle may be placed in.

Q. Does the graduating valve close the exhaust in the emergency position also?

A. No; the brake pipe exhaust cannot be closed in the emergency position.

Q. Why not?

A. Because the brake pipe air exhausts through different ports than those controlled by the graduating valve, and because it is not desirable that it should be shut off in emergency.

Q. What becomes of the air in the supplementary reservoir and chamber "D' in an emergency application?

A. It escapes to the atmosphere through port "W," and the emergency exhaust ports in the slide valve.

Q. Do the piston and graduating valve move in an emergency application?

A Yes, as the reduction of chamber "A" pressure is more rapid than that of chamber "D"—but-its movement has no effect on the operation of the brake valve.

Q. What brings the piston back to its normal position, when brakes are being released?

A. In the release, running and lap positions, an opening is made from the back of the piston—chamber "D" to the atmosphere, which permits enough air to escape from this chamber to reduce it below chamber "A" pressure, which being the stronger, pushes the piston back to its normal position.

Q. What causes the short exhaust of air from the brake valve each time the valve handle is returned to release, running and lap positions?

A. It is the escape of air from chamber "D."

Q. What cuts off this flow of air?

A. The vent valve.

Q. Where is this vent valve?

A. It is attached to the end of the piston stem on chamber "D" side.

Q. Is this part in one piece?

A. No; there are four pieces, the vent valve, the follower cap-nut, vent valve spring and piston cotter.

Q. What is the follower cap-nut for?

A. It slips over the vent valve and is screwed into the end of a stem projecting from the piston on chamber "D" side,—thus holding the vent valve in place on the end of the piston stem. The part of the vent valve which does the seating to close off the flow of air from chamber "D" projects out of the end of the follower cap-nut through an opening in the cap-nut made for the purpose.

Q. What is the vent valve spring for?

A. To permit the vent valve adjusting itself to its seat. It has to be left a little loose in the follower cap-nut, and the spring is to hold it steadily against its seat, when located

Q. What is the piston cotter for?

A. It passes through the follower cap-nut and piston stem, thus preventing the follower cap-nut from getting loose and working off the piston stem.

Q. Where is the port that connects chamber "D" with the atmosphere in release, running and lap positions, located?

A. It starts at the center of the back cap, passes through the cap and is cored through the body of the brake valve and then up to the slide valve seat

Q. Where is the vent valve seat?

A. In the center of the back cap, at the point where this port commences

PIPE CONNECTIONS.

Q. What is the purpose of the small pipe bracket bolted to one side of the brake valve body?

A. It is for straight air pipe connections.

Q. How many, and what are the pipe connections of the B 3 brake valve?

A. Six; as follows: main reservoir, brake pipe, supplementary reservoir, straight air supply pipe, straight air pipe, and accelerator pipe.

Q. Where does main reservoir pipe connect?

A. To the bottom, on the same side as valve handle.

Q. Where is the brake pipe connected?

A. Underneath, on side opposite to valve handle.

Q. Where is the supplementary reservoir pipe connected?

A. At the front end of brake valve on opposite side from handle.

Q. How does it connect with chamber "D?"

A. By a port passing through the brake valve body

Q. Where does the accelerator reservoir connect with brake valve?

A. At the front end on same side as the brake valve handle. There is also a hole drilled and tapped on the handle side near the front end, which may be used if more convenient.

Q. Where does the straight air supply pipe connect to the brake valve?

A. To the rear opening in the pipe bracket at side of valve body.

Q. Where does the straight air pipe connect?

A. At the front opening of the pipe bracket.

CUT-OUT COCKS.

Q. What provision is made for cutting off main reservoir pressure in case it is necessary to work on the pressure controller or brake valve?

A. A cut-out cock is placed in the main reservoir pipe between the pressure controller and the main reservoir.

Q. What provision is made for cutting out the brake valve on the second engine, when running double header?

A. A cut-out cock is placed in the brake pipe below the brake valve for this purpose.

Q. What is the use of the cut-out cock in the straight air pipe?

A. To cut out the straight air pipe on engine and tender.

Q. Can the straight air brake on the tender be cut out without interfering with the driver brake?

A. Yes; by means of a cut-out cock on the straight air pipe under the cab near rear of engine.

Q. What provision is made for cutting out the automatic brake?

A. Cut-out cocks are provided for this purpose.

Q. Where is the cut-out cock for cutting out the automatic driver brake placed?

A. Between the driver brake triple valve and double check valve.

Q. Why is it not placed between the brake pipe and triple valve?

A Because that cuts out the triple valve and prevents the charging of the auxiliary reservoir. With the cut-out cock placed between the triple valve and double check valve, the auxiliary reservoir always remains charged and when cut in, is available for instant use Cock can be placed between brake pipe and triple valve, however, if so desired.

Q. What kind of cocks are used in the straight air pipe, between the brake valve and double check valve, and between the triple valve and double check valve?

A. These two cut-out cocks are of a special style. They have a hole drilled in one side so that when in the cut-out position, they connect the pipe leading to the double check to the atmosphere.

Q. What is gained by this style of cock?

A. When cut out, no pressure can accumulate in the pipe leading to the double check valve, which insures the double check remaining seated.

PRESSURE CONTROLLER.

Q How is brake pipe pressure regulated with the B 3 equipment?

A By means of the pressure controller.

Q What may the pressure controller be said to be?

A. A device for regulating or controlling brake pipe pressure.

Q. What does it take the place of?

A. The feed valve or excess pressure valve that is usually found on other styles of engineers' valves.

Q. Is this valve a part of the engineer's brake valve?

A. Yes, just as much as the feed valve or excess pressure valve is a part of any ordinary engineer's valve.

Q. Where is it located?

A. In the pipe leading from the main reservoir to the engineer's brake valve.

Q. At what point in this pipe is it generally placed?

A. It is generally placed in the cab near the engineer's valve and handy to the engineer.

Q. To what may its principle of operation be compared?

A. To that of the ordinary pump governor.

Q. Of how many portions does it consist?

A. It is generally considered as having two portions—

the supply portion and the regulating portion, which are usually connected with a pipe, but if more convenient, where the single controller is used, the bracket may be dispensed with and the regulating portion screwed into the cap of the supply portion.

Q. Where is the excess pressure confined with this valve?

A. It is confined to the main reservoir.

Q How is it confined to the main reservoir?

A. By placing the pressure controller in the pipe between the main reservoir and engineer's valve, and having it so arranged that it shuts off the flow of air from the main reservoir to the brake pipe when the brake pipe is charged to the maximum brake pipe pressure carried

Q What are the advantages of this method of controlling brake pipe pressure?

A (a) No special position of the brake valve is required to get excess pressure. (b) Excess pressure can be obtained in any position of the brake valve. (c) Brake pipe and auxiliary reservoir pressure cannot be raised above the maximum in any position of the brake valve, and therefore the tendency to overcharge the brake pipe and auxiliary reservoirs in releasing brakes, a common result of leaving the brake valve handle in full release position too long with older forms of brake valves, is overcome.

Q How many sizes of pressure controllers are there?

A. Two; the three-quarter-inch for straight air, and the one and one-quarter for brake pipe pressure regulation.

Q. How many types of these controllers are there?

A. Two; the single, and the duplex.

Q. What is a single controller, and where is it used?

A. It has but one regulating top, and is used on straight air, and on engines where under ordinary conditions the same pressure is carried in both the main reservoir and brake pipe.

Q. What is a duplex controller, and where is it used?

A. The duplex controller has two regulating tops, and is used on engines where the standard brake pipe and main reservoir pressure may be required, or where a higher pressure may be required.

Q. What advantage is gained by the use of the duplex contoller?

A. Either high or low pressure may be cut in or out at a moment's notice, without the necessity of changing adjustment of brake pipe or main reservoir tops.

Q. From whence does the controller take its air pressure?

A. Directly from the pipe between the supply portion and the brake valve.

Q. How is the pressure varied when using the duplex regulating portion?

A By means of appropriate cocks, according to schedule used, placed in the pipe leading from the air supply to the pressure heads.

Q. How is the regulating portion arranged for attachment in position?

A. It is provided with a bracket so it can be bolted fast to the side of the cab.

Q. How is the adjustment of the regulating portion accomplished?

A. The adjustment of the regulating tops or heads is accomplished by means of adjusting the screw which regulates the tension of the spring the same as in any ordinary governor.

Q. Where is the supply portion of the controller located?

A. This is the part that is placed in the main reservoir pipe between the reservoir and brake valve.

Q. In what way does the supply portion differ from the steam portion of an ordinary governor?

A. It has a leather seated supply valve instead of a metal valve, and has a screw entered into the bottom of the body which runs up to the valve seat and is moved by a hand wheel on the outer end of the screw.

Q. What is the use of this screw?

A. By screwing the wheel up, it will lift the valve off its seat, and allow the free passage of air from the main reservoir to the brake valve.

Q. When would it be necessary to use the hand wheel?

A. It can be made use of in the B 3-S equipment, when the engine is called on to handle a train equipped with the high speed brake, and with any of the schedules in case of any defect that would cause a sluggish action of the pressure controller.

Q. What shuts off the flow of air from the main reservoir to the brake valve?

A. In operation, with either a single or duplex regulating portion, as soon as the pressure in the brake pipe, or chamber "B," is great enough to overcome the resistance of the spring which is holding the diaphragm seated over port "B," the air will pass through the port, through passage below this port, and the pipe that connects the regulating and supply portions to the space above the piston in the supply portion, forcing the piston down, which in turn forces the valve to its seat, thus cutting off communication between main reservoir and brake pipe, or chamber "B."

Q. What and where is this small port "C?"

A. It is a small pin hole drilled through a screw called a muffler plug screwed into a vent opening in the neck of the diaphragm, being the same as the vent opening in the diaphragm of any governor.

Q. What attention must be given to port "C" when using the duplex controller?

A. Each regulating head has a vent port "C," therefore one of these should be plugged

Q. What is port "X" in the supply portion of the controller for?

A. It is an exhaust port connecting the under side of the supply portion piston with the atmosphere so that any leakage past this piston may be discharged to the atmosphere.

Q. What care should be taken in locating the supply portion?

A. It should, as much as possible, be away from the boiler head to prevent the drying out of the leather seat.

Q. What is the object of the arrow cast on the outside of the supply portion?

A This is used as a guide to assist in properly coupling up the supply portion in the piping. The air should pass through in the direction indicated by the arrow.

Q What is the object of the letters L. & H, cast on the bracket that holds the regulating heads?

A. These letters signify low and high, and the pressure on the side marked "L" should be set for the low pressure, and the one on the side marked "H," for the high pressure.

DIVIDED RESERVOIR.

Q. What is the divided reservoir?

A. A cast iron reservoir, divided by a partition into two separate chambers,—hence the name.

Q. Is this divided reservoir used with all styles of New York brake valves?

A. No, it is only used when the accelerator valve is part of the equipment.

Q. What is the object of the divided reservoir?

A. As previously explained, it is necessary to have a small reservoir to furnish volume to chamber "D," of the engineer's brake valve, and as will be shown, it is also necessary for the accelerator valve to have a small reservoir The divided reservoir represents these two small reservoirs combined and cast in one piece.

Q. Is there any communication between the two chambers of the divided reservoirs?

A. Absolutely none.

Q. Are the two chambers of equal size?

A. No, one is quite small, as compared with the other.

Q. What is the small chamber used for?

A. It acts as a supplementary reservoir for the engineer's brake valve.

Q. What is the larger chamber for?

A. It acts as the accelerator valve reservoir.

Q. What are the capacities of these two chambers?

A The supplementary reservoir chamber contains 92 cubic inches, and the accelerator reservoir chamber 600 cubic inches.

Q. How may the large chamber be distinguished from the small one?

A. When coupled up the accelerator valve is attached

to the large chamber. When not coupled, by means of the two studs projecting from the large chamber end to fasten the accelerator valve with

Q. To what is the small chamber connected?

A. To the supplementary reservoir.

Q. Where is the divided reservoir located?

A. Usually under the running board, directly beneath the cab.

Q What are the plugs in its bottom for?

A. To drain the chambers, which should be done frequently.

ACCELERATOR VALVE.

Q. What is the function of the accelerator valve?

A. It serves to accelerate discharge of air from the brake pipe in making service reductions on long trains.

Q. When does it operate?

A. Only when service applications are made with the brake valve, and then only when the volume of brake pipe air is sufficient to warrant its use

Q. Is the amount of air discharged from the brake pipe greater when the accelerator valve is used than would be the case if the brake valve alone was used?

A. No.

Q. What controls the flow of air that actuates the accelerator valve?

A. The flow of air to the accelerator which actuates it is controlled by the automatic cut-off of the engineer's brake valve.

Q. Is the action of the accelerator valve automatic?

A. It is

Q. How many cars must be in a train to obtain the action of the accelerator valve?

A. About eight cars.

Q. Why will it not operate with less than eight cars?

A. Because, with less than this number of cars, the automatic lap of the brake valve takes place before sufficient pressure has been accumulated in the accelerator reservoir to move the piston of the accelerator valve down against its spring.

Q. How many pounds pressure is required in the accelerator reservoir to operate the accelerator valve?

A. About ten to twelve pounds.

Q. About how long does it take after the brake valve is placed in a service notch to open the accelerator valve on trains long enough to bring it into use?

A About four seconds.

Q Does it close as soon as the exhaust from the brake valve ceases?

A. No, it continues to blow for about four seconds, after the brake valve exhaust ceases.

Q. Why is this?

A. Because it takes about that long after the brake valve exhaust closes for the pressure in the accelerator reservoir to reduce sufficiently to allow the valve to resume its normal position.

Q. Why not have it so arranged that it will operate on a less number of cars?

A Because the brake valve is capable of taking care of short trains.

Q. Does the accelerator consist of more than one chamber?

A. Yes,—it has two chambers, known as B. & O.

Q Name the working parts of the accelerator valve.

A. The piston, valve stem, slide valve, slide valve spring, valve stem leather seat and spring.

Q Where is the piston located?

A. In chamber "B."

Q. What pressure acts on the piston?

A. The air in the accelerator reservoir acts on the upper side of the piston.

Q What is this piston for?

A. To give motion to the slide valve.

Q. Where is this slide valve located?

A. In chamber "O."

Q. What pressure is always present in chamber "O?"

A. Brake pipe pressure is always present in chamber "O," and around the slide valve.

Q. What prevents brake pipe pressure in chamber "O" from passing the chamber "B?"

A. The leather seat on the valve stem, which rests against the seat formed on valve stem bush, and which is held up to this seat by the spring.

Q. What is the slide valve for?

A. The slide valve is to permit the escape of brake pipe air when moved into the proper position, by the piston in chamber "B," acted upon by the pressure accumulated in the accelerator-reservoir, during a service reduction in a long train, and to shut off this flow of air when the reduction has been made, and the air in the accelerator reservoir has escaped.

Q. What is the shape of the exhaust port in the slide valve?

A It is oblong in shape.

Q. What is the shape of the exhaust port in the slide valve seat?

A. It is triangular in shape, with its point upward.

Q Why triangular in shape?

A. To permit of a slow closure of the accelerator valve exhaust.

Q. Why should the accelerator valve exhaust have a slow closure?

A For the same reason that the service exhaust of the brake valve should have a gradual cut-off to prevent the release of the head brakes.

Q. Of what use is the slide valve spring?

A. To hold the slide valve to its seat and prevent dirt or other foreign substances getting under it, when chamber "O" is not charged with air.

Q. To what pressure is the accelerator valve connected?

A. Brake pipe pressure.

Q. Explain the operation of the accelerator valve.

A. During a service application a portion of the air from the brake pipe passes to the accelerator reservoir and thence to the top of the piston in the accelerator valve. When 10 or 12 pounds pressure has accumulated in the reservoir and on top of the piston, the latter moves down carrying with it the slide valve and stem, and compresses the spring The oblong port in slide valve registers with the triangular port in the seat, the port opening being very small at first, but gradually increasing until piston and slide valve have reached full travel. When the cut-off valve of the brake valve goes to automatic lap, further flow of air to accelerator reservoir is stopped, and the pressure on the piston is reduced until the spring pushes it and the slide valve upward stopping the further flow of brake pipe air to the atmosphere.

Q. What is the result of this action of the accelerator valve?

A. A much larger volume of air is discharged from the brake pipe in a given time than could pass through the service exhaust ports of the brake valve.

Q. Does the accelerator valve exhaust stay open longer with a long train than with a short one?

A. Yes,—because with a long train the volume of brake pipe air to be reduced is greater and the cut-off valve of the brake valve remains open longer.

Q. What is the object of the cut-out cock placed in the brake pipe connection leading to the accelerator, as practised on some railroads using this equipment?

A. So that a quick means may be provided for cutting out the accelerator, if the brake pipe connection should break off at the accelerator or the accelerator become defective.

HIGH SPEED CONTROLLER.

Q. What is the high speed controller for?

A. It acts as a reducing valve for the driver and truck brake cylinders.

Q. What valves does the high speed controller take the place of?

A. It takes the place of the usual compensating or high speed reducing valve, for driver and truck brake cylinders, and the usual safety valve used to prevent the brake cylinder pressure from becoming too high when the straight air and automatic brakes are both in use, and at the same time provides a means of reducing the pressure in the driver and truck brake cylinders to any extent desired or entirely releasing them without interfering with the train brakes.

Q. Of what does it consist?

A. It consists of a cylinder containing a piston and

valve and a lever safety valve screwed into the cylinder.

Q. To what is it connected?

A. On the bottom, to the brake cylinders and on the end, to the brake pipe.

Q. Name the operating parts.

A. In the cylinder are a piston and a piston valve, and in the safety valve, a spring, valve stem, pop valve and lever handle.

Q. Describe the piston and valve.

A. This consists of a piston having a leather seat on each face and is fastened to the piston valve which has two annular grooves, one large and one small.

Q. What pressures act on the piston?

A. Brake pipe pressure on the plain side, and brake cylinder pressure on the piston valve side.

Q. What pressure acts on the piston valve?

A Brake cylinder pressure.

Q. What is the normal position of the piston and valve?

A. Brake pipe pressure pushes it over in the direction of the solid seat and holds it firmly seated so that no brake pipe air can get into the piston valve chamber.

Q. How does the piston valve stand in this position?

A With the large annular groove standing over the opening leading to the brake cylinder and under the port leading up to the safety valve.

Q. Does the piston move during ordinary brake applications?

A. No, it does not, unless the brake pipe pressure is reduced below that in the brake cylinders.

QUICK RELEASE VALVE.

Q. What is the quick release valve?

A. A valve used to hasten the release of the engine brakes after either an automatic or straight air application of the brakes, or if desired after a straight air application only, leaving the release of the automatic brakes normal.

Q. With what schedule is this valve furnished?

A. Usually with the B 3-S equipment.

Q. Can this valve be used successfully on switch engines equipped with the older types of brakes?

A. It can.

Q. What are the operating parts of this valve?

A. A piston, rubber seated valve and spring.

Q. Where is this valve usually located?

A. In the brake cylinder pipe between the cylinders and the double check valve when intended to hasten the release of both straight air and automatic brakes.

Q. Where located when used to hasten the release of the straight air brake only?

A. In the straight air pipe between the brake valve and double check valve.

Q. How many pipe connections has this valve?

A. Three.

Q. How is it connected up when used to hasten the release of either the automatic or straight air brake?

A. The end having the 3/4-inch union swivel and nut is connected to the brake cylinder side of the piping and the opposite side to the double check valve side of the piping. The bottom connection is to take an exhaust pipe if desired.

Q. How connected when used for hastening the release of the straight air brakes only?

A. The side with the union swivel and nut is connected to the piping leading to the double check valve,—the opposite side, to the straight air pipe leading to the brake valve.

STRAIGHT AIR BRAKE.

Q. What is meant by the term "straight air?"

A. Air that passes direct from main reservoir to brake cylinder without first passing through triple valves or auxiliaries.

Q. What brakes only are operated by straight air?

A The locomotive and tender brakes.

Q. How is it admitted to and discharged from engine and tender brake cylinders?

A By means of the combined automatic and straight air brake valve.

Q. Is this air taken from chamber "B" of the brake valve?

A. No; a separate pipe carries it directly from main reservoir to brake valve.

Q. What is this pipe called?

A. The straight air pipe.

Q. Is this pipe connected directly to the main reservoir?

A. No, it is connected to the main reservoir pipe between the main reservoir cut-out cock and the pressure controller.

Q. How is it connected to the brake valve?

A. By means of a pipe bracket bolted to the side of the brake valve.

Q At what pressure is it admitted to the brake cylinder?

A. Forty pounds.

Q. If this air comes direct from the main reservoir pipe, how is it reduced to 40 pounds?

A. By means of a controller valve used especially for this purpose.

Q. Where is this controller valve located?

A. In the straight air pipe between its main reservoir connection and the brake valve.

Q. What kind of a valve is this?

A. It is a ¾-inch controller valve of the same design as the one used to control the brake pipe pressure, but with a single pressure top.

Q. To what is the pipe leading to the regulating top of this controller connected?

A. To the straight air pipe which leads from the brake valve to the brake cylinders at a point between the brake valve and double check valve.

Q. How is the pressure adjusted?

A. By removing the top cap and screwing the adjusting screw down for more pressure, or up for less,—the same as with a pump governor.

Q. What position must the brake valve be placed in to apply the straight air locomotive brakes?

A. In release and straight air application positions

Q. Must the full 40 pounds be admitted each time the brake is applied?

A. Not necessarily. It can be admitted to any extent up to 40 pounds.

Q How is this arranged for?

A. By means of a lap position located about midway between release and running positions.

Q. How would you partially apply this brake?

A. By going to release and then back to the straight air lap position.

Q. Suppose you wanted to apply the brake harder?

A. Would repeat this operation until fully applied or the desired braking force was obtained.

Q. In what position must the brake valve be placed to release the straight air locomotive brake?

A. In running and straight air release position.

Q. Can this brake be graduated off?

A. Yes, if so desired.

Q. How?

A. By moving the handle to running position and letting part of the air escape from the cylinders, then return it to straight air lap. This can be repeated as desired until fully released.

Q. What effect does variation of piston travel have on the straight air brake?

A None. A constant pressure of 40 pounds is maintained in the cylinders, regardless of piston travel.

Q. What effect does ordinary brake cylinder leakage have on the straight air brake?

A. The straight air will keep the brake fully applied in spite of any ordinary brake cylinder leakage.

Q. Why do we get only a partial opening of port "N" in the last service notch?

A This port is purposely restricted in order that main reservoir air may be prevented from passing to the brake cylinders in advance of the auxiliary reservoir pressure, in case the brake valve handle should be moved directly to the last service notch.

Q When the automatic brake is released by moving the brake valve handle to release position, is the automatic driver and tender brake released and the straight air brake applied?

A. Yes and no. The triple valves are moved to release position and the pressure in the cylinders holding the double check valve seated against the straight air pipe connection commences to escape through the triple valve exhaust. At the same time, straight air at 40 pounds pressure is being admitted to the straight air pipe side of the double check valve. As soon as the pressure in the cylinders falls below 40 pounds, the pressure in the straight air pipe pushes the double check over, closes the connection leading to the triple valve exhaust and raising the brake cylinder pressure back to 40 pounds, holds them applied to that extent.

Q. Is the straight air pressure used at any time in connection with the automatic brake?

A. Yes, the straight air ports are open to the locomotive brake cylinders in the last service notch and the emergency position.

Q. What good does this do?

A. If the pressure in the cylinders, supplied by the automatic brake, falls below 40 pounds, the straight air will hold them applied with that amount of pressure.

Q. If the straight air brake was applied and it became necessary to apply the automatic brake without giving the straight air brake time to release, is there any danger of getting too much pressure in the engine and tender brake cylinders, and overheating or sliding the wheels?

A. No, this is provided for by the lever safety valve.

Q. What is the lever safety valve?

A. A valve placed in the high speed controller in such a way that it is in constant communication with the engine brake cylinders, and permits the brake cylinder pressure to escape when it builds up beyond a certain predetermined point.

Q At what pressure is this valve set?

A. At 53 pounds.

Q. Can the locomotive brakes be released without releasing the automatic brakes on train?

A. Yes.

Q How is this accomplished?

A. By holding down the safety valve lever until all, or as much of the cylinder pressure as may be desired, is allowed to escape.

Q. Where is the air that goes to the brake cylinders in straight air applications taken from with the B-2 brake valve?

A. From chamber "B" above the slide valve.

SCHEDULES.

Q. By what names are the different schedules of this equipment known?

A. B-3, B-3-S, B3-HP and B3-HS.

Q. What is the B-3-S equipment for?

A. For switch engines only

Q. What are the principal operating parts of the B-3-S equipment?

A. The B-3 brake valve, single pump governor, single pressure controller, lever safety valve, ¾-inch single pressure controller (for straight air), and quick release valve. With this schedule the accelerator valve is not furnished, and the ordinary supplementary reservoir is substituted for the divided reservoir.

Q. At what pressure are the governor and pressure controller valve set with this equipment?

A. The pressure controller is set at 70 pounds, and

the pump governor at 90 pounds for ordinary switching service

Q. Can an engine, equipped with schedule B-3-S and used in passenger switching service, handle trains charged with high speed pressure without any additional equipment on the engine?

A. Yes, it can.

Q. How is this done?

A. The pump governor would have to be set at 110 pounds pressure, and when handling high speed trains, the ¼-inch cut-out cock, in the pipe between the regulating and supply portions of the pressure controller, closed

Q What is the object of closing this cock?

A. It renders the pressure controller inoperative and allows the full main reservoir pressure of 110 pounds to pass to the brake pipe, so that trains using the high speed brake can be handled without delay, and without additional apparatus on the engine.

Q. What is schedule B-3 for?

A. This is a schedule furnished for engines in passenger or freight service, where but one brake pipe pressure is used.

Q. What are the principal operating parts of schedule B-3?

A. The B-3 brake valve, single pump governor, single pressure controller, accelerator valve, divided reservoir, ¾-inch single controller (for straight air), and a lever safety valve.

Q. At what pressures are the governor, and pressure controller adjusted with this schedule?

A Governor at 90 pounds main reservoir, pressure controller 70 pounds brake pipe.

Q. For what is schedule B3-HP used?

A. For engines in heavy freight service, and heavy grades where loads are handled one way, and empties the other.

Q What are the principal operating parts of this schedule?

A. The B-3 brake valve, pump governor and pressure controller, each with duplex regulating portions, divided reservoir, accelerator valve, lever safety valve, ¾-inch single pressure controller (for straight air), and union three way cocks.

Q. What brake pipe pressures are usually carried with schedules B 3-HP?

A. The regulating portions of the pressure controller are adjusted for 70 and 90 pounds.

Q What main reservoir pressures are usually used with this schedule?

A. The regulating portions of the pump governor are set for 90 and 110 pounds respectively. These may be varied, however, to suit local conditions.

Q. How are these pressures cut in and cut out?

A. By three-way cocks provided in the piping.

Q. How are these operated?

A. Turn the handle in line with the pipe leading to the regulating head, set at the pressure to be used, high or low, as desired. This will cut in the head required to regulate the supply portion and cut out the one not required for use.

Q. What is the schedule B3-HS?

A. This is the high speed brake schedule.

Q What are the principal parts of this schedule?

A. The B-3 brake valve, duplex pump governor, duplex pressure controller, divided reservoir, accelerator valve, ¾-inch single pressure controller (for straight air), high speed controller, one union three-way cock and one union four-way cock.

Q. At what pressures are the regulating portions of the duplex pressure controller set with this equipment?

A. The low pressure is set at 70 pounds, and the high pressure at 110 pounds.

Q. At what pressures are the regulating portions of the pump governor set, with this schedule?

A. 90 and 130 pounds.

Q. How are the regulating portions of the duplex pressure controller cut in and cut out with this equipment?

A. By means of a four-way cock.

Q. Describe this four-way cock.

A. This is a special cock with a connection to each of the regulating portions, one to the supply pipe between the controller and brake valve, and one to the pipe between the brake valve and accelerator reservoir.

Q. What do the letters "L," "H" and "R," cast on the connections of the union four-way cock signify?

A. "L" stands for low pressure position

"H" stands for high pressure position.

"R" stands for reservoir, meaning that this connection should be coupled to the accelerator reservoir pipe connection.

Q. What care must be taken in adjusting the regulating portions of the pressure controller?

A. The pressure portion coupled up to the four-way cock connection marked "L," should be set for the low pressure, and the one coupled to the connection marked "H" should be set for the high pressure. Care should also be taken to see that the sides marked "L" and "H" on the four-way cock lead to the sides of the bracket correspondingly marked.

Q. How is this four-way cock operated?

A. By turning the handle towards the side marked "L" or "H" as required.

Q. What is the purpose of the connection to the accelerator reservoir pipe?

A. To prevent more than the usual predetermined reduction of brake pipe pressure in any graduating notch in a service application with 110 pounds brake pipe pressure.

Q. How is this effected?

A. When the handle of the four-way cock is in position to operate the regulating head adjusted at 110 pounds brake pipe pressure, a small port in the accelerator reservoir connection of the four-way cock is brought into communication with a small port in the four-way cock leading to the atmosphere, which permits a certain quantity of the air passing to the accelerator reservoir to escape to the atmosphere, thus preventing the pressure in the accelerator reservoir rising above the pressure obtained in a service reduction with the low pressure portion cut in.

Q. Why is this port necessary with the high pressure and not with the low?

A. Because the greater velocity of the air at high pressure has a tendency to charge the accelerator reservoir to too high a pressure, and thus cause the accelerator valve to remain open longer than intended.

Q. How are the pump governor regulating heads cut in and out?

A. By means of a union three-way cock having a connection to each of the regulating heads and to the main reservoir pressure

Q. How is this three-way cock used?

A. The handle is turned to point to the "L" or "H" cast on the cock connections, according to which pressure is desired.

TRAIN HANDLING.

Q. In what position should the handle of the brake valve be, while charging up the train?

A. In running and straight air release position, unless standing on a grade where it might be necessary to hold the train with the straight air brake applied on the locomotive, or in recharging on grades when it is desired to hold the slack of the train bunched, by means of the locomotive brake, while releasing. In either case, the brake valve handle may be placed in release and straight air application position.

Q How should the brake valve be handled when testing the brakes?

A. It should be moved slowly to the fourth or fifth service notch, and left there until signal is given to release the brakes.

Q. How should the brakes be released?

A. By placing the brake valve handle in running and straight air release position.

Q. In what position should the brake valve handle be placed when the brake is not being operated?

A. In running and straight air release position

Q. What provision is made to assist the engineer in finding the running position?

A. A small pin projects from the quadrant opposite

the running position notch, so it can be felt by the hand in locating this position in the dark.

Q. In what service notch should the brake valve handle be placed to make a service application of the locomotive and train brakes?

A. In the notch corresponding to the amount of reduction required.

Q. What should govern the initial reduction in making an application?

A. The length of the train, the speed, whether loaded or empty, character of grade and efficiency of the brakes.

Q. When is the first notch of the brake valve used for the initial reduction?

A. Only with short trains of five cars or less.

Q. Why is the exhaust port "G" in the slide valve only partly opened in this position?

A. To prevent the air escaping from the brake pipe fast enough on very short trains, to cause a possibility of undesired quick action of the triple valves.

Q. When is the second notch used?

A. With trains of more than five cars.

Q. What notch should be used for the initial reduction in handling long freight trains down heavy grades?

A. The third notch.

Q After the initial reduction, how much should the following reductions be?

A. As much as circumstances, in the judgment of the engineer, may indicate as necessary.

Q. How long should the brake valve handle be left in any one position?

A. Ordinarily until a further reduction is required. This valve is supposed to make a brake pipe reduction corresponding to the position placed in, and then to lap automatically without being moved, and will do so if not defective.

Q. What should be done if it does not lap itself automatically?

A. The handle should be moved slowly back to positive lap position when the desired reduction has been made.

Q. Why necessarily slowly?

A Because, as previously explained, if the brake pipe is shut off suddenly, there is a tendency for the front brakes to release, which in handling trains, especially long freight trains, might break the train in two.

Q. What is the greatest service reduction obtainable?

A. Twenty-three pounds, in the fifth service notch.

Q. Why is 23 pounds the limit set for the service reduction of the brake pipe?

A. Because, with a reduction of that amount, the pressures in the auxiliary reservoirs and brake cylinders should be equalized.

Q. If, for any reason, a further reduction should be deemed necessary, what could be done?

A. Either return the brake valve handle to lap position, and leave it momentarily, until the exhaust from the back of the piston ceases, then commence again using the notches as if the brake had not been applied at all, or, if desired, move the handle slowly towards emergency position and make the desired reduction by slightly opening the emergency ports.

Q. Would emergency result in this case?

A No, as the brakes have already been applied practically to full service limit.

Q. In what position should the valve handle be placed to release both the locomotive and train brakes?

A. Running and straight air release position.

Q. If it is desired to release the train brakes only and hold the locomotive brakes applied, what position should be used?

A. The full automatic release and straight air application position.

Q. At what time is this method of releasing brakes particularly beneficial?

A. In releasing the brakes on freight trains, for the purpose of holding the slack bunched, while the train brakes are releasing, also for holding a standing train on grades while recharging.

Q. In releasing the brakes on a grade, should the straight air be held applied long after the automatic brakes are released?

A. No; it, too, should be released.

Q. Why is this?

A. To avoid over-heating the driving-wheel tires.

Q. How should it be released?

A. It should be graduated off, by placing the brake valve handle in running and straight air release position for a moment, and then back to the straight air lap, which is midway between release and running positions, alternately, until fully released.

Q. Why is it necessary to release the straight air gradually, when handling a train?

A. If suddenly released, the engine may surge ahead and cause a severe strain on the draft gear and possibly cause a break-in-two.

Q. How is the brake valve used to apply the straight air locomotive brake only?

A. The handle should be placed in the full release and straight air application position.

Q. Should the straight air brake on the engine be used to bunch the slack of the train before applying the automatic brake, or to stop a train without the use of the automatic brake?

A. As a rule, no,—on account of the liability to cause severe shocks at the rear of the train. If used for this purpose, extreme care must be taken to avoid damage, to cars and lading, caused by the slack running in or out too hard, and it should be graduated on with very light increases of pressure.

Q. How is the straight air graduated on?

A. By placing the brake valve handle in full release and straight air application position for a moment, and then returning it to straight air lap, as previously explained.

Q. If it is desired to release the locomotive brakes without releasing the train brakes, how can it be done?

A. By pressing down the lever of the lever safety valve and holding it down until the locomotive brake is partially, or entirely released, as desired.

Q. When is this particularly beneficial?

A. In case of driving wheels sliding or the tires becoming over-heated.

Q. Does the application of the locomotive brakes in full release and straight air application position affect the train brakes in any manner?

A. No.

Q. In what position only can all the brakes be released?

A. The running and straight air release position.

Q. What is the effect of using the fifth or full service notch of the brake valve?

A. In addition to a full service application of the

automatic brakes, straight air is admitted to the locomotive brake cylinders, and the full pressure, at which the straight air controller is set, will be maintained in them, regardless of brake cylinder leakage and long piston travel.

Q. How is an emergency application of the brakes made?

A. By placing the brake valve handle in full emergency position.

Q. What effect does the use of the emergency position have on the locomotive brakes?

A. In addition to the usual more rapid application of the automatic brakes, the straight air port is open to the brake cylinder pipes in this position also, and the brake cylinder pressure will be maintained, at the pressure at which the straight air controller is set, despite cylinder leakage or piston travel.

Q If the brakes should be applied in the emergency from an unknown cause, what should be done?

A. Move the brake valve handle over to the last service notch, or the emergency position, and leave it there until the train stops

Q. What is the object of going to the last service notch or emergency position in this case?

A. To prevent the loss of main reservoir air and to obtain the benefit of the straight air maintenance feature previously explained

Q. How should the brake valve be handled when making a two-application stop with a passenger train?

A. A heavy application should be made while the speed of the train is high, so as to reduce it rapidly. When it has been reduced to about 10 or 12 miles per hour, if a short train, place the brake valve in running position just long enough to start all brakes to release, then return to lap position until ready to make the second application. If the train is a long one, move the brake valve handle to release position for about three seconds, to start the train brakes to release, then to lap position, which will release the locomotive brakes, and leave it there until ready for the second application.

Q. How should the final release of the brakes be made on passenger trains?

A. On short trains, the brakes should be released by moving the handle to running position, just before the train stops. With long trains, the brakes should be held applied until the train stops.

Q. Should the brake valve handle be moved to the full release and straight air application position, after releasing the automatic brakes, to bring the train to a stop?

A. No

Q. Why not?

A. Because this would be liable to cause severe shocks due to the slack running in against the engine.

Q. Can the full release and straight air application be used when handling a light engine?

A. Yes, if desired, except in cases of emergency, when the emergency application position should be used.

Q. Why?

A. Because a quicker application and a higher brake cylinder pressure would be obtained than is possible by the use of the straight air only.

Q. What should be done if an engine with this equipment is run second in double heading?

A. The double heading cock, in the brake pipe, under the brake valve, should be closed, as with all previous types of brake valves, and the brake valve handle placed in running position.

Q. In running trains with two or more engines coupled together, can the engine brakes, on other than the first engine, be used independently of the first engine?

A. Yes, the locomotive brakes of these engines can be applied and released independently of the first engine.

Q. How can this be done?

A. If the automatic brakes are not applied by the leading engine, the straight air brake on any of the following engines and tenders can be applied by placing the brake valve handle in release and straight air application, and release them all by returning the handle to running and straight air release position. If the automatic brakes have been applied on the train, including the helping engines, the engineers on these engines can release the driver and truck brakes, partially or entirely, by using the lever safety valve. They cannot, however, release the automatic tender brakes in this case, as this brake is not connected to the lever safety valve in the cab

Q. What would cause a continuous blow at the brake valve exhaust in release, running and lap positions?

A. A leak past the vent valve or a leaky main slide valve

Q What would cause a leak past this vent valve?

A. Dirt on it or its seat, or the vent valve and seat not ground to make a good joint, either of which permits air to pass to port "O" and through slide valve exhaust to the atmosphere

Q. What would be the effect of this leak in release, running and lap positions, aside from causing a blow at the brake valve exhaust?

A. As this air is coming from chamber "D," which is supplied by the brake pipe, it is a brake pipe leak.

Q. Would a leaky vent valve have any effect on an automatic application of the brakes?

A. Not unless the brake valve handle is returned to positive lap position, when it would cause a leak at the exhaust as before. Except when the brake valve handle is returned to positive lap position, the vent valve is always away from its seat during applications, but air cannot escape by passing the vent valve opening, because in all application positions port "O" is closed to the atmosphere by the slide valve.

Q. What other defect would cause a blow at the brake valve exhaust in release and running position?

A. A leak through the partition of the divided reservoir from the supplementary reservoir to the accelerator reservoir.

Q. How would this leak cause a blow at the brake valve exhaust in release and running positions?

A. Because in these positions, there is a direct opening from the accelerator reservoir through the brake valve to the atmosphere, as well as through port "T" in the accelerator valve.

Q. What might cause a blow at the brake valve exhaust in full release position only?

A. If the slide valve should be badly worn by the graduating valve, it would cause a blow at the exhaust in full release position by being directly over the bridge between chamber "A" and exhaust port "C," and would be a brake pipe leak.

Q. What else, beside the foregoing, could cause a blow in running and lap positions, with brakes not set?

A. In running and lap positions, if the double check is

open to the straight air pipe, a leak past the leather seat on the piston valve side of the high pressure controller.

Q. How could a leak past the seat on the piston valve side of the high speed controller cause a blow at the brake valve exhaust, in running position, and also in lap, if the brake is not applied?

A. Air leaking into the piston valve chamber, unable to escape through the safety valve, would pass into the brake cylinder pipe leading to the double check valve, and if this valve was open to the straight air pipe, would pass up to the brake valve and as the port to straight air pipe is open to the atmosphere, it would escape through brake valve exhaust.

Q Why would this not cause a blow in lap, if the brake is applied?

A. Because the brake would have to be applied with an automatic application to hold in lap position, and in automatic applications the double check would close the straight air pipe.

Q. Why would it not cause a blow in full release position?

A. Because, on account of the straight air being applied in this position, the straight air pipe exhaust is closed.

Q. How could you determine in a general way whether the trouble was in the slide valve or not?

A. If there is a continuous blow in all positions the trouble would be in the slide valve.

Q. How could you determine, in a general way, if the trouble is in the vent valve?

A. If the valve is tight in all application positions, the trouble is likely in the vent valve

Q. If the valve only blows in the release and running

positions, how could you tell, in a general way, whether the trouble is in the divided reservoir or the high speed controller?

A. Disconnect the brake cylinder pipe at the high speed controller. If there is a leak from the controller cylinder, piston seat SA-6 is at fault. If there is no leak there, the trouble is likely in the divided reservoir.

Q. What would cause a continuous blow in the positive lap position, with the automatic brake applied?

A. A leaky slide valve, a leaky vent valve, or a leaky double check valve.

Q. How could a leak in the double check valve cause a blow with the brake applied, and the brake valve in positive lap position?

A There would be a leak into the straight air pipe and as the straight air port is open to the atmosphere in this position, the leakage would escape at the brake valve exhaust.

Q. What would cause a continuous blow at the brake valve exhaust in the different service notches?

A. Failure of the brake valve to lap automatically, a leaky main slide valve, a leaky graduating valve, and in the first four notches, a leaky double check valve.

Q. What would prevent the brake valve from lapping automatically in any of the service notches?

A. A leak to the atmosphere from chamber "D," through the back cap gasket, the pipe connections to the supplementary reservoir, or around the supplementary reservoir, as through a sand hole in the casting, by the reservoir plug, or through the partition of the divided reservoir, due to sand holes, and past the piston packing to chamber "A."

Q. How would leakage past the back head of brake

valve, in pipe connections to supplementary reservoir, or reservoir itself, or through the partition of the divided reservoir, cause this?

A. A leak in any of these places would have the effect of reducing the pressure in chamber "D," and the supplementary reservoir, and when by the movement of the piston, the graduating valve had nearly closed the exhaust port in the slide valve, upon reaching a point where the brake pipe pressure is reducing at the same rate that the pressure in chamber "D" is reducing through leakage at any of the points mentioned, the movement of the graduating valve would cease, and the brake valve refuse to lap itself automatically, and the brake pipe reduction continue until the valve is lapped by hand.

Q. Why does a leak in the piston packing cause the brake valve to fail to lap automatically?

A. For the same reason as given in answer to the preceding question,—only in this case, the supplementary reservoir and chamber "D" air leaks into chamber "A" (brake pipe), past the piston packing, instead of to the atmosphere, as in the preceding case.

Q. What would cause a leak past the piston?

A A poorly fitted or badly worn packing leather and ring, or a bent piston stem.

Q. How does a bent piston stem cause this?

A. It tends to twist the piston in the cylinder and allow the chamber "D" pressure to leak to the brake pipe.

Q. What causes a piston stem to bend?

A. Probably too frequent use of the emergency position.

Q. What effect would a leak past this piston have with brakes not applied?

A. None at all.

Q. What effect would supplementary reservoir, or chamber "D" leaks to the atmosphere, have with brakes released?

A. Such leaks would, in release and running positions, be supplied from the brake pipe, and being, therefore, brake pipe leaks, would in general simply tend to keep the air pump working.

Q. How could you determine if the failure of the brake valve to lap automatically is caused by supplementary reservoir leaks to the atmosphere?

A. By going over the parts previously mentioned, where air could leak to the atmosphere, with soap suds.

Q. How could you test for leak in partition of divided reservoir?

A Ordinarily, with brake valve in release or running position, disconnect the pipe leading from the accelerator reservoir to the brake valve, at either end, and see if any air is escaping from the reservoir. If there is a leak, and at the same time, there is considerable leakage from port "T" in the accelerator valve, make the test recommended later on, as there is a possibility of leakage at both places being from the brake pipe, past valve, instead of through the partition of the divided reservoir.

Q. How does a leaky graduating valve cause the brake valve to blow in a service notch the same as if the valve had not lapped automatically?

A. The graduating valve moves to the cut off position, but on account of not making a tight seat on the slide valve, air continues to escape from the brake pipe, which can only be overcome at the time by lapping the valve by hand.

Q. How would a leak at the double check valve cause a blow at the brake valve exhaust, while the valve is in either of the first four service notches?

A. For the reason previously given, that such leakage would be into the straight air pipe, which is open to the atmosphere in lap and the first four service notches through ports "E," "V" and the brake valve exhaust.

Q. How would you test to determine if it is the double check valve that is causing the blow?

A. With the automatic brake applied, either disconnect the straight air pipe at the brake valve and see if air comes through, or if a special cut-out cock is used in the pipe, close it and see if air comes through the small hole in the side,—in either case it would denote a leaky double check valve.

Q. Is it important that the double check valve be tested occasionally?

A. It is.

Q. Why so?

A. Because, if allowed to become defective, it would allow locomotive brakes to leak off while a service application is being made in any of the first four service notches.

Q. What effect would breaking off the pipe to the supplementary reservoir have?

A. It would prevent the automatic cut-off of the brake valve during a service application.

Q. Why?

A Because it would reduce the volume of the supplementary reservoir to practically nothing.

Q What effect would this have on the braking?

A. The brake valve handle would have to be returned to positive lap position following each service reduction.

Q. There being no leaks in the brake valve, what might prevent the reduction in the first service notch being as great as desired?

A. The brake valve handle, or slide valve lever being loose on the handle shaft, or lost motion in the link pins, which connect the slide valve to the slide valve lever.

Q. How would this make the reduction less than intended?

A. Because, when the handle is moved to the first service notch, it would not, on account of the lost motion, move the slide valve as far as intended,—therefore, the air in chamber "D" would not have to expand to the point intended in order to lap the service port in the brake valve.

Q. All parts being tight, what would make the reduction greater in the first service notch, than intended?

A. Lost motion in the graduating valve lever, at the fulcrum pin or at the connections of the piston stem or graduating valve.

Q. How would this cause the reduction to be greater than was intended?

A. Because the piston would have to travel a certain distance to take up this lost motion, without moving the graduating valve, and then moving the graduating valve the usual distance to close the brake valve exhaust, would allow the pressure in chamber "D" to expand lower than was intended.

Q. What is the trouble when the valve laps automatically on an engine alone, or with a short train, but will not with a long train?

A. Leakage past the piston in the brake valve, probably due to a bent piston stem.

Q. Why will the valve lap on an engine alone or with a short train, under these conditions, and not do it on a long train?

A. Where the brake pipe volume is small, it reduces quite rapidly,—giving a correspondingly quick movement to the piston, which carries it and the graduating valve over to the automatic lap in spite of a slight leak, past the piston, but when the volume is large, the piston moves more slowly on account of the slow fall of brake pipe pressure, and if the piston stem is bent on account of it binding in the cylinder, it gives a better opportunity for the pressure in chamber "D" to leak into the brake pipe without moving the piston far enough to have the graduating valve close the exhaust port in the slide valve

PRESSURE CONTROLLER DEFECTS.

Q. What attention must the vent port "C," in the pressure controller and the straight air controller receive?

A. Special care must always be taken to keep this port open.

Q. When, only, should air escape from it?

A. When the maximum pressure it is set at is obtained.

Q. If air escapes through port "C" before the maximum pressure is reached, what is the trouble?

A. Dirt or scale on seat, or diaphragm does not seat properly on the air valve seat

Q. If no air passes to the brake pipe at all in first charging up, what is probably the trouble?

A. The cut-out cock between the main reservoir and controller valve may be closed.

Q. If, after charging up all right, the controller failed to open when releasing after an application, what would be the trouble?

A. The piston may be stuck down, or vent port "C" in the muffler plug stopped up.

Q. How could port "C," being stopped up, cause this?

A. If the piston and ring in the supply portion are tight, the air admitted to the top of the piston could not escape, if port "C" should be stopped, except by leaking past the piston and passing out of port "X," which would make the controller very slow to open.

Q. If, at any time and for any reason, the pressure controller refused to open, what could be done?

A. Screw up the hand wheel on the bottom of the controller valve.

Q. What effect would this have?

A. It would allow full main reservoir pressure to pass to the brake pipe.

Q. What precautions should be observed when applying the brakes under these conditions?

A. From any notch under these conditions the brake valve handle should be returned to positive lap position as soon as the safety valve begins to blow.

Q. If the controller should not open promptly after light applications of the brakes, where would the trouble be?

A. This would be due to sluggish action of the controller, which should be reported at once for examination.

Q. What would cause the controller to be sluggish in opening?

A. A continuous leak past the diaphragm and the air valve seat, port "C" plugged up, the piston or ring fitted too tight, or the valve fitted too tight in the valve guide.

Q. What would make the pressure controller sluggish in closing?

A. A bad leak past the piston, passage in the air valve seat partially clogged up, the piston or ring fitted too tightly in the cylinder or the valve fitted too tightly in the guide nut

Q. What would cause a blow at the relief port "X" in supply portion when the brake pipe is not fully charged up?

A. A leak past the upper seat on the valve, and a loose fitting valve in the guide nut.

Q. What, in addition to this, would cause a blow at this port when fully charged up?

A. Leakage past the piston.

Q. What would cause a continuous blow at the port "C" in the muffler plug?

A. Dirt or scale, or a poor bearing between the diaphragm and air valve seat, and with the high pressure cut in, perhaps a leaky three, or four-way cock in the controlled pipe connections.

Q. What harm would it do to plug this port up in this case?

A. Plugging this port in any case would probably prevent the pressure controller from working, as air could not escape off the piston except by leaking down past it.

Q. What should be done if the pipe to one of the duplex regulating tops should break off?

A. The broken end should be plugged and if it had been connected to the top that was cut in, cut this top out and cut the other one in, and adjust this one to the pressure being used.

Q. What if the pipe between the supply and regulating portions of the pressure controller should break?

A. It would cut the supply portion off from the regulating portion, and there would be nothing to regulate the brake pipe pressure.

Q. What should be done?

A. Plug the broken pipe to avoid waste of air, and either use the full main reservoir pressure, or cut the main reservoir pressure down to the brake pipe pressure desired, by adjusting the pump governor.

Q. What effect would a leak between the ports in the three-way cock, used in the B-3-HP equipment have?

A. None,—while the low pressure is in use, but if this should be cut out and the high pressure cut in, the air would leak to the low pressure top, but unless the leak is greater than the capacity of port "C," it would not shut the pressure off.

Q. What effect would a leak between the ports in the four-way cock used with Schedule B3-HS have?

A. It would probably cause a constant blow at the accelerator pipe exhaust port, and if the high pressure top was cut in, perhaps at port "C."

LEVER SAFETY VALVE AND HIGH SPEED CONTROLLER DEFECTS.

Q. If there should be a continuous blow at exhaust openings in the spring case of the lever safety valve, either when using the safety valve alone or in connection with the high speed controller, while the brake is applied, where would the trouble be?

A. It would denote a leak past the pop valve seat in

the safety valve, either due to dirt or scale on it or a poor bearing.

Q. What is the trouble if it opens and blows before the brake valve handle is placed in the last service notch?

A. Except when using more than 70 pounds brake pipe pressure, this would indicate that the valve was not properly adjusted, or spring had become weak, or that the piston travel was too short.

Q. What would be the effect of a leak past the seat on the piston valve side of the high speed controller?

A. Brake pipe pressure could leak into the piston valve cylinder and pipes leading to the driver and truck brake cylinders.

Q. What effect would this have with the brakes released?

A. Being unable to escape at the safety valve, the air would travel back to the double check valve, and finding an opening through it, either to the straight air pipe or triple valve, or both, would cause a blow either at the brake valve or triple valve exhaust, or perhaps both.

Q. What effect would this leak have with the brakes applied?

A. In light service applications, it would tend to build the driver and truck brake cylinder pressure up higher than it should be, with the reduction made.

Q. Why should it not do this with a brake pipe pressure of 70 pounds and a full service reduction?

A. Because a full service reduction from 70 pounds would bring the brake pipe pressure down to, if not lower than, that in the brake cylinders, and brake pipe pressure could not leak into a pressure equal to it, or higher.

Q. Why would it raise the cylinder pressure when using the high brake pipe pressure?

A. Because then, the last service notch, when using more than 70 pounds, brake pipe pressure, would still leave the brake pipe pressure higher than 53 pounds, and thus permit a leak from the brake pipe to the locomotive brake cylinders,—if this seat should be very bad.

Q. How could you be sure that the trouble is in this seat?

A. With brakes released, disconnect the brake cylinder pipe from the high speed controller and see if air is blowing from it. If so, the seat on the piston valve side is leaking and must be replaced.

Q. What effect would this defect have if the brake pipe fell below the brake cylinder pressure?

A. None,—as it is the seat on the opposite or plain side of the high speed controller that makes the joint then.

Q. If the brake pipe pressure was reduced lower than the pressure of the engine brake cylinders, and the seat on the plain side of the piston leaked, what would occur?

A. Brake cylinder pressure would leak into the brake pipe and reduce the braking power correspondingly.

Q. How could you test for a leak of this kind?

A. Empty the brake pipe and disconnect the brake pipe from the high speed controller, and see if air blows out of the controller at this point, with brakes applied.

ACCELERATOR VALVE DEFECTS.

Q. If there is a continuous blow at the exhaust elbow of the accelerator valve, what is the trouble?

A. The slide valve is leaking, due to a bad seat or dirt on the seat.

Q. If this leak should be a serious one, what could be done?

A. Cut out the accelerator valve if it has a cut-out cock in the brake pipe connection, if not, put a blind gasket in the brake pipe connection to the accelerator valve, or screw a plug into the exhaust elbow.

Q. If, in making a service application with a light engine, or a short train of less than six cars, there is a blow at the accelerator exhaust elbow, what is the trouble?

A. Either the spring is weak, or port "S" in the piston is plugged up with dirt or gum.

Q. If there is a continuous blow at port "T" in the accelerator valve, what is the cause?

A Probably a leak past the seat,—due to dirt on seat, or seat being worn.

Q. If this blow only exists when the brake valve handle is in lap position, where would the trouble probably be?

A. A porous wall in the divided reservoir.

Q. If, when using the high speed pressure, the accelerator valve should cause a greater reduction than desired, where would the trouble be?

A The small exhaust port, in the four-way cock, plugged up.

OTHER DEFECTS.

Q. If there is a continuous blow from exhaust opening "X" in the quick release valve, with the brake applied, what is the trouble?

A. The valve seat is leaking,—due to being in poor condition, or dirt on it.

Q If there is a blow at the driver brake triple valve

when brakes are either applied or released, what is the trouble?

A A leaky triple slide valve, due to dirt on the seat, or a defective seat.

Q. If there is a blow at the driver brake triple valve in release only, what is the trouble?

A. A leak past the seat on piston valve side of the high speed controller in all probability.

Q. If it blows only when the straight air brake is applied, what is the trouble?

A. Straight air pressure is leaking past a bad seat on the triple valve side of the double check valve.

NEW YORK PRESSURE RETAINING VALVES.

The function of the retaining valve, and its construction and operation have already been discussed at some length in the section on the Westinghouse air brake

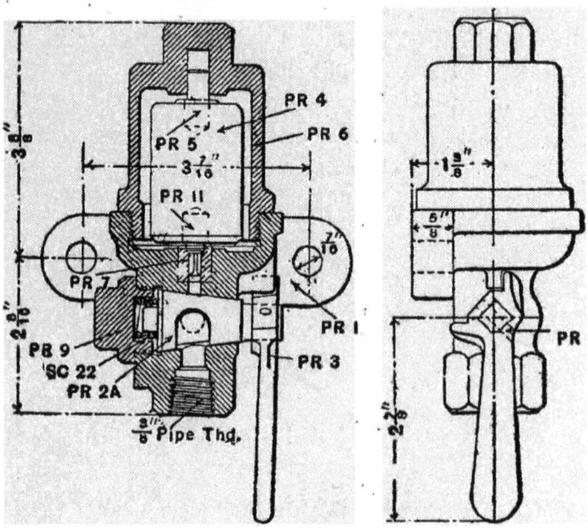

Fig. 136—Freight Car Pressure Retaining Valve.

system, and it will not be necessary to continue the discussion in connection with the New York system, for the reason that the design and action of these valves are practically the same in both systems. In the New York air brake there are four forms of retaining valves used. Fig. 136 illustrates the most common form. This valve is used on freight cars. Fig. 137 shows style PV-retaining valve for use in passenger service. This valve has a shaft extended from the retaining plug for the handle so that the retainer can be located outside the vestibule, and still be operated from the inside. This feature constitutes the main difference between style P

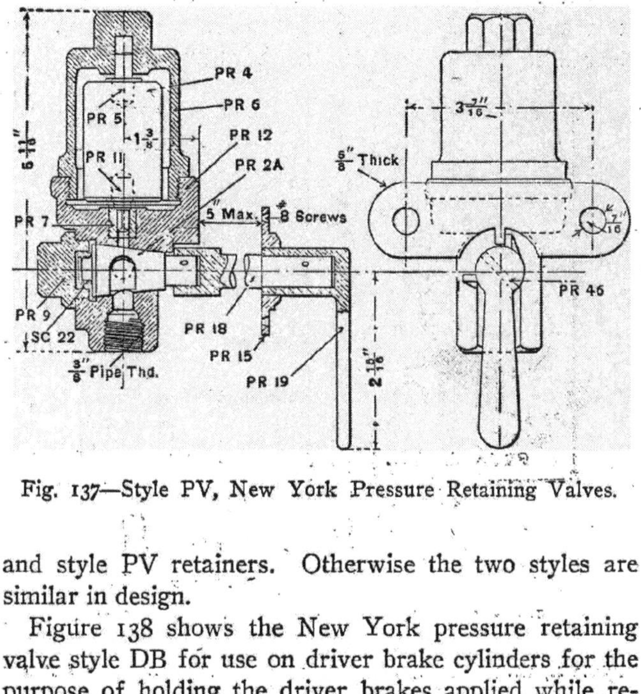

Fig. 137—Style PV, New York Pressure Retaining Valves.

and style PV retainers. Otherwise the two styles are similar in design.

Figure 138 shows the New York pressure retaining valve style DB for use on driver brake cylinders for the purpose of holding the driver brakes applied while releasing the train brakes, and thus keep the train bunched. This method greatly lessens the danger of the train breaking in two from the slack running out. The style DB retainer has three positions, as follows: vertically downward, full release; horizontal, to retain 15 pounds;

vertically upward, to retain all brake cylinder pressure. In order to obtain efficient service from retaining valves,

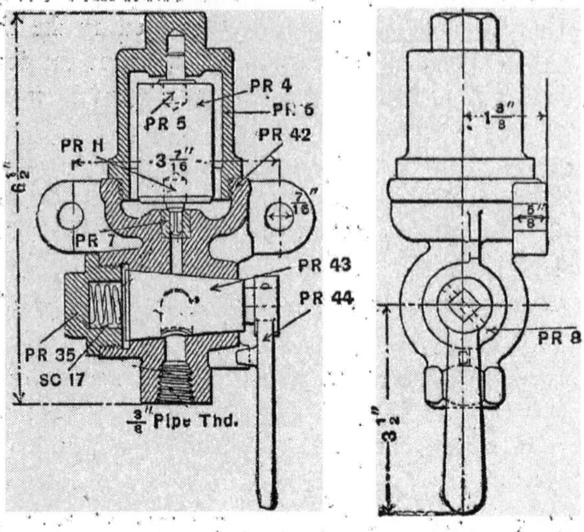

Fig. 138—Style DB, Pressure Retaining Valve.

it is absolutely necessary that the pressure retaining pipe, and all joints be air tight; also the brake cylinder packing leather must be free from leaks.

BRAKE LEVERAGE.

Brake leverage is a combination or system of levers coupled up and arranged in such a manner that when actuated by the brake piston pressure, such combination will deliver pressure on the brake shoes and thus arrest the rotation of the wheels.

Three kinds of levers are used in modern air brake practice, and they are known as levers of the first class, second class, and third class. The difference between these three classes of levers is determined by the three points in the lever at which the application of the forces is made. Fig. 139 shows the three classes of levers, the view at the top representing a lever of the first class, the intermediate view a second class lever, and the bottom view shows a lever of the third class. The first section of the formulæ accompanying each illustration, $W = \frac{F \times a}{b}$ means that, the force applied multiplied by the force-applied arm, and divided by that portion of the lever between the fulcrum and the force-delivered arm, gives the force delivered. The next formulæ, viz., $F = \frac{W \times b}{a}$, means that the force delivered multiplied by the distance in inches between the fulcrum point, and the force delivered point, and divided by the distance in inches between the force applied and the fulcrum point equals the force applied. The letters have the same meaning in each formula; as follows:

W = force delivered, in pounds.

F = force applied, in pounds.

a = distance in inches between force applied point and fulcrum point.

b = distance in inches between fulcrum point and force delivered point.

Although the location of letters a and b changes with the different classes of levers, their meaning remains the

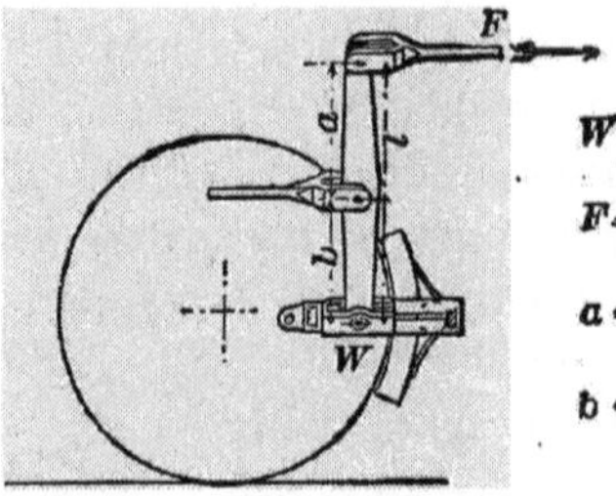

$$W = \frac{F \times a}{b}$$

$$F = \frac{W \times b}{a}$$

$$a = \frac{W \times b}{F} \text{ or } a = \frac{W \times l}{F+W}$$

$$b = \frac{F \times a}{W} \text{ or } b = \frac{F \times l}{F+W}$$

FULCRUM BETWEEN APPLIED AND DELIVERED FORCES.

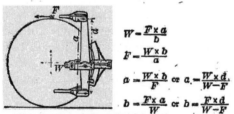

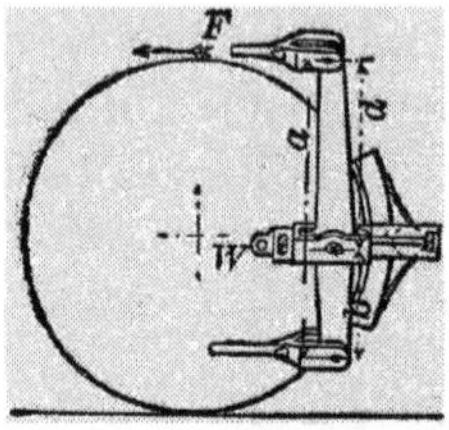

$$W = \frac{F \times a}{b}$$

$$F = \frac{W \times b}{a}$$

$$a = \frac{W \times b}{F} \text{ or } a = \frac{W \times d}{W-F}$$

$$b = \frac{F \times a}{W} \text{ or } b = \frac{F \times d}{W-F}$$

DELIVERED FORCE BETWEEN FULCRUM AND APPLIED FORCE.

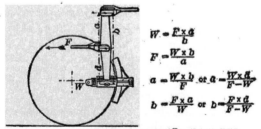

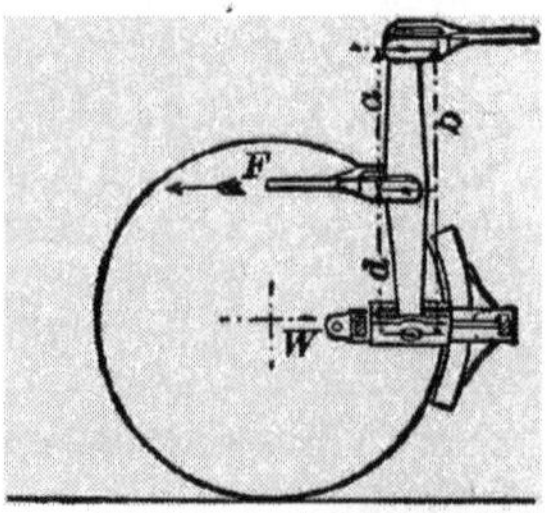

$$W = \frac{F \times a}{b}$$

$$F = \frac{W \times b}{a}$$

$$a = \frac{W \times b}{F} \text{ or } a = \frac{W \times d}{F-W}$$

$$b = \frac{F \times a}{W} \text{ or } b = \frac{F \times d}{F-W}$$

APPLIED FORCE BETWEEN FULCRUM AND DELIVERED FORCE.

Fig. 139—Brake Levers.

same. The fulcrum point is the stationary point on which the lever gets its purchase.

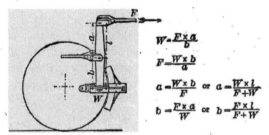

TOTAL LEVERAGE.

The total leverage in a combination of brake levers, is that applied force which would be produced by using one long lever if it were possible to do so, but owing to inability to do so under a car, a series of several shorter

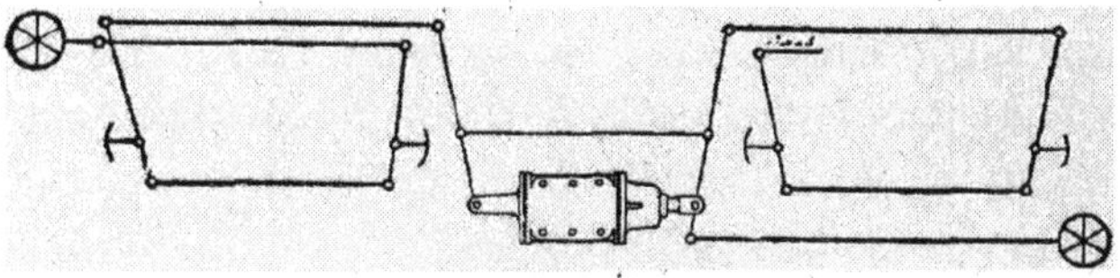

Fig. 140.

levers must be employed, which will produce the same result. For instance a total leverage of 7 to 1 means that with one long lever the force delivered is seven times greater than the force applied, or that a system of shorter

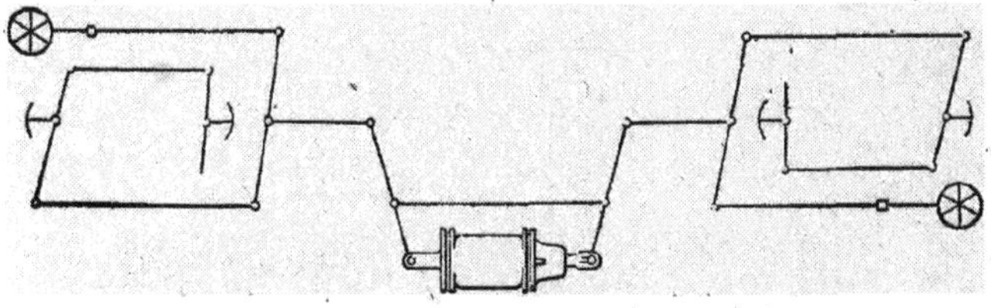

Fig. 141—Hodge System of Car Brake Levers.

levers used on a car is capable of delivering a pressure at the brake shoes seven times greater than the pressure applied to the piston in the brake cylinder. The total leverage on a car should never he higher than 10 to 1, and if possible as low as 7 or 8 to 1. These limits are necessary because of the small clearance between the brake shoes and wheels, and the excessive piston travel when the brakes are released. If the total leverage be too high the brake shoe clearance will be too small, resulting in the rubbing of the brake shoes on the wheels when the brakes are released.

Figure 140 shows the Stevens system of foundation brake gear. The Hodge system of leverage is outlined in Fig. 141. In this system an equalizing lever is required for the hand brakes, as shown. Tender brake levers and their arrangement are shown in Fig. 142.

BRAKING POWER.

The braking power of any system of air brakes is the power applied at the brake shoes through the medium of the leverage and the pressure on the air piston.

The percentage of braking power is the ratio of the total braking power to the total weight of the car. It is

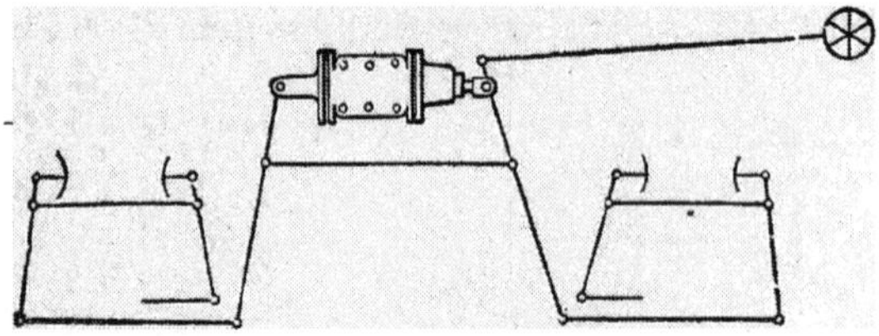

Fig. 142—Tender Brake Levers.

based on the light weight of passenger and freight cars, and also the tender; but is based on the loaded weight resting on the drivers, and on the truck wheels for the reason that the weight of the engine in working order does not vary much. The percentages are as follows:

On passenger cars, 90 per cent; on freight cars, 70 per cent; on tenders, 100 per cent, and on drivers and engine truck, 75 per cent

RULES FOR CALCULATING BRAKE POWER.

The force exerted upon the piston depends upon the size of the cylinder and the air pressure in the cylinder.

To get the number of pounds push at the piston, multiply the number of square inches on the piston by the number of pounds pressure per square inch on the cylinder. For example, an 8-inch piston contains 50 square inches, which multiplied by 50, the cylinder pressure, would give a push of 2,500 pounds at the end of the piston-rod

To find the number of square inches on a piston, multiply the diameter by itself, and by the number thus obtained multiply .7854, and cut off the last four figures from the result, and the remainder will be the number of square inches For example, 8 times 8 is 64, and .7854 multiplied by 64 equals 50 2656, or 50 inches and 2,656 ten-thousandths of an inch The decimal can be dropped unless it equals 5 or more, as for instance, a 10-inch cylinder would be counted as having 78½ square inches.

A short method is to multiply the diameter by itself, and the result by 11 and divide by 14

The following table gives the force exerted upon the pistons of the different sized cylinders with pressures of 50 and 60 pounds per square inch:

Size of cylinder,	6"	8"	10"	12"	14"	16"
50 lbs. pressure,	1,000	2,500	4,000	5,650	7 700	10,059
60 lbs pressure,	1,700	3,000	4,700	6,700	9 200	12,050

The braking power of a car after it has been equipped may be calculated in the following manner:

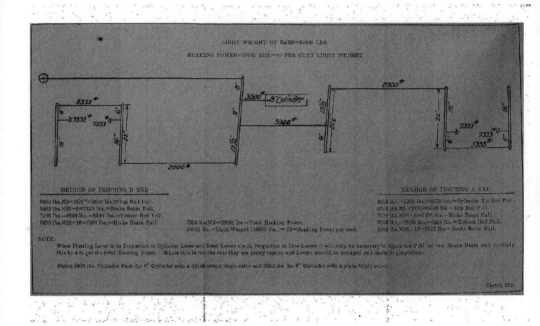

LIGHT WEIGHT OF CARS=36600 LBS.

BRAKING POWER=29332 LBS.=80 PER CENT LIGHT WEIGHT

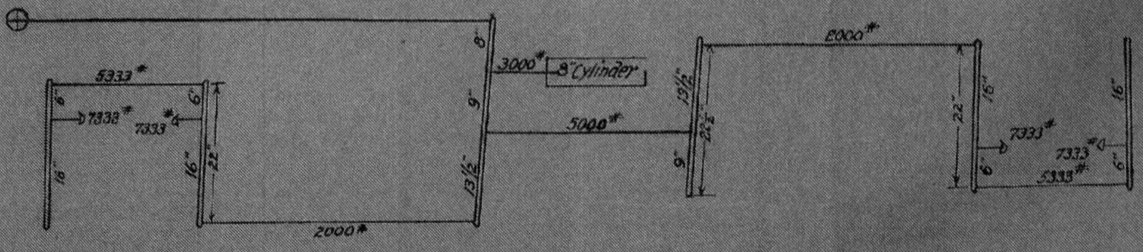

METHOD OF FIGURING B END

3000 lbs.×9÷13½″=2000 lbs.=Top Rod Pull.
2000 lbs.×22÷6=7333 lbs.=Brake Beam Pull.
7333 lbs.—2000 lbs.=5333 lbs.=Bottom Rod Pull.
5333 lbs.×22÷16=7333 lbs.=Brake Beam Pull.

7333 lbs.×4=29332 lbs.=Total Braking Power.
29332 lbs.÷Light Weight (36600 lbs.)=.80=Braking Power per cent.

METHOD OF FIGURING A END

3000 lbs.+2000 lbs.=5000 lbs.=Cylinder Tie Rod Pull.
5000 lbs.×9÷22½=2000 lbs.=Top Rod Pull.
2000 lbs.×22÷6=7333 lbs.=Brake Beam Pull.
7333 lbs.—2000 lbs.=5333 lbs.=Bottom Rod Pull.
5333 lbs.×22÷16=7333 lbs.=Brake Beam Pull.

NOTE:

When Floating Lever is in Proportion to Cylinder Lever and Dead Levers are in Proportion to Live Levers it will only be necessary to figure the Pull on one Brake Beam and multiply this by 4 to get the total Braking Power. Where this is not the case they are wrong repairs and Levers should be changed and made in proportion.

Figure 3000 lbs. Cylinder Push for 8″ Cylinder with a quick action triple valve and 2500 lbs. for 8″ Cylinder with a plain triple valve.

Sketch 223.

(1) Multiply the total piston pressure by the force-applied arm in inches. (2) Divide by the force-delivered arm to find the force exerted on the outer end of the lever; also the force on the opposite end of the tie rod which connects to the middle of the Hodge lever. (3) Divide the pull on the middle hole of the Hodge lever by 2. On a freight car omit this division. (4) Multiply by length of lever between force applied and the fulcrum point, and divide by that portion of the lever lying between the fulcrum point and brake shoe. (5) If the proportions are alike in the live lever and dead lever of both trucks multiply by 4 to get the total braking power. (6) Divide the total weight of the car into the total braking power to get the percentage of braking power. (7) Divide the total braking power by the total piston pressure to get the total leverage.

The insert sheet sketch 223 illustrates the process of calculating braking power.

BRAKE SHOE FRICTION.

Friction is the resistance to motion between two bodies in contact due to the interlocking of projections on the surface of each which interrupt or oppose each other, and must be broken off, bent or crushed out of shape before the two rubbing surfaces can pass each other.

The friction of a brake shoe against the wheel is expressed by the term co-efficient of friction, meaning the result obtained by dividing the actual pull of the brake shoe tending to stop the rotation of the wheel, by the load pressing the shoe against the wheel, as for instance if a brake shoe is pressed against the wheel with a load of 4,000 pounds and exerts a pull on the wheel of 500 pounds, the co-efficient of friction is 500 divided by

4,000 or .125. For convenience in use, however, this figure is expressed as 12.5 per cent. Conversely if a brake shoe, having a co-efficient of friction of 12.5 per cent., is applied with a braking force of 4,000 pounds, the retarding effect of the shoe will then be 12.5 per cent. of 4,000 = 500 pounds.

The co-efficients of brake shoe friction covering the various types of brake shoes in general use have been determined by carefully conducted shop tests with full sized shoes and wheels and from these tests have been developed the following laws:

(1) The co-efficient of friction of the brake shoe decreases with increase of pressure; that is, the co-efficient of friction of a cast iron brake shoe, acting under a load of 3,000 pounds against a wheel moving at 30 miles an hour, averages 28 per cent., whereas with the same shoe applied with a load of 6,000 pounds against the wheel at 30 miles an hour, it is only 23 per cent.

(2) The co-efficient of friction of the brake shoe decreases with increase of speed; that is, the co-efficient of friction of a cast iron shoe with a load of 3,000 pounds applied to a wheel at 30 miles an hour is 28 per cent. With the same shoe acting under the same load on a wheel moving at 54 miles an hour, the co-efficient of friction is 20 per cent.

(3) At a constant speed, the co-efficient of friction of a brake shoe diminishes with increase of time of application.

(4) The retarding effect of the brake shoe at very low speeds and just before the wheel stops, rises very rapidly as the wheel stops.

Experience has demonstrated that the pressure applied to the ordinary brake shoe cast iron should not exceed

ST. CLAIR
BRAKE VALVE

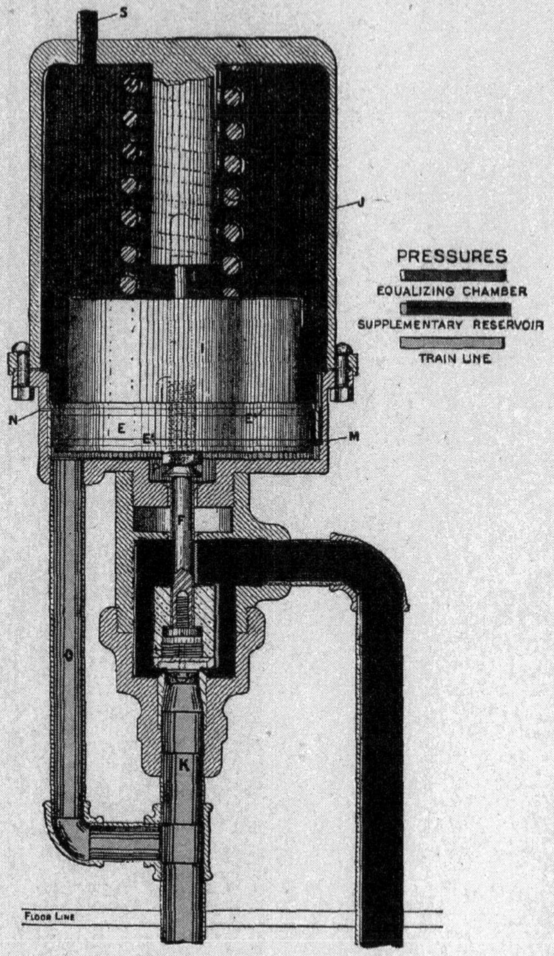

Locomotive Firemen and Enginemen's Magazine.

ST. CLAIR AIR BRAKE SERIES

PLATE I—REAR END RELEASE AND QUICK RE-CHARGE VALVE—(Running Position)

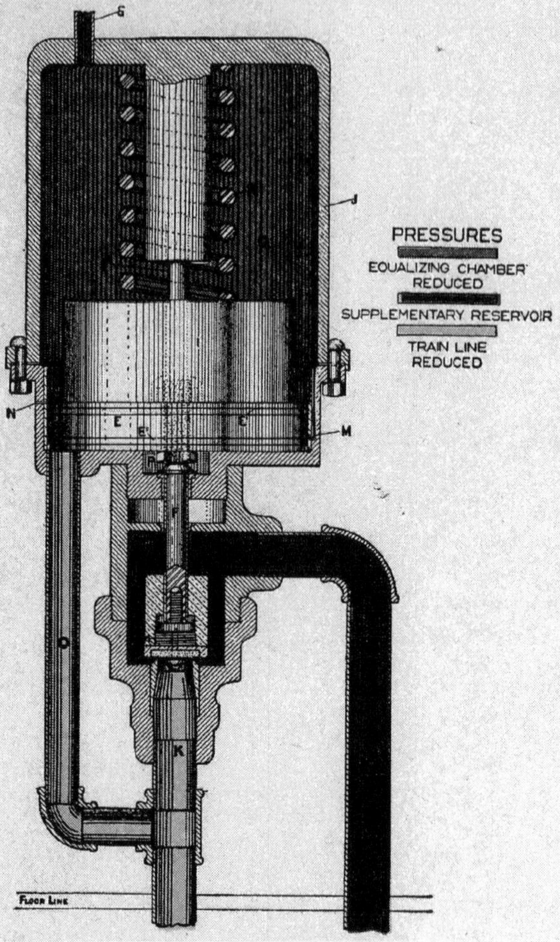

Locomotive Firemen and Enginemen's Magazine.

ST. CLAIR AIR BRAKE SERIES

PLATE II—REAR END RELEASE AND QUICK RE-CHARGE VALVE—(Application Position)

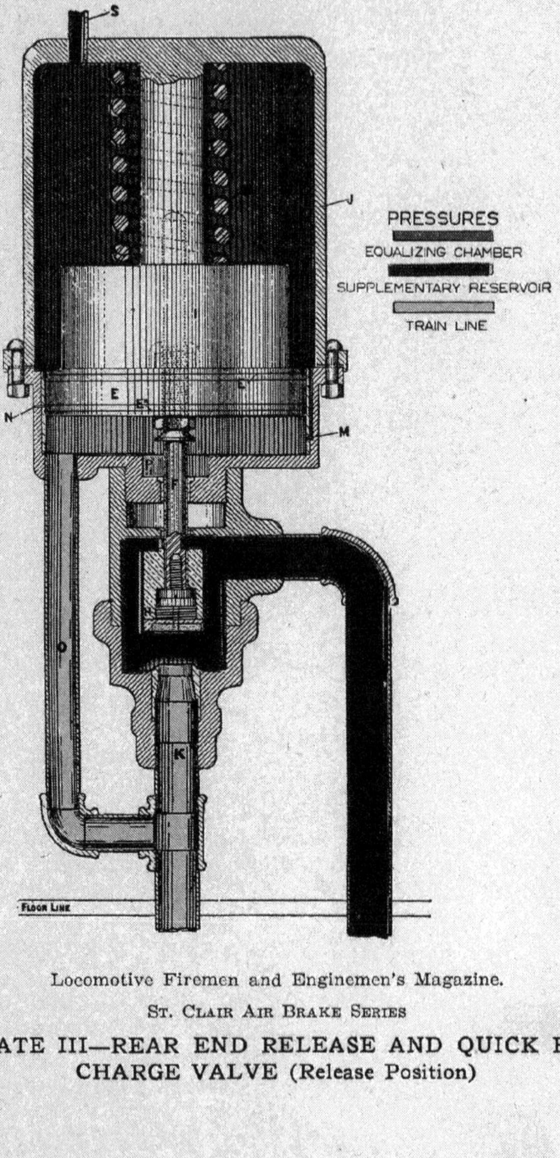

Locomotive Firemen and Enginemen's Magazine.

St. Clair Air Brake Series

PLATE III—REAR END RELEASE AND QUICK RE-CHARGE VALVE (Release Position)

90 per cent. of the weight holding the wheel to the rail, or the brake shoe would stop the motion of the wheel before the train came to a stop. This is because there is a greater area of contact between the shoe and the wheel. The brake shoe pull should always be less than the pull of the rail, to avoid sliding the wheel.

QUESTIONS AND ANSWERS.

NEW YORK TYPE J TRIPLE VALVE.

Q. For what conditions of service has the Type J triple valve of the New York air brake company been designed?

A. For all conditions and classes of passenger train service.

Q. How many, and what are the styles in which this valve is made?

A Two, Style "A," and Style "B."

Q What is the principal difference between the two styles?

A. Style "A" is fitted with a high emergency pressure cap, safety valve and supplementary reservoir; Style B is not

Q. What are the main features of the Type J triple valves?

A. The maximum braking pressure is available at all times, provided of course that the air pump is running.

Q Why is this?

A. Because the auxiliaries are recharged in about the same time required to release the air from brake cylinders.

Q. How many and what are the positions of this valve?

A. Five; as follows: Full release and charging, service, lap, release and recharge, and emergency.

Q. Is there any danger of obtaining an emergency application when making a service application?

A. No. The service ports are so proportioned as to prevent this.

Q. Briefly describe the action of the J triple valve in release and recharge.

A. When brake pipe pressure is restored after a service application, or when the valve is in lap position, the piston, slide valve and graduating valve are returned to full release and recharging position.

Q. Describe the action of the safety valve used in connection with this valve?

A. It is set for 60 pounds, and its action is practically the same as it is with other triple valves.

NEW YORK TYPE K TRIPLE VALVE.

Q. How many, and what are the sizes in which this triple valve is made?

A. Two. The K-5 for 8-inch brake cylinders, and the K-6 for 10-inch brake cylinders.

Q. Do these valves perform all the functions of the older type of quick action triples?

A. Yes; and three additional functions, vix: quick service, restricted release and uniform recharge.

Q. Can they be used in the same train with the older type of triples?

A. Yes; and they serve to improve the action of the latter when so used.

Q What is the difference between the K-5 and K-6 triple valves?

A. With the exception of the slide valve, the moving parts in both valves are identical.

Q. For what class of service are the K triple valves well adapted?

A. Long trains.

Q. How many, and what are the positions of this triple valve?

A. Six; as follows: Normal release and recharging, service, service lap, restricted release, normal release after restricted release, and emergency.

Q. When it is desired to make a service application how should the brake valve be handled?

A. Make a gradual reduction of brake pipe pressure.

Q. How is service lap position brought about?

A. By the automatic action of the triple after the desired brake pipe reduction has been made.

Q. If it is desired to make a heavier application how is it obtained?

A. By making a further reduction of brake pipe pressure, which causes the valve to automatically uncover the feed port allowing additional air to pass from the auxiliary to the brake cylinder.

Q. When the auxiliary pressure is reduced below brake pipe pressure, what occurs?

A. The graduating valve will again close the feed port.

Q. Can this action be repeated?

A. It can, until brake pipe and auxiliary pressures equalize.

Q. How is restricted release obtained?

A. By admitting a sufficient volume of air to the brake pipe to cause the parts of the valve to assume a position in which the flow to the atmosphere is limited to one small port.

Q. How is normal release again obtained?

A. When during the time the triple is in restricted release the auxiliary pressure becomes nearly equal to brake pipe pressure, the parts of the valves will again assume the position of normal release.

Q. How is release of the brakes after an emergency application brought about?

A. In the same way as following a service application.

NEW YORK PRESSURE RETAINING VALVES.

Q. How many forms of pressure retaining valves are there in use?

A. There are four.

Q. Which is the most common?

A. The freight car retainer.

Q. What are the other forms?

A. The styles P, PV and DB.

Q. For what are the style P and PV retainers used?

A. For 12, 14 and 16-inch passenger car cylinders.

Q. What is the difference between the style P and the style PV?

A. Style PV has a shaft extended from the retaining plug for the handle, so that the retainer can be located outside of the vestibule and be operated from the inside. Otherwise they are alike.

Q. Why is it necessary to use a special pressure retainer on passenger cars having 12-inch or larger brake cylinders?

A. As the style S triple valve used on 12, 14 and 16-inch cylinders has a larger exhaust port than the smaller triples, it was necessary to make the retainer larger to correspond in order to reduce the pressure from the larger brake cylinders as fast as the smaller pressure retainer did from the smaller cylinders.

Q. Where are the retaining valves usually located?

A. They are placed at points about the cars and locomotive, easily accessible by trainmen and enginemen, where they may be conveniently operated.

On freight cars they are usually located close to the hand brake; on passenger cars, at the end and inside of vestibule; and on locomotives inside the cab and on the tender; near the gangway.

Q. How are the retaining valves piped?

A. They are piped to the exhaust port of the triple valve, so that when the triple valve goes to release position, the exhaust air from the brake cylinder must pass through this pipe to the pressure retaining valve before it can escape to the atmosphere.

Q. Where are pressure retaining valves mostly used?

A. In mountain service to assist in letting trains down grades safely.

Q. How do they operate to increase the facility and safety of train handling?

A. In mountain service, when the engineer desires to recharge the auxiliaries without allowing the train speed to increase materially, they retard the exhaust of air from the brake cylinder until the pressure reduces to about 15 pounds, and then retain this latter amount. To do this, however, the pressure-retaining valve handle must be turned to a horizontal position.

In level grade service, pressure retaining valves are used to advantage in holding the slack bunched in long trains while releasing the automatic brakes, to prevent breaking in two.

Q. If the handle of the freight car retainer is turned up to a horizontal position, how much pressure will it hold, or retain, in the brake cylinder?

A. About 15 pounds.

Q. Does the passenger car retainer hold the same amount of pressure?

A. Yes.

Q. With a freight car retainer handle turned up, how long should it take the brake cylinder pressure to blow down to 15 pounds from 50 pounds, with 8-inch piston travel and an 8-inch cylinder?

A About 58 seconds.

Q. How long will it take to blow down under the same conditions with a 10-inch passenger car cylinder; 14-inch; 16-inch?

A. About 62 seconds.

Q. When freight car pressure retainers are used on 14-inch brake cylinders, on long trains, where there are cars without retainers, what is the result in making the stop even though these retainers are not turned up?

A. It is almost impossible to make the stop without a shock, and possibly breaking in two The cars which have no retainers will have their brakes released before those which have retainers.

Q. When a small retainer is used on cars that have large brake cylinders, and the retainer is turned up on a long grade, what is likely to occur?

A. As the retainers take longer to blow the pressure down, the wheels are likely to overheat.

Q. Where is the style DB retainer used?

A. On driver brake cylinders, for the purpose of holding the driver brakes applied while releasing the train brakes.

Q. Why is it desirable to operate retainers on driver brakes?

A. To keep the train bunched while releasing at slow speeds, and thus prevent it from breaking away into two or more pieces.

Q. How many positions are there for the handle of the DB style retainer?

A. Three; vertically downward, full release; horizontal, to retain 15 pounds; vertically upward, to retain all brake cylinder pressure.

Q. In order to have the pressure retaining valve operate efficiently, what conditions must be observed?

A. The pressure retaining pipe and all the joints must be absolutely air tight, as must also be the brake cylinder packing leather.

BRAKE LEVERAGE.

Q. What is understood by the term "leverage?"

A. When taken in connection with car braking, it is a combination or system of levers, so coupled up and arranged, that when actuated by the brake piston pressure, delivers pressure on the brake shoes to arrest the rotation of the wheels.

Q. Are levers always used in combination in air brake work?

A. Yes; generally speaking, but in the study of leverage, it is found advantageous to divide up the combination and treat each lever therein as a single, simple lever.

Q. How many kinds of levers are used in modern air brake pactice?

A. Three. They are known as levers of the first class, second class and third class.

Q. What is the difference between these three classes of levers?

A. The location of the three points in the lever at which the application of the forces is made determines the class of the lever.

Q. Describe a lever of the first class.

A. It is a lever in which the fulcrum point is between the points where force is applied, and force delivered.

Q. What is a lever of the second class?

A. One in which the point where force is delivered is between the fulcrum and the point, where force is applied.

Q. Describe a lever of the third class.

A. In a lever of the third class the point where force is applied is between the fulcrum and the force delivered point.

Q. What is meant by the proportion of levers?

A. The ability of the lever to deliver a certain force in proportion to the force applied upon it

Q. How is the proportion of a lever found?

A. By dividing the force-applied arm by the force-delivered arm.

Q. What is the force-applied arm?

A. The length in inches of that portion of the lever lying between the force-applied point and the fulcrum point.

Q. What is the force-delivered arm?

A. That portion of the lever in inches between the force-delivered point and fulcrum point.

Q. Give a formula for calculating the force in pounds delivered by a lever.

A. $W = \frac{F \times a}{b}$ in which W is the unknown quantity (viz.: force delivered); F is the force applied in pounds; a equals distance in inches between force applied point, and fulcrum point, b equals distance in inches between fulcrum point and force-delivered point.

Q. Give method of calculation.

A. F multiplied by a, and this product divided by b, all

of which are known quantities, will equal W, the force delivered.

Q. Explain the formula, $F = \frac{W \times b}{a}$

A. In this formula the value of F is to be ascertained; therefore, W multiplied by b, and this product divided by a, all of which are known quantities, will equal F, the force applied.

Q. Is there not a general rule which can be used, disregarding the class of the lever?

A. Yes, it is very simple, worth memorizing, and is as follows: Multiply the force applied by the force-applied arm, in inches, and divide that product by the force-delivered arm, in inches.

Q. What is meant by force-applied point?

A. That point on the lever where the pressure, or power, is first introduced.

Q. What is meant by the force-delivered point of the lever?

A. That point of the lever where the force practically leaves the lever, through the connecting rod, to proceed to the next connecting lever.

Q. What is meant by the fulcrum point of the lever?

A. That point which is practically used as a stationary point on which the lever gets its purchase, or, as is commonly known, gets its "prying" point.

TOTAL LEVERAGE.

Q. What is meant by total leverage?

A. Total leverage, in the continuous combination of brake leverage in the foundation brake gear of a car, is an equivalent to one single, long lever, if it were possible to use such a lever; but, on account of the inability to do so, a series of several shorter, or lower proportioned levers must be employed and be connected up into a system to produce the same result that one very long lever would.

Q. What is meant by a total leverage of 7 to 1?

A. In car leverage it means that a system of short levers used in combination is capable of delivering a pressure at the brake shoes seven times greater than that applied by piston in the brake cylinder.

Q. About what should the total leverage on a car be?

A. Never higher than 10 to 1, and if possible, as low as 7 or 8 to 1.

Q Why are these limits placed on the total leverage?

A. On account of the very small clearance between the brake shoes and wheels, and to prevent rubbing of the brake shoes on the wheels when brakes are released.

BRAKING POWER.

Q. What is meant by the term "braking power?"

A. The power applied at the brake shoes, through the medium of the leverage and the pressure on the air piston, to arrest the rotation of the wheels.

Q. What is meant by braking power per pair of wheels?

A. The pressure delivered by the brake shoes on one pair of wheels.

Q. What is meant by total braking power?

A The total pressure expended on all the wheels of the car.

BRAKING POWER PERCENTAGE.

Q. What is meant by percentage of braking power?

A. The ratio of the total braking power and the total weight of the car. This percentage is found by dividing the total braking power by the weight of the car.

Q. What percentage of braking power is ordinarily employed?

A. On passenger cars, 90 per cent; on freight cars, 70 per cent; on tenders, 100 per cent; on locomotive driving wheels, 75 per cent; on engine truck wheels, 75 per cent.

Q. Is the percentage of braking power based on the light or loaded weight of the car, tender and engine.

A. It is based on the light weight of the passenger car, freight car and tender; but is based on the loaded weight resting on the locomotive driving wheels and on the truck brake wheels.

Q. Why is the braking power based on the light weight of the car and tender and on the loaded weight of the engine?

A. The higher percentage of braking power on the passenger car is designed because the loaded weight and light weight of the car do not vary a great deal; hence, a high braking power is permissible. The freight car varies greatly between its light and loaded weight; hence, the braking power must be placed lower than with the passenger car. Also the freight car runs at lower speeds, where the co-efficient of brake shoe friction is higher than on the passenger car at high speeds, and a lower braking power must therefore be used, to prevent the skidding of wheels when the car is empty.

Q. Why is 75 per cent used on the engine driving wheel and truck wheel brakes?

A. The weight of the engine in working order does not vary much, and the working weight is really the loaded weight; hence, the braking power of the engine is comparatively high, although it may seem low when we consider the figures only

Q. Why is the tender braked at 100 per cent?

A. Because it has been found that this percentage can be safely used, on account of the tender always carrying a certain amount of coal and water above the light weight.

Q. How have these practices been determined and adopted?

A. By actual service conditions.

Q. Is there a different percentage in braking power on a car when it is loaded and when it is light?

A. Yes; if a car is braked 70 per cent, and be given a load equal to its own weight, the car will be then braking at only 35 per cent

Q. What cylinder pressure is used as a basis for computing the braking power?

A. Sixty pounds where the quick action triple valve is used, and 50 pounds when the plain triple is used.

Q. How is the piston pressure in the cylinder calculated?

A. The diameter of the piston is first multiplied by itself, then that product multiplied by the decimal .7854 and that product in turn multiplied by the pressure exerted in pounds per square inch on the piston. Thus, the calculation of a 60-pound pressure on the piston of an 8-inch cylinder would result as follows:

$$8 \times 8 = 64;\ 64 \times 7854 = 50;\ 50 \times 60 = 3000 \text{ lbs.}$$

Q. What is understood by the term "foundation brake gear?"

A. That part of the air brake system under the car, comprising the levers, connecting rods, jaws, pins, brake beams, hangers, hanger supports, lever guides and supports.

PART 1

INDEX

A

C

D

I

J

K

L

N

P

Q

R

S

T

V

W

INDEX

EXAMINATION QUESTIONS AND ANSWERS NEW YORK AIR BRAKE

A

O

P

Q

R

S

T

V

W

Lightning Source UK Ltd.
Milton Keynes UK
UKHW021858290720
367391UK00011B/346